# The Other Rāma

SUNY series in Hindu Studies

---

Wendy Doniger, editor

# The Other Rāma

## *Matricide and Genocide in the Mythology of Paraśurāma*

BRIAN COLLINS

SUNY PRESS

Cover image: Indian axe (18th–19th century) from the Metropolitan Museum of Art Collection (public domain).

Published by State University of New York Press, Albany



For information, contact State University of New York, Albany, NY
www.sunypress.edu

**Library of Congress Cataloging-in-Publication Data**

Names: Collins, Brian, author.
Title: The other rāma : matricide and genocide in the mythology of paraśurāma / Brian Collins, author.
Description: Albany : State University of New York Press, [2020] | Series: SUNY series in Hindu Studies | Includes bibliographical references and index.
Identifiers: ISBN 9781438480398 (hardcover) | ISBN 9781438480381 (pbk.) | ISBN 9781438480404 (ebook)
Further information is available at the Library of Congress.

10 9 8 7 6 5 4 3 2 1

# Contents


| | | |
|---|---|---|
| List of Figures | | vii |
| Abbreviations | | ix |
| Acknowledgments | | xi |
| Preface: The Other Rāma | | xv |
| Introduction: God with an Axe | | 1 |
| Chapter 1 | The Brahmin Warrior: Paraśurāma *in Extremis* | 33 |
| Chapter 2 | Matricide I: The Broken Pot | 79 |
| Chapter 3 | Matricide II: The Severed Head | 105 |
| Chapter 4 | Varṇicide I: The Extermination of the Kṣatriyas and Its Aftermath | 149 |
| Chapter 5 | Varṇicide II: Blood and Soil in Malabar and Maharashtra | 183 |
| Conclusion: Introducing Paraśurāma | | 219 |
| Notes | | 257 |
| Works Cited | | 279 |
| Index | | 303 |

# List of Figures


| | | |
|---|---|---|
| Figure I.1 | Pāṇḍavas and Niṣādas Ranked with Implicit Reference to a Hierarchy of Values | 23 |
| Figure 1.1 | The Descents of Paraśurāma and Viśvāmitra | 63 |
| Figure 1.2 | Comparison of the Pṛthu and Paraśurāma Myths | 67 |
| Figure 2.1 | Comparison of the Matricide Myth, the Vedic Sacrifice, and the Tamil Exorcism | 102 |
| Figure 3.1 | A Painted Plaster Sculpture Showing Jamadagni Ordering Paraśurāma to Decapitate Reṇukā | 106 |
| Figure 3.2 | The Contextual Layers of the *Brahmāṇḍa Purāṇa* Recitation at the *Bhadradipāpratiṣṭā* | 120 |
| Figure 3.3 | Comparison of the Gaṇeśa, Paraśurāma, and Gaṇeśa-Paraśurāma Stories | 121 |
| Figure 3.4 | Comparison of the Ahalyā, Reṇukā, and Cirakāri Stories | 127 |
| Figure 3.5 | Structural Comparison of Reṇukā Myths and Rituals in South India | 132 |
| Figure 3.6 | The Triangle of the Dead Mother Complex and the Triangle of the Reṇukā Myth | 141 |
| Figure C.1 | The Inversion and Reestablishment of the Analogic Key | 231 |
| Figure C.2 | A Synchronic Representation of the Paraśurāma Myth | 232 |
| Figure C.3 | The Four Cycles within the Paraśurāma Myth | 235 |
| Figure C.4 | The Four Cycles Interpreted with the Analogic Key | 238 |

Figure C.5 The Brahmin Warrior Motif 241

Figure C.6 The Matricide Motif 242

Figure C.7 The Varṇicide Motif 243

Figure C.8 The Libidinal Triangles Representing the Two Murders in *Psycho* 250

Figure C.9 The Libidinal Triangles Representing Paraśurāma's Matricide and Cattle Theft 251

# Abbreviations

| | |
|---|---|
| AV | Atharva Veda |
| BḍP | Brahmāṇḍa Purāṇa |
| BhP | Bhāgavata Purāṇa |
| BVP | Brahmavaivarta Purāṇa |
| HV | Harivaṃśa |
| KaP | Kalki Purāṇa |
| KG | Kṛṣi Gītā |
| MBh | Mahābhārata |
| MSRM | Mukapiṭhavāsiṇī Śrī Reṇukā Mahātmya |
| PP | Padma Purāṇa |
| Rām | Rāmayaṇa |
| ṚV | Ṛg Veda |
| ŚB | Śatapatha Brāhmaṇa |
| SkP | Skandha Purāṇa |
| TS | Taittirīya Saṃhitā |
| VāP | Vāyu Purāṇa |
| VDhP | Viṣṇudharmottara Purāṇa |
| ViP | Viṣṇu Purāṇa |

# Acknowledgments

My thanks in providing invaluable assistance for this project go first to my University of Chicago Divinity School dissertation advisor Wendy Doniger, whose advice, encouragement, and mentoring have extended long past the expiration date and whose student I will always be. I am also extremely grateful to David Dean Shulman, now retired from the Hebrew University of Jerusalem, and Alf Hiltebeitel, now retired from George Washington University, the latter of whom assigned me the editorship of the *Oxford Bibliographies in Hinduism*'s entry on "Rāma Jāmadagnya/Paraśurāma" when I was looking for academic work just after finishing my PhD and was also kind enough to read and comment on this manuscript in 2019. Both Alf and David served as readers of my dissertation and graciously extended to me some of their invaluable insights into and knowledge of the *Mahābhārata* and its traditions.

My *baḍa bhai* in Paraśurāma studies, Pradeep Kant Chowdhary, formerly of Delhi University, has been doubly helpful, first for publishing his wonderful *Rāma with the Axe: Myth and Cult of Paraśurāma* in the same year in which my dissertation came out and then for being so generous with hospitality and feedback during my two visits to see him in New Delhi. Likewise, another great Paraśurāma scholar, Nicolas Dejenne of the Université de la Sorbonne Nouvelle in Paris, was kind enough to share with me his work on modern interpretations of the Paraśurāma story and its contemporary political significance.

Swagata Pandit did an amazing job turning around a rush translation of some Marāṭhī texts, and Anne Feldhaus of Arizona State University gently dispelled some of my ignorance on matters of the worship of the Goddess in Maharashtra. I am also thankful to Patrick Olivelle from the University of Texas at Austin for his provocative and compelling arguments on the status of *varṇa* in the time leading up to the epic's composition. Gratitude is also owed to Adheesh Sathaye of the University of British Columbia, Borayin Larios of the University of Vienna, and James Mallinson of the School of Oriental and African Studies for each assisting me in various ways, as well as Keralan filmmaker Jayan Cherian, my former SUNY editor Chris Ahn, my subsequent SUNY editor James Peltz, and the two anonymous reviewers who took such great care in reading, commenting upon, and immeasurably improving the manuscript in 2018.

From the Gopikabai Sitaram Gawande College in Umarkhed, Maharashtra, Someshwar Vadrabade, Vitthal Kadam, Yadaorao Raut, and Sakshi Jamde assisted me in getting to the Shri Renuka Devi Mandir in Mahur and showed me boundless kindness and generosity. With her deep and broad knowledge of the rituals surrounding Māriyammaṉ, Perundevi Srinivasan of Siena College helped me to rethink and clarify some of the ideas in chapter three. G. H. Visweswara shared with me his labor of love, the *Mahābhārata Spectroscope*, which was a great help in navigating the Southern recension of the epic. Madhavi Kolhatkar, retired from Deccan College, thoughtfully shared with me a paper of hers on Paraśurāma during a visit to Athens in the summer of 2015.

I am immensely grateful to Marcello De Martino and Claudia Santi for inviting me to present portions of this work at the second Comparative Mythology Today Conference, "*Nomen Numen*: Expressions of the Sacred between History of Religions, Linguistics, and Archeology," held on April 15, 2019, at the University of Campania "Luigi Vanvitelli," in Santa Maria Capua Vetere, Italy.

My graduate students Emily McPherson and Glynnis "Gabby" Gunnett have my sincere appreciation for performing various acts of drudgery in service of this project in the 2017–18 school year. From the Department of Classics and World Religions at Ohio University, I wish to thank my past and present colleagues Cory Crawford, Loren Lybarger, Myrna Pérez Sheldon, William Owens, James Andrews, Ruth Palmer, Neville McFerrin, Neil Bernstein, Fred Drogula, Tom Carpenter, Lynne Lancaster, Steve Hays, Elizabeth Collins, and Jaclyn Maxwell for helping to provide the supportive working environment that was necessary to bring this book to fruition.

Additionally, I am eternally grateful to the Gawande family: Sushila, Meeta, Atul, and the late Sitaram, who made this book possible. Sushila and Meeta should receive special thanks, Sushila for being unfailingly supportive of me and my family since I took the Drs. Ram and Sushila Gawande Chair in Indian Religion and Philosophy in 2013 and Meeta for seeing the wisdom of writing a provision for research funds into the endowment in this time of austerity for the humanities. This book is for them, as well. Finally, I thank my family for their love and support, especially my wife Jennifer and our daughter Arwyn (may she never bear an axe!).

Brian Collins
Athens, Ohio

# Preface

## *The Other Rāma*

Leveling accusations against a god requires some delicacy. This is true even of the three rabbis with *chutzpah* enough to give the Deity his day in court in Elie Wiesel's "*purimschpiel* within a *purimschpiel*," *The Trial of God.* It requires far more delicacy than Richard Dawkins displays in his oft-quoted diatribe calling that same God a "vindictive, bloodthirsty ethnic cleanser" (2006, 51). Even the second century heretic Marcion had more subtlety than that.[1] It requires the judiciousness of a Plato, who argues that "the doings of Cronus, and the sufferings which in turn his son inflicted upon him, even if they were true, ought certainly not to be lightly told to young and thoughtless persons" (*Republic* 2.378). Let me then be as delicate as I can: Paraśurāma, incarnation of the high god Viṣṇu and the subject of this book, is best known for systematically exterminating twenty-one successive generations of human beings solely because they were born into the martial Kṣatriya class. Twenty-one generations. That is roughly the number of generations separating this author (b. 1975) from Thomas Aquinas (b. 1225). Paraśurāma is also said to have decapitated his mother. But I have no intention of putting him on trial.

The primary purpose of this book is to provide anyone interested in Indian mythology and religion with a wide-ranging study of the myths of Paraśurāma, a hero of the *Mahābhārata* epic, a progenitor and patriarch in Malabar and Maharashtra, and the sixth *avatāra* of Viṣṇu. Born a "mixed-up" Brahmin with the dual nature of an ascetic and a warrior, Paraśurāma decapitates his mother Reṇukā at his father's command after her eye wanders to a handsome bathing *gandharva* prince when she is supposed to be collecting water. Then, in response to a Kṣatriya king's cattle raid gone wrong that leaves his father Jamadagni dead, Paraśurāma goes on to launch a campaign of annihilation against the entire Kṣatriya class, wiping out the aforementioned twenty-one successive generations.

This book is called *The Other Rāma* to distinguish our hero (as mythmakers sought to do when they added the "Paraśu-" to his name and thus made him "Rāma with the Axe") from Rāma Dāśarathi ("Rāma the Son of Daśaratha"), that divine king of the Solar Dynasty and hero of the *Rāmāyaṇa* epic worshipped throughout South and Southeast Asia, whose noble figure and visage are instantly called to mind by anyone who hears the word "Rāma." Even speaking his holy name by accident is said to bring blessings to the speaker.[2] Despite a few foibles (exiling his wife, for one), Rāma is the ideal king, husband, and god. The greatest compliment a Hindu couple can get on their wedding day is that they look like Rāma and his equally perfect bride, Sītā.[3]

Our Rāma is not that Rāma. Our Rāma is Paraśurāma—the Other Rāma. He has no wife, no children, no kingdom, and comparatively few devotees. But both Rāma and Paraśurāma are incarnations of Viṣṇu. When the two Rāmas meet in the *Rāmāyaṇa*, sparks fly, and not only because Rāma uses his superhuman strength to break the divine bow of Paraśurāma's guru, Śiva. There can only be one Viṣṇu incarnate at a time, and since Rāma is the hero of the *Rāmāyaṇa*, it is Paraśurāma who must surrender his power and walk out of the poem and into permanent exile. This lonely, wandering Other Rāma and his violent career are what concern us here.

It may be a special kind of delusion peculiar to historians of religion to hope that (absent a fortuitous book-banning campaign) any nonspecialist would read a monograph about a figure from Indian mythology whose name has five syllables and two diacritical marks. Nevertheless, I have undertaken the writing of this book with that delusion firmly in place. Because, although I aim to keep my promise not to put Paraśurāma on trial, I am convinced that his expert testimony demands our attention, if only because of all that he must have witnessed over the millennia for which he has watched the world from his lonely home on Mount Mahendra. Paraśurāma's myth cycle speaks to deep, possibly universal, elements of the psyche. It also speaks to equally deep, but historically contingent, structures in a widely shared and continually influential Indic worldview. It also speaks to the political realities of our "unnamable present," to borrow Roberto Calasso's apt phrase. And if it does not speak directly to my reader, I hope, at least, that my reader understands that it speaks to me.

# Introduction

## *God with an Axe*

Thou art my battle axe and weapons of war: for with thee will I break in pieces the nations, and with thee will I destroy kingdoms.

—Jeremiah 51:20

Thine axe is bloody; what hast thou done?

—*Njals Saga*

## The Paraśurāma Cycle

What follows is my own telling of the Paraśurāma cycle incorporating as many elements as possible taken from all of its collected variants. It is what Wendy Doniger calls a "macromyth" (1998, 93). The immediate purpose of this synoptic macromyth is to serve as a thematic key to the available corpus of Paraśurāma literature. First in this list is the *Mahābhārata*, a massive Indian epic composed between 500 BCE and 500 CE that tells the story of a dynastic war between the noble Pāṇḍavas (the brothers Yudhiṣṭhira, Arjuna, Bhīma, Nakula, Sahadeva, and their shared wife Draupadī) and their treacherous cousins the Kauravas. Second is the *Rāmāyaṇa*, the other great Sanskrit epic, composed between 400 BCE and 400 CE, that tells the story of the heroic Rāma Dāśarathi's quest to rescue his wife Sītā from her kidnapper, the demon king Rāvaṇa. These are followed by the Sanskrit and vernacular regional compendia of myth, legend, and liturgy called the Purāṇas; subsequent temple legends and collected oral traditions; as well as modern plays, poetry, novels, films, television mini-series, and comic books.

The summary below will serve to introduce the figure of Paraśurāma along with the main characters and the basic sequence of events in his mythology. Some of the elements in this admittedly artificial telling of the story take significantly different forms in other versions (sometimes, for reasons that will become clear later, it is the king Kārtavīrya instead of the *gandharva* Citraratha who distracts Reṇukā at the river; sometimes the two women embrace the wrong trees instead of eating the wrong bowls of rice pudding, etc.), but all of the major episodes are present.

> There was once a king named Gādhi who was the incarnation of Indra, the king of the gods, who had decided to take human form after Gādhi's pious father prayed for a divine son. In time, Gādhi had a beautiful daughter named Satyavatī, who one day caught the eye of the Brahmin ascetic Ṛcika. Although Ṛcika was a priest of the famous and powerful Bhārgava clan, Gādhi thought that an ascetic (even a Bhārgava ascetic) was too poor to marry his daughter, a member of the royal Kṣatriya class. After Ṛcika made two requests for Satyavatī's hand in marriage, Gādhi finally said that Ṛcika could marry his daughter only if he could pay the bride price of one thousand fast white horses each with one black ear. To Gādhi's surprise, Ṛcika paid the price (with help from the god Varuṇa), married the princess, and took her to live with him in the forest.
>
> After their marriage, Ṛcika's clan patriarch Bhṛgu came to visit the couple. As a wedding gift to his new daughter-in-law, Bhṛgu offered Satyavatī whatever she desired. Satyavatī asked that she might give birth to a righteous Brahmin son, and that her mother might give birth to a son who would be a powerful Kṣatriya warrior. Bhṛgu agreed and for Satyavatī he infused a *caru* (a bowl of rice pudding) with saintliness, piety, wisdom, and all the qualities that make a good Brahmin. For her mother he infused another *caru* with valor, strength, martial prowess and all the attributes of a brave warrior. He then told each woman to take her *caru* and consume it after performing the ritual for giving birth to a son.
>
> The women did what they were told, but they accidentally mixed up the dishes and each ate the rice pudding meant for the other. Some time later when Bhṛgu had returned, he perceived their mistake and predicted that Satyavatī would give birth to a Brahmin who would act like a Kṣatriya and her mother would

give birth to a Kṣatriya who would act like a Brahmin. Satyavatī was horrified and begged Bhṛgu to defer the prediction for one generation, to her grandson. Bhṛgu agreed and Satyavatī gave birth to the Brahmin Jamadagni, while her mother gave birth to Viśvāmitra, a king who would later become a Brahmin ascetic.

Jamadagni, like his father, married a princess. Her name was Reṇukā and after they were wed she went to live with him in his forest hermitage, where she gave birth to five sons, of which Paraśurāma, inheritor of the mixed nature intended for his father, was the youngest. One day Reṇukā went out to the stream to collect some water, and as she was filling her pot, she saw a *gandharva* (a celestial musician or forest spirit) named Citraratha bathing in the water and engaging in erotic play with his concubines a little farther downstream. Distracted by her momentary attraction to Citraratha, Reṇukā spilled the water she was collecting and left a wet spot on the front of her clothes.

When she returned to the hermitage Jamadagni saw the wet spot on his wife's clothes and deduced her mental infidelity. He became enraged and one by one he ordered each of his sons to cut off his mother's head. The four oldest were too horrified at their father's words to speak, let alone obey, so Jamadagni cursed them to become dumb like animals. Only Paraśurāma obeyed his father's command without hesitation and cut off Reṇukā's head with his axe (*paraśu*). Pleased with his son's loyalty, Jamadagni granted the boy whatever he desired, and Paraśurāma asked him to resurrect his mother, lift the curse on his brothers, and cause everyone to forget the entire incident. Jamadagni granted all this, along with long life and victory in battle.

Some time passed and a Kṣatriya king named Arjuna Kārtavīrya, who had received one thousand arms as a boon from the gods, came to the hermitage of Jamadagni while on a hunting trip and demanded hospitality from Reṇukā. With the help of her husband's divine "Wishing Cow" that could magically provide anything its owner desired, Reṇukā was able to provide the king and his hunting party with an elaborate feast. Impressed with her abilities, Kārtavīrya decided he wanted the cow and stole it from the hermitage.

Paraśurāma, who was away on a journey, returned to find the cow missing and went after Kārtavīrya to avenge the theft. When he caught up to him, Paraśurāma cut off Kārtavīrya's thousand arms with his arrows before finally killing him. But while he was still away and the hermitage was unprotected, the slain king's sons sneaked in and killed Jamadagni in retaliation. When Paraśurāma returned to find his father dead, he swore revenge on all Kṣatriyas, vowing to wipe them out twenty-one times over. In fulfillment of his vow, he killed twenty-one generations of Kṣatriyas and filled five lakes with their blood before, his rage spent, he made a sacrifice in which he gave away the earth that he had conquered and went into exile to spend the rest of his days in meditation. Meanwhile, Brahmin men impregnated the Kṣatriya widows to produce a righteous generation of kings.

Some of the Kṣatriyas had been saved by sages or animals that hid and protected them in the forest. And when Paraśurāma was through killing, they came out of hiding and repopulated the earth, which had been suffering with no warriors left to protect it. Later, Paraśurāma intervened in the events of the great *Mahābhārata* war that would once again nearly wipe out all the Kṣatriyas on earth. He trained the warriors Bhīṣma and Drona in the martial arts and the use of magical weapons. He also trained the warrior Karṇa, but cursed him to die in battle after learning that Karṇa had hidden the fact that he was a Kṣatriya during his tutelage.

Forced into exile because he had given away the earth in sacrifice, Paraśurāma went to the ocean and hurled his axe out into the water, forcing the ocean to recede and create a new strip of land on which he could live, since it had not been part of the earth when he gave it away. Paraśurāma settled the new place by establishing temples, bringing in Brahmins to perform the Vedic rituals, and setting up schools to teach martial arts. Eventually he returned to his meditations and withdrew from the world, where he has the status of an undying *cirañjīvin* (immortal).

## The Argument, Purpose, and Structure of This Book

### Argument

The first part of my argument is this: The Paraśurāma myth was created by Brahmins as a narrative response to the decline of sacrificial performance and the rise of post-Vedic sectarian religions after the Buddhist Mauryan empire collapsed in the second century BCE. It provided a fantasy of Brahmin power with which the mythmakers could identify and a model of the proper Brahmin-Kṣatriya relationship that they hoped Kṣatriyas would emulate. But this is the beginning of an understanding, not the totality of it. Every Paraśurāma myth is not adequately explained by tracing it straight back to this historical genesis. Myth transmission is not like a row of dominos; it is a diffusion through language, theology, ritual, state formations, psychology, natural philosophy, folklore, life patterns, institutional authority, religious experience, technology, and collective identity. Understanding a myth means understanding its place in these discourses, which is at least as important as where it began.

The raw material for the Paraśurāma myth is drawn from elements of the Vedic worldview. This is significant because by the time of the Paraśurāma myth, the Vedic tradition encompassed its own commentarial literature, produced by generations of sustained reflection on the meaning of the text employing an exegetical practice based on homology and analogy. Thus, it was already the case that mythic symbols and tropes of the Vedic tradition had multiple referents in an array of domains that included the ritual, the natural, the somatic, and the divine, resulting in the Paraśurāma myth being dense with overlapping (and imported) meanings from the start.

This brings us to the second part of my argument: After the end of the period of epic composition (around 500 CE), subsequent variants of the Paraśurāma myth expanded, elaborated, and sometimes inverted its thematic content, providing the narrative equivalent of an exploded-view drawing of the myth with an open-ended structure (there is no conclusion for a figure who never dies). These expansions, elaborations, and inversions of the myth reflect the particular needs of actors according to their social, political, religious, and economic situations, such as the Citpāvan Brahmins in eighteenth-century Maharashtra or early medieval Vaiṣṇava theologians in Kashmir. But they also illuminate certain cross-culturally relevant concerns and psychic structures, such as a personality formation André Green has identified as the "Dead Mother Complex" and the general fear of rebounding, retributive violence, made more acute as technologies of war have grown more sophisticated.

Finally, let me be clear on one point. The Vedic worldview that I will be referring to throughout this book is just that—a view of the world, not a world itself. Chauvinistic colonial historians and Hindu nationalists alike have made the mistake of taking the textual evidence we have of how a small class of educated intellectuals saw the world from the little corner of it in which they were ensconced and presenting it as the essence of a Hindu civilization, which these colonial historians and Hindu nationalists then compare to (or conflate with) the South Asia of their own day. The texts and traditions I will treat in this book are significant not because they provide some kind of a window into the fundamental nature of the Indian mind or the true form of its civilization, but rather because they demonstrate the conflicts, contestations, and ambiguities that marked the movement of ideas across diverse South Asian cultures over a period of two thousand years.

## PURPOSE

The purpose of this book is to serve as a guide to the Paraśurāma mythos for those who want to learn something about this comparatively little-studied figure and also to provide some interpretations of this mythos proceeding from my central argument. In this respect, the *raison d'être* of book is not the argument itself, but a question, namely, "Why is Paraśurāma an *avatāra* of Viṣṇu?" Of course, we could ask this of any *avatāra,* but so much the better! Asking why Narasiṃha the Man-Lion, Kurma the Tortoise, or Matsya the Fish are *avatāra*s would no doubt lead to some wonderful insights about the development of Viṣṇu worship. But the question of Paraśurāma's *avatāra*-hood raises a different set of issues than would most. Paraśurāma's heroism is characterized by behavior that is excessive, and the tradition seems to have seen it this way for a long time.

The unavoidable question of why it matters what anyone thinks or has thought about Paraśurāma also deserves an answer. It matters because answering that question is an opportunity to make a series of bigger and more broadly applicable observations. A close reading of Paraśurāma's mythology as it develops over the centuries will illuminate the social tensions and religious ferment that have shaped that development and thereby enrich our picture of Indian intellectual history. Specifically, understanding Paraśurāma's enduring role in Indian mythology will lead us to some important insights about the complexity of Indian attitudes toward women's bodies and retributive violence. But the Indian mythmakers who created and propagated stories about Paraśurāma were not naive agents. They did not unknowingly reproduce their social structures in myths in the same way that dinosaurs left behind their fossilized bones, all so that these myths could then be interpreted and explained to their descendants by later Western scholars. To the contrary, they were often perspicacious and sublimely creative observers of the human condition who may well have as much to say about us (in the broadest sense) as we have to say about them.

## STRUCTURE

To make organization of the material easier, I have identified three major motifs that belong to the structure of the myth. The first is Paraśurāma's mixed nature as a Kṣatriya and a Brahmin, almost always as the result of a ritual mistake. The second is matricide, that is, Paraśurāma's decapitation of his mother, the Kṣatriya princess Reṇukā, who is herself worshipped as a goddess in parts of India. The third motif is the vengeful annihilation of the Kṣatriyas in an act of mass extermination often characterized as "genocide," which is in many ways the defining characteristic of Paraśurāma's mythos.

In chapter 1, "The Brahmin Warrior: Paraśurāma *in Extremis*" I will employ a trope originated by the philosopher Slavoj Žižek to explore three levels or aspects of Paraśurāma's split identity: the universal-ontological, the particular-sexual, and the singular-subjective. At the universal-ontological level, I will focus on the cosmic implications of Paraśurāma's overcoming of dualities, beginning with Phillip Lutgendorf's characterization of the Hindu notion of the *avatāra* as a '"compression' of infinitude into a mortal frame" and a *cirañjīvin* ("long-lived one") as "just the reverse: an endless extension of corporeal life" (2007, 279). As both an *avatāra* and a *cirañjīvin,* Paraśurāma is a mythicization of the simultaneous compression and extension of time, something like a narrative counterpart to the infinite set of numbers between zero and one.

The particular-sexual level of the myth, I will show, is best illustrated in stories of Paraśurāma's coming into being as a hybrid figure, so I will focus on myths of his conception (which I will refer to, following Freud, as "primal scenes") modeled after fertility rites involving the hugging of trees and the ingestion of rice pudding. To understand Paraśurāma on the singular-subjective level, I will turn to the late–twentieth-century Malayalam poem *Maḻuvinṟe Katha* ("The Story of the Axe"), which endows him with both individuality and interiority. In the poem, Paraśurāma's hybridity binds him to his problematic actions irrevocably and defines him as a unique figure. Paraśurāma has the power of a Brahmin and the temper of a Kṣatriya, and that causes all the trouble.

Another point I will consider is what *kind* of Brahmin Paraśurāma is. He is a member of the Bhārgava clan that includes the warlike Brahmins Aurva, Śukra, and Cyavana, all of whose stories are used to illustrate prominent themes in the epic without actually being integral to its plot. Next, I will examine the concept of *varṇa,* the ancient Indian class system whose boundaries Paraśurāma transgresses, balancing the normative concepts expressed in the Sanskrit law texts against what we know about ancient Indian realities, including the reign of Puṣyamitra Śunga and what some historians have claimed was a Vedic restoration that followed the Buddhist Mauryan empire.

Returning to a philosophical reading, I will next explore the Paraśurāma myth's elaboration of the concepts of dislocation, excess, and becoming by analyzing it alongside those of three other liminal figures from Hindu mythology: Droṇa, Dattātreya, and Viśvāmitra, each of which illuminate a different facet of Paraśurāma. Droṇa's story, I will argue, illuminates Paraśurāma's temporal and spatial exceptionalism; Dattātreya's story illuminates his embodiment of excess; and Viśvāmitra's story illuminates his embodiment of the vanishing mediator of "becoming." To see how Paraśurāma exemplifies the "sovereign exception" of the lawmaker beyond the law, I will examine the discussion of sovereignty in the Hindu myth of the first king Vena as well as the writings of the twentieth- and twenty-first-century European political philosophers Carl Schmitt and Giorgio Agamben. Finally, I will use another idea from philosophy, that of the double negation, to reread Paraśurāma alongside the European myth of the Wandering Jew.

The second chapter, "Matricide I: The Broken Pot," is the first of two chapters devoted to Paraśurāma's decapitation of his mother. Because the story of Reṇukā's decapitation is so popular in its own right and is so significant a part of her own separate but related mythology, it seems proper to treat the episode as a myth in itself. Therefore, this is the approach I will take in the matricide chapters, beginning with establishing the form of the matricide "micromyth":

1. A married woman sees an attractive man, becomes sexually aroused involuntarily and loses control, after which her husband sees evidence of her arousal and perceived infidelity.

2. The sons refuse their father's command to kill their mother and are cursed to become animals or idiots as a result, losing the power of speech.

3. The youngest son obeys his father's command to behead his mother.

4. The father/husband restores and resurrects the mother/wife, and the youngest son asks for the whole incident to be forgotten.

In "The Broken Pot," I will focus on the first element of the matricide micromyth, looking at the ways in which Reṇukā's perceived incontinence at the river—imagined by the seventeenth-century *Mahābhārata* commentator Nīlakaṇṭha as a reference to the involuntary production of vaginal lubrication when a woman becomes sexually aroused—reflects ancient Indian values and anxieties that come together in notions of the fluidity of female sexual desire, defined against the yogic ideal of semen retention. I will also look at Reṇukā's ordeal in light of the topic of split identity treated in the previous chapter, since she is the nominal source of Paraśurāma's Kṣatriya half. To explore some nonobvious but significant aspects of this trope, I will analyze it through the lenses of the Aristotelian concept of *akrasia,* or self-control; the Indian folkloric motif of the woman waylaid at the well; myths about the nonhuman beings known as *yakṣa*s and *gandharva*s; and the Sanskrit sexological literature. I will also think about the breaking of Reṇukā's water pot in terms of the symbolic significance of the pot in Indian poetry and philosophy. Finally, I will compare the story of Reṇukā's encounter with the bathing prince with two Indian rituals: the Vedic *varuṇapraghāsa* rite and a contemporary Tamil exorcism.

Chapter 3, "Matricide II: The Severed Head," focuses on the other elements of the matricide micromyth: the curse Jamadagni places on the sons who refuse his command to behead Reṇukā; the matricide itself; and Reṇukā's recapitation and resurrection. To fully explicate these episodes, I will follow in the footsteps of venerable scholars such as Girindrasekhar Bose, Sudhir Kakar, Robert Goldman, A. K. Ramanujan, Gananath Obeyesekere, Wendy Doniger, Jeffrey J. Kripal, and Alf Hiltebeitel in applying the tools of psychoanalysis to the study of South Asian religion. Specifically, I will employ the theories of Jacques Lacan, Julia Kristeva, Stanley M. Kurtz, and André Green to examine the psychological aspects of Paraśurāma's matricide.

The chapter begins with the fate of the disobedient sons who either are cursed to die, are rendered dumb "like animals," are reduced to beggary, or else become renouncers. Following Kristeva's explanation of matricide as the developmental moment in which a child must reject the mother and submit to the law of the father, I will look at variations of the consequences suffered by Paraśurāma's brothers in Vaiṣṇava *purāṇa*s and South Indian temple legends. Next, I will address the matricide itself by returning to "The Story of the Axe" before looking at some condemnations of and parallels to Paraśurāma's matricide from Śaiva traditions in Tibet and Tamil Nadu. I will also give a lengthy treatment of the episode in which Paraśurāma's mythic trajectory most deeply penetrates the Śaiva universe: Paraśurāma's fight with Śiva's adopted son Gaṇeśa.

Following that is a digression in which I look at the myth of Cirakāri, another son who is ordered to decapitate his mother by his father, but spends so long considering the matter that it gives his father a chance to cool off and withdraw the command. As I will show, this myth, found in the epic and the *Skanda Purāṇa*, combines elements of the story of Indra and Ahalyā with that of Reṇukā in order to make an implicit critique of Paraśurāma's hasty matricide. In the next section, I will spend some time with myths from Maharashtra and Tamil Nadu focusing on Reṇukā as a goddess in her own right, often identified with the headless goddesses Chinnamastā and Lajjāgauri. In the last part of the chapter, I will use the psychoanalytic theories of Green, Lacan, and Kurtz to understand the matricide micromyth and put forward my most developed interpretations of the decapitation of Reṇukā.

Like the matricide episode, the annihilation of the Kṣatriyas is also at the core of the Paraśurāma myth cycle, and so it will also require two chapters to fully explicate. The mass killing the myth describes, I will argue, deserves its own nomenclature. Since the criterion Paraśurāma uses to select his victims is their membership in the second tier of the fourfold hierarchy of *varṇa,* I have chosen to call it "varṇicide."

The book's fourth chapter, "Varṇicide I: The Extermination of the Kṣatriyas and Its Aftermath," will address the varṇicide itself, beginning by contextualizing the episode in the larger myth cycle of the rivalry between the Bhārgava Brahmins and the Haihaya kings. Then I will look at discussions of Paraśurāma by contemporary Hindus on internet message boards to examine how the modern reception of the myth, shaped by notions of race, genocide, total war, and terrorism, has given Paraśurāma a new relevance while also giving us new lenses through which to view him. Next, I will compare Paraśurāma to Aśvatthāman, the epic's other immortal, accursed, father-avenging, Brahmin warrior figure, with special attention to the modern depiction of the latter in a twentieth-century Bengali play.

The second half of the chapter will treat the sanitization and theologization of Paraśurāma's varṇicide in the literature produced by the early Vaiṣṇava sect called the Pāñcarātrins in Kashmir around 500 CE. I will argue that, along with developing their theology of a personal and omnipotent deity, the Pāñcarātra variant of the Paraśurāma myth, which turns his human victims into demons, serves the purpose of connecting local and regional sacred history to the late Vedic mythic structure of the war between the gods and the demons. I will conclude with a look at a "countermyth" produced by the Śvetāmbara ("White-Clad") Jainas in the twelfth-century Gujarati *Triṣaṣṭiśalākāpuruṣacarita*. For the Jainas, Paraśurāma represents the dangers of excessive wrath and, for the benefit of an audience transitioning from Śaiva to Jaina hegemony, they portray him as a cruel killer of men whose actions lead to the Brahmins (not the Kṣatriyas) being annihilated twenty-one times by the eighth world ruler of Jaina mythology, Subhūma.

In the next chapter, "Varṇicide II: Blood and Soil in Malabar and Maharashtra," I will begin by weighing the strengths and weaknesses of D. D. Kosambi's Marxist reading of the Paraśurāma myth as pure Brahmin ideology. Then, using the Vedic idea of the sacrificial remainder as starting point, I will look at some of the ways in which mythmakers imagine the Kṣatriyas to have survived the varṇicide campaign in order to rise again. As part of this discussion, I will examine the myth-histories of some of the castes in India that trace their descent from this surviving remnant, including the Fire Clan Rajputs and the Khaṇḍelvāl Vaiśyas of Rajasthan. Next, I will discuss the land creation submotif in which Paraśurāma uses his axe or some other projectile to drive back the sea and create a new strip of land to settle. I will argue that this event functions as what Lacan has called a *point de capiton,* or "quilting point," being the intersection and knotting together of the fluid motif from the matricide stories and the sacrificial remainder motif from the varṇicide stories.

I will then look at Paraśurāma's role in the Sanskrit *Keralamahātmya* and the Malayalam *Kēraḷōlpatti,* in which he is celebrated as a culture hero of Kerala's Malabar coast, the same piece of land he is most often said to have reclaimed from the sea with his axe. Paraśurāma is also credited with originating some of the region's most distinctive cultural features: matrilineal succession; the political institution in which a provisional king called the Perumal serves at the pleasure of the Brahmins for a period of twelve years; and the practice of *kalarippayattu,* a system of kicks, throws, punches, blocks, pressure points, healing techniques, and the use of various weapons that is a mixture of Tamil martial traditions and northern *dhanurveda.* We shall see that in Kerala, at least, Paraśurāma's myth is also an indisputable piece of propaganda used to legitimize the land rights of the Nambudiri Brahmins.

Finally, I will argue that this is also the case in Maharashtra. With a close reading of the *Paraśarāma Caritra,* a semihistorical account of the rule of the Brahmin Peśwās, or Prime Ministers, composed around 1772, I will show how Paraśurāma's story is used to lend legitimacy to the Brahmins of the Citpāvan clan who ruled Maharashtra in the eighteenth century. In concluding this chapter, I will examine exactly how Paraśurāma's violent act of destruction became an act of creation in places like Malabar and Maharashtra, where new stories were needed to undergird new power structures, and compare the ideology of these Paraśurāma myths with other recent "blood and soil" mythologies from the United States.

In my conclusion, I will attempt to tie all of these re-descriptions, observations, analyses, and interpretations together with some graphic representations and three arguments. First, I will argue that the "doubling" of Paraśurāma's conception narrative (first appearing in the story of the ritual mistake, then in the story of Jamadagni and Reṇukā's Brahmin-Kṣatriya marriage) is intentional, meant to establish an "analogic key" that we can represent as *Paternal : Maternal :: Brahmin : Kṣatriya*. Second, I will argue for the existence of four subcycles within the Paraśurāma myth that I identify as the cycle of the primal scenes, the Kārtavīrya cycle, the *kṣatra* cycle, and the *avatāra* cycle. Third and finally, I will argue that the open-ended structure of the Paraśurāma cycle is a mythogenetic element that contributes to the different paths taken in the variants.

Those who want to get straight to the Paraśurāma myths can do so by proceeding to the first chapter. The remainder of this introduction is dedicated to methodology and it mostly sticks to examples not taken from the Paraśurāma cycle in order to demonstrate what I think is the broader applicability of my approach. I will lay all my cards on the table with respect to what I think myths are, what I think we can learn from them, and why I think comparison and psychoanalysis are valid tools for reading Indian myths in general and the Paraśurāma myth in particular.

## A Note on Method: How Myths Make Sense

In 2008, Jonathan Z. Smith was asked why he studied religions. He answered: "Because they're funny. . . . They relate to the world in which I live, but it's like a fun house mirror: Something's off" (Sinhabu 2008). Smith's somewhat glib, but no doubt honest, characterization of the study of religion is useful here. When I am reading Paraśurāma's story, I find that it is *strangely familiar* in the literal oxymoronic sense. On one level, the themes of the myth are deeply rooted in the conflicts and concerns of the very different world that was ancient India: class identity versus clan identity; temporal power versus spiritual authority; sacrificial religion versus devotional religion. But on another level, Paraśurāma's story revolves around the familiar perennial and cross-cultural issues of mothers, fathers, and the desire for revenge. And on still another level, the myth of Paraśurāma's protracted repetitive campaign of killing seems to speak directly to our own modern world in which every victory in war only demoralizes the populace further and creates a power vacuum in which a new enemy can and usually does arise. What are we now to make of the strangely familiar story of Paraśurāma that has been delivered to us from a different time and place? And just as important, how do we unpack it without damaging it in the process?

By comparing a wide array of variants, we will trace the intertwining developmental arcs of the three motifs I have identified above (mixed birth, matricide, and genocide/varṇicide) and seek to draw some conclusions based on the transformations the myth undergoes. We will see that some transformations are of limited significance and serve only to clarify an underlying outline (such as whether the curse Jamadagni inflicts on Paraśurāma's disobedient brothers causes them to die or become mute), while other transformations are of great significance and speak to something specific about the myth's structure (such as the myths that identify the bathing man Reṇukā sees at the river as Jamadagni's killer Arjuna Kārtavīrya).

At this point the reader may rightly ask: Does it not seem capricious to say that the changes in one variant speak volumes while another variant is just one among many? Am I not picking and choosing which parts of the myth to read maximally and which ones to read minimally in order to support any interpretation I want? Ultimately, the reader will answer those questions for herself. I will only reply that I make these decisions informed by the myth's larger cultural and historical context. But this explanation is not enough to fend off all further questions on method. So, before we proceed, I will turn away from Paraśurāma in order to outline the theory and method of comparative mythology as I practice it. But first, a preemptive warning and a critique.

## A Warning: The Politics of Speculative Arguments

In the introduction to *Man into Wolf: An Anthropological Interpretation of Sadism, Masochism and Lycanthropy*, the Austrian polymath Robert Eisler prepares his readers for the coming onslaught of (highly) speculative arguments he is about to unleash upon them with this borrowed quote: "If I am in the wrong, my errors may set the minds of others at work, and may be a means of bringing both them and me to a knowledge of the truth" (Macaulay 1910, 568–69 in Eisler 1978, xxiii). Eisler is one of my favorite authors and *Man into Wolf*, flawed is it is, is one of my favorite books.[1] Even so, I find that there is something deeply disingenuous in this quote. At first glance, the line appears to express the very spirit of intellectual humility, of being a worker among workers in the production of knowledge. It suggests offering up outrageous ideas that may be wrong and humbly accepting it if they prove to be so, all in the interest of shaking an intellectual community out of its stupor and forcing it to creatively rethink the issues at hand. And I have no doubt this is what Eisler intended when he quoted it. But on closer inspection we can see how it can easily be used as a ploy to muddy the waters of good-faith scholarship with arrant nonsense like "intelligent design," racial pseudo-science, and Hindutva history. Not all errors bring one closer to the truth, after all. Some just waste everyone's time and cheapen the discourse.

Even more problems arise when we consider the source of the quote: the nineteenth-century British peer, politician, and scholar Thomas Babbington Macaulay. The line comes from a letter Lord Macaulay wrote from Calcutta on November 26, 1836, to his friend Macvey Napier, the editor of *The Edinborough Review*. The letter accompanied an essay Macaulay had written on the sixteenth-century English philosopher Francis Bacon in which he disputed the degree to which the Baconian method (often considered the start of the scientific method) was truly an original use of inductive reasoning. But as the line suggests, when it came to Bacon, Macaulay may well have been prepared to amend or even reverse his contrarian position if presented with better arguments. On the subject of the Baconian method, Macaulay was prepared to be corrected by other white men with whom he considered himself on equal footing. He even took the trouble to establish his authority with scholarly *bona fides*, announcing that his opinion was formed "not at second hand, like nine tenths of the people who talk about Bacon, but after several very attentive perusals of his greatest works, and after a good deal of thought" (568).

In other matters he was much less open-minded. On the subject of Indian religion, for one, he did not hold himself to the same standards and had no such compunctions about "second hand" knowledge. His opinions on matters of Indian religion were unexamined, unassailable, and backed up with considerable political power. One year earlier, he had famously written:

> I have no knowledge of either Sanscrit or Arabic. But I have done what I could to form a correct estimate of their value. I have read translations of the most celebrated Arabic and Sanscrit works. I have conversed both here and at home with men distinguished by their proficiency in the Eastern tongues. I am quite ready to take the Oriental learning at the valuation of the Orientalists themselves. I have never found one among them who could deny that a single shelf of a good European library was worth the whole native literature of India and Arabia. (1835, 10)

Macaulay's imperious attitude would have been one thing coming from an armchair scholar, but Macaulay was more than that, serving as a member of the Council of India, a board created by charter in 1833 to advise the Governor-General of India. In a letter he had written to Napier in August, Macaulay informed him about the goings-on in the subcontinent that year:

> You have probably heard of the *Thugs,* a species of robbers and murderers who infest this country. Vigorous efforts have lately been made to put them down; and in the course of these efforts, the real nature of their confederacy has for the first time been discovered. I think that you will agree with me in pronouncing the long existence and the vast extent of this fraternity to be a phenomenon without parallel in history. The government here have printed, but not published, a volume of papers respecting this strange race of men. The book is so ill arranged that, even if it were published, few people would read or understand it. But the information which is dispersed through it is in the highest degree curious and amusing. Lord Auckland observed to me the other day that it would be a matchless subject for a review. (567–68)

The writings of William Sleeman to which Macaulay refers and which accompanied this letter were introduced to the world in the pages of *The Edinborough Review* the next year, kicking off the feverish British Thugee suppression campaign in earnest. It was likely Macaulay himself who subsequently penned legislation allowing the British to imprison any suspected Thug for life on the basis that the Thugee cult was a religion (not to mention a threat to the opium trade) and its murderous practices an inherent aspect of its members' personalities (Rappaport 2012, 22n14 and Rushby 2002, 178).

Macaulay's double standard should serve as a warning to Western scholars. Making a speculative argument and challenging others to disprove it is rarely done in good faith (how many scholars have we ever seen rejoicing at the success others have attained by proving them wrong?). And even when it is, it presupposes that others are in a position to do so. While contemporary Western scholars' writings are nowhere near as consequential as Macaulay's were, we should keep in mind that we are still writing from his side of the table. This does not mean, however, that we should steer clear of Indian religion unless we are affirming its irreducible particularity (or its objective supremacy as some might want), for we should also keep in mind that the

Indian prisoners Macaulay deemed to be irremediably evil would have certainly been better off if he had placed less emphasis on cultural differences and more on commonalities.

## Critiques of Comparison

The Macaulay case is an extreme example of comparison being used as cudgel by an arrogant colonial power. But some scholars have made a case against comparison *tout court.* Bruce Lincoln and Cristiano Grottanelli's critique represents such a case that requires addressing. Of their twelve "Theses on Comparison," number six really sums up the argument: "Wide-ranging comparison—comparison of the strong sort—has consistently disappointed" (Lincoln 2018, 25–26). It has done so, they contend, because its practitioners "consistently misrecognized products of their own imagination and desire ('the human mind,' 'tripartite ideology,' 'homo religiosus') for objects having historic, prehistoric, and/or transhistoric actuality" (26). Leaving aside the question of *who* exactly has been "disappointed" (more than once, apparently) by Lévi-Strauss, Dumézil, and Eliade—the three strong comparativists named in the essay—I will address the idea of misrecognition because it raises a very important question.

I should begin by noting that Lincoln makes no distinction between organizing principles and what we might call "master discourses." But we should make that distinction, because they are very different things. The former are ways of partially analyzing a narrative whose meanings are so dense and multifaceted as to defy any description that does not resemble the prose of James Joyce. The latter are overarching metanarratives that subsume and exhaustively explain all other narratives. Master discourses are a virtual guarantee of misrecognition on the part of the interpreter, but I would submit that it is much harder to characterize an organizing principle as a product of the scholar's own imagination and desire, misrecognized as an object with "historic, prehistoric, and/or transhistoric actuality."

Constellations may be misrecognitions of random groupings of stars seen from particular point in space, but they have guided sailors for millennia. That does not mean, however, that they are never the occasion for conflict. According to the anthropologist and historian Marshall Sahlins, just such a conflict occurred in the winter of 1779, when Captain James Cook arrived in Hawai'i as the Pleiades appeared on the horizon at sunset, marking the start of the Makahiki festival and setting off a chain of events that led to his murder—a "historical metaphor" for the "mythical reality" of the death of the god Lono at the end of the season (Sahlins 1981, 17–28). This old conflict then became the basis of a new conflict in the 1990s between Sahlins himself and fellow anthropologist Gananath Obeyesekere over who has the authority to explain how "natives" think and whether the story of Captain Cook should be viewed through the lens of Hawai'ian or European mythology (see Borofsky 1997).

Constellations are organizing principles, albeit organizing principles loaded with meanings (astrological and otherwise) that one has to contend with in order to navigate with them. Throughout this book, I will use organizing principles originated by Lévi-Strauss, Dumézil, Freud, and Kristeva to highlight certain features of the myths in question. The danger, I admit, is that one could misrecognize the Oedipus complex or tripartite ideology as essential and ahistorical features of myth. But picking out patterns is not, in itself, either essentializing or reductive. It is instead a simple necessity when one tries to drink from the proverbial firehose of myth.

"Weak" comparison, the good kind, according to Lincoln and Grottanelli, "refrains from imagining that universal themes, a shared prehistory, or a process of diffusion are responsible for the similarities between mythic narratives" (129). Instead, the two myths being compared are understood to be situated in their respective historical and cultural contexts. Lincoln continues: "Such common features as they share are not accidental, however. Rather, they reflect similar points of tension in the social structure of the peoples among whom these stories circulated" (ibid.). This seems to me to be inarguable, but it leaves us asking: Are we not now comparing something else? Are we incurious enough not to ask about the origins of the parallel "points of tension" that give rise to these similar myths? Are social hierarchies supposed to be less historically contingent, less interested, less idiosyncratic, and more concrete than myths? Surely they are not. So how does this get us past whatever problems are created by comparing myths?

Another line of critique, that comparison always employs a "muted third term" (e.g., "the sacred") and never fails to find exactly what it is looking for, is not wrong. But neither is it devastating. We can separate our epistemology from our ontology and remain agnostic about the real-world correlates of our heuristic devices. The humanities, at least in my mind, are meant to creatively re-describe the world rather than explain it. These two aims are confused when Aaron W. Hughes, also criticizing comparison, describes it as "a literary conceit: an activity that selects, juxtaposes, and manipulates two or more *unrelated objects* that an individual perceives to share one or more similar or overlapping characteristics" (2017, 9; my emphasis).

This understanding of comparison rests on an unexamined use of the word *unrelated* and its nominal root form, *relation,* which is a property held symmetrically or asymmetrically between two things (a concept that philosophers have been attempting to understand since the *Phaedo*). In this sense, "unrelatedness" is a specific type of relatedness rather than the absence of it. In other words, unrelatedness is also a relation. Simply put, there is no real definition of what *unrelated* means in the study of religion. Are two religions (the kind of "objects" here under discussion) unrelated because they do not overlap in mental or physical space? If we could find two religions unrelated in that way, then the situation would end at that same moment in the mind of the observer, something like Lévi-Strauss's fabled attempt to find an uncontacted South American tribe. Are two religions unrelated because they do not share a time or place of origin? That seems like an arbitrary distinction and if true, it would make modern Asatru unrelated to the practices of pre-Christian Europe that it emulates.

If two things can be compared (and any two things can be compared), they are comparable by definition, which is not the same thing as saying they are the same or even analogous. Those who want to see a more rigorous, context-attentive, and theoretically grounded practice of comparison in the study of religion (and I count myself among them) may object to this characterization or they may want to insist upon a narrower range of comparable objects and add their own qualifications in order to disallow questions like, "How is a raven like a writing desk?" That is all to the good, but I think this will always be an exercise in arbitrary rule making if it is done outside of the context of a particular project. As I understand it, any comparison can be fruitfully made if it illuminates some new aspect of the myth one is creatively re-describing.

I am also wary of the idea that comparison is a kind of experimental laboratory where one can test hypotheses, as Ivan Strenski has suggested in his otherwise illuminating article on the subject (2016, 51). Testing hypotheses is a way to construct, by process of elimination, an objective account. And, beyond a very circumscribed realm that would include the relative dating of texts and establishing the earliest uses of ideas such as "karma" and "rebirth," I do not think the humanities are best equipped to do that. I will therefore spend more time re-describing these myths than testing my hypotheses on them.

This is not a step back from relevance, however, since imaginative re-description is at least as important a form of knowledge production as hypothesizing is. The physicist Phillip Ball has written of contemporary works of science fiction based on more or less accurate understandings of quantum physics that, while there will always be hits and misses, "it is right that there should be imaginative responses to quantum mechanics, because it is quite possible that only an imagination sufficiently broad and liberated will come close to articulating what it is about" (2018, 10). And when it comes to being counterintuitive, obscure, and mystifying, religion may not beat quantum physics, but it certainly gives it a run for its money.

The comparative method is the proper exercise of the training one receives as an historian of religions. One may well argue that just because one has been trained to do something is no reason to do it, or even to assume it has any use at all. This is true in many cases, but does not apply to the project of the humanities, which is to gain a better understanding of what it is to be human. In this project, any disciplined way of thinking that is rigorously self-critical and is practiced among a group of sufficiently diverse scholars (diversity being not a mere sop to public relations in our case, but a vital necessity for the well-being of the field) will produce insights and perspectives that will be of use to others. But the proof, ultimately, is in the pudding. Now, on to the nuts and bolts of the kind of re-descriptions and comparisons I will be doing in this book.

## Myth/Myths/Mythos/Mythology

Throughout this book, I will be using the terms *myth, myths, mythos,* and *mythology* (as well as *myth cycle*) interchangeably to spare the reader from ploddingly repetitive prose. But they all mean the same thing in my usage. The word *myth* can both refer to something that is commonly believed but is not true and to a story that, while fictional, nonetheless is held to contain some profound truth about the human experience. This double meaning of myth is the product of an argument that goes back to Ancient Greece and Plato's distinction between the truth of *logos* and the falsity of *mythos,* the latter of which he admits may nonetheless be useful in indoctrinating children too young to appreciate a good argument.[2] This idea of myth as falsehood more or less held until the sixteenth and seventeenth centuries, when it was overturned by humanist thinkers such as Francis Bacon and Giambattista Vico, who saw myth as an important category for understanding human thought and culture.

In the interest of compressing an enormously complicated narrative better treated elsewhere (e.g., Feldman and Richardson 1972; Lincoln 1999; Johnston 2018), we can quickly move on to the early nineteenth century when Georg Friedrich Creuzer developed a psychological theory of myth, writing that its purpose was "to transpose what has been thought into what has happened" (1819–21, 99).[3] Continuing into the twentieth century, the philosopher Ernst Cassirer understood comparative mythology as a way to explore the human capacity for creating symbols. For Cassirer, understanding myth was tantamount to understanding the workings of the mind. This idea was shared by the anthropologist Claude Lévi-Strauss, for whom myth was not merely fanciful but instead employed the sophisticated manipulation of symbols to resolve the binary contradictions of social life, which are an expression of the binary nature of human consciousness. Taking a different view of the myth-mind connection, the psychoanalysts Freud and Jung saw myths as representations of personality development, with Freud focused on the Oedipal conflict while Jung built his theory around mythic archetypes as expressions of the collective unconscious.

We do not need to go any farther to establish that the study of myth, indeed the very idea of myth, is a product of the Western tradition stretching from fifth-century-BCE Athens to twentieth-century Europe. So what purpose can it have in looking at Indian myths? Is there even such a thing as an Indian myth? The Paraśurāma stories we will be reading were not "myths" to the people who made them, but *itihāsa* ("history"), or *purāṇa* ("ancient tales"), or something else. Why call them myths then? And why compare them with non-Indian myths?

To answer the last question first, I would say that the study of myth is always-already comparative; even if one is studying a single variant in isolation, studying myth is always an implicitly comparative enterprise because designating a story as "myth" requires one to place it in the same category alongside stories already accepted as mythological. It would be nonsense to say that Kwakiutl myths are nothing like Egyptian myths, since one is already referring to them both as "myths." To my mind, being explicitly comparative is a more transparent way to go about it.

As to the question of nomenclature, we can call these Paraśurāma stories "myths" for practical reasons. We need not presuppose the psychic unity of humankind to see that using the category of myth allows for some creative re-descriptions that would not be possible otherwise. I will therefore call the Paraśurāma stories "myths" because they fit my definition, which I freely admit is purely heuristic and will not enable one to pick a myth out of a lineup when it is presented alongside folktales, legends, and tragedies. Nevertheless, here it is: *A myth is a narrative about events not witnessed by the teller or the audience, existing in more than one variant, that expresses the values, anxieties, and worldview shared by the group of people who receive and reproduce it.*

## MYTHS ARE NARRATIVES

To begin with, I specify that myths are narratives about events not witnessed by the teller or the audience but are understood to have happened in the past that lies beyond conventional historical memory, or sometime in an imagined future. I also specify that they must exist in more than one variant, following Hans Blumenberg's characterization of them as "stories that are distinguished by a high degree of constancy in their narrative core and by an equally pronounced capacity for marginal variation" (1985, 34). I also specify that myths are narratives in order to distinguish them from other communicative forms that do much the same work. Pierre Bourdieu was surely right when he argued that acculturation through embodied practices (e.g., the way we are taught to sit, stand, look people in the eye, or not look people in the eye) was among the most effective ways of constructing a disciplined subject, writing:

> The principles embodied in this way are placed beyond the grasp of consciousness, and hence cannot be touched by voluntary, deliberate transformation, cannot even be made explicit; nothing seems more ineffable, more incommunicable, more inimitable, and, therefore, more precious, than the values given body, made body by the transubstantiation achieved by the hidden persuasion of an implicit pedagogy, capable of instilling a whole cosmology, an ethic, a metaphysic, a political philosophy, through injunctions as insignificant as "stand up straight" or "don't hold your knife in your left hand" (1977, 94).

Not discounting table manners and the like, mythic narratives are also highly effective ways of communicating implicit cosmologies, ethics, metaphysics, and political philosophies. But unlike the process Bourdieu describes above, myth's double polyvocality—both internal in the plurality of voices belonging to different characters inside the myth and external in the plurality of voices belonging to different mythmakers producing variants of the myth—gives people an opportunity to elaborate upon these unstated principles through supplemental narratives or to critique them through counternarratives. Thus, the narrative form of myths is a type of plasticity in the sense developed by Catherine Malabou: it both gives form (like plastic surgery) and receives form (like plastic explosives) (2008, 4–5). By dint of their narrative plasticity, myths become sites where worldviews are presented as well as contested and sometimes blown apart.

We should note, however, that contestation of a worldview in a myth can inadvertently reify or affirm it, which is why myth is so often equated with ideology. I will illustrate with an example from the *Mahābhārata*: the story of the outcaste Niṣāda archer Ekalavya (*MBh* 1.123.10–39), here summarized by Simon Brodbeck.

> (1) Verses 10–14. Droṇa is the martial tutor of the young Pāṇḍavas and Kauravas; Ekalavya, son of the *niṣāda* chief Hiraṇyadhanus (golden-bow), also comes for tuition, but Droṇa refuses him because he is a *niṣāda*. Undeterred, he lives in the woods, makes a clay model of Droṇa, practices under its unseeing eye, and becomes an expert archer.
>
> (2) Verses 15–24. When the Pāṇḍavas are out hunting, their dog discovers Ekalavya in the forest. Ekalavya shoots the Pāṇḍavas' dog in the muzzle with seven arrows, and the Pāṇḍavas witness his skill. When interrogated, he says he is Droṇa's pupil.
>
> (3) Verses 25–39. After Arjuna has complained to him of Ekalavya's skill, Droṇa comes to see Ekalavya, who receives him as his guru. Droṇa says that to gurus a fee is due; Ekalavya says he will give whatever Droṇa wants; Droṇa chooses Ekalavya's right thumb; and Ekalavya severs and gives it willingly, thus sacrificing his archery skills (2006: 2).

In making the heroic Pāṇḍavas triumphant in this situation, the myth normalizes and naturalizes the dominance of the noble *aryas* (which they represent) over other groups. But it also creates a martyr in Ekalavya and gives form to the resentment of the dispossessed stemming from the unfairness of this inequality. Indeed, in the modern age, Ekalavya has become something of a symbol of the *Dalit* resistance against caste oppression (see Doniger 2014, 547–55). However, by reimagining Ekalavya as the truly noble one who obeyed his guru without thought for himself and the Pāṇḍavas as petulant princes who went whining to their teacher when they were bested fair and square, this critique also affirms the correctness of rigid obedience to one's superiors (Droṇa), even though they are usually in charge of maintaining the hierarchy. Indeed, it is Droṇa who puts Ekalavya in his place. While the heroically reimagined Ekalavya may lend dignity to the *Dalit* cause, it leaves the hierarchical structure that maintains caste oppression untouched and even strengthened.

## Myths Express Values

Shared values, whether they are economic, aesthetic, utilitarian, spiritual, or ethical, are mediated by culture and are typically ranked with respect to one another on a hierarchical scale. Mythmakers can (and frequently do) manipulate the ranking of values to paint an idealized or aspirational picture of the world.[4] Returning to the Ekalavya myth to demonstrate this process, we should begin by noting the origin story (which also seems to originate in the epic) of Niṣāda, the eponymous ancestor of Ekalavya's tribe. In the variant that appears in *MBh* 12.59.99–103, a group of Brahmins have collectively murdered the evil king Vena. The Brahmins then use their ritual expertise to bring forth an heir from the childless king's corpse. First, they create from his thigh a dwarfish being (*harasva*) with the complexion of a burned stake (*dagdhasthūṇā*) named Niṣāda, so named because the Brahmins told him to "sit down" (*niṣīda*) after he was created. Next, they create from his right arm the good king Pṛthu, who attempts to undo all the evil his father has wrought by preventing the mixing (*saṃkara*) of peoples.

Thus, in the *Mahābhārata*, although both are princes, the semi-divine Pāṇḍavas (whose name means "Sons of the Pale One") are ranked higher than the Niṣāda Ekalavya with implicit reference to a hierarchy of values:

| | Niṣāda | Pāṇḍava |
|---|---|---|
| Descent | Monstrous/Chthonic (–) | Divine (+) |
| Body Part | Thigh (–) | Arm (+)* |
| Place of Origin | Forest (–) | Palace (+) |
| Color | Dark (–) | White (+) |
| Training | Self-taught (–) | Guru-taught (+) |
| Social Structure | Tribal (–) | Dynastic (+) |

*Although the Pāṇḍavas are not identified as descendants of Pṛthu *per se*, they are so by default when compared to the Niṣādas's eponymous ancestor.

Figure I.1. Pāṇḍavas and Niṣādas ranked with implicit reference to a hierarchy of values.

Each time the mythmakers reaffirm what is already expressed at the level of narrative (the superiority of the Pāṇḍavas) with language that obliquely refers to an implicit hierarchy of values like the one laid out above, they add another layer of reification onto that hierarchy and push it farther beyond the reach of criticism. The active, formative plasticity of mythic narrative derives in part from the unstated value systems that undergird them. The study of myth thus requires some variety of the hermeneutics of suspicion to pick out the implicit hierarchies it relies on. We could think of this as "decoding," but since that implies the false premise of some original message in the myth—an *ur-myth*—that can be uncovered, it is better to think of an interpretation arrived at in this way as a self-conscious and creative act of critically informed re-description—a "myth with footnotes" to use Lincoln's memorable phrase (1999, 209).

## Myths Express Anxieties

Anxieties are the flip side of values. While ranked values present a normative vision of the world, anxieties imagine what mythmakers fear could be. Sometimes mythmakers express these anxieties without being aware that they are doing so. Sometimes the anxieties they express are unconscious. This is a claim that requires some explanation on my part. I will get into specific models of this later, but for now I will say that human beings have a large, energy-expensive brain with more cognitive capacity than there is any reasonable use for. What is more, our awareness can only focus on a small amount of all that cognitive activity at a time. But, as Nietzsche, Freud, and Girard have taught us, outside of our limited awareness, conflicts are constantly going on, born out of the compromise made in every ordered society between the individual will and the common good. Appreciation of myths derives, at least in part, from the fact that they serve to externalize, and sometimes resolve, the anxieties that accompany these conflicts beneath the level of consciousness.

In the story of Ekalavya, some expressed anxieties are immediately apparent. The Pāṇḍavas are fearful of the prospect of another archer equal to or better than Arjuna. This is also tied to a more specific anxiety that in the coming war the Pāṇḍavas' enemies might be able to use such an archer to cancel out the advantage conferred by Arjuna's proficiency with the bow. But even after the crafty Droṇa has effectively undone the black swan event that was Ekalavya's supremacy in archery, there still remains a lingering anxiety about the hierarchical ranking of values and the potential instability in them that this episode has revealed. This anxiety is tied to a question of order, or dharma, which will require much more bloodshed than a mere severed thumb to answer.

Here I invoke, as I will again, the principle expressed in a quotation often attributed to President Dwight D. Eisenhower: "Whenever I run into a problem I can't solve, I always make it bigger. I can never solve it by trying to make it smaller, but if I make it big enough, I can begin to see the outlines of a solution." Myths make problems (anxieties) bigger—often, *much* bigger. The Paraśurāma myth focuses and enlarges a number of anxieties: the child's anxious struggles to understand their role in a family, the anxieties men feel about women's sexual desire, and Brahmins' uneasiness over the relationship of their class to coercive violence. We will return to these anxieties again and again throughout this book.

## Myths Express Worldviews

What I mean here by "worldview" is the set of common assumptions, expectations, and structuring metaphors that any hearer or reader of the myth must hold in common with the mythmaker in order for the intended meaning to be communicated. In an individual myth or even an epic, this worldview is almost always expressed only in part (the *Mahābhārata* is unusual in its claim to contain everything that can be said). We could, therefore, think of myths as windows giving us a glimpse of one small part of the worldview lying on the other side of them, but that would imply that, like windows, myths are transparent (i.e., neutral, which they are not) and that worldviews exist somewhere beyond the myths so that they can be seen through them (they do not). Rather than windows, myths are much more like projectors, shining out a partial image of a worldview. Myth and worldview exist in a mutually constitutive relationship: a myth's "making sense" (to use a phrase that mimics the idea of the middle voice, in which something "gets itself done") and its expression of a worldview against which that myth *can* make sense are one and the same action.

Let us return to Ekalavya and the Pāṇḍavas one last time. To make sense of this myth, or for this myth to make sense, one must have in mind a particular aspect of the *Mahābhārata*'s worldview: the dynamics of the guru-disciple relationship. In the world of the epic, the disciple is in debt to the guru from the time of tuition and obligated to pay whatever price the guru asks for the knowledge he has received. It is for this reason that

Ekalavya is willing to go through with the supremely self-defeating gesture of cutting off his right thumb when Droṇa asks for it. But since the myth tells us that Droṇa refused to take on Ekalavya as a disciple and was thus never truly his guru, more context is required. *MBh* 1.123.14 makes clear that Ekalavya's skill was acquired through his own great faithfulness (*parayā śraddhayā*) and greater discipline (*yogena paramena*). But Ekalavya's act of making a clay image of Droṇa and then treating it with the respect due to a teacher (*ācāryavṛttiṃ*) in 1.123.12 turns him into a disciple of Droṇa anyway. This makes sense when read in light of a worldview in which graven images of divine beings function more like conduits than representations. Through the process of *darśan* (seeing and being seen) Ekalavya has indebted himself to Droṇa just as surely as if he had learned at the master's feet.[5] Thus, the Ekalavya story has shown us, without telling us, something about the nature of both *mūrti* worship and social obligations in the epic worldview.

## MYTHS ARE RECEIVED AND REPRODUCED[6]

Admittedly, my definition of myth as a narrative about events not witnessed by the teller or the audience, existing in more than one variant, that expresses the values, anxieties, and worldview shared by the group of people who receive and reproduce it suffers from what Lincoln has rightly observed is a common problem in such definitions: I have used the verb *shared* to avoid the question of who made the myth. I have made it anonymous and impersonal and therefore beyond critique, which is how traditions themselves often represent their myths (Lincoln 2012, 54–55). But I, as a scholar, am very concerned about the authors of these myths and their intentions. Indisputably, each individual variant of a myth has an author, whether we know that author's name or not. And every author has a reason to make a variant, which gives each variant an intentional meaning.

There are many questions one can ask of a myth to determine this intentional meaning: Who made it? When did they make it? Where were they (geographically, socially, economically, politically) when they made it? Whom did they want to hear or read it? What did they want those people to think or feel? All of these questions have to do with a myth's point of origin. But we cannot always determine a myth's point of origin. What is more, myths do not always stay at their points of origin. They tend to travel, like the Wandering Jew or Paraśurāma. So, when we find a myth that looks strangely familiar or strangely out of place (or both), such as the story of the Buddha in medieval France, it raises some new questions: Who brought this alien myth to this new community? Did the myth resonate with existing cultural values or did it serve to express new imported or developing cultural forms (ritual, aesthetic, economic, social, demographic)?

Added to that, myths often live far beyond their temporal origins, persisting from age to age, like the Wandering Jew or Paraśurāma. So, when we see a later variant of an older myth, we have to ask: What external circumstances caused the author to change this myth variant from its earlier form? And if the myth's narrative seems relatively stable, has the community of readers or hearers changed to the point that they would derive new meanings from it that would have been foreign to its original historical context? Inevitably, we bring meaning to a myth from our own experiences. As my use of the word *genocide* in the title of this book suggests, it is difficult to read Paraśurāma's extermination of Kṣatriyas without thinking about more recent historical extermination campaigns. This is true not only for scholarly readers, but for contemporary Hindus, as I demonstrate in chapter 4. These new meanings generated by the act of reading Paraśurāma in a world that has the concept of genocide exist in tension with what we understand about the meaning of the myth for its previous audiences, and the more we know about a myth's history, the greater that tension grows.

Myths are not so much retold as deployed, sometimes (though not always) for political reasons. They are meant to have an effect. It is therefore necessary to look beyond the questions about a myth's production and look at questions about its reception. A useful case study is found in the reception history of Hercules as a symbol in Revolutionary France. Hercules—another highly problematic mythical hero, like Paraśurāma—had long been a popular symbol of sovereign power for the French monarchs, especially Henri IV (r. 1589–1610). And at the Festival of the Unity and Indivisibility of the Republic in August 1793, an event conceived to improve morale during a time of war, food shortages, and rebellion, a giant statue of the hero standing astride the defeated Hydra was erected at Les Invalides. Three months later, the National Convention in Paris followed the suggestion of painter Jacques-Louis David (best known for "The Death of Marat") and decreed that an even larger Hercules be erected at Pont-Neuf as a symbol of the people. The classical hero would also grace the new Great Seal of France as the national symbol.

But soon the darker elements of Hercules (who famously murdered his wife and children when possessed by madness) began to creep into the discourse. A newspaper editorial suggested that the new Hercules statue should portray him devouring a diminutive crowned figure representing the king. Popular street performances featured Hercules attacking puppet effigies of the nobility and the clergy. Most unsettling of all, commentators waved off the massacres perpetrated during the Terror by comparing them to Hercules clearing out the Augean Stables. In 1795, the plans for the Pont-Neuf statue were abandoned and talk of putting him on the Great Seal ceased. By 1798, the Upper House of Parliament was describing Hercules as "an allegory whose conception and execution were not fortunate" (Blanshard 2005, xi–xvii).

In the case of Revolutionary France, why did the darker elements of Hercules's mythology overwhelm the ready-made appeal of his strength, notoriety, and non-Christian origins that caused the National Convention to adopt him in the first place? One can only speculate, but, as part of the classical heritage, Hercules's story was in the public domain, not tied to any particular group. Because of this, there was nothing to stop others from using him as a symbol in ways that may have been either directly opposed to those of the original adopters or "helpful" in an unhelpful way, like an unrequested public endorsement from a wildly unpopular figure. Hercules also fell victim to the same relentless critique of discourse that propelled him into popularity, just as antiestablishment movements will vote their antiestablishment candidates into office in one election cycle and then quickly attack them in the next, decrying them as part of the establishment.

It is important to note that people can find meaning in a myth without knowing its context. People "respond" to myths. They fill in the gaps created by lack of familiarity with the values, anxieties, and worldviews expressed in the myth by supplying their own values, anxieties, and worldviews. The mutually constitutive relationship of myth and worldview can survive this disjunction, causing the meaning of the myth to change in light of the new worldview it is being used to express. But at the same time, it is exerting its own influence on that worldview, having, to revert to an optical analogy, a distorting and sometimes magnifying effect. Something like this seems to have happened with Hercules in France, where he was ultimately *too* apt a symbol, in ways that were surely unintentional. His descent into a madness in which he murdered his own wife and children too closely reflected the violent purges of the Terror (Robespierre loved the idea of Hercules).

As the Hercules and Ekalavya stories indicate, "values," "anxieties," and "worldviews" are fuzzy conceptual categories that cannot be easily disentangled and the dynamics of reception and reproduction can upend their relationship to each other. These dynamics manifest in the multiplicity of a myth's variants and are best explored by looking at each variant's historical context and the intentional meaning given to it by the mythmaker.

But apart from the variants is the myth itself, which really is anonymous. As Lincoln explains,

> Where most variants agree—that is, commonalities of plot, character, incident, moral, or whatever it is that unites these and makes them variants of a single story (rather than an anthology of different tales)—is the portion that is rightly anonymous, for this shared content is a collective possession and product, also an ancestral heritage that can belong to no individual author. (2012, 55)

Doniger designates this shared anonymous narrative the "micromyth" (1998, 88). The micromyth or myth structure stands apart from the myth variants and cannot be attributed to any particular mythmaker or connected to any particular audience. We could dismiss this as a scholarly construct with no objective reality like the Proto-Indo-European language, but that seems to me a way of sidestepping what should be the most important part of any discussion of mythology. The questions of who, what, when, where, how, and why are of little use to us here, and so we must turn to a different conceptual register, that developed by Freud and the psychoanalytic thinkers who came after.

## Myth Reception: Psychoanalysis, Structure, and Subjectivity

When we talk about people receiving and reproducing myths, we know now that those myths are not transparent neutral windows that reveal a worldview beyond them, but have been given intentional meanings by interested parties and tend to magnify and distort. We know that myths "make sense," but what about the people who make sense *of* those myths? It turns out that the situation is just as complicated on our side of the textual boundary as it is on the side of the mythmakers. This brings us to what will surely be a controversial part of my argument, the recourse to psychoanalytic theory as developed by Freud, Lacan, Kristeva, and Green.

By way of justification, I will return to that large, energy-expensive brain I promised to say some more about earlier. The ancient Indians who first told and heard the Paraśurāma myth had this same kind of brain and, in the interface between those brains and the world, developed notions of being a self, which I will call "subjectivity." Jessica Frazier has identified at least three major types of subjectivity in Indian thought: one that is closed off from the world; one that is separate from the world but interacts with it; and one that is open to the world and continuous with it (2017, 31). As this plurality of understandings demonstrates, subjectivity is neither given nor natural, but is at least partially a product of social construction. Thus, we can speak of a history of subjectivity.

I am using the concept of a history of subjectivity in two senses: First, each individual subjectivity has a history of how it came to be, which psychoanalysis attempts to describe. Some of these attempts are better than others, clearly. But it would be wrong to dismiss the conceptual framework Freud developed because of its limitations. Freud was a brilliant thinker, but he was nonetheless an early–twentieth-century thinker who knew what he did not know about the functioning of the brain (see Jabr 2018). In light of new discoveries, psychoanalysis may not work at the level of the neuron, but neither does Newtonian physics work at the level of the neutron. And we still need them both. Most importantly, Freud's models still give rise to useful re-descriptions.

Second, subjectivity itself has a history, which Western thinkers such as Hegel, Heidegger, and Sartre (and more recently, Julian Jaynes, David Chalmers, and Daniel Dennett, to name a few) have attempted to describe. Those who would make sense of myths have to also consider the history of the subjectivity of those subjects that received and reproduced them. Thus, to be of any value, creative re-descriptions of myths have to go beyond theories of myth into theories of subjectivity, since it cannot be the case that the structure of myths created and comprehended by historically constituted subjects bears no relationship to the structure of their subjectivity.

When we go beyond the external realities of a particular myth variant's deployment to see how the narrative has changed, we are asking what circumstances are inherent to the anonymous core of the myth itself, (i.e., its inner logic or structure) that may have caused it to change. To take a well-known example, we can look at the collapsing of two different figures—the unnamed serpent in the Garden of Eden in Genesis 3:1 and the adversary who tempts Jesus in the desert in Mark 1:12–13, Matthew 4:1–11, and Luke 4:1–13—into the single figure of Satan. This superimposition is exemplified in the myth, well known in the Orthodox Churches, of Adam and Eve signing a contract with Satan after their expulsion from the Garden (see Stone 2002). At some point, some historically situated actor started connecting these two clearly different figures from the garden and the desert, but he (probably not a she) did so under pressure created by unconscious acquiescence to the parallel structures of these two temptation events and their positions as bookends for the Christian understanding of human salvation history. In the Christian worldview, the serpent in the garden and tempter in the desert must be related. It *makes sense.*

This kind of associational thinking, which we will see repeated as we delve into the Paraśurāma mythos, is also common to both the unconscious as conceived by Freud and to the speculative poetics of the Sanskrit Brāhmaṇas and Upaniṣads. To do a thorough job of creatively re-describing what is happening inside the structure of our myth, we will therefore make use of Indian hermeneutics, along with those developed in psychoanalysis and certain philosophical notions developed by Hegel and his successors, including a path of inquiry taken from Žižek, in whose thought psychoanalysis and Hegelian dialectics come together in strange ways.

In concert with these theoretical models, I will also introduce comparative and contextual materials. This means I will tack back and forth between synchronic and diachronic readings of the myth to demonstrate the ways in which an inchoate element in the myth structure is developed in a particular variant or a variant is so influential that it reshapes the myth structure. I will be interpreting myths through rituals that enact and perform the values, anxieties, and worldview that both the myth and the ritual share. I will also be interpreting myths through other myths as well as (occasionally) others' myths. But I am not interested here in strong comparison per se. My purpose in liberally sprinkling this book with comparative material and punctuating it with epigraphs from Kierkegaard and Kabir, Scandinavian sagas and Hebrew prophets, is to poke points of entry into Paraśurāma's myth cycle, opening it up to the broadest construal possible so that we can learn something from it.

1

# The Brahmin Warrior

## *Paraśurāma in Extremis*

[The] general is not thought about with passion but with a comfortable superficiality. The exception, on the other hand, thinks the general with intense passion.

—Søren Kierkegaard, *Repetition*

About things that are untrue and composed of the five elements, the scripture says, "Not this, not that."

—*Avadhūta Gītā* 1.25

### Universal, Particular, Singular: Paraśurāma's Fractured Identity

The two epigraphs that introduce this chapter represent two distinct hermeneutical principles, one external to Indian thought and one central to it, both of which are needed to understand Paraśurāma's identity, so ordinary in its strangeness. Kierkegaard's observation that the exception "thinks the general with intense passion" helps us to understand the utility of stories like Paraśurāma's for constructing, not exceptional spaces, but general principles. The quotation from the *Avadhūta Gītā*, a text attributed to Dattātreya, Paraśurāma's legendary guru and fellow exemplar of divine hybridity, illustrates the nondualistic principle of discrimination, successively determining all of the things that a thing is not in order to finally arrive at the truth of what it is: *neti, neti* ("not this, not that"). We will need both Kierkegaard and Dattātreya as we move between the three levels of Paraśurāma's split identity: the universal, the particular, and the singular. In order to connect Paraśurāma to the distinctive aspects of the various worldviews to which he belongs we will be following a model in which, as Žižek has it, "Universal stands for ontology, Particular for sexuality, and Singular for subjectivity" (2017, 1).

On the universal-ontological level, the figure of Paraśurāma embodies a whole list of oppositions. He is an *avatāra* and a *cirañjīvin* (a "long-lived one"), a Vaiṣṇava deity and a Śaiva devotee, a Brahmin and a warrior, a sage and an epic hero.[1] To simplify things, my fellow Paraśurāma enthusiast Nicolas Dejenne opts to exclusively use the term *hero* to refer to him.[2] Yes, Paraśurāma is anomalous. But let us not make too much of this. In Hindu myth, anomalies are ubiquitous. Śiva is a god of contradictions, as Doniger (1973) has demonstrated with an unassailable thoroughness. But so is Viṣṇu. And this is especially true in the myths of his *avatāras*, the paradigmatic examples of which are the Brahmin dwarf Vamana, who contains the transcendent overlord of the cosmos in his diminutive frame, and the man-lion Narasiṃha (that God of the Fine Print, that Devil in the Details) a custom-made hybrid created to slip through all the loopholes in the invincibility boons granted to the demon Hiraṇyakaśipu (see Soifer 1991 and Dębicka-Borek 2015).[3]

I would even argue that terms such as *paradox* and *contradiction* have been somewhat overused in the study of Indian religion to emphasize the presence of complexity. Taken in the sense of vastly different qualities common to the same object, I could describe myself as a paradox: sometimes awake, but also frequently asleep; sometimes happy, other times bitterly disappointed; known to fly through the air in a jet but also sometimes to ride along under the ground in a subway train. What we really mean when we talk about paradoxes in mythology (and what I will mean when I use the term throughout this book) is that a mythological figure is presented in such a way as to hold in tension two contrasting ideas for the purposes of thinking through those ideas in a culturally specific way.

With this characterization in mind, I argue that Paraśurāma is anomalous and paradoxical in a way that demonstrates some important aspects of an Indian worldview that can be applied in a larger context. The contradictions he embodies are not natural oppositions (although mythmakers do tend to map natural oppositions such as earth and water onto the myth's existing oppositions) but rather culturally determined ones. On the ontological level, the Paraśurāma myth is a site in which different abstractions and their relationships are used to create a picture of the world that resonates with Vedic thought. The fissure in Paraśurāma's nature replicates the ontological "break" in the world that corresponds to what Jan Heesterman refers to as the "broken world" of Vedic sacrifice (1993, 44).

The particular-sexual level of the myth, in which Paraśurāma is a representation of the conflicts that come along with being born into a family, is best illustrated in the stories of Paraśurāma's conception (which I will later refer to as "primal scenes") in the Critical Edition of the *Mahābhārata*. In the version of the story that Akṛtavrana relates to the epic's protagonist Yudhiṣṭhira at Mount Mahendra, he explains his guru Paraśurāma's mixed-class identity as a case of two women being unable to distinguish between *Ficus religiosa* and *Ficus racemose* (in their defense, both are types of fig trees):

> When the wedding [of Satyavatī, the Kṣatriya daughter of King Gādhi, and the Bhārgava Brahmin Ṛcīkxa] was done, Your Majesty, the oldest of the Bhṛgus [Bhṛgu, the progenitor of the line and the great-grandfather of Ṛcīka] came because he wanted to see the bride. When he saw his son [that is, his great-grandson Ṛcīka], he was happy. The pair honored the sitting guru, who was revered by the gods, with folded hands and remained prostrate. Being happy, Lord Bhṛgu said to his daughter-in-law [Satyavatī], "Choose a wish, good woman, and I will give you what you want." She asked the guru for a son and he granted the favor to her and to her [unnamed] mother, also a Kṣatriya. Bhṛgu said, "In your fertile season, you and your mother must go to bathe for the son-ritual and each embrace a tree, she the *aśvattha* and you the *uḍumbara*." But in embracing, Your Majesty, they did it backwards. When the glorious Bhṛgu came there on another day, he detected the reversal. He told his daughter-in-law Satyavatī, "Your son will be a Brahmin who acts like a Kṣatriya. Your mother's son will be a Kṣatriya with the nature of a Brahmin." Then she begged her father-in-law again and again, "Don't let my son be this way, let it be my grandson instead!" He said, "So be it," and she was comforted. (*MBh* 3.115.19–26)

Later in the epic, Yudhiṣṭhira hears the story of Paraśurāma's conception again, this time from his own fallen guru Bhīṣma, who is lying on his deathbed of arrows (compassion for the unfortunate circumstances of the storyteller and Yudhiṣṭhira's legendary circumspection conspire to keep him from pointing out the differences):[4]

Then the Bhārgava [Ṛcīka] was pleased, son of Kuntī, joy of the Kurus. Then he cooked a *caru* (rice pudding) in order to obtain a son for himself and also for Gādhi. Then Ṛcīka the Bhārgava called his wife and said, "You are to use this *caru,* and that one is for your mother. To her a shining son will be born, a bull of the Kṣatriyas. He will be invincible in the world of kings, killing the bulls of the Kṣatriyas. But this *caru,* good lady, will procure for you a calm, austere son who will have inner peace and be the best of the twice-born." After saying this to his wife, the wise Ṛcīka, joy of the Bhṛgus, went to the forest to generate *tapas* [inner heat derived from asceticism].

At the same time, King Gādhi, out touring the pilgrimage sites, arrived with his wife at Ṛcīka's hermitage. Then, Your Majesty, Satyavatī took the two *carus* in hand. She had not misunderstood her husband's words, but she was excited in her mind. Then, son of Kuntī, the mother gave her own *caru* to her daughter and ingested her daughter's *caru.* Satyavatī bore the embryo of the Kṣatriya-destroyer with the blazing form and the terrifying countenance. Then, Tiger Among Kings, Ṛcīka saw that through his yogic concentration and said to his fair-complexioned wife, "You were deceived, my lady, when your mother mixed up the *carus*. A powerful son will be born to you who will perform cruel deeds, and your brother will be born as a renouncer absorbed in Brahmin-ness. I put all the Brahmin-ness in [the *caru*] through the power of my *tapas.*"

When her husband had said this, the noble Satyavatī, trembling, placed her head on his feet and said, "My Lord, great sage, do not let the final word be that 'You will obtain a son who is a mixed-up Brahmin.'" Ṛcīka said, "This is not the outcome I intended for you, my lady. Your mother and the *caru* will be the cause of your son's violent deeds."[5] Satyavatī said, "O sage, you can produce worlds at will. What about me? I want a son who is peaceful and righteous, O Best of Priests." Ṛcīka replied, "My lady, I have never told a lie, even when it would be inconsequential. How could I do so having kindled a fire to make a *caru*?" "Please let our grandson be this way [instead]," continued Satyavatī, "I want a son who is peaceful and righteous, Best of Priests."

"There is no difference to me between a son and a grandson, fair woman," replied Ṛcīka, "so it will be as you have said, my lady."

> [Vāsudeva said] "Thus Satyavatī gave birth to her son, the Bhārgava Jamadagni, who was calm, peaceful and absorbed in austerities. And Gādhi, Joy of the Kuśikas, received Viśvāmitra, equal to a Brahmin sage and embodying the totality of Brahmin-ness itself. Ṛcīka's son Jamadagni fathered the great hero [Paraśurāma], who was knowledgeable of all the sciences and was a master of the science of archery and who like a blazing fire destroyed all the Kṣatriyas." (12.49.8–22)

The image from the first story of Satyavatī and her mother embracing the two trees is an evocative one with at least two possible sources. One possibility is that this is drawn from the embrace of the *uḍumbara* post central to the *audambarī* rite that forms part of the *agniṣṭoma* (Gerrety 2016). Another possibility is that this scene alludes to a fruit- and flower-picking pastime popular in depictions of young women in eastern India around the second century BCE that subsequently became part of the myth of the Buddha's birth. When it was depicted in nativity scenes at Buddhist monasteries and temples, the image was introduced into widespread use in art and poetry as the *śālabhañjikā*, or "woman-and-tree motif," in which a woman clings like a vine to the trunk of a tree to promote pregnancy (Roy 1979, 3–5). It is also possible that it is a reference to one of the many indigenous fertility rites involving trees like those attested among the Coorgs, Bhīls, and others (see Frese and Grey 2005, 9339).

But trees symbolize more than fertility. Because they provide wood to make the implements and fuel for the sacred fire, trees are essential for sacrifice, the central institution of ancient Indian religion. However, as with people, only certain kinds of trees are eligible to participate in sacrifice. In the late Vedic imagination, trees, like people and gods, belongs to one of the four *varṇas*. The *uḍumbara* tree Satyavatī was meant to embrace is associated with nourishment, abundance, and the creator god Prajāpati (Gerrety 2016, 166). The *aśvattha* tree that Satyavatī mistakenly embraces belongs to the Kṣatriya class, which explains why Bhṛgu had ordered her mother to embrace it to give birth to a mighty warrior. The Kṣatriya-like attributes of the *aśvattha* tree include the hardness of its wood and its mythic identification with the thunderbolt weapon of Indra (Smith 1994, 224). *Atharva Veda* 3.6 compares the *aśvattha* to a raging bull that subjugates nearby trees and calls upon it to destroy the sacrificer's enemies: "[The] vessel made of pipal [*aśvattha*] is said to procure *apaciti* for the sacrificer—perhaps meaning 'retribution' or 'revenge' which is exacted by force" (ibid.).[6]

But Ariel Glucklich also notes that there is some ambiguity in the tradition's understanding of the *aśvattha* tree.

> It is the destructive warrior-like powers of the tree that produce benefits, a symbol for the powers of the sacrificing Kṣatriya, or for the royal Kṣatriya who wields that Khadira *daṇḍa* [staff] in the court of law. . . . It is the destroyer of enemies, the one who splits open the head of the enemy in a military conquest of other trees (AV 3.6.6). And yet it is also a remover of curses and protector from enemies, including the Kṣatriya's Brahmin rivals. . . . The Aśvattha is both Kṣatriya and Brahmin (Vedic hymns), heaven and earth, destroyer and healer; it is the world (cosmos) and humanity's place in the cosmos. (1988, 101)

Leaving trees out of the picture entirely, the other story of Paraśurāma's conception blames the mixed birth on switched *carus*, bowls of a seminal rice pudding infused with power by the sage Bhṛgu.[7] The *carus* introduce the possibility of deliberate deception. Trees are morphologically distinct from one another, whether one can properly identify them by name or not. But the *carus* are identical in appearance and can be switched with no one being the wiser. In the version from *MBh* 12.49 it is Satyavatī who switches the *carus*. In a third version found in *MBh* 13.4 that combines elements from the other two, Satyavatī's mother convinces her to switch her *caru* with the one that Ṛcīka prepared for his own son because she assumes that he would have made that one more powerful.[8] In all cases, the element of trickery that comes with the *carus* reinforces the idea that Paraśurāma is the victim of someone's actions more than merely the result of them.

Taken in narrative order, the *carus* are also the first instantiation of the theme of fluidity (congealed with rice starch, in this case) that runs throughout the myth and which we will examine in later chapters (and to underscore this point, Satyavatī herself becomes a river after giving birth in many of the Purāṇic versions of the myth). The fluidity theme continues with the telltale vaginal secretions of Reṇukā (euphemized as water), which provoke her husband to order her murder, and with Paraśurāma's reclamation of dry land from the ocean in a reversal of his mother's inability to control her own water. Perhaps most importantly, the fluidity theme also appears in the collected blood of the Kṣatriyas that consecrates the Kurukṣetra battlefield after Paraśurāma's extermination campaign.

Returning to the differences in the *caru* story and the tree story in the Critical Edition, one strange and telling element stands out as common to both. Satyavatī, who is Paraśurāma's near-miss of a *first* mother, rejects the very idea of him and passes him down another generation, to Reṇukā's womb, even when, as in the case of the *caru* story, he is already present in her womb as an embryo. The postponed nativity in these stories raises some important questions about Reṇukā and Paraśurāma's relationship. What is she to him? Can we call Reṇukā Paraśurāma's mother if it is not her ritual mistake but Satyavatī's that creates him? Can Reṇukā be his mother if, due to this generation-skipping, Paraśurāma's own father has taken *his* place as her husband?[9] Beyond that, Satyavatī is a mother who effectively aborts her son because he will be the wrong kind of child (a faint echo of the modern Indian practice of sex-selective abortion). Does this original maternal abandonment (a louder echo of the queen Kuntī's abandonment of her son Karṇa, Paraśurāma's future pupil and victim of his curse) set up a violent relation between mother and son that leads to the matricide? These questions we will reserve for a later chapter.

Continuing our inquiries into the particular-sexual level of the myth, we should observe that although Paraśurāma may not be terribly unconventional in his hybridity, he *is* unconventional in his relationship to time. Lynn Thomas has argued convincingly that Paraśurāma is a "strangely atemporal figure" whose presence at crucial moments across the vast span of cosmic time represents a deliberate anachronism on the part of Indian mythmakers in order to frame Paraśurāma as a symbol of the turning of the cosmic ages, or *yugas* (1996, 64, 83–85). A Marāṭhī rescension of the *Mahābhārata* names three male-female pairs that mark the transition from one *yuga* to the next: Paraśurāma and his mother Reṇukā are placed at the juncture of the first and the second *yugas*, Rāma Dāśarathi and his bride Sītā at the juncture of the second and the third, and Kṛṣṇa and Kṛṣṇā (i.e., the Pāṇḍava queen Draupadī) at the juncture of the third and the fourth (Karve 1932, 18). Significantly, though Paraśurāma, Rāma, and Kṛṣṇa are all regarded as incarnations of Viṣṇu, only Paraśurāma is born into the world as a Brahmin (with a Kṣatriya mother), while Rāma and Kṛṣṇa are of the Kṣatriya class. More significantly, Paraśurāma is the only one who, so to speak, comes to the dance with his mother (or at least with her reanimated body). We see in this anomaly, as in many others in the Paraśurāma cycle, a superimposition of thematic frames. In this case, the superimposed themes are matricide and class mixing, compelling us to read his hybrid identity through his relationship to his mother and vice versa.

To understand Paraśurāma on the singular-subjective level—Paraśurāma *as* Paraśurāma—we turn to the late-twentieth-century poem, *Maḻuvinṯe Katha* ("The Story of the Axe"), one of the well-known works of the female poet Nalapat Balamani Amma, the celebrated "poet of motherhood" (Subramanian 2016, 119).[10] The first-person narrative is a deep dive into the inner life of Paraśurāma (called Brigurama here), in which he reflects on his exile and his nature. It is composed in Malayalam and comprises seventeen stanzas, telling the story of Paraśurāma in a way that unifies the elements of his mythology and connects them directly to the poet's native region of Kerala.

In the first two stanzas, the long-lived Paraśurāma is sitting atop Mount Mahendra, looking down and contemplating the land of Kerala in the present day. Stanza three narrates Paraśurāma's idyllic childhood in the forest, where he spends his time meditating beneath the trees. In stanza four Paraśurāma decapitates his mother (without reviving her), an act for which he goes into his first exile in stanza five. As he wanders, Paraśurāma finds that he feels kinship neither with the meditating Brahmin seers he meets nor with the warmongering and haughty Kṣatriyas. About his encounters with the latter, he recalls:

> Their arms clanking and their robes glistening,
> Smashing and destroying all that came in their way
> And enjoying through plunder
> All that they had lusted for,
> (The innate frailty of that robust race
> Became the sword that slaughtered my mother!)
> An inner voice asked me:
> "Should this matricidal axe
> Do nothing against these pleasure-mongers?" (1980, 127)

Neither his father nor any sacred pool has cleansed him of his sin of matricide. Even so, as the last lines of this stanza indicate, over the course of his wanderings Paraśurāma has found a way to displace both his own guilt and that of his mother. As he reflects back on his actions, he effaces his mother's personal responsibility by naming the "sword" of her weak, pleasure-loving Kṣatriya nature as the direct cause of her death. He displaces his own guilt by naming as the indirect cause of her death the poem's titular "matricidal axe," which now has a voice of its own and is lusting for more Kṣatriya blood.[11]

The poem uses the metaphor of fire to express Paraśurāma's murderous rage. It appears as "the burning kiln of [Paraśurāma's] soul" in stanza four and takes up the entire body of the very brief sixth stanza describing Paraśurāma's decision to return home after his penance, which moves from the dying embers of Paraśurāma's anger to the welcoming fires of home:

As the flames flared and died down in embers and ash
In my mind,
The earthen lamps of the hermitage,
Their flames darting heavenward,
Beckoned to me. (127)

In stanza seven, after he finds his home ravaged by Kārtavīrya and his men, Paraśurāma takes up his axe against them and describes his unstoppable fury:

There arose in me
The invincible power of *tapas*,
My dormant heritage.
Like fire in the hands of a child. (Ibid.)

It is clear here that the fiery destructive power Paraśurāma unleashes to destroy Kārtavīrya and his army comes from the Brahmin part of his nature rather than the Kṣatriya. His father even castigates him for expending the stored-up energy of the Bhṛgus so rashly. His *tapas* is "fire in the hands of a child" because the Kṣatriya half of him makes Paraśurāma unable to use the Brahmin power with wisdom or restraint.

The episode of Paraśurāma's annihilation of the Kṣatriyas closely resembles the destructive campaigns of Aśvatthāman and Aurva. But while we can separate the mass destruction from Paraśurāma, it is harder to see how we can separate Paraśurāma from this mass destruction. In the epic, his twenty-onefold elimination of the Kṣatriyas constitutes the main part of his identity. And in the later tradition that we see represented in Balamani Amma's poem, Paraśurāma's dual inheritance continues to bind him to his actions irrevocably—he has the power of a Brahmin and the temper of a Kṣatriya, and that causes all the trouble.

Here the Dattātreyan formula of "*neti, neti*" will help us: The neither/nor-ness of Paraśurāma is precisely what allows him to wield superior Brahmin power but also renders him unable to control it properly. Balamani Amma connects his mother's and father's voices to representative objects to underscore their natures: his weak Kṣatriya mother speaks to him through the axe that killed her, while the voice of eternal dharma, wafting over holy basil-scented winds, speaks to him through his Brahmin father.

As I entered the ashram yard fragrant with *tulsi* plants,
My blood-stained axe held aloft,
There came into my ears the message of eternal *dharma*
Through my father: "The guilt of heinous sin is on you, poor child!
To avenge a trifling harm
You squandered the massed soul-force of ancestors.
The spiritual wealth our fathers earned
Is for the welfare of the world,
And not for empty vanity.
Love of war may well [behoove]
The weak Kshatriya clan,
But in greater men with added strength from *tapas*
It will spell the ruin of the three worlds." (Ibid.)

It seems that, as the tradition expands, the inner life that is only hinted at in the epic version of Paraśurāma is created in later stories by the internalization of his external struggles, a development that logically comes out of Paraśurāma's always-already conflicted dual nature. Adheesh Sathaye has pointed out a parallel development in the case of Paraśurāma's sometimes-cousin, the Kṣatriya-turned-Brahmin Viśvāmitra, who becomes "unmoored" from his Vedic and Śāstric framework as medieval mythmakers flesh him out and incorporate the figure into their regional Purāṇas (2015, 139).

Finally, when trying understand him, one point to consider is what *kind* of Brahmin Paraśurāma is. He comes from the Bhārgava Brahmin clan, like Aurva, Śukra, and Cyavana, all of whose stories are used to illustrate prominent themes in the epic without actually being integral to its plot. To explain the presence and role of the Bhārgava myths in the epic, V. S. Sukthankar theorizes that nonmythical, that is to say, actual and historical, Bhārgavas appropriated an older version of the epic, infused it with Bhārgava myths unrelated to the core narrative, and turned it into the Bhārgava-centric *Mahābhārata* we have today (1936, 75–76). Following Sukthankar, Robert Goldman argues that through their use of consciously constructed "metamyths," "Bhārgava mythmakers and epic redactors were able to elaborate the Bhṛguid myths and integrate them, for their own ends, into the pseudohistorical framework of the Mahābhārata" (1971, 105).[12] Goldman concludes that the Paraśurāma cycle, which he describes as "a pastiche of Bhārgava motifs and themes" (135), is "the culmination of the epic Bhārgava cycle" (138), "a deliberate creation of the epic bards intended to incorporate, in one complex, almost every highly charged feature of the Bhṛguid cycle" (136), and finally, "a mythic record of the earliest attested case of sanskritization in India" (144).

Using M. N. Srinivasan's concept of "sanskritization" (the strategic adoption of Brahmin values and identity by a group in order to increase its prestige), Goldman is arguing that the violent stories of Paraśurāma and other Bhārgava heroes are evidence that at one time they were a non-Brahmin group that—unlike traditional Brahmins whose authority derives from their ritual purity, education, and professed abstention from bloodshed—practiced some sort of non-Vedic magic, used weapons, and possibly drank alcohol. Why then, one could ask, would they want to keep a record of their heterodox past, which would seem to undermine the purity-based Brahmin authority they want to exert? Hiltebeitel asks himself the same question and concludes that "the answers one might expect—their portrayal expresses the Bhārgavas' power over the text, perhaps in combination with an omnipotence fantasy, or the determination to convince others of their omnipotence—are, I think, hardly plausible" (1999, 162).

He argues instead that "Bhārgavas are portrayed for defining, and if necessary correcting, the status relations *of* Brahmans" (ibid.). Likewise, Johannes Bronkhorst also disputes Sukthankar's "Bhṛguization" thesis, arguing instead that "the important roles played in the *Mahābhārata* by Bhārgavas and Aṅgirasas have nothing to do with the participation of these two groups of Brahmins in the composition, or brahmanisation, of this text, but rather are concerned with the image its redactors wished to project of Brahmins" (2016, 240). Far from unconventional Brahmins, the Bhārgavas are consummate Brahmins—even, I would argue, idealized exemplars stemming from a Brahmin fantasy of political power. They are the exception thinking the universal with an intense passion.

## Brahmin Power and Kṣatriya Puissance

At this point in our discussion of Paraśurāma's fractured identity, we should ask about this epic version of the myth: Who made it? When did they make it? Where were they (geographically, socially, economically, politically) when they made it? Who did they want to hear or read it? What did they want those people to think or feel? At this early stage in the discussion, I am prepared to make a few preliminary observations. Brahmins made this myth, first of all. They made it in the centuries following the rule of the Buddhist emperor Aśoka Maurya (r. 272–232 BCE). And just as important as the period of historical time in which we can place them is the period in which they understood themselves to be—namely, on the wrong side of a golden age in which their homeland had been ruled by righteous Brahmin-supporting kings. Geographically, they were somewhere in North India, but socially, economically, and politically, they were in a perceived position of diminished power and prestige compared to their imagined past. The audience for the Paraśurāma myth, both inside and outside the epic, was the ruling Kṣatriya class. Accordingly, the mythmakers wanted their audience to feel awe at the power of the Brahmin sage and obligation to maintain the proper order of society with Brahmins at the top.

With these general coordinates established, we can now enlarge upon some of these answers. Expanding our answer to the question of who made the myth requires us to spend some time with the suggestive work of Georges Dumézil. Citing myths from taken from India, Iran, Northern Europe, Greece, and Rome, Dumézil argues that the Indo-European society that formed the basis of Indian civilization was early on divided (perhaps more in theory than practice) into a tripartite scheme. This scheme consists of three interdependent functions that he identifies in the composition of both the pantheons and social hierarchies of Indo-European societies. The first function is a magico-sovereign class that the figure of Mitra-Varuṇa represents in the Vedic pantheon and the Brahmins represent in ancient Indian society. The second function is composed of military specialists represented by the god Indra and the Kṣatriyas, and the third function consists of economic producers, called Vaiśyas in ancient India and associated with the Aśvin twins, gods of horses and medicine.

Following Dumézil's model, the escalation of conflict in the Vedic commentarial literature of the Brāhmaṇas between the martial sovereign god Indra and the magical-contractual sovereign god Varuṇa (who is also the father of Bhṛgu and thus the ancestor of all the Bhārgavas) represents the struggle for sovereignty between the first and second functions and highlights the differences between them. "Indra," writes Dumézil, "in contrast, for example, to Varuṇa, keeps no tight accounts, acknowledges no blind path of justice" (1970, 66). Varuṇa, on the other hand, is the guarantor of the oath with the power to "bind" those who transgress it. It is in his role as a binder that Varuṇa comes into conflict with Indra's warrior ethos (1988, 104–105).

Heesterman argues that the Indian case is different from other divisions of religious and political power in the Indo-European world because in India, "[it] is in the sphere of world renunciation that the Brāhmaṇa and the ultimate authority he stands for belong. Society and its king have no claim on him beyond what he is willing to concede and he can—ideally, he even should—withdraw from society" (1978, 5).[13] By the time of the Dharmaśāstras, a collection of law books from the sixth century BCE, the roles of Brahmins and Kṣatriyas were clearly demarcated, at least in the literature. Brahmins had come to see the necessary "dirty work" of making war and enforcing order that accompany statecraft as polluting and impure. Kṣatriyas, in their turn, had come to rely on the Brahmins, through their performance of the sacrifice, to cleanse them of the pollution they accrued through the duties of kingship. Insofar as their increasing ritual specialization and the spreading practice of renunciation freed Brahmins from worldly ties, it also divorced them from the realities of political power, a situation that might have been unacceptable to some Brahmins, ambivalent though they may have been about kingship.

This is a picture of the social tensions lying beneath the surface of ancient Indian political life as the Brahmins understood it until those tensions erupted under the pressure caused by the arrival of the Buddhist Mauryan empire in the fourth century BCE: Brahmins depended on kings, but regarded them with an ambivalence that became a mixture of dread and disdain when imperial patronage of the Buddhist *sangha* started to threaten their claim to complementary spiritual authority.

But who were these Brahmins we have been talking about, really? And how did they react to the rise of Buddhism as a competitor for patronage and the arrival of a Buddhist empire with the reign of Aśoka?

> For some fifty years the [Buddhist] Mauryan kings continued to rule in Magadha until, about 183 B.C., Puṣyamitra Śunga, a brāhmaṇ general of Bṛhadratha, the last Mauryan king, succeeded in gaining power by a palace revolution. Puṣyamitra was a supporter of the orthodox faith, and revived the ancient Vedic sacrifices, including the horse-sacrifice. (Basham 1967, 57)

Or so writes A. L. Basham in his still-unsurpassed masterpiece *The Wonder That Was India*. The Brahmin warrior called Senapati ("General") Puṣyamitra is supposed to have been the scourge of Buddhist heretics, savior of the ancient Vedic tradition, and ruler (if usurper) of large parts of the Mauryan empire. We can find mentions of him in the Purāṇas, the plays of Kālidāsa and Baṇa, the grammatical treatise of Patañjali, and a handful of inscriptions (Bhandare 2006, 70). In the *Aśokāvadāna*, the story of Aśoka, Puṣyamitra offers money for the heads of Buddhist monks, inspiring one monk to use his magic power to create heads to bring to the king so he can claim the rewards (Strong 1989, 293). In the very late *Bhāviṣya Purāna*, Puṣyamitra causes a new race of Kṣatriyas to rise up from the altar of his royal sacrifice and also uses magic weapons to kill four million Buddhists himself.

About a decade ago, when I was writing the dissertation on which this book is based, I was quite convinced that Puṣyamitra's resurgent Vedism, his identity as a Brahmin warrior, and his reestablishment of Vedic order by overthrowing a heretic king all figured large in the historical backdrop for the Paraśurāma myth. Paraśurāma's matricide made sense when analyzed alongside Puṣyamitra's historical regicide and in light of James Fitzgerald's convincing argument about the politics of the *Mahābhārata*, namely, that its "quasi-parricides" in which pupils kill their gurus "would seem to demonstrate to their audience that the required annihilation of the old order involves the awful sacrifice of something cherished, fundamental to, and formative of, oneself" (1983, 625). Danielle Feller goes as far as suggesting that "Brahmin massacres at the hand of kings are not pure fiction, but did take place historically. Even though it is impossible to prove, it cannot be ruled out that these historical events inspired legends depicting feuds between kings and Brahmins" (2014, 101n9). To my mind, Puṣyamitra's historical overthrow of his own Mauryan patron-king looked like an inspiration for the Bhārgavas' war against the greedy Haihaya clan which they had served as family priests. Likewise, the new generation of Kṣatriyas spawned by Brahmins in the epics and in the myths of Paraśurāma's state building in Maharashtra and Malabar seemed to be reimaginings and repetitions of the Śunga "restoration."

But now all of this seems a bit too neat. For one thing, the *Viṣṇu Purāṇa*, which actually does compare epic heroes to historical figures, does not connect Paraśurāma to Puśyamitra. Instead, it describes the emperor Mahāpadmānanda, born to a Śudra woman, as being "like a second Paraśurāma" (4.24.3).[14] And more recently, through his study of the coins that date to the immediate post-Mauryan period, Shailendra Bhandare has made the unwelcome (to me) pronouncement that " 'Śungas,' if they ever existed, were probably as localized as the rest of the groups we know from coins in terms of their political prowess" (2006, 97). Judging from the numismatic evidence, it was the emergence of local urban economies and power centers that marked the end of the Mauryans. And this kind of small-scale localized political and economic organization is antithetical to the ideals of sovereignty and dominion encoded in the Horse Sacrifice that supposedly initiated Puṣyamitra's rule and does not generally coincide with stable and centralized imperial power. It would seem, then, that Puṣyamitra Śunga's Vedic restoration (or his enlightened secular reign, as Hindu nationalist fellow traveler Koneraad Elst would have it) is probably as mythical as Paraśurāma's destruction of the Kṣatriyas.[15]

Both the Puṣyamitra story and the Paraśurāma myth speak to a fantasy of Brahmin rule, an anxiety about mixing classes, and the desire to return to a previous way of life. But what if that earlier way of life never existed? Citing the notable absence of its mention in the Aśokan edicts, which we can date to the third century BCE, Patrick Olivelle has recently raised serious doubts about the importance of the *varṇa* system before the early centuries CE. If society were actually conceived of as being stratified into the four classical *varṇa*s of Brahmins, Kṣatriyas, Vaiśyas, and Śūdras in any meaningful way, he argues, Aśoka should have had something to say about it. And Aśoka does not. His stone edicts mention Brahmins, but not as the top tier of a *varṇa* or caste system. In fact, he contrasts them not with Kṣatriyas but with *śrāmaṇas*, renouncers who live in forest *āśramas*, which makes Jamadagni and Paraśurāma sound far more like *śramaṇa*s than Brahmins. What does this mean? Did Brahmins imagine themselves as half of the Brahmin-Kṣatriya pair, vying for power, while kings like Aśoka saw them as half of the Brahmin-*śramaṇa* pair, living relatively inconsequential lives of religious devotion on the outskirts of the social order?

The figure of the twice-born Brahmin's absence from the datable inscriptions is one thing, but what about its absence from the literature? "If any properly ideal (*santa*) Brāhmaṇas have ever existed," goes Shulman's dry observation, "they seem not to have made their way with any prominence into the vast corpus of Hindu myth and legend" (1985, 149). If there are no proper Brahmins either in the historical record or in the mythological record, whence comes this idealized essence of Brahmin-ness, or *brahman,* that becomes corrupted in Paraśurāma? In the epic, Brahmin nature is always distinct from that of the Kṣatriya, and one need only glance through Bhīṣma's deathbed speech in the Mokṣadharma Parvan (*MBh* 13) to see how clearly the text separates the duties of Brahmins from those of Kṣatriyas. And yet, when it comes to *pakka* Brahmins, one can hardly see the rule for the exceptions.

It is undeniable though, that the Brahmins somehow "won" in the centuries following the collapse of the Mauryas. After all, Buddhism disappeared almost completely from India but Brahmins are still around today. And, as Alexis Sanderson notes, between the fifth and eighth centuries, Indian kings who had converted to new non-Vedic sectarian movements commonly proclaimed in inscriptions their commitment to upholding the *varṇa* system that put Brahmins on top (2009, 41). "Moreover," he goes on, "there is abundant epigraphical evidence of kings throughout this time bringing Vaidika [Vedic] brahmins into their kingdoms by making them grants of tax-exempt land, thereby extending the penetration of brahmanical culture while facilitating the administration of their territories and promoting agricultural development" (43).

Describing how the Brahmins pulled off their cultural victory, Bronkhorst notes the importance of narrative, and especially of some of the story elements recognizable in the Paraśurāma myth. He describes as a recurring feature of the epics, "Brahmins who live in their hermitages (*āśrama*) in the forests, where they occupy themselves with rites and Vedic recitation" (2017, 364). He continues, "The stories make clear that these holy men in the forest possess extraordinary powers, which they can, if need be, use for or against others" (ibid.). The mythical *āśrama*s in which these powerful Brahmins dwell thus become the models for the real-life *agrahāra*s (income-earning estates) granted to Brahmins by kings (Bronkhorst 2016, 411).

When considering how Paraśurāma might fit into this story, it is worth noting Sanderson's observations that the post-Vedic cults most frequently subscribed to by the early medieval kings who made land grants to Brahmins and promised to enforce the *varṇa* hierarchy were those of Viṣṇu, Śiva, the Goddess, and the solar deity Sūrya (2009, 43). Paraśurāma's association with Śiva goes back to the epic, as does his relationship to Sūrya, with a story found in *MBh* 13.97–98 as well as the *Viṣṇudharmottara Purāṇa* (the first post-epic account) that connects Paraśurāma's birth to a prophecy the god gives to Jamadagni. Additionally, though it is not attested in the earliest textual references, to the extent that Paraśurāma has become a cultic figure, it has usually been in his role as a protector deity for the Goddess in the form of his mother, Reṇukā. I am not prepared to say anything definitive on this point, but if Brahmins wanted a narrative that could appeal to the four major forms of devotion *au courant* among the early medieval kings, they could have done a lot worse than the Paraśurāma myth.

This much is clear to any king who hears the story of Kārtavīrya's encounter with Paraśurāma and his family: If a king asks politely, a Brahmin can feed his army. But if he gets greedy, a Brahmin can wipe him and his kind off the face of the earth, and then do it another twenty times for good measure. However, as powerful as they have proved to be in establishing and supporting cultural hegemony, these outward images of powerful magicians that accompanied the Upaniṣadic-yogic inward turning of Brahmin ritual are difficult to connect to any historical reality. They appear rather to conform to Lincoln's notion of myth as "ideology in narrative form" (1999, 147).

I cannot therefore accept Joydeep Bagchee's argument that a reading of the Paraśurāma myth as "historically explicable propaganda" does not work (2018, 100). Bagchee gives three reasons for dismissing such an interpretation, all of which require responses: First, he makes the claim that there is no evidence of any historical Brahmin-Kṣatriya conflict. Even if we leave aside Feller's suggestion above, this still runs into trouble as a straw man argument. There is no need to demonstrate any historical conflict to argue that Brahmins responded negatively to the social shifts occasioned by the rise of the Mauryan empire and expressed their displeasure in mythmaking. Indeed, the Paraśurāma story (along with the Puṣyamitra story, which also seems to have been more imagined than real) is itself the evidence for this kind of an attitude among Brahmins, and it would be perverse to ignore this most obvious reading. To draw a parallel, anti-Semitic propaganda is not proof of the Jewish conspiracies that it describes, but it is proof of anti-Semitism itself.

Second, Bagchee cites evidence that there existed, instead of conflict, "a great deal of harmony between a king and his priest" (99–100). But the sources he uses for this claim are dubious at best. He refers to a 2003 article by Raf Gelders and Willem Derde, arguing that European scholarship with its Protestant bias invented the idea, later adopted by nineteenth-century reformers, that Brahmins and their "priestcraft" were responsible for debasing and corrupting what had once been a "rational" Hindu religion (4614). Even if Gelders and Derde are right in their conclusion that Protestant scholars made things up based on their anticlerical prejudice, their assertion says nothing about what kind of relationship Brahmins and Kṣatriyas actually had between 500 BCE and 500 CE; proving that one claim is made with bad evidence is not the same as proving that the opposite claim is true.

Bagchee also invokes the work of Madeleine Biardeau, which he reads as evidence that the king and his Brahmin priests represented "two poles of the same universal socio-cosmic order" (100). But in the very section that Bagchee cites, Biardeau's description of the Brahmin-Kṣatriya relation does not seem harmonious, but extremely fraught:

> In practice, the Brahman has modelled himself on these contradictory demands, while taking account of harsh reality: he has consented to officiate in the various sacrifices and rites in which his presence was required, accepting the fees associated with them; he has even become priest-in-charge of a temple, which is even more degrading, but may be extremely lucrative. He has

> demanded proportionately greater remuneration when the function entailed greater risks for his status, for example in funeral rites. Occasionally he may have been greedy. (1989, 63)

Finally, Bagchee points to the ambiguity with which the epic treats Paraśurāma as a strike against the historical propaganda reading. I agree with Bagchee here, but propose that we must distinguish between vulgar propaganda, which the Paraśurāma story would exemplify if it ended with the Bhārgava's simple apotheosis, and a far subtler form of narratized ideology, more in line with what we would expect from the epic that repeatedly tells us that dharma is subtle (*sūkṣma*). Ambiguity is, after all, the currency of both the epic mythmaker and the Brahmin. Would we not expect a figure used to focus and reflect their discontent to be at least as ambivalent and conflicted as they imagined themselves to be with regard to the questions of power and pollution? In the end, while there is no reason to suggest that the Paraśurāma story is merely or solely a piece of Brahmin propaganda, there is ample textual evidence that it functions *on some level* as propaganda, or at least as a mythological *cri de couer*. I am very sympathetic, however, with Bagchee's (and Vishwa Adluri's) position that the *Mahābhārata* is—whatever else it is—a philosophical text with some important things to say about being and becoming, as I will show in the next section. With all that said, let us start to pull Paraśurāma loose from his epic moorings and open up our discussion a bit wider.

## Droṇa, Dattātreya, and Viśvāmitra: Symbols of Dislocation, Excess, and Becoming

Writing on Hegel's *The Phenomenology of Spirit*, John Russon remarks that "the sense of ourselves as equal participants in a shared world with which we normally live is itself a developed view, a view accomplished through . . . negotiation" and is "perhaps Hegel's most distinctive contribution to our philosophical heritage." He continues,

> *The Phenomenology of Spirit* demonstrates that the sense of ourselves that we typically live with—a coherent sense of ourselves as independent agents, coherently integrated with the human and natural world—is an achievement (indeed, a complex negotiation with the conflicting infinities of reality, desire, and others) and not

> our "given" state. The achieving of this coherent, integrated sense of self is accomplished only through interpersonal negotiation, and Hegel demonstrates, in his descriptions of the "struggle to the death" and "master and slave," the ways in which we can fail to cooperate in allowing each other to live as equal selves. (2011, 57)

With all due respect to Hegel, as distinctive as this contribution is, it is not unique.

As I have already argued, India long ago developed its own narrative formulations of the integrated sense of self. One such narrative formulation, while substantially different from it, is nonetheless recognizable as an analogue to Hegel's master and bondsman discussion in which he describes "two opposed configurations of consciousness: one, a self-sufficient consciousness for whom being-for-self is essential; the other, an un-self-sufficient consciousness for whom life, or being-for-another, is essential. The former is *lord,* the latter *bondsman*" (quoted in Neuhouser 2009, 49).

*Śatapatha Brāhmaṇa* 4.1.4, a commentary that purports to explain the reason for offering a portion of the pressed *soma* plant to the paired gods Mitra and Varuṇa (the gods of the treaty and the oath, respectively) understands the integrated self as a product of interpersonal relation at a social level that is itself a repetition of a divine order.

> Mitra and Varuṇa are the *kratu* ["formulator of desire"] and the *dakṣa* ["executor of desire"] of (the sacrificer) and thus they belong to his self (*adhyātma*). Whenever he desires in his mind (saying) "Perhaps this (should be) mine. I will do this," that is *kratu*. When that is accomplished, that is *dakṣa*. Mitra is the *kratu* and Varuṇa is the *dakṣa*. Mitra is the Brahmin class (or Brahmin nature) and Varuṇa is the Kṣatriya class (or Kṣatriya nature). The Brahmin class is the *abhigantṛ* ["conceiver"] and the Kṣatriya class is the *kartṛ* ["doer"]. In the beginning the Brahmin class and the Kṣatriya class were separate. Mitra, the Brahmin class, could stand in the law (*ṛte*) without Varuṇa, the Kṣatriya class. But Varuṇa could not stand without Mitra and whatever he did without Mitra's aid did not succeed. Varuṇa the Kṣatriya class called on Mitra the Brahmin class, saying, "Unite yourself to me! I will put you before me. Helped by you, I will be able to accomplish something!" Mitra said, "So be it!" And from that came the offering to Mitra and Varuṇa. (*ŚB* 4.1.4.1–4, see Collins 2014, 93–94)

There is a kind of weak parallel here to Julian Jaynes's controversial theory that, until the mid-to-late second millennium BCE, humans did not possess what we now think of as consciousness. Jaynes describes consciousness as being marked by two distinct functions. The first is "mind-space" that allows us to experience thinking "in" our heads and consider contents in a metaphorically visual field. The second is an "analog I," or a thinking self, that makes such introspection possible (Sleutels 2008, 308). Before the dawn of consciousness, according to Jaynes, humans had a "bicameral mind" in which the left and the right hemispheres did not send electric impulses across the corpus callosum. In the bicameral mind the right hemisphere of the brain communicated to the left hemisphere with auditory hallucinations, which the left hemisphere—the site of language and identity—experienced as commands from gods, ancestors, and dead rulers. For Jaynes, the bicameral mind is the only reasonable explanation for the rise and persistence of monumental religion in China, Egypt, and Mesopotamia. Viewed through the lenses of Jaynes's theory (which is, as I said, controversial), the *kratu* and the *dakṣa* seem to point to some intuition of the two-ness of the mind, also reflected in the description of the two birds in the *pippal* tree in *Ṛg Veda* 1.164 (see Calasso 2016, 201).

The significance of the *ŚB* narrative for our discussion is that the concrete social hierarchy, much more culturally specific than Hegel's *Herrschaft und Knechtschaft*, is the same one that is negotiated in the Paraśurāma myth, providing a scriptural warrant for reading it as a "symbol of epic philosophy" as Bagchee has it (2018, 113).[16] Accordingly, in this section we will examine Paraśurāma alongside three other mythical figures: the epic warrior-sage Droṇa, the Deccan folk god Dattātreya, and Viśvāmitra, the Kṣatriya king who becomes a Brahmin sage by practicing austerities after a humiliating defeat at the hands of the Brahmin Vasiṣṭha. All three figures could have their own scholarly books devoted to their mythology—and they do, in the cases of Dattātreya (Rigopoulos 1998) and Viśvāmitra (Sathaye 2015)—and Paraśurāma's relationship to each would take an entire chapter in this book to really explore in any meaningful way. So instead of attempting that, I will briefly use each figure to illuminate some aspect of Paraśurāma's exceptionality so that we can spend the rest of this chapter using his myth to think through the concepts of sovereignty and exclusion.

## Crossing Paths and Streams with Droṇa

In the *Mahābhārata,* the Brahmin warrior Droṇa is the teacher of the Pāṇḍava and Kaurava princes, a fellow Brahmin warrior, and the father of an another important Paraśurāma-related figure, Aśvatthāman. Droṇa's thematic connection to Paraśurāma is evident from the beginning of his narrative. Keeping with the epic's crystalline nature, the story of Droṇa's birth from the spilled seed of the Brahmin ascetic Bharadvāja reflects Reṇukā's episode of incontinence upon seeing the *gandharva* in the river. This tale is found throughout the *Mahābhārata* and is one of many myths that relate the accidental emission of an ascetic's semen. The version from *MBh* 1.154 has Bharadvāja going to the Gangā to bathe and getting a glimpse of the celestial dancer Ghṛtācī's naked body, at the sight of which he becomes erect and spills his seed into a vessel (*droṇa*).

In both this story and the Reṇukā episode, there is a seductive celestial figure glimpsed bathing at a river and something suggestive that happens to a pot. But, as Lévi-Strauss notes in *Totemism*, "it is not the resemblances but the differences that resemble each other" (1963, 77). Droṇa is conceived when his Brahmin father accidentally ejaculates while watching a celestial female figure bathe. And while Paraśurāma is not *actually* conceived when his Kṣatriya mother experiences the female equivalent of an involuntary ejaculation while watching a male celestial figure bathe, he is *figuratively* born then, since the events that immediately follow "activate" the latent martial characteristics of Paraśurāma's personality.

Along with their birth stories, the two figures are also closely associated at the level of clan. Droṇa is born into the Bharadvāja clan, while Paraśurāma is, of course, a Bhārgava. Fittingly, in *MBh* 12.181 it is the eponymous sages Bharadvāja and Bhṛgu who have a sustained discussion about the *varṇa*s and *varṇa* mixing. And in the Paraśurāma tradition from Kerala, Paraśurāma fills the void created by his annihilation of the Kṣatriyas by turning Brahmin clans into armies, against their objections. He further specifies the Bharadvāja clan as the one to share his burden of having killed all the Kṣatriyas (Menon 2003, 30).

This connection between the two figures established throughout the epic serves to focus our attention on the episode, just a few verses after his birth story, when the adult Droṇa encounters Paraśurāma as the latter is on his way from the post-varṇicide sacrifice at Kurukṣetra and heading for exile in the mountains. Droṇa has evidently gotten a garbled message about what Paraśurāma has been doing, since he comes looking for him with the idea that he is giving away all his property (*vitta*) rather than the earth he has just conquered by slaughtering twenty-one generations of Kṣatriyas. When he meets Droṇa, Paraśurāma explains that he has no property to give and offers him a choice between his body and his *astrāṇi,* a word denoting "spells" or offensive magic (*MBh* 1.154.10).[17] This is reminiscent of the choice Rāma Dāśarathi will force Paraśurāma to make after they meet in the *Rāmāyaṇa*, when Paraśurāma describes himself as having departed Kurukṣetra for Mount Mahendra "possessing only his ascetic power" (*Rām* 1.74.26).

Droṇa chooses the *astrāṇi,* of course, because he thinks his magically obtained martial power will impress his boyhood friend, the Kṣatriya Drupada, who is also the recently crowned king in Ahicchatrā.[18] But when the newly empowered Droṇa comes to visit him, Drupada rebuffs the Brahmin with a cold and dismissive adage: "No man of learning is a friend to the unlearned, no man with a chariot to one who has none, no king to a man who is not. An old friend—who needs him?" (*MBh* 1.153.15, van Buitenen 1973, 315). Droṇa then hatches a plot to avenge this insult, conquering Drupada's kingdom with the help of the Pāṇḍavas. After overthrowing him, Droṇa throws his former friend's insult back in his face, saying, "You know, no king can be friend to a man who is not! Therefore, [Drupada], I have toiled for your kingdom. You shall be king on the southern bank of the Ganges, and I north of the river" (*MBh* 1.154.23–24, van Buitenen 1973, 316). The denouement is a scene Paraśurāma would appreciate: a proud Kṣatriya (Drupada) bound in fetters before an armed Brahmin (Droṇa) who then brings down an axe—an axe of the verbal variety, in this case.

As it turns out, this kind of humorous humiliation is also part of the larger Paraśurāma tradition. As one twentieth-century Varanasi Brahmin puts it: "The satirist is like Paraśurāma. He brings down the *paraśu.* Sanskrit jokes are always cruel. They can be deadly" (Siegel 1987, 161). Unfortunately for Droṇa, Drupada does not appreciate his brand of hatchet-blade wit and this joke does indeed turn deadly when the king goes out to perform the rites that eventually result in the birth of Dhṛṣṭadyumna, the warrior by whose hand Droṇa will die at Kurukṣetra. Unfortunately for everyone else, Dhṛṣṭadyumna's actions will also set in motion the terrible revenge inflicted on the Pāṇḍavas by another Brahmin warrior, Paraśurāma's near-double and Droṇa's son, Aśvatthāman.

Fitzgerald places the encounter with Droṇa alongside the story of Parasūrāma training Karṇa in magic weaponry as another example of the Bhārgava's generosity, or at least his generous attitude toward training and sending out non-Kṣatriya warriors into the world (2002, 89–132). But the Droṇa episode is somewhat different in that it is all wrong temporally. Though the details are vague on when this meeting happens, the text seems to place it directly after Paraśurāma's campaign of varṇicide. For when else does he have anything worth giving away other than during the brief period after he has conquered the earth and before he gives it up? This varṇicide (much less successful than previous versions, given the large number of Kṣatriyas blissfully unaware that they have all been killed) is therefore many generations later than it is supposed to be. Droṇa is the only one said to have encountered Paraśurāma at this point in his story and the recounting of their meeting completely throws off the timeline. Paraśurāma's varṇicide is supposed to have happened in a prior age, but if we take this story into account, the Pāṇḍavas and the Kauravas (Kṣatriyas all) are both alive right after the massacre, as is the king Drupada, Droṇa's childhood friend whom he meets directly after seeing Paraśurāma. This story is inconsistent with Paraśurāma's temporal relationship to the events of the epic. The only reason for its inclusion is to build on Paraśurāma's connection to Droṇa and the older generation of warrior gurus who are to be wiped out in the battle at Kurukṣetra. Since he is still dwelling on earth in the present day, Paraśurāma's connection to this past generation thus underscores his identity as a figure always out(side) of time.

## DATTĀTREYA AND PARAŚURĀMA

Like Paraśurāma's mother Reṇukā, Dattātreya is a figure of devotion in the Deccan plateau. Identified as a yogi, a Muslim Sufi *pīr,* and a locally recognized *avatāra,* the three-faced Dattātreya, like Paraśurāma, is the son of one the seven Vedic sages, Atri. Like Paraśurāma, Dattātreya is a nominally Vaiṣṇava deity who also embodies some form of Śaiva excess. While Paraśurāma embodies excessive violence and sacrificial destruction, Dattātreya embodies sensual indulgence in wine, women, and meat. In the goddess-worshiping Śākti Tantric tradition, he is also the guru of Paraśurāma and reveals to him the secret teaching of the goddess Tripurā in the *Tripurā-rahasya* (Rigopoulos 1998, 169).[19] In some lists of the ten *avatāra*s, Dattātreya actually takes the place of Paraśurāma, which leads Rigopoulos to suggest that the Paraśurāma-Dattātreya alternation in the *avatāra* lists comes from their shared connection to Kārtavīrya (42). But the interchangeability of these two figures may also come from the qualities of excess and hybridity that they both embody. While Dattātreya does not share Paraśurāma's dual identity of Brahmin and Kṣatriya, both Paraśurāma and Dattātreya combine the figures of the Vaiṣṇava deity with the Śaiva/Śākti devotee and of the Vedic sage with the Tantric practitioner.

Other disciples of Dattātreya are also central figures in Paraśurāma's story. In the *Bhāgavata* and *Garuḍa Purāṇa*s as well as the *Sutra-pāṭha* of the heterodox Mahānubhāv sect in Maharashtra, it is Dattātreya who teaches yoga to Alarka, the demon whom Bhṛgu curses to be born as an insectoid hell-being and who is set free only when Paraśurāma discovers him boring into Karṇa's thigh in the story from *MBh* 12.3 (Choudhary 2010, 154; Rigopoulos 1998,

91).[20] And it is also Dattātreya who grants Paraśurāma's enemy Kārtavīrya one thousand arms in some versions of the *Mahābhārata*. According to the *Sahyādri-lila*, another Mahānubhāv text composed during the second half of the fourteenth century, after Kārtavīrya propitiates Dattātreya for a boon the latter grants him one thousand arms and invincibility as long as he does not anger a Brahmin, a cow, or a woman. Kārtavīrya, of course, transgresses against all three prohibitions when he storms into Jamadagni's hermitage, rejects the hospitality of his wife Reṇukā, and steals his cow, thereby bringing his destruction at the hands of Paraśurāma down upon himself.

Later, when Reṇukā is on her deathbed, she makes Paraśurāma promise to enlist Dattātreya to perform her funeral rites. After she dies, Paraśurāma takes his mother's corpse and goes to find Dattātreya, who is disguised as a hunter and accompanied by two dogs. Paraśurāma is able to recognize the disguised figure as Dattātreya because green shoots immediately grow out of his staff when they meet. At first, Dattātreya refuses to perform Reṇukā's rites, but then agrees at the insistence of his divine consort. He then makes an offering of meat and liquor, establishing the Tantric Śākti traditions that are connected to the worship of Reṇukā in South India (Rigopoulos 1998, 93–94). As Dattātreya becomes integrated into more mainstream Vaiṣṇava groups, another figure (and another link to Paraśurāma) appears in his iconography: the "Wishing Cow" or Kāmadhenu, sometimes identified as the cow stolen from Jamadagni's *āśrama*. For Rigopoulos, "[Dattātreya's] connection with the two opposite poles of cow and dog—indicating the spectrum of purity and pollution—portrays the full, all-embracing sanctity of the *trimukhī* [three-faced] deity" (1998, 232).

The last figure we will examine in this section, the Kṣatriya-turned-Brahmin Viśvāmitra, is also connected to dogs (he almost eats one) and cows (he almost steals one). So that we can better understand the Paraśurāma-Viśvāmitra connection, we will first spend some time thinking about the significance of the cattle raid, which is not only a widespread Indo-European myth motif, but also the act that sets into motion the events leading to Paraśurāma's annihilation of the Kṣatriyas.

## Kings and Cattle

> Mother cow is in many ways better than the mother who gave us birth.
>
> —M. K. Gandhi

> It's not about my cows, I'll tell you that much. It's about freedom and liberty . . . and above all it's about our policing power. Who has policing power today?
>
> —Nevada rancher Cliven Bundy, three days before armed standoff with the U.S. Bureau of Land Management on April 12, 2014

Throughout the Indo-European world, cattle and cattle raiding have taken on deep significance in the social and individual imagination, especially in the establishment of sovereignty over land. Looking at material from the British Isles, home of the Irish cattle-raiding epic *Táin Bó Cúailgne* ("The Cattle Raid of Cooley"), Cozette Griffin-Kremer observes:

> [Medieval] tales of the *Táin Bó Cúalgne* and the avatars of the swine-herds in their topological heritage can be seen as recapitulating a ritual process for the appropriation of territory—as expressed in the Icelandic term of *landnáma*—in which each feature of the landscape and its name have a primordial event as precedent. (2001, 168–69)

Lincoln, analyzing myths from the Indo-European societies studied by Dumézil, has reconstructed a Proto-Indo-European cattle-raiding narrative that he identifies as the foundational myth of the second function, the Kṣatriyas, in the same way that the myth of the first sacrifice is the foundational myth of the first function, the Brahmins (1976, 24). He sums up this reconstructed myth as follows:

> [An] Indo-European hero whose name was *Trito, "Third," suffered at the hands of a monstrous creature, a three-headed serpent who was originally identified with the aboriginals of the area in which the myth was told. In the first encounter, the serpent stole some cattle belonging to the hero or to someone close to him, but in a second meeting, (when—according to the Indo-Iranian version—the hero was aided by a warrior god and fortified by an intoxicating drink) he defeated the monster and recovered the cattle. (1976, 18)

Lincoln's argument and his reconstructed myth present three very significant points relating to the myth of Paraśurāma. First, the claim that this cattle-raiding myth functions for the Kṣatriya just as the myth of the first sacrifice functions for the Brahmin is a persuasive one. "When Indian or Iranian warriors undertook an expedition," he writes, "they looked to the mythic [*Trito] as their prototype, and various texts show them identifying themselves with this hero" (1981, 132). In the *Ṛg Veda* specifically, Jarrod Whitaker has demonstrated that the motif of the god Indra's cattle raiding provided a model for masculinity and heroism for the Vedic poets and warriors alike: "Since cattle raiding is manly, whether in the cosmic or human realm, then poets presumably act in a manly way when they free cattle with their ritual speech, albeit in an auxiliary role" (2011, 47).[21]

Lincoln's proto-myth bears a strong resemblance to the events that set Paraśurāma's massacre of the Kṣatriyas in motion. After Kārtavīrya abducts Jamadagni's cow in many Purāṇic versions of the myth, Paraśurāma, often through *śakti* ("power") bestowed by Śiva, chases down Kārtavīrya, kills him, and gets the cow back.[22] Although the *Trito myth involves a herd of cattle and the Paraśurāma myth has only a single cow (sometimes with her calf), the similarities strongly suggest that the story of Kārtavīrya's theft of is a variant of the ancient cattle-raiding myth, but featuring a Brahmin rather than a Kṣatriya as the protagonist.

Sanskrit literature is filled with stories—some self-serving, others satirical—about the origins of kingship. Themes of cattle theft and cattle protection dominate, from hymns about Indra in the Vedas to regional cycles such as the Rajasthani epic of Pabūjī, revered by the Rajputs "because 'he sacrificed his life to save cows,' the mainstay of their existence" (Wicket 2010, 11). *Atharva Veda* 5.19.10 clearly lays out the rules for kings regarding the cows of Brahmins: "No king who lays his hands on a Brahmin's cow can protect his kingdom." By this standard, stealing Jamadagni's cow has compromised Kārtavīrya's ability to rule, making him little more than a cattle rustler or bandit and lending some justification to Paraśurāma's initial act of regicide, if not to the wholesale slaughter of Kṣatriyas that follows.[23]

All of this makes the case for a strong and stable connection between cattle raids and kingship. As the Brahmin-Kṣatriya hybrid, Paraśurāma becomes the figure responsible not only for sacrifice, the function of the Brahmin class, but also for the paradigmatic Kṣatriya practices of leading raids to recover stolen cattle-wealth and protecting the cattle of Brahmins. This annexation of the Kṣatriyas' defining narrative represents what could be an attempt to undo the bifurcation of temporal power and spiritual authority and to restore the imagined magico-sovereign role of the first function.

Dejenne calls our attention to a similar theme in K. M. Munshi's 1946 Hindi novel *Bhagavān Paraśurāma*, which "thanks to the prestige of its author has proved extremely influential for most of the later rewritings of Paraśurāma story and, as such, largely determines the current conceptions of this figure" (2007, 17):

> In [*Bhagavān Paraśurāma*], Rāma seems to be returning to the ancient Bhārgava tradition of "priest-warriors" who, in the years preceding his birth, had split between a purely "spiritual" and peaceful tradition, that of Jamadagni, and another warrior [tradition], that of Cāyamāna—and it is therefore Rāma's Bhārgava identity that would explain the coexistence in him of *brahma-tejas* and *kṣatra-tejas*. . . . The reader is then invited to think that Rāma's visionary plans to extend the Sindhu Āryavarta to Simhala and to unify all Āryans into one *gotra* stem from his unique and inspired understanding of the fate of the Bhārgavas. (241)

This brings us to Viśvāmitra.

## The Royal Sage versus the Brahmin Warrior

The rivalry of the Kṣatriya-turned-Brahmin Viśvāmitra and the pure Brahmin Vasiṣṭha, who appear in the Vedic hymns as *ṛṣis* equal in rank to Jamadagni, finds its fullest expression in the epics and Purāṇas. At the center of this rivalry is the Kāmadhenu, the "Wishing Cow," or (stretching it a bit), the "Desire Cow." The episode begins with a king on a hunting trip who comes to the *āśrama* of a Brahmin and is amazed to find that a forest-dwelling ascetic is able to feed his entire royal retinue with a magic wishing-cow, here referred to with the proper name Nandī or Nandinī. The Kṣatriya Viśvāmitra tries to buy the cow but the Brahmin Vasiṣṭha refuses to give her up. Sathaye translates the argument:

> Vasiṣṭha replied, "This cow is used for the gods, for guests, and for the ancestors, and also to make ghee for the sacrifice; this Nandinī of mine cannot be given away, not even for your kingdom, good sir." Viśvāmitra said, "I am a Kṣatriya, and you are but a mendicant, engaged in ascetic practice and contemplation. How could Brahmins have any valor with their placid and subdued

> nature? If you don't give me the cow that I want for a hundred million (coins), then I will not be deviating from my personal moral code as I take away your cow by force."
>
> "You are a powerful king," said Vasiṣṭha. "A Kṣatriya of great valor. Just do whatever you want, but do it quickly—don't deliberate on it."
>
> The Gandharva said: When he received this reply, Pārtha, Viśvāmitra forcefully seized the cow Nandinī, who had the appearance of a swan or the moon. Struck by whips and goads, being pushed around here and there, Vasiṣṭha's blessed Nandinī began to bellow. She came before him and stood there looking up expectantly. And even though she was being repeatedly beaten, she did not move away from his hermitage. "I hear you crying, my dear," said Vasiṣṭha, "as you scream out again and again. But, my Nandī, you are being stolen away by force, and I am just a passive Brahmin." (*MBh* 1.165.17–24)[24]

Following this exchange, Viśvāmitra's men try to take the cow's calf, which proves to be the last straw for the irritated bovine. The cow grows enraged and produces enormous foreign armies from her dung, urine, and spittle. It is a moment in which a maternal figure's release of body fluids spells destruction for a Kṣatriya, as it does (in a less direct fashion) in the story of Reṇukā. Viśvāmitra surrenders to the overwhelming forces arrayed against him, and is convinced by what he has seen to renounce his Kṣatriya status in order to become a Brahmin (1.165.35–45).

According to the *Rāmāyaṇa*'s version of the story, the cow is called Śabalā, which means "dappled" or "brindled" and is also a pun on *sabala,* or "powerful" (Sathaye 2015, 73). She is referred to as a "jewel," prompting competing *varṇa*-based claims on the cow that are worth examining. Viśvāmitra insists: "She is indeed a jewel (*ratna*) and the earthly lord is the jewel-bearer (*ratnahārin*). Give Śabalā to me, Brahmin. She is mine according to dharma" (*Rām* 1.52.9). But Vasiṣṭha is equally adamant that the cow belongs to him as a Brahmin, listing all of the sacrificial rituals for which he needs her and concluding, "all my actions are based upon her" (1.52.24). Vasiṣṭha claims the cow as a sacrificial implement necessary for life as a Brahmin while Viśvāmitra claims the cow as wealth belonging to a king.

In his analysis of this myth, Lincoln picks up the ambiguity of Viśvāmitra's self-identification as a *ratnahārin,* which could mean either "jewel-bearer" or "jewel thief" (1981, 143). In the *Mahābhārata* tradition, as Sathaye points out, "most Telugu and Grantha manuscripts . . . also give Vasiṣṭha's rebuttal to Viśvāmitra's contention that a king may seize jewels from his subjects: 'A king on this earth is not supposed to seize two kinds of jewels belonging to a Brahmin: the cow used for his *agnihotra* rituals or his incomparable wife, the mother of his children' " (2015, 7n4 website). The set of associations here is worth examining. The jewels that belong to a Brahmin are his cow and his wife, both connected to the sacrifice. Kings have no claims on either.

The *Mahābhārata* version of Viśvāmitra and Vasiṣṭha's struggle over the Kāmadhenu foreshadows the Paraśurāma myth in two ways that extend beyond just the anti-Kṣatriya cattle raid motif. To begin with, the teller of the story is none other than the *gandharva* Citraratha, forbidden apple of Reṇukā's eye in the Critical Edition, whom the Pāṇḍavas, in an act of intrusion extremely reminiscent of the Reṇukā episode, surprise while he is bathing at the river with his women at the evening hour appointed for *gandharvas* (1.158.1–15). Violence ensues and the Pāṇḍavas overcome the *gandharva* by force and burn up his chariot, after which he goes from being Citraratha ("Excellent Chariot") to Dagdharatha ("Burned Chariot"). He then surrenders and begins to tell stories to the Pāṇḍavas (1.58.35–55). This encounter with Citraratha is an obvious parallel to Reṇukā's encounter in the matricide micromyth, but with a very different ending that segues into a cattle raid story featuring a Kṣatriya-Brahmin hybrid (Viśvāmitra) that is itself part of the frame for a telling of the myth of the Bhārgava Brahmin Aurva's averted varṇicide (1.169–71). The resonances with the Paraśurāma myth ring loud and clear, especially in light of the other narratives in close proximity. The "problem" is set up here, awaiting Paraśurāma to solve it.

Sathaye has shown that the "counternormative" figure of Viśvāmitra has long served as a way for Brahmins to institutionalize and mediate Brahmin power. In the epics, Viśvāmitra and his rival Vasiṣṭha serve as representations of the "Brahmin Other" and the "Brahmin Self," respectively, setting up an orthodox interpretative framework for the story. The early Purāṇas do not stray too far from this model when they deploy the Viśvāmitra story in order to create Vedic-Brahminical legitimacy for sectarian temple-based practices. But the later *Skanda* and *Brahma Purāṇas* witness the "unmooring" of Viśvāmitra from his Vedic and Śāstric framework as medieval mythmakers weave his narrative into their regional Purāṇic traditions and map his story onto local sites of pilgrimage, just as similar traditions will absorb and transform the Paraśurāma myth.

Viśvāmitra enters the Paraśurāma story in Bhīṣma's account of Paraśurāma's conception, during which Bhīṣma explains that the Bhārgava sage Cyavana, along with the king Kuśika, orchestrated the ritual mistake that resulted in Paraśurāma's birth because Cyavana wanted the martial teachings of the *dhanurveda* (the science of archery), long passed down by the Bhārgavas, to finally be unleashed upon the Kṣatriyas (*MBh* 13.52–56). By introducing predestination and displacing the causes for Paraśurāma's rage onto events that predate and supersede the proximate cause of the cattle theft at the hermitage, this telling sets the stage for later variants of the myth that imagine Paraśurāma as an *avatāra* of Viṣṇu and ascribe cosmic and dharmic necessity to his destruction of the Kṣatriyas. And in naming Paraśurāma as the last repository of the Bhārgavas' secret teaching, this variant also contains the seeds of much later stories that describe him as the founder of the four branches of the Keralan martial art called *kalaripayattu,* which practitioners believe is derived from *dhanurveda* (Bālakrishnan 1995, 18).

The other reason for intentionally mixing up the *carus* in this story is so that the king Kuśika can get his wish of having a Brahmin born into his family. But Cyavana has foreseen that granting Kuśika's request will have negative consequences, and intentionally abuses his host's hospitality to try and provoke him into backing out of the arrangement. However, since Kuśika's royal generosity is not diminished when Cyavana reduces an offered meal to ashes and forces his host to make him a chariot, the Brahmin finally relents, making the prediction that "by the hostility between the Brahmins and Kṣatriyas there will occur a mixture of races," using the term *kulasaṃkara* (referring to a mixture of clans) rather than *varṇasaṃkara,* the mixing of *varṇa*s (*MBh* 13.55.11). Viśvāmitra comes into the narrative when he is explicitly named as Paraśurāma's mixed-class counterpart in the Kauśika line (*MBh* 13.56.12).

There are some major factors, as Robert Goldman observes, that keep Viśvāmitra from being a true counterpart to Paraśurāma. First, Viśvāmitra actually *becomes* a Brahmin, while Paraśurāma never becomes a Kṣatriya—he just acts like one (and kills them). Second, because the curse skips a generation only in the Bhārgava line and not in the Kauśika, Viśvāmitra is a contemporary of Jamadagni, not Paraśurāma. And third, Viśvāmitra and Paraśurāma do not contend with each other as one would expect. Instead, Viśvāmitra's strife is with the sage Vasiṣṭha and with the kings of the solar dynasty to whom Vasiṣṭha serves as preceptor.[25]

Exploring the philosophical ramifications of the myth, Sathaye writes that Viśvāmitra "stands for the [Brahmin-Kṣatriya] boundary itself, perpetually *becoming* rather than being Brahmin" (2015, 106). It is here, in the ontological

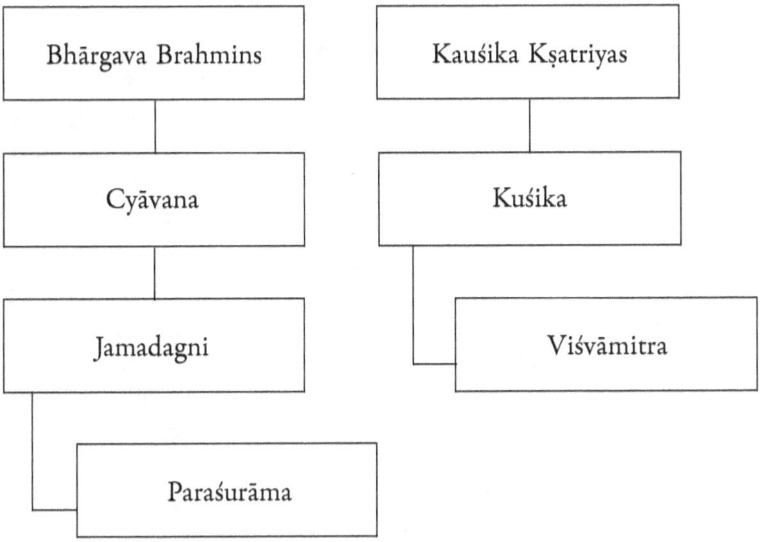


Figure 1.1. The Descents of Paraśurāma and Viśvāmitra.

distinction of being and becoming, that the figure of Viśvāmitra is the most significant in understanding Paraśurāma. As we have already seen, in the Hindu tradition myths are often tools to express subtle and profound arguments that we might classify as "metaphysical." To continue the conversation with Hegel from above, we can revisit his famous pronouncement:

> The truth is neither being nor nothing, but rather that being has passed over into nothing and nothing into being—"has passed over," not passes over. But the truth is just as much that they are not without distinction; it is rather that they are not the same, that they are absolutely distinct yet equally unseparated and inseparable, and that each immediately vanishes in its opposite. Their truth is therefore this movement of the immediate vanishing of the one into the other: becoming, a movement in which the two are distinguished, but by a distinction which has just as immediately dissolved itself. (2010, 60)

Shulman notes that the eighteenth-century Tamil *Kāñcippurāṇam* is most interested in Paraśurāma's "unending oscillation between poles, his creative and energizing imbalance" and argues that inside Paraśurāma's divided identity "both upper and lower limits are themselves refracted or divided further, for the two boundaries can interpenetrate and coincide" (1985, 128–29). Shulman also connects this aspect of the myth to Śiva: "Like Rudra-Śiva, the Brahmin is both outside and in, Untouchable remnant and symbolic center, ideal and its antithesis, guardian and destroyer" (129). I would argue that this element of the story is present in almost all Paraśurāma narratives, especially when read alongside the becoming-Brahmin figure of Viśvāmitra.

To wrap up this discussion, I will observe that each of the three figures we have briefly treated here has shined a light on a significant aspect of Paraśurāma's ontology: Droṇa's story illuminates Paraśurāma's temporal and spatial exceptionalism; Dattātreya's myth illuminates his quality of excess; and Viśvāmitra's story illuminates Paraśurāma's embodiment of the vanishing mediator of "becoming." All three of these elements will come into play when we move the Paraśurāma story into a broader context and take a closer look at its underlying political theology.

## Sovereign and Supplement

> Take but degree away, untune that string,
> and hark, what discord follows! Each thing meets
> in mere oppugnancy: The bounded waters
> Should lift their bosoms higher than the shores,
> And make a sop of all this solid globe . . .
>
> —*Troilus and Cressida*, Act I, Scene 3

The Shakespeare quote above is spoken by Ulysses as he laments the growing discontent and listlessness of the Greek army as the siege of Troy drags on. In his pivotal *Violence and the Sacred*, René Girard takes the increasingly dangerous situation Ulysses describes to represent what he calls the "sacrificial crisis," the loss of social distinctions that precedes a cataclysmic eruption of violence (1977, 53).[26] In ancient India, the equivalent for this loss of distinctions would be the dreaded *varṇasaṃkara,* the mixing of classes foretold by Cyavana in *MBh* 13.55.11.

The thirteenth-century *Bṛhaddharma Purāṇa*, composed in Bengal (like the *Kalki Purāṇa* that we will examine shortly), relates the myth of the wicked first king Vena, whom we have already seen in the introduction. Vena is an "atheist" who causes "Brahmins to beget sons in Kṣatriyas, Kṣatriyas in Vaiśyas, and so forth." The text describes the evils of Vena's reign in familiar terms of social breakdown: "When Vena left the path of dharma, all classes and all castes became mixed for when the sages told him that mixing castes led to hell, he announced his intention to cause them to intermarry thoroughly" (Doniger 1976, 327). Attributing the sin of *varṇasaṃkara* to the evil king Vena calls to mind the origin of the Latinism "miscegenation," coined in a fraudulent 1863 American pamphlet called *Miscegenation: The Theory of the Blending of the Races, Applied to the American White Man and Negro*, purported to be an outline of the Republican Party's plan for forcing the races to mix through marriage.[27]

In the version of the myth from the *Bhāgavata Purāṇa*, Vena's mourning mother preserves his body with magic spells after the Brahmins kill him. Later, the Brahmins begin to feel the terrible consequences of murdering a king (even a bad king) when the social order disintegrates even further, with thieves plundering the people and the Brahmins unable to stop them. After learning that the ability to spot fault in another is insufficient to keep the world in line, the Brahmins return to the preserved corpse of their victim and bring forth an ugly black dwarf named Niśāda (whom we have also already met in the introduction). Then they produce the king Pṛthu from the corpse in order to restore order, proclaiming the new king to be Viṣṇu himself (*BhP* 4.14.45). Born from the destruction of his evil father Vena, the prototypical good king Pṛthu comes to earth in order to end the famine and *varṇa* confusion brought about by his father's adharmic reign. He does this by subjugating the earth in the form of a cow, "milking" her, and using her to provide sustenance for men and gods, creating the social ordering framework of the four *varṇa*s and the four stages of life at the same time.

In other versions, the people install Pṛthu as their king because the Earth no longer spontaneously generates food and drink to meet their needs and they need someone to "milk" the earth to provide sustenance. As in another great lactic myth, the oft-told story of the churning of the Ocean of Milk, the milking of the earth provides much more than mere dairy products. Among the things Pṛthu milks from the earth are grain and agriculture, which provide sustenance to a population that can no longer rely on magic wishing trees for food (Bailey 1981, 107). Some myths have Pṛthu acting in a more Kṣatriya-like fashion, shaping the earth's landscape with his bow and arrows or forcing her to yield up her bounty on pain of death. In a version that appears in the *Viṣṇu Purāṇa* and the *Samarāṅgaṇasūtradhāra*, the earth turns into a cow and runs to the creator god Brahmā for protection. Brahmā, in turn, strikes a compromise and charges Pṛthu with protecting the earth while the earth agrees to provide sustenance (Gonda 1966, 106).

Another set of myths name Brahmā rather than Pṛthu as the milker of the earth. One such story appears in the *Mārkaṇḍeya Purāṇa*:

> Afflicted with hunger, [the people] went to see Brahmā. He knew what the Earth had done, and accordingly, milked her, using Sumeru as the calf. After the cow was milked, corn reappeared along with seventeen types of seeds and fourteen types of plants for use in the sacrifice. These plants had to be cultivated, so Brahmā taught the people the art of cultivation as a means of livelihood. Then he established bounds of propriety (*maryādā*) according to a plan . . . and the characteristics of the people. After that, in order, he established the *varṇas, āśramas* [life stages], laws to protect people and the respective heavens applicable to the *varṇas* and certain classes of sages. (Bailey 1981, 106)

Both of these sets of myths reflect the familiar struggle for dominion of the earth, conceived as a cow, with the conquest of the earth conceived as a kind of cattle raid and the end result being a hierarchically segmented society.

The way that Pṛthu's birth results from his father Vena's death marks this story as an Oedipal myth, and even more so with the inclusion of the earth/mother/cow to complete the triangle. The Earth's transformation into a cow is a clear indication of her maternal status, but she also becomes the wife of Pṛthu when he is named as *vasudhāpati* ("husband or lord of the earth") in *Śatapatha Brāhmaṇa* 5.30.21, and she becomes his daughter in versions of the story from the *Brahmāṇḍa* and *Bhāgavata Purāṇas* and the appendix to the Droṇa Parvan of the *Mahābhārata* (Bailey 1981, 116n). By the time we get to the *Lakṣmī Tantra*, composed by the Pāñcarātrins between the ninth and tenth centuries CE, the earth has been given as a consort to Paraśurāma (Gail 1977, 228).

Whether conceived of as wife-mother, cow-mother, or earth-mother (which are also coincidentally the three respective female roles in the matricide, cattle theft, and varṇicide episodes), the mother is not a passive object. She plays hard to get, either by hiding in her father's house or withdrawing her fruits, and will only yield either to the martial sovereignty of the second function (Pṛthu and his bow) or the magical-contractual sovereignty of the first function (Brahmā). This overlap of the cow and the earth in the earth-milker myth echoes the Paraśurāma myth's trajectory from a raid to win back a stolen cow to a massive varṇicidal campaign to take sovereignty over the earth. Likewise, both myth cycles portray an ambivalence toward Kṣatriya power, seen as both frightening and necessary, and a fantasy about a reconstituted Kṣatriya class under the power of the Brahmins. Figure 1.2 shows the structural analogues of the Pṛthu/Brahmā and Paraśurāma myths (not represented in narrative sequence).

The parallels between Pṛthu and Paraśurāma strongly suggest once again that the Paraśurāma myth is drawing on the connection between cattle raiding and sovereignty, but replacing the paradigmatic Kṣatriya with a Brahmin warrior. In his analysis of the text Ryosuke Furui writes:

> The [*Bṛhaddharma Purāṇa*] can be seen as an attempt by *brāhmaṇa*s to design a framework of social systematization, through which they give a meaning and explanation to the social reality perceived by them and try to impose a social order compatible with their own world view. The tension between them and other social groups which accompanied this attempt is recognisable by the fact that the composers need to incorporate the episode of the defiance and subjugation of the *saṃkara*s for legitimising their authority to decide matters related to these social groups. (2013, 211)

| Pṛthu/Brahmā | Paraśurāma |
|---|---|
| Vena steals the earth and the sacrificial gift | Kārtavīrya steals the cow used for sacrifice |
| Brahmins kill Vena | Paraśurāma kills Kārtavīrya/Kṣatriyas |
| Earth cries out for kings | Earth cries out for kings |
| Brahmins churn Vena's corpse | Brahmins impregnate Kṣatriya widows |
| Pṛthu born from Vena's corpse | Paraśurāma becomes a warrior when he swears vengeance after Jamadagni's murder |
| Pṛthu subjugates earth/cow | Paraśurāma wins back cow and conquers earth |

Figure 1.2. Comparison of the Pṛthu and Paraśurāma Myths.

To restore dharma and fix the situation, the Brahmins then classify all of the mixed races (*saṃkaras*) created by Vena and absorb them into the hierarchical social system. The Brahmins in this miscegenation myth become the arbiters of social order for these new, bastardized classes created in defiance of dharma. They decide on the state of the adharmic exception and thereby restore dharma. Ultimately, as we shall soon see, the kind of sovereignty Paraśurāma exercises in the state-founding myths of Maharashtra and Malabar is likewise based precisely on his ability to decide the exception.

## Dharma and the Sovereign

The subject of the exception leads us to the work of Carl Schmitt, "Crown Jurist of the Third Reich," whose 1922 essay "Definition of Sovereignty" begins with his oft-quoted dictum, "Sovereign is he who decides on the exception" (1985, 15). Writing in the context of the political instability and threatening civil war that plagued Weimar Germany in the 1920s, Schmitt seeks to develop a theory of the state that reinstates the transcendent omnipotent lawgiver in the form of the totalitarian sovereign.[28] Building on Thomas Hobbes's theory of the social contract and his own insistence that "[all] significant concepts of the modern theory of the state are secularized theological concepts," Schmitt argues that liberal democracies cannot guarantee security from external threats (and, more significantly, from internal threats) that could undermine their stability without a theistic idea of the state (31). Elucidating the "borderline concept" of sovereignty, Schmitt writes:

> Contrary to the imprecise terminology that is found in popular literature, a borderline concept is not a vague concept, but one pertaining to the outermost sphere. This definition of sovereignty must therefore be associated with a borderline case and not with routine. It will soon become clear that the exception is to be understood to refer to a general concept in the theory of the state, and not merely to a construct applied to any emergency decree or state of siege. (5)

The paradox of Schmitt's definition of sovereignty is that the borderline concept of the sovereign is at the very center of the legal order. Underlying the force of law is the state of exception, the place where law is totally absent and the sovereign wields absolute power. Thus, all law comes from lawlessness and "authority proves that to produce law it need not be based on law" (31).

In many ways, Paraśurāma's relation to dharma is like that of the Schmittian sovereign to the law. His existence as a Brahmin warrior is itself a violation of dharma, as are his subsequent acts of violence. But their result, paradoxically, is a restoration of dharma. He exists outside of dharma, but transcends it while at the same time embodying it, at least temporarily. Paraśurāma closely resembles the sovereign in that, "although he stands outside the normally valid legal system, he nevertheless belongs to it" (7).

In a related line of argument, Italian philosopher Giorgio Agamben posits a connection between three figures of Indo-European law and folklore: the werewolf, the Germanic *friedlos* or "man without peace," and the *homo sacer,* the banished man of ancient Roman law (1998, 63). All of these figures are cast out from the city and are living under the "ban" of the sovereign, reduced to the status of "bare life." "In Western politics," Agamben argues, "bare life has the peculiar privilege of being that whose exclusion founds the city of men" (12).

Paraśurāma seems to reflect elements of both the *homo sacer* and the sovereign who bans him; he conquers the earth only to give it away in sacrifice, an act that immediately results in his being exiled from it. In the case of the myths of Malabar and Maharashtra that we will treat later, his exclusion from the world after his destruction of the Kṣatriyas necessitates his creation of a new land and a new society over which he exercises a new sovereignty, making Brahmins into warriors and corpses into Brahmins.

The powerful secret of sovereignty's paradoxical nature and the lawlessness in the center of order is an overriding preoccupation of the authors of the Vedic, Śāstric, and Tantric traditions. And its practical application, setting up the mutually constitutive worlds of dharma and *adharma,* is the central concern of the epic. This proves to be difficult, because dharma, as the epic tells us repeatedly, is subtle. Ariel Glucklich puts his finger on it when he writes:

> The subject of dharma eludes almost every attempt to develop a system of conceptualization. This may be due to the fact that dharma is not a "subject" at all. Dharma is not a *what,* it is a *how.* (Glucklich 1994, 8)

If, as Glucklich argues, dharma is less a rigid system than a "normative 'world view' " that is transitive, temporal, and experienced in terms of "boundaries in space and time," (ibid.) how are we to conceive of its opposite, *adharma*? In much the same way as we conceive of dharma, as it turns out. *Adharma,* for Glucklich, is "not the binary opposite of dharma, because this would imply the absence of a temporal relation. Instead, *adharma* is the temporal ranging of consciousness across boundaries, and over the world felt by the body" (9). As we have already seen, Paraśurāma's relationship to temporality is one of the things that makes him unique. In the next section, we will take a closer look at how Paraśurāma's embodied, free-ranging *atemporality* fits into his identity.

## Between Two Deaths: The Cirañjīvin, the Wandering Jew, and the Double Negation

According to most lists, there are ten *avatāras* of Viṣṇu: Matsya the fish, Kūrma the tortoise, Varāha the boar, Narasiṃha the man-lion, Vāmana the dwarf, Paraśurāma, Rāma, Kṛṣṇa, the Buddha, and Kalki. There are also seven *cirañjīvins*, or "immortals": Droṇa's son Aśvatthāman, the demon king Bali, the monkey god and model Rāma devotee Hanumān, the Kaurava warrior Kṛpa, the demon Rāvaṇa's righteous brother Vibhīṣaṇa, the sage Vyāsa, and Paraśurāma. As the reader has probably noted, Paraśurāma's is the only name found on both lists.

Comprising meddlesome sages, pious monkeys, blessed demons, and cursed warriors, the *cirañjīvins* are a disparate bunch, to be sure. But all seven (sometimes eight, with the Bhārgava sage Mārkaṇḍeya as a common alternate) are supposed to live until the end of the current cosmic cycle. Writing about another member of this select group, namely, Hanumān, Phillip Lutgendorf observes:

> The concept of bodily immortality invites us to ponder a condition that, once again, situates Hanuman on a boundary, this time between human mortality and divine eternality. If an avatara is, so to speak, a "compression" of infinitude into a mortal frame, a *cirañjīvī* is just the reverse: an endless extension of corporeal life. And if the problem of mortals is (as the saying goes), "so much to do, so little time," that of an immortal is . . . potentially just the opposite: a deathless being has, literally, "all the time in the world." (2007, 279)[29]

Lutgendorf's observation about the inverse temporal values of the time-compressing *avatāra* and the time-expanding *cirañjīvin* calls our attention to a paradox in Paraśurāma's identity that is particularly dense with meanings: the implications of Paraśurāma's dual identity of both *cirañjīvin* and *avatāra*.[30]

The *cirañjīvin-avatāra* paradox (and here the word is appropriate) also illuminates Paraśurāma's dual identities as a Śaiva devotee and a Vaiṣṇava deity by indexing the Śaiva theme of *coincidentia oppositorum* (e.g., Śiva as the erotic ascetic) and the Vaiṣṇava variation of that theme: the infinite contained within the finite (e.g., the universe seen in the mouth of the child Kṛṣṇa in *BhP* 10.8.37–38). That is to say, the *cirañjīvin-avatāra* paradox is Śaiva insofar as it *juxtaposes* "time expanded" with "time condensed" and it is Vaiṣṇava insofar as it *encloses* the expanded time of the *cirañjīvin* within the condensed time of the *avatāra*.[31]

This paradox is mythically resolved, through an act of negation, in the *Nṛsiṃha* and the *Brahmāṇḍa Purāṇas* as well as several *Rāmāyaṇa* commentaries. All recount an episode (one that mirrors his own mother's loss of power as a result of her encounter with the bathing prince at the river) in which Paraśurāma gives up his *avatāra* power to Rāma Dāśarathi when the two Rāmas meet after the latter's wedding to Sītā (see Thomas 1996, 65). Disarmed and neutralized, Paraśurāma must now go on existing without any reason to do so. He is made a landless wanderer twice over, already in exile from the world and now in exile from the cosmos as constituted by the endless struggles of the gods and demons. At this moment, as after his inability to defeat Bhīṣma in the *Mahābhārata*, Paraśurāma's status as a *cirañjīvin* seems more like a curse than anything else.[32]

## The Vengeance of Aśvatthāman

Paraśurāma's curse of long life is mirrored in the epic story of his fellow *cirañjīvin* Aśvatthāman, whose father Droṇa is slain during the *Mahābhārata* war when Yudhiṣṭhira tricks him into wrongly thinking that Aśvatthāman has been killed, after which he lays down his weapons in despair. After the war, Aśvatthāman vows to avenge his father's cruel and deceitful slaying by making one last raid on the Pāṇḍavas to exterminate them completely while they are asleep.

The Sauptika Parvan, the brief tenth book of the epic, is devoted to Aśvatthāman's revenge for Droṇa's death, which takes the form of this gruesome night raid on the Pāṇḍava camp. Duryodhana, mortally wounded, has been defeated in a duel with Bhīma and the remaining members of the Kaurava army—Aśvatthāman, Kṛpa, and Kṛtavarman—are hiding in a forest. While his two companions sleep soundly, Aśvatthāman is unable to sleep at all, consumed with anger and shame over the death of his father and the supposedly noble Pāṇḍavas' dishonorable trickery. As he lies awake, Aśvatthāman witnesses a single monstrous owl attacking and killing a group (a murder?) of crows sleeping in the branches of a fig tree. Inspired by this omen and ignoring the objections of Kṛpa, he goes to the Pāṇḍava camp (located, significantly, *off* of the Kurukṣetra battlefield where everyone who dies automatically goes to Heaven). There he invokes the god Śiva and offers himself as a sacrifice so that Śiva can possess him and give him the power to destroy what is left of his enemies. As the remnant of the Pāṇḍava army is sleeping, Aśvatthāman descends on the camp and murders every last man in their sleep, including Draupadī's sons, father and brother, while Kṛpa and Kṛtavarman set the camp on fire. At the end, only the five brothers and Draupadī are left alive.

When the Pāṇḍava brothers and their wife, who have been away, hear what has happened, Draupadī demands Aśvatthāman's death and the jewel that has been on his forehead from birth as proof. Aśvatthāman and Arjuna square off in a duel and Aśvatthāman releases the most terrible of all the magic weapons, the *brahmaśiras*. Kṛṣṇa then instructs Arjuna, who possesses the weapon as well, to launch his own *brahmaśiras* to counteract it. At this point, the sages Nārada and Vyāsa arrive to try and defuse the situation and prevent the two weapons from annihilating the entire universe. Arjuna withdraws his weapon, but Aśvatthāman only redirects his into the wombs of the Pāṇḍava women, making them barren and killing the unborn child Parikṣit. To preserve the royal lineage, Kṛṣṇa uses his power to resurrect Parikṣit and then deprives Aśvatthāman of his forehead jewel before sending him into exile. Kṛṣṇa then explains to Yudhiṣṭhira that this massacre was not the work of Aśvatthāman alone, but Śiva's way of finally taking his share of the sacrifice of battle just as he did with the sacrifice of his father-in-law Dakṣa, which he destroys in a famous Śaiva myth.

Equal parts brooding and brutal, Aśvatthāman is the epic's other rampaging Śaivite Brahmin warrior seeking bloody vengeance for his slain father. Besides their shared desire to avenge their respective fathers' deaths and each one's propensity to go overboard in that vengeance, Paraśurāma and Aśvatthāman are alike in other ways. Both are born of fathers closely associated with fire. Both are exiles. Both direct their attacks at the "seed" of their enemies. Both are Brahmin warriors—Aśvatthāman attributes his mixed nature to *mandabhāgya* or "bad luck" (*MBh* 10.3.21). Both are closely linked to Śiva. The sacrificial massacres each of them perpetrates serve as bookends for the *Mahābhārata*'s great battle. The epic places the two figures in the same category when Bhīṣma says that Paraśurāma and Aśvatthāman, though the "sons of Munis," were kept out of Heaven because of their actions (*MBh*

13.06.33). Both, Shulman observes, present "an 'anomalous paradigm'—a conceptual device which seems to be particularly prominent in the worlds of Hindu Epic and myth" (1986, 423). And like Paraśurāma, Aśvatthāman also remains a figure of devotion in popular religion (though a far more marginal one) into the modern era, if this report is to be believed:

> It is easy to verify that a large section of Indian householders perform the daily ritual of sprinkling drops of oil on the ground before bathing. Scholars believe, this endless reiteration has a long-standing relationship with the legend of Aśvatthāmā; it speaks of a deep bonding between the common people and the hero still roaming the wilderness; the reflex-like action is a token of (forgotten but frozen) remembrance of Aśvatthāmā's continual suffering; the gesture of good-will evinces the wish to mitigate the agony . . . of the loss of his jewel, the physical pain that still consumes him. (Chakrabarty and Bhattacharya 1964, 160, quoted in Bandyopadhyay 2012, 488–89)

Both Paraśurāma and Aśvatthāman are mirrored in the medieval Christian story of the Wandering Jew, cursed to walk the earth until the Second Coming of Christ. This legendary figure has been alternately traced back to the Teutonic Wotan (Blind 1986, 169–89) and the Buddha (Edmunds 1913, 47).[33] Like Aśvatthāman, he receives liquid alms from the common folk, but in the form of beer rather than oil (Anderson 1986, 80–81). He is also known for wandering around disguised as a beggar, as Paraśurāma does in the *Kalki Purāṇa*, and has the power to curse, as Paraśurāma curses not only Karṇa, but anyone who needlessly summons him and disturbs his exile. Salunkhe reports that a favorite Marāṭhī phrase of Paraśurāma devotees is "*śāpādapi, śarādapi,*" meaning that he kills as easily with curses as with arrows (2001, 212).

But for our purposes the most salient connection to the Wandering Jew story is Hyam Maccoby's understanding of the figure as a "sacred executioner." Maccoby traces the origins of the story to the tale of Pontius Pilate's doorkeeper Cartaphilus, who strikes Jesus on his way to the cross and tells him to hurry. In a moment of off-the-cuff literalism that would fit well into the *Mahābhārata*, Jesus tells him, "I go, and you will wait for me until I return," effectively cursing him to remain on earth until the end of time (1986, 237). Maccoby notes that the Wandering Jew's mythology borrows heavily from the story of Cain, but takes on a new meaning in the context of medieval

Christian-Jewish relations. His wandering is the wandering of the Jewish people; his longevity is their unlikely survival; and his role, like theirs, is to witness the truth of Christianity by waiting for the Second Coming (251).

Paraśurāma takes on a similar apocalyptic witness role in the *Kalki Purāṇa*, a very late minor Purāṇa that was probably composed in early-eighteenth-century Bengal (Hazra 1958, 303–308). In the *Kalki Purāṇa*, Paraśurāma and three other *cirañjīvins* (Vyāsa, Aśvatthāman, and Kṛpa, all veterans of the *Mahābhārata* war) disguise themselves as wandering mendicants and go and visit the nativity of Kalki ("Ender of Kali"), the future and final *avatāra* of Viṣṇu, born to bring the Kali Yuga to its close and the exterminate the race of *mleccha*s or barbarians. 1.2.29 tells us that the four wanderers know of Kalki's destiny and, before departing, they perform his naming ceremony, consecrating him to his divinely destructive purpose.

After undergoing his sacred thread ceremony to mark his coming of age, Kalki goes to live and train at Paraśurāma's *āśrama*. When his training is concluded, Kalki offers the guru payment for services rendered. Paraśurāma declines, saying that it will be payment enough if Kalki fulfills his destiny of obtaining a magic bow from Śiva and conquering the world by overthrowing the Brahmin-oppressing king Kali—destroying many sinful kings and Buddhists in the process—before handing it over to the Kṣatriya-turned-Brahmin Devāpi and the Kṣatriya Maru, the two figures destined to rule over the reestablished Golden Age (*KaP* 1.3.7–10).[34] It is not difficult to see the parallels between Kalki's actions and those of his preceptor. Kalki's actions seem to be a perfected and cosmically elevated repetition of Paraśurāma's varṇicide, with none of the ambivalence, resulting in a true reign of dharma.

We can also interpret Kalki as the Christ to Paraśurāma's Wandering Jew, who has waited on earth for his return. But there are two "Christs" in the Christian legend, the Christ about to be crucified at the tale's beginning, and the risen Christ who returns to usher in the Millennium at the tale's end. In the larger Paraśurāma myth cycle, analogous roles to that of these two Christs are performed by two *avatāra*s. The first is Rāma, who turns Paraśurāma into a walking unassimilable remainder when he takes over the role of *avatāra* and effectively casts Viṣṇu out of him in an act of negation.[35] The second "Christ" in our myth is Kalki, who presents an inversion of Paraśurāma's relationship to Rāma when Kalki takes Paraśurāma as his guru and fully becomes his *avatāra* self under his guru-ship. It seems that Kalki, the last *avatāra*—technically, the not-yet *avatāra*—is powerfully connected to the no-more *avatāra*.

In the *Vāyu* and *Brahmāṇḍa Purāṇas*, which describe Paraśurāma as "consisting of *brahma* and *kṣatra,*" his father Jamadagni is said to have "swallowed the fire of Viṣṇu," which he must have then passed on to his son (*VāP* 2.4.93–94; *BḍP* 3.1.96–97). And in the epic, as we have seen, he is created by the addition of either a tree or a *caru* (or both) into the typical pairing of father and mother during conception. Whether we are talking about the fire of Viṣṇu or the *kṣatra* infused in the *caru,* from before his birth, Paraśurāma is "supplemented" and that supplement is taken away when he meets Rāma.

The episode of Rāma's defeat of Paraśurāma appears throughout the Purāṇas and in many regional versions of the *Rāmāyaṇa*. Typically, it ends with Rāma either destroying Śiva's bow, representative of the power lent to Paraśurāma by Śiva (as in Vālmīki's and Kṛttivāsa's *Rāmāyaṇa*, and the *Rāma Nāṭaka*); destroying Paraśurāma's Brahmin power (as in the *Kaṃban Rāmāyaṇa*); or cutting off his path to Heaven permanently (as in the Oriya *Jagamohana Rāmāyaṇ*, the Marāṭhī *Śrī Rāmavijaya*, and the *Madhava Kandali Rāmāyaṇa*).[36] The theme is echoed in the *Brāhmāṇḍa Purāṇa* and in the legend connected with the Paraśurāma temple in Pedhe, Maharashtra (Mate 2001, 103). It also occurs in Bhavabhūti's eighth-century drama the *Mahāvīracarita*, where a bellicose Paraśurāma (who boasts about killing Kṣatriyas still unborn in the womb) starts the fight after he becomes angry that Rāma has broken Śiva's bow and threatens him with his axe. Here the axe is identified as having been broken off from Śiva's own and given to Paraśurāma as a gift in an episode that earned Śiva the epithet Khaṇḍaparaśu, "He of the Broken Axe" (Mirashi 1974, 119–22). In nearly all cases, the encounter with Rāma ends with Paraśurāma being reduced in some way and his exile status being made permanent. Whatever supplement Paraśurāma is born with, in whichever protean form it is understood, is taken away when he meets Rāma. An inversion takes place, and Paraśurāma himself, made redundant by the presence of Rāma and cut off from Heaven, becomes the supplement himself.

Why then does Kalki choose the demoted Paraśurāma as his guru? Why not take his training under the immediately previous incarnation of Viṣṇu? Why does he skip over the intervening *avatāras* (the Buddha, Kṛṣṇa, and Rāma) and go to Paraśurāma? Obviously, one reason is that Paraśurāma, unlike them, is still alive. But we must remember that his long life is inseparable from his negated status. He is a *cirañjīvin* only because he is no longer an *avatāra.* In undertaking his training at his *āśrama,* Kalki is asking Paraśurāma to pass on to him the thing he cannot give because it is the thing taken from him by Rāma. But in asking, he interpellates (to repurpose a term from Louis

Althusser), or "calls up" that very thing in Paraśurāma. When the training is over, Kalki takes the already-taken (by Rāma) thing from Paraśurāma in a double negation. Negating the negated thing brings it back, but only so that it can vanish in that same instant. This double negation serves as a kind of death for Paraśurāma, leaving him in a state of limbo like the Wandering Jew awaiting the Second Coming. The period that follows is the time between the two deaths.

The concept of two deaths can be understood with reference to mourning and funerary rituals. In the ordinary course of things, a person dies a biological death that then requires a ritual, social, and legal death to remove him or her from the world. Sometimes, the orders of the two deaths are reversed, with a person experiencing a social death, as in cases of banishment or renunciation, that leaves them still physically alive, but no longer part of the world. Žižek explains:

> Recall the two symmetrically opposed modes of the "living dead," of finding oneself in the uncanny place "between the two deaths": one is either biologically dead while symbolically alive (surviving one's biological death as a spectral apparition or symbolic authority of the Name), or symbolically dead while biologically alive (those who are excluded from the sociosymbolic order, from Antigone to today's *Homo sacer*). (2014, 248)

Like Jesus's words to the impatient guard, Rāma's defeat of Paraśurāma is a first death of the exclusionary type, leading to an extended period of undeath that only concludes with a second death granted at the end of the world itself. Lacan describes the second death using similarly apocalyptic imagery, calling it "death insofar as it is regarded as the point at which the very cycles of the transformations of nature are annihilated" (2016, 248). In Sanskrit, this is called the Great Dissolution, or Mahāpralaya.[37]

On his way to the cross, Christ gives the Wandering Jew his first death in the sense of "removal from life" but does not grant him true extinction until he returns as the risen Christ in the Second Coming. Christ and the Wandering Jew become mirror images of each other: one waits in Heaven to live while the other waits on earth to die, with each event scheduled to occur at the exact same point in time. In our story, Rāma gives Paraśurāma his first death by stripping him of his *avatāra* status and Kalki gives him symbolic extinction at the end of the age. Both Rāma and Kalki are forms of Viṣṇu, while Paraśurāma exists during the period between the two as a *negated* form of Viṣṇu, awaiting the double negation of the final (and always future) *avatāra*. Paraśurāma is unique in this way, existing on earth as an indestructible trace of what was once Viṣṇu: an *avatāra*-shaped void.

## Conclusion

In this chapter, we began with the three levels or aspects of Paraśurāma: the universal-ontological, especially his dual identity as *avatāra* and a *ciranjīvin*, in which he symbolizes the simultaneous compression and extension of time; the particular-sexual, best understood through myths of his birth describing fertility rites involving the hugging of trees and the ingestion of rice pudding as well as his unusual relationship to temporality; and the singular-subjective, in which his conflicted nature bequeaths him both individuality and interiority as well as irrevocably binds him to his actions.

We then examined the Paraśurāma myth as it appears in the Critical Edition of the *Mahābhārata*, observing that it was probably produced by Brahmins in North India after the ascent of the Buddhist emperor Aśoka. The mythmakers believed themselves to be in a state of reduced influence and importance as a result of the spread of Buddhism and they wanted their Kṣatriya audience to recognize the power of Brahmins and support a class system with Brahmins at the top. The Paraśurāma myth is therefore a reaction to a real historical shift, but only reflects this historical reality as it was experienced by a small corner of the population—one with a very highly developed intellectual system based on analogy and intensely focused on the questions of purity and pollution, life and death, that arose from their sustained reflection on the Vedic sacrifice. The Brahmin warrior Paraśurāma's internal contradictions, reflecting anxieties situated in a specific time and place, thereby became fertile ground for metaphysical speculation, as my creative re-descriptions of the synchronic macromyth have shown.

We then explored the Paraśurāma cycle as narrative symbolic philosophy. First, we analyzed the Paraśurāma myth alongside those of Droṇa, Dattātreya, and Viśvāmitra, respectively illuminating Paraśurāma's temporal and spatial exceptionalism, his embodiment of excess or saturation, and his embodiment of the vanishing mediator of "becoming." To see how Paraśurāma exemplifies the "sovereign exception," we brought in the myth of the first king Vena and the theoretical models of Carl Schmitt and Giorgio Agamben. Finally, we utilized the concept of the double negation to interpret his nature in the context of his relationship with the Purāṇic Kalki, the epic hero Rāma, and the epic anti-hero Aśvatthāman. Finally, we (fruitfully, I hope) reread Paraśurāma's story alongside the European myth of the Wandering Jew.

I began by writing that Paraśurāma is an *avatāra* and a *cirañjīvin* (a "long-lived one"), a Vaiṣṇava deity and a Śaiva devotee, a Brahmin and a warrior, a sage and an epic hero. But it might have been more accurate to say that he is "not this, not that." As we have seen in what so far has largely been a synchronic discussion of the Paraśurāma macromyth, he is the exception: the flickering, vanishing mediator between opposing poles, sovereign and supplement, indestructible but not really there. In the next two chapters, we will examine Paraśurāma's first, exceptional act of violence, his decapitation of his mother Reṇukā.

# 2

# Matricide I

## *The Broken Pot*

Then the little spring from which the water was flowing said, "Girl, why did you break your little water pitcher?"

"Why should I not break my little water pitcher?"

"Oh," said the spring, "then I will begin to flow," and it began to flow furiously. And everything drowned in the water.

—Adapted from Jacob and Wilhelm Grimm,
"Little Louse and Little Flea (Grimm 033)"
as told by Dorothea Catharina Wild

It's just as well that my pitcher has broken.
I am free from hauling water!
An obligation removed from my head!

—Kabir

### The Matricidal Micromyth: "Death to all that flows"[1]

The episode of Paraśurāma's decapitation of Reṇukā functions as an independent, detachable component that does not affect the narrative structure of his war against the Kṣatriyas and it is often either left out of the Paraśurāma myth (as in *MBh* 12.48–49, the version narrated by Kṛṣṇa) or told as a separate story with Reṇukā as the main figure. Nevertheless, it is not unrelated to the thematic nexus of the myth because it serves to crystallize the anxieties and nostalgia expressed in the stories of Paraśurāma's mixed birth and charges them with erotic energy. It also serves as Paraśurāma's first trauma, the dress rehearsal for his varṇicide.

To read the episode better on its own terms, we will first break it down into its most basic elements, rendering the story into a micromyth, elegantly described by Doniger as "a beam of pure light that seems colorless until it is refracted through the prism of a particular cultural telling" (1998, 88). Admittedly, for most readers, "colorless" is not the first word that comes to mind upon hearing a story about a woman wetting herself with desire and a son decapitating his mother. But micromyths are not always bland, as the four elements of the matricide micromyth demonstrate:

1. A married woman sees an attractive man, becomes sexually aroused involuntarily and loses control, after which her husband sees evidence of her arousal and perceived infidelity.

2. The sons refuse their father's command to kill their mother and are cursed to become animals or idiots as a result, losing the power of speech.

3. The youngest son obeys his father's command to behead his mother.

4. The father/husband restores and resurrects the mother/wife, and the youngest son asks for the whole incident to be forgotten.

The first element—in which a married woman sees an attractive man, becomes sexually aroused involuntarily and loses control—expresses cross-cultural themes of incontinence and the loss of magical power through transgression. It connects, too, to the themes of varṇicide and mixed birth. I have already argued that the story of Paraśurāma is much concerned with class mixing and that the conflict of *varṇa*s within Paraśurāma mirrors the conflict in the social order in which he exists, so that the mixed-class theme and the varṇicide theme act as transformations of one another. But what I did not consider until I had a conversation with a colleague about discussions of libido in scientific debates about race in nineteenth century America, is how deeply the concern with *varṇa* is also tied to the myth's focus on female sexual desire. Also at work here is the mythological and folkloric motif of the "woman waylaid at the well," or the *paṇaghaṭa-līlā*, especially popular in women's songs, but also appearing in the erotic strains of both Hindu and Sufi devotional songs and Hindi cinema (Pauwels 2010, 3).

The second element, the refusal of the enraged father's sons to kill their mother and their subsequent curse to lose the power of speech, is central to a psychoanalytic interpretation of the myth. The idea, originated by Freud and modified by Jacques Lacan, Julia Kristeva, Diane Jonte-Pace, and Madelon Sprengnether, that a rejection or expulsion of the mother and a submission to the law of the father marks the child's entrance into the realm of language provides an explanation for the fate of the disobedient brothers.[2]

The third element, the youngest son's murder of his mother, is the crux of the micromyth, the sinful act that demands expiation and the foreshadowing of Paraśurāma's extermination of the Kṣatriyas. We have finally arrived now at the reason for the subtitle of this book: Paraśurāma's act of matricide provides a blueprint for his extermination of the Kṣatriyas because his mother's *varṇa* is the same as that of his Kṣatriya victims and because his attempt to annihilate them is an extension or an iteration of his matricidal impulse. I will go into much more detail about this in the conclusion.

The fourth and final element, resurrection, connects the Paraśurāma myth to the larger myth cycle of the Bhārgava clan to which he belongs. As Goldman notes, myths commonly associate the descendants of Bhṛgu with the power to raise the dead (1977, 86). Also, in connection with Paraśurāma's desire for the incident to be forgotten, the resurrection represents a denial and attempted undoing of the matricide and mirrors the psychological processes of repression and sublimation.

## The First Element: "Incontinent the Void"[3]

In a footnote to his translation of the matricide episode found in the epic, Goldman examines the compound *klinnāmbhasi* ("soaked in water"), which is used to describe the state of Reṇuka's clothes after she has seen another man sporting in the river:

> The intent of the phrase *klinnāmbhasi* is not clear. In what sense is Reṇukā soaked in water? Is the idea that, having "lost her senses" (becoming *vicetanā*) she falls in the water? Perhaps, but as she was bathing anyway, she would have already been wet. Some later Purāṇic versions have an elaborate story, perhaps based on this phrase, according to which Reṇukā, through her chastity, fidelity,

> and austerity, had achieved the power either to bathe without getting wet or to roll water back to the ashram in a ball. She loses this power and so Jamadagni comes to know of her erotic fantasy. This story seems clearly derivative and moreover would be a slight on the sage's powers of omniscience. Nīl[akaṇṭha] gives a purely erotic interpretation, citing the following curious verse: *sundaraṃ puruṣaṃ dṛṣtvā bhrātaram pitaraṃ sutam/ yonir dravati nārīṇāṃ satyaṃ satyaṃ janārdana//* "When she sees a handsome man, whether it be her brother, father, or even a son, a woman's [vagina] grows wet. This is the truth, the truth, Janārdana." (1971, 22)[4]

It is important to point out that, although Reṇukā is described as going to bathe in the *Mahābhārata*, subsequent versions of the myth often have her going to collect water, which gives her no logical reason to come back wet. We should also note well the double meaning of incontinence as both lack of sexual restraint and inability to control body functions. In the classical literature of both North and South India, as Doniger argues, "the fluidity of the human body is seen by Hindus as a source of danger" (1980, 58). Āyurvedic practitioners in Sri Lanka in the 1970s were in the habit of examining a woman's urine for cloudiness to see if she was leaking any fluids she should not have been. Obeyesekere explains:

> [The] white discharge in females, which may be secretions due to vaginitis or to hormonal changes in pregnancy or puberty, are interpreted as the pathological emission of *dhātu* [body components], though not exclusively semen. The reported wetness in the vagina may be lubrication caused by masturbation or sexual fantasies, or simply a normal physiological condition of moistness, but it is generally interpreted as pathological semen loss. (1977, 212–13)

In yogic physiological terms, the loss of fluid represents a loss of potency and it is by retaining their sexual fluid that yogis and other spiritual adepts gain their great power. In the Haṭha Yoga tradition in particular, female sexual fluid is called *rajas* and a male yogi can draw it up into his body through his urethra during sex (Mallinson 2018, 190–99). The opposite of yogic self-control is licentiousness (or incontinence), and both opposing themes are plentiful in the Śaiva mythology that inform the traditions of Paraśurāma.

One interpretation of the matricide episode explicitly links incontinence with loss of power. According to this explanation, the myth is an allegory in which Reṇukā represents semen, the forest represents the mind, and the bathing *gandharva* prince stands for lust. Reṇukā's five sons are the five bodily centers and Paraśurāma represents the purest of these, located behind the forehead. Read as a prescriptive yogic allegory, the myth's message is this: When lust occurs in the mind, the yogi will lose his seed unless he is able to channel it upwards through the chambers of his body to the highest point of purity, where it will be safe (Donaldson 1995, 162). By identifying Reṇukā with semen, this yogic interpretation of the episode reinforces the widespread notion in India that women, like semen, represent power when controlled and peril when released. A wise man controls women as carefully as he controls his own semen, a notion that goes back to the Vedic rituals in which the sacrificer's wife must always stay behind a screen to mediate the danger of her (necessary) presence (see Jamison 1996, 256).

## DEFILEMENT AND *AKRASIA*

"The representation of defilement," writes Paul Ricoeur, "dwells in the half-light of a quasi-physical infection that points toward a quasi-moral unworthiness" (1967, 35). In Ricoeurian fashion, the matricide episode establishes a clear link between the "quasi-physical" and the "quasi-moral," connecting Reṇukā's mental lapse to a physical manifestation related to some form of symbolic incontinence. The adultery Reṇukā commits in her heart manifests itself as a wet spot on the front of her clothes, but the stain becomes significant only when her husband Jamadagni perceives its import.[5] Jamadagni's harsh judgment, sometimes represented as an omniscient yogic eye, connects Reṇukā's stain to her infidelity and results in a swift punishment. Ricoeur concludes, "Thus it is always in the sight of other people who excite the feeling of shame and under the influence of the word which says what is pure and impure that a stain is defilement" (40).[6]

Aristotle, in *Nicomachean Ethics* VII:1–10, expounds on *akrasia*, "lack of self-control," or "incontinence." *The Stanford Encyclopedia of Philosophy* explains:

> The two kinds of passions that Aristotle focuses on, in his treatment of *akrasia,* are the appetite for pleasure and anger. Either can lead to impetuosity and weakness. But Aristotle gives pride of place to the appetite for pleasure as the passion that undermines

> reason. He calls the kind of *akrasia* caused by an appetite for pleasure "unqualified *akrasia*"—or, as we might say, *akrasia* "full stop"; akrasia caused by anger he considers a qualified form of *akrasia* and calls it *akrasia* "with respect to anger." We thus have these four forms of *akrasia*: (A) impetuosity caused by pleasure, (B) impetuosity caused by anger, (C) weakness caused by pleasure (D) weakness caused by anger. (Kraut 2018)

Building on the Greek tradition, Saint Paul gives *akrasia* as a reason for regular marital sex, giving couples this advice: "Do not deprive each other except perhaps by mutual consent and for a time, so that you may devote yourselves to prayer. Then come together again so that Satan will not tempt you because of your lack of self-control [*akrasia*]" (1 Cor. 7:5). Based presumably on his understanding of *akrasia* as the unqualified variety, Paul's warning resonates strongly with the themes of the Reṇukā myth, in which a married woman loses sexual control at the sight of another man. We should note that in Hindu myth, sages such as Jamadagni are not known for their physical attractiveness and tend to be the cuckolds when it comes to marital infidelity.

*Akrasia* as understood by the Greek philosophical tradition provides a framework that allows us to transform and externalize Paraśurāma's fundamental internal division yet again, opposing a Kṣatriya's lust to a Brahmin's wrath. Thinking in terms of *akrasia,* we can connect Reṇukā's lapse at the river with Jamadagni's burst of anger at the ashram, the two events that bookend the decapitation. Each fall on opposite sides of the Aristotelian rubric—Reṇukā's as sex-related *akrasia* and Jamadagni's as anger-related *akrasia*. Paul's idea that marital sex functions as a prophylactic against *akrasia* also resonates with the idea of Reṇukā's weakness as a kind of insult to the old ascetic Jamadagni's virility (she would not be cheating if you could keep her happy in bed!), a motif that is drawn from the Bhārgava myth of Cyavana and Sukanyā in *MBh* 3.121–24.

The Greek word *akrasia* comes from *kratia*, whose Sanskrit cognate *kratu* is a word that the reader will recall came up in the last chapter in connection with the *Śatapatha Brāhmaṇa*'s myth of the Brahmin god Mitra and the Brahmin-Kṣatriya symbiosis deployed as a way to understand subjectivity. In Greek, *kratia* means "mastery" and gives the English lexicon words like "democracy" (or better still, "autocracy," "kleptocracy," and the playful but sadly apt neologism "idiocracy"), while the Sanskrit *kratu* means "intention" and "will" as well as "ability" and "power." In regional variants of the Reṇukā myth, the identification of Reṇukā's power with some kind of ability (usually to control water) connected to her social status is explicit. But the language in the epic's Reṇukā story does not describe her reaction to seeing the bathing *gandharva* in terms of mastery or loss of control but rather describes her losing her consciousness or "sense" (as in "common sense"), employing a form of the word *cit* ("consciousness") that is repeated later to describe Paraśurāma's brothers' dumbfounded reaction to being asked to kill their mother.[7] Losing control, losing purity, losing consciousness, and losing power all find their signifier in Reṇukā's defiled wet clothing.

What is the difference or the connection between Reṇukā falling into the water and the water falling out of Reṇukā? The Sanskrit sexological tradition is filled with conjectures about what kind of sexual fluid women possess and how it functions in orgasm and conception.[8] According to *Suśrutasaṃhita* 2.36, female discharge, called *ārtava* or *strībīja* ("female seed") flows like melted butter during intercourse (Das 2003, 222). One commentator, Āḍhamalla, argues that women must produce ejaculate or they would not be able to obtain sexual pleasure, and that female ejaculate is produced "steadily upon arousal, irrespective of actual stimulation due to intercourse or other means" (221–22). Another, Ḍalhaṇa, holds that two women can produce a "boneless child" by having sex with each other and mixing their sexual fluids through tribadism (228). Texts that postdate the *Kāma Sutra* employ a general idea that sexually excited women can squirt out some kind of lubricating fluid called *kāmaśila* ("passion-water") or *mada* ("passion"), either involuntarily upon orgasm or at will in order to fake one (396–97). By way of illustration, Das repeats the story of an Indian gynecologist whose ministrations inadvertently cause a woman to ejaculate in a stream so powerful that it blows up a light bulb in his office (399n1347).[9]

The Purāṇic interpretation of *klinnāmbhasi* ("soaked in water") as suggesting a special ability regarding liquid on Reṇukā's part and the subsequent kaleidoscopic expansion of this idea into a wide array of variants revolving around fluidity, incontinence, and images of collapse and dissolution are the products of thematic superimposition. Reṇukā's incontinence simultaneously indexes the perilous Brahmin-Kṣatriya balance of power, Indian discourse on the sexual failings of women, concerns about the danger women present through the transgression of their bodily boundaries (exemplified in the unwilled eruption of fluid), and the idea of women as a threat to external social boundaries (exemplified by Reṇukā's disastrous contact with an outsider).

Contact with an outsider is the occasion of her incontinence, and, in a later instance, of her husband's death.[10]

In a variant from Cholavandan, Tamil Nadu, Reṇukā is in the habit of collecting water every morning in a pot made out of sand that is held together by magic. One day, the god Indra is flying over her and looks down to admire his reflection in the water she is carrying, causing the pot to break apart. When Reṇukā is unable to reform the pot and returns to the hermitage without water, her husband orders their sons to behead her (Foulston 2002, 94). In another South Indian variant Reṇukā has the power to make water temporarily solid so that she can carry it, a power she can only retain as long as her heart is pure (Jouveau-Dubreuil 1937, 114).

In a version of the myth told by goddess worshippers at the Reṇukā temple in Savadatti, in the southern state of Karnataka, Reṇukā again has the power to fashion sand from the riverbank into a pot. To add to her impressiveness, instead of putting a folded bolt of cloth under the magically constructed pot to balance it on her head, she uses a coiled cobra as a head cushion. When she sees the handsome prince in the river and is overcome with lust she finds that she is no longer able to magically make a pot out of sand. Paraśurāma does not appear in this variant and so there is no one to behead her, but her husband does banish Reṇukā and she becomes a diseased old hag. She remains in this state until the Aśvin twins, Vedic horse deities and physicians to the gods, find her and restore her to her state of youthful beauty, after which Jamadagni accepts her back into the hermitage. The version that local Viṣṇu worshippers tell has a different ending. After the Aśvins restore her, Reṇukā returns to the hermitage, where Jamadagni orders Paraśurāma to behead her (Gurumurthy 2005, 32).[11]

Reṇukā's physical appearance and spiritual power are also linked in the *Mahābhārata,* where Jamadagni reprimands his wife when he notices that she has lost her aura of virtue and beauty. Goldman translates the phrase the text uses, *brāhmyā lakṣmyā vivarjitām,* as "bereft of her spiritual power and her beauty" and gives a gloss, writing, "Brāhmī is the energy she had acquired as a brahman's wife through her chastity. Lakṣmī may be taken as her beauty and splendor as a princess" (1973, 22). Here Goldman's reading is instructive, pointing out an easily overlooked instance in which the text picks up and sexualizes one of the main contradictions that the Paraśurāma cycle attempts to resolve: the imagined coexistence of Brahmin and Kṣatriya at the top of the hierarchy.

Reṇukā is a Kṣatriya living the life of an ascetic, acting the part of the dutiful wife of a forest sage because her husband is a Brahmin. Throughout her life with Jamadagni, Reṇukā has been able to hold in balance her royal identity, given at birth, and her Brahmin identity, imposed at marriage. When the text tells us that Reṇukā has simultaneously lost both her royal splendor and her virtue as a Brahmin wife, it presents a picture of a constructed identity encompassing two opposites, once held in tension but now collapsing and canceling each other out. Images of a ball of water perilously suspended in the air (like a quivering globe of liquid in zero gravity) or a pot of sand dissolving into tiny grains and falling to the ground are compelling metaphors to represent and visualize this moment, and these images demonstrate the way that variants of the matricide myth understand Reṇukā's composite personality as a natural tension made into an unnatural cohesion and held together by the exertion of power.

There is another way to look at Reṇukā's desire, if we take it as a desire to be *like* the handsome prince rather than to be *with* the handsome prince. Some mythmakers have seen an element of nostalgic longing in Reṇukā's desire, as this story recounted about the Paraśūrāma temple in Pedhe, Maharashtra illustrates:

> Parashuram's mother and the wife of the great Kshatri king, [Kārtavīrya], were sisters. The sage Jamadagni was poor, and his wife was forced to do all the household duties with her own hands. One day, fetching water, she thought of her sister's grandeur and her own poverty. As she was thus thinking the pitcher became empty. The sage asked her why her pitcher was empty, and when she told him how the water had leaked away, he blamed her for thinking her sister's state better than her own. She said: "If I want, to ask my sister there is hardly food for ten men." "I have," the sage replied, "food for ten thousand, but I do not think it wise to call a Kshatri to dinner." She pleaded that they should be asked, and her sister and her husband came with a large following. From his wish-fulfilling cow and never-empty jar the sage satisfied the king and all his men. Learning the source of the sage's store of food, the king carried off the cow and the jar and killed the sage, forcing him to lie on a bed of pointed nails. (*Gazetteer of the Bombay Presidency, vol. X (Ratnagiri District)* 1885, 355n4)

Reṇukā's desire here is not so much to frolic with a handsome man but to display that most Kṣatriya-like of values, the warrior's generosity, which is praised in so many Vedic hymns of gratitude. Through his own generosity, Indra, the Kṣatriya par excellence, earns the epithet Maghavā ("The Munificent") (see Whitaker 2011, 89–90).[12] Generosity is the virtue of nobility because it is capricious and unbound; blows come as easily as gifts from the noble warrior's open hand.[13] In the myth from Maharashtra given above, Reṇukā has a Tantalus moment when she looks down and sees that the water she has collected has drained out of her pot, not because of her unbidden sexual response, but because she envies the wealth of her sister, who is married to Kārtavīrya. This myth conflates Kārtavīrya with Citraratha and has Reṇukā admiring the idea of his wealth rather than the appearance of his body. Subsequently Jamadagni replaces Reṇukā's empty pot with his own magical bottomless pot. Here, overflowing is imagined not as incontinence, but munificence. However, munificence is the wrong virtue for a Brahmin, and so the Kṣatriya Kārtavīrya (made here into Jamadagni's brother-in-law) steals the pot and the cow and inflicts on Jamadagni the appropriately ascetic death of forcing him to lie on a bed of nails.

## *Gandharvas*, the *Chora*, and the Woman Waylaid at the Well

In the Paraśurāma cycle, Reṇukā is the one who first sees an outsider in the form of the bathing prince, and the mere sight of him proves disastrous. Later in the myth cycle, this moment of the wife's first contact with the outside repeats with deadly results. The second time, the stranger Reṇukā encounters is Kārtavīrya, who ignores Reṇukā's attempt at a hospitable welcome and proceeds to ransack the hermitage, setting into motion the events that lead to the slaughter of the Kṣatriyas (*MBh* 3.116.20). The parallel structure of these opening sequences and their reliance on the wife's role as dispenser of hospitality in Vedic myth and ritual makes a connection between the matricide episode and the destruction of the Kṣatriyas.

From the very beginning of the Paraśurāma cycle, the world outside the family is associated with disaster, peril, death, and the Kṣatriya class. In the Tamil *Kāñcippurāṇam*, the bathing prince is explicitly identified as Kārtavīrya, the same man who kills Paraśurāma's father. This identification, which also relates to the above story from Ratnagiri district that identifies Kārtavīrya as Reṇukā's brother-in-law (not a stranger, but someone in the family who arouses desire for what he has) is key to my understanding of the myth, as I will explain later. But the fact that the *Mahābhārata* identifies the handsome man that Reṇukā encounters at the river as Citraratha, king of the *gandharvas*, places the river episode in the context of a large body of myths about relations between humans and wilderness beings. And we should take a closer look at that context.

Traditionally in Indian myth and epic, the forest has been the home of dangerous animals and spirits, religious ascetics who have renounced the world, and those who have been banished. The wild *araṇya* is the opposite of the settled *grāma* (and the cultivated *kṣetra,* as we shall see) and is the setting for stories of "hunting, asceticism, exile, the testing of heroes, and romantic adventures" (Rosella 2010, 147). Rosella's description of the forest as a place that "can enact erotic wishes" and "promotes . . . erotic wish-fulfilment and libidinal freedom" makes it an appropriate setting for Reṇukā's encounter (157). The motif of erotic attraction overwhelming the hero or heroine's mind in a forest landscape (and often near a river) is of course familiar from Kṛṣṇa mythology centered on the god's dalliances with Rādhā and the cowherd girls. It has since been employed in modern Indian cinema (see Ciolfi 2010) and in folk songs sung by women. The folkloric motif of the "woman waylaid at the well," or the *paṇaghaṭa-līlā*, portrays a married woman bringing a pot to collect water and meeting a handsome and often sexually aggressive stranger. In these songs, "the women are usually portrayed as victims, mostly as subjected to a test of their virtue, which they pass" (Pauwels 2010, 6). Unlike Reṇukā, the women in the folk songs tend to fend off the advances of a stranger, not become aroused from afar. Pauwels recounts a reading of the motif as an allegory for women's need for self-control:

> [The] full waterpot (*ghaṭa, gagarī, kalaśa*) stands for the auspiciousness of the *suhāginī* (virtuous married woman), and the broken pot is a bad omen and symbolizes the breaking of the rules of *maryādā* or normative constraints on women. The arduous road (*ḍagara*) is the difficult path of life for the young *bahū* or daughter-in-law in a joint family. The basic images that occur in the songs then stand for concerns with which women are confronted in their daily lives. Obviously, there are also sexual implications, with the broken pot symbolizing lost virtue (or virginity), and possibly also signifying fertility. (Joshi 2000 in Pauwels 2010, 6)

Now we have arrived at the broken pot of this chapter's title, which we can see in a broader context using psychoanalysis.

Kristeva writes that (symbolic) matricide, conceived as a horror toward and rejection of the maternal body, is "our vital necessity" and the prerequisite for entrance into the realm of language represented by the father (1989,

28). Despite the mother's unwillingness to let go of the special bond she has with the child, the body of the mother is forbidden to the child by the incest taboo and thus the maternal body is a site of conflicting desires that Kristeva terms the *chora,* or "vessel." This characterization is especially apt in the Paraśurāma myth, since, as we have seen, it is a (spilled) vessel that betrays Reṇukā to her husband.

When discussing the village sectarian practices centered on Reṇukā and related goddesses in South India, Brubaker writes, "The most common temporary embodiment of a goddess is some form of that universal symbol of the feminine, the vessel or pot" (1978, 81). In the festivals held in Pudhucherry, the goddess is frequently represented as a *karakam*, "[water] in a pot with the key ingredients of turmeric, vermillion, a lemon, a one rupee coin and margosa leaves immersed in it" (Srinivasan 2009, 362). The full pot itself is a popular symbol of auspiciousness in Hindu, Jain, and Buddhist art throughout South and Southeast Asia and its roots go back to the later Vedas (Coomaraswamy 1993, 161–65). *Atharva Veda* 10.8 uses the image of the full water jar to think out the metaphysics of *pūrṇa* or "fullness," identifying a woman bearing a jar as the rising sun (Jurewicz 2016, 293–96). Jurewicz has included it in a list of "superordinate categories" or "general domains" of Vedic ontological thought, most of which find some expression in the Paraśurāma myth:

> These [superordinate categories] are Water And A Rocky Hill, A Vessel Filled With Liquid, Procreation, Creation of Space, Finding The Hidden, Freeing Cows and Cleansing By Heat. They are evoked by verbal phrases or words denoting everyday experience (natural phenomena, objects and activities). Their aim is to endow complex concepts with a simple frame and scenario which will [facilitate] mental associations between different concepts. (52)

We should also note that later heterodox Tantric poets employ the motif to criticize religious dogma. In one such poem, or *dōha,*

> the water in the well is God; all humans are the water-fetchers, and their containers may differ, but God is manifest just the same in all of them. The pots are to be broken to see the underlying unity. This can be understood to refer to the Sufi concept of *fanā'* or "absorption" in God. The broken pot then is not something negative but a positive indicator, signifying transcendence above worldly concerns. (Pauwels 2010, 8)

Against this psychoanalytic, folkloric, and philosophical background, Reṇukā's encounter at the forest sets up a mesocosmic representation of the struggle that pervades the myth: the struggle between Brahmin and Kṣatriya. The forest setting is in fact what makes the micromyth such a productive site for commentary and self-commentary. As Pauwels explains:

> [As] a chronotope, the forest becomes the existential locus of the creature in *statu viae,* and the inner theatre of an iterated and cyclic psychomachy. In fact, the forest's time-space is a special sort of "everyday time": That is, both a series of moments of presentness that contain specific meanings contained within a particular combination of time and space (cultural, social and also emotional and psychological), and, simultaneously, an accumulation of meanings that go far beyond specific presentness, and that include the past utterances of others. In brief, the forest is the setting of space-time fusion, that is, of the alternation between flashback (*analexis*) and flashforward (*prolexis*). The forest is the locus through which one learns to give meaning to the vastness of the events that have occurred, are occurring or will occur in the real world. (160)

Reṇukā's encounter at the river is purposely staged in a setting charged with erotic and metaphysical significance. The broken water pot, or the loss of the power to control water, is a superimposition of sexual incontinence in the body on top of the fragility of dharma in the human realm, which will be demonstrated more acutely the next time Reṇukā greets a Kṣatriya stranger. And when we read the story in light of the speculative philosophy in *Atharva Veda* 10.8.14, in which the sunrise is a woman bearing a jar of water that some perceive with their eyes and others apprehend with their mind, there is a metaphysical third domain of meaning to be superimposed on top of human consciousness and cosmic order.[14]

Adding a fourth dimension to our analysis, Nancy Falk has identified a political model in the "complex relationship between wilderness and kingship" that occurs in both Buddhist and Hindu myths and rituals.[15] In some cases, this relationship is one of conquest and domination of the forest by the king. In other cases, the wilderness represents a seat of power and wilderness beings are royal patrons and protectors (1976, 9). Falk argues that the wilderness and the beings therein represent a form of chaos that must be tamed by the king, who can then use his mastery over the wilderness as a source and symbol of his power. Using this pattern, she gives a unique interpretation of the famous story of the Buddha's victory over Māra under the *bodhi* tree:

> [A] *yaksha* engages a prince in battle over the *yaksha*'s seat—which also seems in this instance to be the throne and symbol whose possession authorizes a kingship. The prince wins, and as a result of his conquest he gains mastery over the world. Later the throne becomes an image of him, as a kind of prototypical king. Another king devotes a cult to it and his personal well-being becomes dependent on its maintenance. (12)

Falk's analysis of the Buddha myth as a ritual struggle between a Kṣatriya and a forest spirit finds a faint echo in the story of Reṇukā's encounter. But unlike the Buddha, who defeats the *yakṣa* and takes his throne as a symbol of his own power, Reṇukā's psychological struggle with the *gandharva* results in her disastrous fall from grace. However, in the South Indian rituals based on the myth, a venerated object (the sacrificial post) does in fact represent Reṇukā's tempter at the river just as Falk's Buddha myth describes the building of a *stupa* that represents the throne of the defeated *yakṣa*. While the *stupa* explained by Falk's myth represents the victory of a prince over a forest spirit, the sacrificial post represents a forest spirit who has been turned into a sacrificial victim (Biardeau 2004, 188).

Franklin Edgerton hypothesizes that *gandharva*s may once have been a type of Indian incubus, a demonic being who takes the form of a handsome man to seduce and sleep with women (1965, 79). We should note too that in the Upaniṣads, *gandharvas* are known to possess and speak through women (Black 2007, 156–58). One *gandharva* in particular, Viśvāvasu, has the *droit de seigneur* over all newlywed brides. The specific *gandharva* that Reṇukā encounters, though, is not Viśvāvasu (also the name of one of Paraśurāma's brothers, coincidentally) but Citraratha, described as the foremost of the *gandharva*s in the *Bhagavad Gītā* (*MBh* 6.32.25).

Stutley gives this general description of *gandharva*s drawn from Sanskrit materials:

> Although these beings are usually benevolent, they may be dangerous to meet at twilight when they roam about lonely places and haunt forest pools. On the other hand, they possess great healing powers, they cured Varuṇa of impotency by using the

> penis-erecting plant (*Feronia elephantum*)—but also they cause insanity. They have a magnetic power over women. (2019, 37)

This characterization of *gandharvas* as seducers of women and their association with sexual potency explains Reṇukā's reaction to the sight of Citraratha in a way that complements Biardeau's reading of the bathing prince as a catalyst that triggers Reṇukā's momentary longing for the life of a princess (Biardeau 1989, 187). Citraratha, as king of the *gandharvas*, is after all as much a figure of royalty as a seductive forest-dwelling spirit, and some part of Reṇukā's dissatisfaction with her marriage to Jamadagni must lie in the lack of sensual pleasure in the life of an ascetic's wife (as per Saint Paul's warning to the Corinthians).

Both the *yakṣas* Falk mentions in the passage above and *gandharvas* such as Citraratha in the Reṇukā story are associated with water. In the *Ṛg Veda*, "Gandharva" refers to one particular being connected to waters, as well as to fertility and the sacred substance Soma (which is itself often depicted as a stream or a spring). L. D. Barnett writes of the "fundamental" connection of the *gandharvas* to water (and thereby to the god Varuṇa) and also to Soma:

> Water to the ancient Hindu represented life, animal and vegetable, fertility, health, generative power; Sōma was its quintessence, the elixir of immortal life and vigour. Both the waters and the Sōma are in the highest heaven, the dwelling of Yama; and thence the waters, divine life-saps, are brought to earth by Gandharvas and Apsarases, who therewith impregnate men, animals, and vegetation. (1928, 706)

Drawing on the sexual imagery in Vedic myth and ritual, Sadashiv Ambadas Dange argues that the figure of Gandharva in the *ṚV* is the solar god Adityā, who "is only another aspect of the sun, controlling all sucked up waters in his orb" (1974, 30). We should take note also of another Tamil version of the myth from Pudhucherry that places the *gandharva* between the water and the sun:

> As [Reṇukā] was gathering the water in the form of a pot in her hand, in the water she saw the "shadow" (reflection) of a Gandharva flying in the sky. For a moment she thought that the Gandharva was as beautiful as Manmatha, the god of love.

> Jamadagni saw this in his vision and in his anger he made the water-pot that was gathering in her hand break and get dissolved in the water. (Srinivasan 2009, 21)

One Indian film about Reṇukā provides a visual to illustrate the connection between Reṇukā and Gandharva-Adityā.[16] In the 1960 Telugu "mythological" *Renuka Devi Mahatyam*, when Reṇukā goes to the river she sees—reflected upside down on the surface of the water—the *gandharva* and his consort doing a song and dance number up in the clouds. Afterward, the pot shatters on her head, soaking and loosening her hair.[17] The element of this film that is most salient here is the reflection of the *gandharva* in the water as he dances in the sky, recalling the natural image of the sunlight reflecting on the water as well as the Tamil story of Indra admiring his reflection in Reṇukā's pot (Foulston 2002, 94).

In the case of *Renuka Devi Mahatyam*, the capacity of film to create visual effects allows the filmmaker to draw upon the Vedic myth and ritual forms preserved in folk traditions. A story in *Ṛg Veda* 3.53.15–16 links Jamadagni to the sun and to Viśvāmitra and also prefigures the curse of the disobedient sons treated in the next chapter of this book. In this myth, Viśvāmitra is cursed by the son of Vasiṣṭha to lose his power of speech and is unable to complete the sacrifice, so Jamadagni takes from the sun a mantra called the *sasarpari* and gives it to Viśvāmitra, restoring his voice.[18]

Chapter 35 of the *Viṣṇudharmottara Purāṇa* tells a story, also found in *MBh* 13.97–98, that connects Paraśurāma's birth to the sun. The text says that one day Jamadagni is firing arrows into the woods for sport and sending Reṇukā out to find the arrows and bring them back so he can shoot them again.[19] When the heat of the midday sun makes her so exhausted she has to rest, Reṇukā is late bringing back a batch of arrows. Jamadagni becomes angry and asks her what had taken so long, to which Reṇukā replies that the beating down of the sun caused her to have to stop and cool her feet in the shade. This explanation causes Jamadagni to become angry at the sun god Sūrya and threaten to start shooting arrows at him.[20] Sūrya then tells Jamadagni that it is his nature to beat down on the earth and Jamadagni cannot rightly blame him for doing what it is in his nature to do. Then Sūrya offers to give Reṇukā his umbrella and shoes for protection and decrees that from then on, an umbrella and shoes will be the best gift to give.[21] Further, Sūrya tells Jamadagni and Reṇukā that he will be born as a son to Reṇukā and do great things on the earth.

Whether we attribute Reṇukā's identity crisis to pent-up sexual energy (as most variants of myth suggest) or to a twinge of regret at her renunciation of royal privilege and splendor, it is clear enough that the elemental figure of Citraratha presents a temptation doubly powerful because it calls to both the sexual and the royal natures of Reṇukā, both of which she is forced to repress as the wife of a renouncer. As we will soon see in the next chapter, though, Citraratha mostly serves as a placeholder for another figure—that of Arjuna Kārtavīrya himself.

## Reading Myth through Ritual

Variants of the matricide myth conceptualize Reṇukā's incontinence as a loss of youth and beauty, the disappearance of a kind of aura, the failure of a magical ability having to do with the transportation of water—which, as Brubaker notes, is to be used for Jamadagni's sacrificial rites whenever its use is specified (1978, 113)—or simply being late for the daily rituals or *yajña*s it is her duty as a Brahmin wife to attend. This last conceptualization, Reṇukā's lateness for the *yajña,* is intimately connected with her inability to control (her) fluid. In the version recounted in the *Bhāgavata Purāṇa*, Reṇukā is late for the *homa* ritual, but does not spill the water, keeping the jar in front of her as she approaches her husband.[22] The strategic positioning of Reṇukā's jar between the front of her clothes and Jamadagni in this variant suggests what is explicit in the *Mahābhārata* version, namely, that she has wet herself.

This thematic nexus is also apparent in the Tamil oral tradition recorded by Perundevi Srinivasan, in which Reṇukā appears covered with fluid (blood) that extinguishes Jamadagni's fire and causes him to spill his water and ultimately lose his own power of celibacy after inflicting a deferred curse on her that would eventually result in her decapitation:

> After killing a female demon, with blood on her body, Renuka climbed the hill and reached the hut of Jamadagni. But as soon as her shadow fell on the hut, the sacrificial fire was doused and Jamadagni's pot of water rolled down, spilling the water on the floor. Jamadagni got angry and cursed her that she would become *utalmari* ("the one with her body transformed") in the final days of her life. Renuka pleaded with him to remove the curse, but the *rishi* said he could not withdraw it. Instead, he granted her a boon, and Renuka asked him to marry her. Jamadagni first refused

> saying that he was a *brahmachari* (a celibate), but eventually he agreed. (2009, 221)[23]

Reṇukā's lateness for the *homa* sacrifice and its connection to her incontinence place the matricide element of the Paraśurāma cycle in a ritual context best understood with a look back at Vedic rites. Stephanie Jamison writes on the role of the wife in Vedic ritual:

> Sacrificer's Wife (Patnī in Sanskrit) is a *structural role* in ritual with particular duties and activities that cannot ordinarily be performed by anyone else. . . . A ritual without a wife is no ritual at all. . . . The first major duty of a wife is to serve as a ritual partner, and this requirement is so strong that, according to some legal authorities, a wife may not be repudiated once the couple has jointly kindled the fires that establish them as Sacrificers. (1996, 30–31)

Significantly, the officiating priests must exclude the wife who is menstruating from the ritual and purify her, along with everything she has touched, before it can begin again. It is not too much of a stretch to connect menstrual blood with the sexual fluid metaphorically present in the Reṇukā story, a connection about which classical Sanskrit and Tamil writers were constantly theorizing in the classical literature (see Doniger 1980, 35 and Das 2003, *passim*). The superimposition in variants of the myth of sexual fluid, incontinence, and lateness for the *yajña,* along with the connection that many versions make between the incident at the river and the ritual to be conducted at the hermitage, all suggest that Reṇukā's defilement can also be read as a disruption or polluting of the sacrifice.

There are also several other elements of the Vedic rituals themselves that suggest that Reṇukā's experience at the river is connected to sacrifice. The first is the queen's obligatory listing of sexual infidelities in a ritual performed at the beginning of the rainy season called the *varuṇapraghāsa*. In this ceremony, there is a ritual confession in which the priest interrogates the queen and she is made to list her lovers of the past year (Jamison 1996, 88). To remain eligible to take part in solemn sacrifice, both wife and husband are bound by the mythic noose of Varuṇa to remain chaste. The penalty for breaking this obligation, coincidentally, is the affliction of dropsy, in which the body retains fluid (48).

The second element occurs after this confession, which takes place under the abusive questioning of the priest, when a pair of ram and ewe statues is sacrificed. Jamison explains:

> Though the offering of the mock ram and ewe seem at first to have little if anything to do with the wife's confession, the conjunction of these two ritual events is not by chance. The hypersexed ovine pair, with their exaggerated dough genitalia, are animal stand-ins for the wife and her "lover." (95)

This ritual explanation goes along with the common conception of sacrifice as substitution, in which a life is given in exchange for the life that deserves to be taken, in this case, that of the queen.

The third element connecting the ritual to the Reṇukā myth—the infidelity—takes place well before the confession and "offstage," so to speak. Jamison makes it clear that it is not an option for the queen to maintain that she has had no lovers in the past year. The ritual is incomplete without a confession, and therefore it necessitates that the king has been made a cuckold at least once in the period since the last sacrifice.

While the cuckolding in the *varuṇapraghāsa* takes place outside of the ritual sphere and precedes the ritual itself, there is another Vedic ritual in which the queen is made to have an extramarital sexual encounter *during* the ritual, the ceremonial cuckolding of the king at the climax of the Horse Sacrifice, or *aśvamedha*. Jamison connects the sexual elements of the *varuṇapraghāsa* to the Horse Sacrifice, describing the confession and sacrificial substitution as "tidy and manageable simulacra of rampant sexuality, in a yearly repeated ritual where the real thing, in the mode of the Horse Sacrifice, might be too much" (96).

The "real thing" is an apt term for the sexual element of the Horse Sacrifice. After the sacrificial horse has returned from a year of wandering and is killed by being smothered with a sheet, the queen is required to have (probably, but *only* probably, feigned) sexual intercourse with the dead animal, presumably in a state of postmortem tumescence (64). Following his wife's ritual copulation with the dead horse, the king's power, maintained through the retention of his semen, is affirmed.

> The king is a cuckold, witness to the act and even required to urge it on verbally, while remaining sexually inactive. *But* he is

> the master, and his power is increased by the sexual act in which he does not take part. (84)

While it is very rare in the mythology for Reṇukā to commit real adultery, Jamadagni clearly construes her admiration of and desire for the man at the river as a defilement of the marriage bed and, unlike the king at the Horse Sacrifice, Jamadagni is not empowered but enraged by his wife's actions. An unlike in the *varuṇapraghāsa,* where substitutes for the wife and her lover (a ram and ewe, or vegetarian versions thereof) are sacrificed, Reṇukā herself is the victim in the matricide episode. While the queen's extramarital sexual activities lend power to the king in the ritual, Reṇukā's symbolic infidelity causes her either to delay and miss the appropriate time for the ritual, soil herself with (sexual) fluid, or lose her status as a proper wife and thus become ineligible to sacrifice, all of which serve to destroy the sacrificial pair of which Jamadagni is the other half.

As Jamison observes, many of the rules and restrictions placed upon the sacrificer's wife are designed to contain and mediate her sexuality. In the case of Reṇukā, sexuality, identified with control of her vaginal fluid, is depicted as out of the control of either her or her husband. The myth sequence concludes, not with the sacrifice of a substitute, but with the killing of the wife herself. The matricide episode, recalling elements of Vedic ritual, represents a commonly occurring trope in epic and Purāṇic literature, that of the sacrifice gone out of control, killing the people it was meant to protect.

In her analysis of a seventeen-day-long festival that takes place in the Dharapuram district of Tamil Nadu, Biardeau notes the close relation of fluid to the sacrificial post representing Pōttu Rāja, servant of the goddess and guardian of her temple.[24] He is typically shown holding a human head, which is usually the last head of the hundred-headed demon slain by Devī that would kill her were he to allow it to hit the ground (Hiltebeitel 1988, 76–82). This particular festival is dedicated to the goddess Māriyamman, a popular version of Reṇukā. At the beginning of the festival, a group of astrologers find a banyan or pipal tree and cut from it a post with a fork of three branches on top. After they cut the post, the astrologers install it underneath the tree from which they have cut it and then take it to the home of the wealthiest man in the village, where they install the post again and collect a monetary offering. At that point, the astrologers take the post through the village, collecting their fees door to door before depositing the post in the water at the nearby Royal Canal. At the canal, six temple priests, a prominent villager, and the local official who oversees the distribution of canal water for irrigation hold a celebration in honor of the post before installing it near the goddess temple where it will stay for the rest of the festival. For the next eleven days, worshippers continually pour offerings of water over the post. Then, for the next two days, the watering stops and temple priests and devotees make offerings to the goddess herself. On the final day of the festival, a temple priest pulls the post out of its hole and throws it into the canal. After the disposal of the post, the officiants report that the goddess's temporary ritual marriage to the post is ended, and she has become a widow again (Biardeau 2004, 209–11).

Of the post in the ritual described above, Biardeau writes that "it alone, has here also a real affinity with water. Perhaps it might also contain a hidden fire that is to be kept latent by pouring water on it" (211). In the search for a tree from which to cut the post, she notes:

> [One] has the choice between two varieties of *Ficus* figuring among the "trees with milk." But this sap—above all when it is a matter of the pipal—is almost certainly the symbol of śukra, semen. The water that will inundate it for fifteen days could thus represent a "feminine" complement intended above all to contain its virile ardor in appropriate bounds. . . . At the same time, it is not unfitting to recall that the common enemy of Reṇukā and Jamadagni is Ārjuna Kārtavīrya, king of the marshes in his capital at Māhiṣmatī and that the seducer Buffalo . . . is also fond of water." (211–12)[25]

In the ritual above, the theme of fluid occurs as water offerings (from the canal and the goddess's sacred jar), as the canal itself (represented by the official who participates in the ritual), as milky sap resembling semen (present in the wood from which the post is made), as the wet marshes of Kārtavīrya, and as the water associated with the seducer buffalo. These last two figures are especially important in the matricide motif: Kārtavīrya is sometimes the same figure who causes Reṇukā to spill her water at the river, who is here identified as the "seducer Buffalo," and who becomes the ritual victim in the Buffalo Sacrifice (Shulman 1985, 120). In my conclusion, I will make much of the identification of Kārtavīrya with Citraratha, which I think is the most telling transformation in all the Paraśurāma variants.

An exorcism ritual from South India provides another point of comparison. After documenting twenty-four exorcisms of sexualized demons (*pēys,* from the Sanskrit *preta*) from married women, Isabelle Nabokov argues against prevailing notions that "a major function of Hindu 'ghosts' . . . is to express women's dissatisfaction with husbands, in-laws or female roles."[26] She also rejects anthropologists' conclusions that women are seen to be subject to possession because of their connection to menstrual or other impurities, or because they share the trait of emotional insatiability with demons, or because their mediating position between nature and culture renders them vulnerable (1997, 298). Nabokov instead sees in these exorcisms a function similar to the end result of Vedic ritual and argues that "it is the function of exorcisms to force women publicly to repudiate this behaviour and to recommit themselves to the cultural expectations of a 'good wife' " (299).

A few aspects of these rituals and the folklore connected to them speak directly to the themes of the matricide micromyth. First, these *pēy*s are "dominated by an unrelenting yearning to fulfil their frustrated desires for sexual intimacy." Second, they are found in "a zone which people call *taricu nilam*, or the 'wasteland' (also *katu,* or 'forest')." Nabokov describes these forest haunts and the timing of the *pēy*s' attacks:

> Sometimes this forbidding territory is depicted with imagery symbolic of the demon's untimely death: a pool of stagnant water where he originally drowned, or a tamarind tree from which he hanged himself. . . . It was within this desolate landscape that virtually all my informants imagined *pēy*s to launch their attacks. They also concurred that the timing of the attacks is at high noon, when there is maximum heat and light. Their victims are usually travelling "alone" outside their community: or as I heard more than once. "The girl gets caught on her way to the fields." (300)

The landscape inhabited by the *pēy* is quite different from that of the *gandharva,* but the social background of the typical possessed woman is resonant with that of Reṇukā:

> We have seen how my informants imagine that women are attacked when walking alone and away from the normative landscape and its focal point, the family home. Their escapade leads them to a forbidden space which—whether filled with stagnant pools and tamarind trees or with bus stands and cinemas—is unincorporated, undomesticated and lacking the features essential for the establishment of social life. Once estranged from their constitutive

> relationships, women appear seduced by this desolate reality. For although their absorption into this alien world is represented first and foremost as the consequence of the *pēy*'s aggression, women are seen as setting themselves up for being "caught." We recall that they are always said on the day of the attack to be dressed in their best attire as if to lure the demon. Moreover, during exorcist dialogues the *pēy*s often emphasize the visibility and sexual availability of their victims. (308)

The most striking resonance of all is the element of decapitation in the rite. After the exorcist has interrogated and identified the *pēy* possessing the woman, the ritual concludes with the real decapitation of a chicken and the symbolic decapitation of the *pēy,* after which the victim is freed and the *pēy* driven out. Nabokov connects this to Tamil versions of the myth of Śiva's decapitation of Brahmā that results in him becoming a "skull-bearer" until he can be cleansed of his sin by Devī.

> In the South Arcot ritual I am describing here, the exorcism likewise opens with a blood offering: the chicken's crude decapitation. This offering is problematic for the *pēy,* who immediately cries for help. He has good reason to fear, since, as I interpret it, the sacrifice foretells his own beheading. The victim runs frantically and drops the stone, the symbolic head of the *pēy,* near the tamarind tree. With this act, she, like the Goddess, beheads her own imposter-husband. Now she is free of her demon at last. . . . Most Tamil myths which feature decapitation usually conclude with the head's reattachment, only rarely to the original body. In exorcisms, it seems that the demon's head is symbolically detached from his victim but reconnected by a nail to another body, that of the tamarind tree. (310–11)

South Indian temple myths frequently connect Reṇukā to a low-caste goddess whose head is also decapitated by accident, resulting in a switching of body and head for both women. We will revisit this motif later, but the brief mention of it now as a variant of the recapitation element in the micromyth is enough to point out that in this exorcism ritual, the *pēy*'s decapitation occurs at the point in the myth in which Reṇukā herself is decapitated. Like the Vedic sacrifice, the Tamil exorcism provides a sacrificial substitution to save the life of the straying wife.

| Matricide Myth | Vedic Sacrifice | Tamil Exorcism |
|---|---|---|
| Reṇukā is excited by a stranger | Queen takes lover (offstage)/ horse (on-stage) | Wife is possessed by *pēy* |
| Jamadagni examines Reṇukā's stain | Priests interrogate queen about her infidelity | Exorcist interrogates *pēy* |
| Reṇukā is decapitated and recapitated (sometimes to the wrong body) | Substitutes for wife and lover are sacrificed | *Pēy* is decapitated and recapitated (usually to the wrong body) |

Figure 2.1. Comparison of the Matricide Myth, the Vedic Sacrifice, and the Tamil Exorcism.

## Conclusion

The subtitle of this chapter's first section, "Death to All that Flows," is taken from Klaus Theweleit's *Male Fantasies, Volume I: Women, Bodies, Floods, Histories*. Theweleit connects modern Europe's ambivalent obsession with female fluidity to the eventual eruption of extreme violence and fascism. In the Paraśurāma myth, we have traced the fluid motif from the fraught tension regarding his mixed birth and dual nature in which an anxious desire to redraw and police the boundaries of *varṇa* exists in a *coincidentia oppositorum* with a Brahmin nostalgia for an imagined past before those borders, when a Brahmin could exercise temporal as well as spiritual power. Now that theme of fluidity leads us into the stories of Reṇukā's sin and the reasons for Paraśurāma's matricidal axe murder, the myth's first act of violence.

We began this chapter by laying out the four elements of the matricidal micromyth, which is, above all, a story about domestic violence against a woman. But it is also an externalization, charged with erotic energy, of the Brahmin-Kṣatriya conflict inherent in Paraśurāma's mixed nature. In this chapter, we have seen Jamadagni threaten to pierce the sun with his arrow. We have also seen an Indian woman blow up a light bulb in her gynecologist's office with a forceful ejaculation of vaginal fluid. And as we learned from the Brothers Grimm, when the little girl breaks her pitcher, the spring begins to flow and everything drowns. We continued with a discussion of notions of defilement, especially the Aristotelian idea of *akrasia*, and then attempted to contextualize Reṇukā's "wetting" at the river in light of Indian ritual, folklore, and sexology. In the next chapter, we will continue examining the matricide micromyth but we will turn our attention away from what happens below Reṇukā's waistline to what happens above her neck.

3

# Matricide II

## *The Severed Head*

> When the daughter of Herodias came in and danced, she pleased Herod and his dinner guests. The king said to the girl, "Ask me for anything you want, and I'll give it to you." And he promised her with an oath, "Whatever you ask I will give you, up to half my kingdom." She went out and said to her mother, "What shall I ask for?"
>
> —Mark 6:22–24

> Ah, what am I seeing? What is this that I carry in my hands?
>
> —Euripides, *The Bacchae*

The reader will have noticed that in the past chapter, our analysis dealt only with the first element of the matricide micromyth: "A married woman sees an attractive man, becomes sexually aroused involuntarily and loses control, after which her husband sees evidence of her arousal and perceived infidelity." In this chapter, we will proceed to the rest of the micromyth and in so doing begin the delicate task of assessing Paraśurāma's divine violence. We will now examine the elements of the micromyth that follow the encounter at the water's edge: Jamadagni's curse of the disobedient sons, Reṇukā's decapitation, and her resurrection. We will finally let the axe fall.

Figure 3.1. A Painted Plaster Sculpture Showing Jamadagni Ordering Paraśurāma to Decapitate Reṇukā.

## Abjection, Repression, Renunciation: Language and the Law of the Father

The events that follow Paraśurāma's matricide are all destructive ones: the theft of the family cow, the killings of Kārtavīrya and Jamadagni, the twenty-one-fold annihilation of the Kṣatriyas, and Paraśurāma's own exile. But the fact that anything happens to Paraśurāma at all contrasts sharply with the stultified and stultifying fate of his brothers who are unable to obey their father's command. What do we know of the exploits, or even the tribulations, of Jamadagni's other sons, Rumanvat, Suṣeṇa, Vaśu, and Viśvāvasu? On this, the tradition remains as mute as they themselves were rendered after disobeying their father.

The authors of the Paraśurāma cycle represent this punitive curse on the disobedient sons in a variety of ways. These representations can be placed along a continuum from a startlingly direct recapitulation of the psychoanalytic Oedipal model to various transformations of the model using distinctly Indic symbols. In this way, the matricide episode reveals roots in unconscious psychological processes as well as in the "pool of signifiers" (to use Ramanujan's well-known phrase) welling up from Indian myth and ritual.

A psychoanalytic reading of the curse that Jamadagni places on Paraśurāma's brothers when they refuse to behead their mother reveals a structural affinity between the matricide episode and the developmental moment that Kristeva describes in which a child must reject the mother and submit to the law of the father, marking his transition into the world of language and subjectivity. But the matricidal expulsion of the maternal that is a prerequisite for entering the realm of the father and language is never truly complete. The maternal remains present at some level of consciousness, where it acts as the ambivalent subject's object of simultaneous attraction and repulsion.

In the story of Paraśurāma, the mother is identical to the *kṣatra,* both as the Kṣatriya nature within Paraśurāma himself and the Kṣatriya *varṇa* in the outside world.[1] Paraśurāma's act of matricide is followed by a "return of the repressed" in the form of another Kṣatriya whose violent arrival inspires him to try once again to kill the *kṣatra*-maternal object within himself by annihilating all the Kṣatriyas on earth twenty-one times. This final abjection of the maternal *kṣatra* allows him to permanently leave the forest and become a man of the field (*kṣetra*), creating Kuru-*kṣetra* in the epic myth, creating Paraśurāma-*kṣetra* in the myths from the Malabar coast, and developing an association with both social engineering and farming, including an identification with the agricultural deity Saṃkarṣaṇa in the Pāñcarātra tradition. He is "Rāma with the Axe," after all, and besides killing, what is the purpose of an axe if not to clear the forest for cultivation?

Viewed through the lens of Lacanian psychoanalysis, the matricide episode is a mythic representation of the child's entry into the realm of speech and the consequences of its failure. When Paraśurāma's four brothers are unwilling or unable to submit to the law of the phallus and fully separate from their mother, their father curses them to remain outside of social order or deprives them of language. In variants of the matricide episode in which Paraśurāma's brothers appear, the failure on the part of the four older sons to behead their mother is represented in terms of loss; as loss of speech, loss of humanity, loss of social standing, and loss of life. In the version of the matricide episode from the *Kālikā Purāṇa*, for example, Jamadagni's disobedient sons stand confused and motionless "as if stupefied" when their father gives his order (82.14). The earlier version of the myth in the *Mahābhārata* reads:

> Then Jamadagni's eldest son, Rumaṇvat by name, came in, and so did Suṣena, Vasu, and Viśvāvasu. The venerable [Jamadagni] told them one after the other to kill [their] mother. Completely bewildered and witless, they said nothing. In his fury he cursed them. When they were cursed, they lost their minds and instantly they were like things with the nature of animals or birds. (3.116.10–12)

Unlike his cursed brothers, Paraśurāma obeys Jamadagni's command to kill Reṇukā, "knowing the power of Jamadgni's austerity" (*MBh* 3.116.13). Shulman understands this verse to refer either to Jamadagni's power (*vīryaṃ*) to kill or curse Paraśurāma or to his power to resurrect the dead, or possibly both (1985, 116–17). The power of the father is to give or take life as he sees fit. And in the dominant Indian Oedipal pattern described by Ramanujan, that power is often directed against the son, which would support the idea that Paraśurāma acted in fear that Jamadagni's power would be directed against him (Ramanujan 1984, 253).[2] But, given the Bhārgavas' family history of bringing the dead back to life, there is good reason to argue that the paternal power Paraśurāma has in mind is not the power to kill, but the power to resurrect. The clan patriarch Bhṛgu restores his own wife's severed head with a *satyakriyā* or "truth act" in *Matsya Purāṇa* 47. The Bhārgava sage Śukra (or Kāvya Uśanas), chief priest of the *asuras,* is known to possess the *mṛtasaṃjīvinī vidyā,* the "resurrection spell" and employs it in *MBh* 1.71 to help them in their war against the gods.[3] Presumably, all Bhārgava sages know this spell; it is the family secret.

In her reading of the episode, Rashmi Desai provides an interpretation that bolsters the idea that Jamadagni's power is something to be identified with the Bhārgava clan:

> If one were to wonder why Jamadagni himself does not mete out justice/punishment but involves his sons, the answer would be that he interprets the slight as besmirching the family (i.e. Bhṛgu) honour. Therefore, the act of murder has to be carried out collectively with Jamadagni as the judge and Paraśurāma as executioner. . . . The message here is that of lineage solidarity. In other words, the betrayal affects the sons as much as it does the husband. (2008, 71)

Reṇukā, like all wives, is a perpetual outsider. Her sin offends her husband's clan, the Bhārgavas. Her death is dealt out by those same Bhārgavas. And the power to resurrect her lies only with the Bhārgavas.

Goldman argues that the motif of resurrecting a dead woman by rejoining her severed head to her body is "borrowed by the Rāma myth from the myth of Śukra" but also notes that Jamadagni's resurrection of Reṇukā "is alone among the numerous Bhārgava episodes in which this power is manifested in its disregard for technique" while "[in] other stories, the techniques, which vary, are felt to be of great significance" (1971, 81, 87). In some later variants, Jamadagni sprinkles water on the bodies to revive them, but there is no mention of this in the *Mahābhārata*. Why is Reṇukā's resurrection so perfunctory in the epic? Why is there so little attention given to this power of Jamadagni's in which Paraśurāma has enough confidence to swing the axe without a second thought? In *BhP* 9.16.20–24, Paraśurāma himself performs a resurrection rite on his decapitated father (killed by the sons of Kārtavīrya) and it is described in great detail, with sacrifices to the four classes of Vedic priests, acts of worship, and ritual bathing. For this reason, it is somewhat dubious that this enormous and anomalous ability to resurrect the dead, which is either described in detail or plays a pivotal role in the other Bhārgava myths in which it appears, is precisely what is being referred to when the texts talk about this vague power of Jamadagni of which Paraśurāma is aware when he chops off his mother's head.

Whether one understands him to be acting with knowledge of Jamadagni's power to curse or his power to resurrect, either of these interpretations seem to mitigate Paraśurāma's actions to a lesser or greater degree, indicating that he is acting either out of fear of punishment or with confidence that his actions can be reversed. There is a third possibility. In psychoanalytic terms, Paraśurāma's knowledge of his father's power could mean an acceptance of the superiority of paternal authority over maternal love, a necessary precondition to the rejection of the maternal symbolized by his act of matricide. One way to resolve the Oedipal conflict is to defect to the winning side and submit to the law of the phallus, or *liṅgam*.

Devdutt Pattanaik reports a practice among the sacred prostitutes connected to the temple of Reṇukā-Yellama in Belgaum that derives from the story of the disobedient sons' curse in which

> the male children dedicated to [Reṇukā-Yellama] are forced to wear female apparel and adopt a female identity. These are the gender-variant male-priestesses known as Jogappas, who are also called the servants (devadasis) of Yellamma. They carry the image of the goddess on their head and travel from place to place offering blessings on behalf of the goddess and seeking alms. (2002, 108)

Combining the questions of family relations and sectarian loyalties, Gurumurthy gives an intriguing if not entirely convincing reading of Jamadagni's curse in the context of the Reṇukā-Yellama tradition:

> [This] is not really a story [of] conflict between two individuals, *Rēṇukā* and *Jamadagni*, but between two religious traditions, the male-dominant [and] the female-dominant, the folk vs. the classical and even the *Sanskritized*, etc. It may be remembered that the first three sons of *Jamadagni* who, one by one, were ordered to do the beheading, did not comply. More than three sons, they belong to three different female-dominant religious ways. They, respectively, worship a Mother Goddess (*Ekkama*—a local one or *Yellama*—a *sanskritized* but cursed one) and *Mātangi* (the transforming-middle position of *Śaiva-Vaiṣṇava* traditions) and the ideal wife in the manner of the *Śaivaite*'s [*sic*]. So the three disobey their father as he is now a *Vaiṣṇavite*. (2005, 195)

Two variants from Savadatti reported by Gurumurthy use sexual terminology in describing the punishment of Paraśurāma's brothers. In both stories, Jamadagni first curses Reṇukā to lose her youth and beauty and to wander the forest alone instead of beheading her.[4] Then the Aśvins, themselves frequently connected to the myth of the headless sacrifice (see Collins 2014, 214–17), restore her and Reṇukā returns to the hermitage. But, Gurumurty recounts,

> Her husband *Jamadagni* was never fully reconciled to *Rēṇukā*. That she sought someone else's help in ridding herself of the curse he had placed on her was an insult to him, he thought. He orders his sons, one by one, to behead her. The first three refuse. Furious, he curses them to "impotence."
>
> In another myth, as desired by his son, *Jamadagni* restores *Rēṇukā* to life. But he refuses to live with her as one who has lost her pristine purity, her special status, and he departs for the Himalayas. With her gift of a second life, *Rēṇukā*, painfully aware of the suffering bestowed upon her sons on her account, [decides] to be with them and protect them. That land became a shrine. Her impotent sons became mendicants. They dedicated themselves to spreading her name. At this, devotees laden with gifts and bound by vows came to her to serve her. (2005, 33–34)

Without knowing the precise meaning of "impotence" in the first variant, it is difficult to make with any confidence a sexual interpretation, but in the second variant the fact that the impotent brothers become (presumably celibate) renouncers makes a stronger case. In this telling, Jamadagni does not wipe away the memory of the matricide after resurrecting his wife. Neither does he restore the disobedient sons he has cursed. He simply leaves the family altogether and for good. This denouement is very close to a child's fantasy fulfillment of the Oedipal conflict, although a neurotic failure in the developmental sense: the father leaves, the mother agrees to stay forever (elevated now to a goddess) and protect her son, and Paraśurāma no longer has even his older brothers to contend with for his mother's love, since they have been emasculated and become renouncers.

The centrality of this idea of renunciation in Indian life is, for Stanley Kurtz, what makes Hindu mythology so ideal for psychoanalytic reading. Although repression plays an obvious role in the matricide micromyth (the forgetting of the deed), Kurtz points out that in the Indian context, we must not overlook the role of renunciation:

> [The] relative explicitness of Hindu collective representations is tied to a culturally characteristic defensive structure based on renunciation rather than on repression. This process of renunciation permits symbolic gratification to lie relatively close to the surface so that it can be overtly sacrificed. Thus, the character of the defensive process underlying Hindu myth and ritual can be said to provide clearer access to the unconscious than the more roundabout, repression-based symbolism characteristic of Western collective representations. (1992, 178)

Near the Reṇukā (Yellama) temple at Savadatti sits a smaller and more simply decorated Paraśurāma shrine. In it, Paraśurāma is represented as an upright figure with a lion's head holding an axe in his right hand and a stringed instrument in his left. In front of him are a *lingaṃ* and a *yoni* placed together in sexual union (Assayag 1992, 112). Within the sanctuary of the Yellama temple itself, Paraśurāma and the goddess are represented as a couple by an axe placed to the left of a decapitated head (120). Even though there is also a small temple to her husband Jamadagni nearby, it is the goddess's son, represented by the weapon that beheaded her, whom the temple presents as her male consort. The presence of a joined *yoni* and *lingaṃ* in Paraśurāma's own sanctuary lends still more support to an Oedipal reading, presenting a symbolic representation of the child's ideal resolution. It is, however, also an extremely common Śaiva symbol.

In one variant from South India connected to the five-day festival of the goddess Usuramma, Reṇukā loses her virtue as the result of a trick and not because of a brief and involuntary impure thought. Reṇukā is going to visit Jamadagni at his hermitage, where he lives with his sons, in order to ask his permission to lead her father's army against an army of demons. As she travels to see her husband, Reṇukā carries on her head seven pots full of rice mixed with water. Because of the power of her virtue (frequently associated with heat in the Hindu tradition), the pots of rice and water on her head begin to boil and cook.[5] Then, in a wager straight out of the book of Job, the god Viṣṇu asks the sage Nārada to see if he can overcome her virtue. Nārada appears first as a beggar and asks her for some of her rice. Reṇukā complies. Next Nārada reappears as a happy and playful child, the sight of whom causes Reṇukā to burst into laughter. In meditation at the hermitage, Jamadagni becomes aware through yogic telepathy of his wife's activities, and summons his sons to behead her (Elmore 1915, 83; Hiltebeitel 1988, 351).

In the myths we have examined so far, the water that Reṇukā spills or is unable to control evokes female sexual fluid. Rice, on the other hand, is a well-known example of a male-gendered seminal substance, like the *caru* in the story of Paraśurāma's conception. The fact that the heat of Reṇukā's virtue cooks the pots of rice also suggests a male sexual element, since it is by recycling the semen in his body, heated through asceticism, that renouncers like Jamadagni gain their power (see Kaelber 1989, 144–45). W. T. Elmore recounts:

> In accordance with [his and Viṣṇu's] plan, Narada appeared in the way before Renuka as a beggar and asked for food. She had compassion on him and gave him a little from the pots on her head. A little further on Narada again appeared, this time as a charming little child with rattling ornaments. When Renuka saw the child she burst into merry laughter. Jamadagni considered that these were wicked acts because he was doing penance, and he determined that his wife must be punished. (1915, 83)

The trick element that characterizes the temptation of Reṇukā also extends to Jamadagni's encounter with his sons:

> Jamadagni believed these [things that Reṇukā did] were wicked acts because he was doing penance, and he determined that

> his wife should be punished. He thought of his eldest son and immediately the son stood before him. His father addressed him affectionately, and asked his son what should be done if anyone were found guilty within their premises. "Forgive him thrice," answered the son.
>
> "But suppose the offender commits a sin beyond forgiveness, what would you suggest?" asked the father.
>
> "Why father, if such a one is found, you must certainly remove his head from his body," answered the son.
>
> "Well, my dear son," said the father, "look now! Your mother is coming. She laughed at that little boy as she came toward our retreat. Do to her according to the judgment which you have pronounced."
>
> "No! no! father," said the son, "I have been nursed by her and I can never do such an atrocious deed with my own hands."
>
> Then Jamadagni was very angry, and said, "Wretch, I will curse you for your failure to keep your word."
>
> "All right father," replied the son, "I am ready for your curse. Kill me, or turn me into a beggar as suits you, but I will never do this deed." (83–84)

When he first appears as a starving beggar, Nārada asks for and receives the rice Reṇukā is carrying on her head and which is cooking from her inner heat. Reṇukā's surrender of the sexualized substance (now male rather than female) goes along with other versions of the matricide episode dealing with women's lack of sexual control, being a transformation of the motif of Reṇukā's spilling the water at the sight of the bathing prince. However, Reṇukā's second encounter with Nārada disguised as a child is somewhat puzzling, especially since it is her laughter at the child and *not* her giving away the rice that Jamadagni deems an "unforgivable sin." In any event, here we have a case of a disobedient son not frozen with terror or indecision, but simply unwilling to follow the order and explicit about his reason.

Whether they are killed, rendered mute, reduced to beggars, or become renouncers, the disobedient brothers of Paraśurāma pay a price for failing the test of filial piety. But, unlike them, Paraśurāma recognizes the power of his father and falls into line. He counts on that power to bring his dead mother back to life and, often, to repress the memory of his act. But, following Kristeva's model, his matricide is ultimately incomplete. Reṇukā, the source of his Kṣatriya nature, returns to life, and the *kṣatra* she represents comes back to wreak havoc in the form of the embodied Kṣatriya Arjuna Kārtavīrya, whom Paraśurāma can only overcome by releasing the Kṣatriya within himself.

## The Matricidal Axe

Although Reṇukā's decapitation is the heart of the matricide episode, it is also the one that requires the least description. Even in Sanskrit, there are only so many ways to say, "And then he cut off her head with his axe" (something like "*tata ādāya paraśuṃ ramo mātuḥ śiro 'harat*," as it appears in *MBh* 3.116.14b). Reṇukā's decapitation (unlike her resurrection) is therefore not really subject to the elaboration and inversion the other elements undergo in the many variants of the myth, robbing us of the chance to mount a broad comparison.[6] To find a psychological explanation of Paraśurāma's act of matricide from within the tradition (in its broadest sense), we now return to the "The Story of the Axe," whose imagery, as we have seen, internalizes Paraśurāma's external conflicts to create the only "interior" that he has: "the burning kiln of [his] soul." And, as Wayne Booth has demonstrated, giving the reader access to a character's thoughts and feelings also tends to create sympathy for that character (1987, 245–49).

The matricide episode occurs in stanza four of the poem. After Reṇukā has committed her mental infidelity and enraged her husband, Paraśurāma does his filial duty:

> High rose my axe, Lord Siva's gift, and
> My mother's head rolled on the ground.
> There lay, at our feet
> That face ever so gentle,
> That body which stood for humility,
> That hot blood which yearned for the pleasures of the world.
> Her wide open eyes like those of a sacrificial animal
> Held only hurt and astonishment.
> [My] brothers, mad with sorrow, wailed aloud;
> Even my father, for a moment, paled.
> But I stood there, unperturbed,
> Brooding over dharma.
> My eyes riveted on the axe's edge.
> Into the burning kiln of my soul,

Restless with simmering agony
Did my father enter to ask:
"What can I grant you, my son?"
"O virtuous and wise,
May my mother live in your thoughts
Not as a sinner
But chaste as of old!"
"So be it," said the compassionate sage,
For he knew the sublime purity
Of the human soul.
Yet, never afterwards did I sit in that shade of the grove,
Nor did the earth melt into shadows. (1980, 125–26)

In the language of the poem, we see Reṇukā's idealized exterior contrasted with her problematic interior. The image of the decapitated Reṇukā presents a head with "a face ever so gentle" rolling on the ground and a body "which stood for humility" lying beside it. In the poem her eyes convey hurt and astonishment, which she could only express if she had died with no knowledge of her fault. Where then, if the head and the body both appear innocent, is the source of Reṇukā's sin? It is her blood (that most basic of bodily fluids) that is clearly guilty, being "hot blood which yearned for the pleasures of the world." In the previous stanza, her living body displays the telltale signs of the restlessness awakened in her blood, but as a corpse out of whom the blood is leaking, Reṇukā's body is pacified and desexualized. The imagery suggests a connection between Reṇukā's blood and her sexual fluid that also serves to exonerate her body and head.

"The Story of the Axe" imagines a different kind of resurrection for Reṇukā. Instead of bringing her back to life physically with his Bhārgava power and expunging her sins (along with those of Paraśurāma and his brothers) from the historical record, Jamadagni leaves her dead and agrees to Paraśurāma's request that he only remember Reṇukā as the sinless woman she was before her fateful trip to the river. In the absence of her living body, Reṇukā becomes a perfect and untouchable ideal of chastity in the eyes of her husband, but not—strikingly—in the eyes of Paraśurāma. Obviously, since he is the narrator, Paraśurāma does not receive the boon of forgetting his matricide. Instead of having the slate wiped clean as it so often is in the Sanskrit tradition, Paraśurāma has to live with the result of his actions, the irretrievable loss of the primal tranquility previously described in stanza three:

In the atmosphere fragrant with burning *samit*
And pervaded with deep peace,
I grew up,
The beloved son of sage Jamadagni.
Though imbued with my mother's Kshatriya culture,
I adored my father, the great Brahmin seer.
While immersed in meditation beneath the ashram trees,
To me, the earth was just a cool shadow. (1980, 125)

The axe, often a gift from Śiva, is the most popular of Paraśurāma's iconographic features. There is even one temple located at Hiremagalūr in the Kaḍūr district of Karnataka that is dedicated to the *paraśu* itself (Janaki 1966, 70). In the poem, the axe is used to disassociate Paraśurāma from the matricide. He is "brooding over *dharma*" with his "eyes riveted to the axe edge" while his brothers wail and his father pales over Reṇukā's headless body. Paraśurāma himself, on the other hand, has retreated into "the burning kiln of [his] soul," which his father has to "enter" to reach him. This image establishes the axe as a representation of cool, dispassionate dharmic violence, at least compared to the fiery and uncontrollable violence of his *tapas,* soon to be unleashed on the Kṣatriyas of the world.

## Axe Murdering and Mother Killing in the Śaiva Tradition

Throughout his myth cycle, Paraśurāma's matricide draws much more condemnation than his Kṣatriya slaughter ever does. One critique of Paraśurāma in the Purāṇic tradition (*BḍP* 2.3.23.65-66) comes from the ultimate outsider, Śiva himself. Similarly, in the *Kāñcippurāṇam*, Śiva appears to Paraśurāma disguised as an Untouchable and mocks his folly at believing that any amount of pilgrimage or penance could wipe away the sin of matricide, which he refers to as *brāhmahātya,* or "Brahmin-killing" (Shulman 1985, 123). Both dialogues are laced with irony, since Śiva himself famously commits that very sin and expunges it with the same kind of penance he is deriding Paraśurāma for performing. In addition to being a well-known seducer, Śiva is also an infamous Brahmin killer.

More irony comes from the Tibetan Buddhist tradition, where it is Śiva (known by the name of his Vedic antecedent Rudra) who is associated with matricide, and is also produced by a kind of mixed birth. The *Mdo dgongspa 'dus-pa*, a Tantra of the rNyingma school, tells the story of the birth of "Matricide Rudra."

> There was a whore named "Wanders About."
> In the evening she slept with a devil, at midnight with a king,
> And at dawn with a god.
> In her womb he was conceived.
> Because there were three fathers—god, devil, and man
> After eight months a three-headed son was born. (Kapstein 2000, 174)

Rudra's mother dies in childbirth and is taken along with her triply sired offspring to the charnel ground, where the infant devours her corpse and emerges as a powerful demon. Eventually the *bodhisattva* Avalokiteśvara destroys Rudra by shrinking himself down small enough to enter the demon's anus and then returning to full size, tearing him apart from the inside. Avalokiteśvara then resurrects Rudra, who is now subjugated to the Buddha in this founding myth of the Tantric Buddhist tradition.[7] In one variant, Rudra actually becomes the consort of the "cannibal queen of Sri Lanka," but the Tantric magician Padmasambhava takes on Rudra's shape to cuckold him, resulting in the queen giving birth to a son who looks like Rudra on the outside but is Padmasambhava on the inside (Paul 1982, 153–56). The presence of these themes in the Śaiva stories that proliferated in Tibet casts new light on the degree to which Paraśurāma is a Śaiva figure.

The *Kālikā Purāṇa*, composed by goddess-worshipping Tantra practitioners in Assam around the eleventh or twelfth century, tells the story of Paraśurāma's pilgrimage from the Sahyādri mountains in the Western Ghats to a pilgrimage site called Brahmakund on the Brahmaputra river in search of a sacred pool where he could wash off the sin of Reṇukā's murder. After walking all the way to Brahmakund, Paraśurāma is finally able to expiate the sin of matricide with a dip in its sacred waters. Then, so that the whole country might benefit from the *kund*'s grace, Paraśurāma opens a channel with his arrow and floods the Kamrup Valley, turning it lush and green—a complete reversal of his actions pushing back the water on the Konkan Coast, though with the same effect of producing new arable land. Although the *Kālikā* does not report it, later legends say that the axe Paraśurāma used to decapitate Reṇukā stayed stuck to his hand until he reached the pool (Behera 1988, 36–39). This motif is surely borrowed from the stories of Śiva Kāpālika, who is unable to drop the skull of Brahmā from his hand after he has decapitated the deity (see Doniger 1973, 123–27).

Part of Paraśurāma's identity is his role as a pupil of his guru Śiva. This guru-pupil relationship is as significant as the father-son relationship in the Hindu imaginary (Goldman 1978, 325). In one myth cycle, this devotion to Śiva puts Paraśurāma into conflict with Śiva's adopted son Gaṇeśa, the son of Pārvatī, whom she creates in Śiva's absence to guard her door. The Paraśurāma-Gaṇeśa conflict appears in the *Brahmavaivarta* and the subsequent *Brahmāṇḍa Purāṇa*, both of which are also noteworthy because they connect Paraśurāma to Śiva through the gift of the axe. The popular cultic figure of Gaṇeśa, we must note, is sometimes understood as decapitated Hindu deity, since in some versions of his origin, Gaṇeśa's elephant head is placed on his shoulders by Śiva after the angry god strikes it off (Courtright 1985, 33–34).

In the *Brahmāṇḍa Purāṇa*'s lengthy account of the Paraśurāma story (among other details, it provides us a back story for Akṛtavraṇa as a Brahmin boy whom Paraśurāma once rescued from a tiger) his conflict with Gaṇeśa takes place after the Brahmin sage has destroyed Kārtavīrya and his sons, along with their army of demons, and has arrived at Śiva and Pārvatī's chamber to thank Śiva for the gift of the axe and pay his respects. But Gaṇeśa stops him at their chamber door and quotes scripture to the effect that anyone who witnesses a couple naked or in the act of copulation will be cursed to become separated from his wife for seven lifetimes. Paraśurāma becomes angry and points out that this proscription does not apply to a *nirvikāra śiśu,* a phrase we will examine below, and that, anyway, Pārvatī and Śiva are not just Gaṇeśa's parents to protect but rather the parents of the whole world (*jagatāṃ pitarau pārvatīparameśvarau,* in the formulation found throughout the tradition).

When Paraśurāma then tries to continue past him, Gaṇeśa picks him up, whirls him around, and throws him onto the ground. Enraged, Paraśurāma then hurls his axe at Gaṇeśa, who takes the blow on his tusk so that his father's weapon may not be used in vain. The sound of Gaṇeśa's broken tusk hitting the ground brings Śiva and Pārvatī out to see the cause of the commotion. When Pārvatī learns what has happened, she blames Śiva for favoring his disciple—whom she mockingly says has come to pay his guru-fee with his son's broken tusk—over his own family. Kṛṣṇa and Rādhā arrive at that moment to calm the situation by reminding everyone of what roles they each have to play in the great cosmic drama (2.3.41.30–2.3.43.42).

In the mid-eighteenth century, the *Brahmāṇḍa Purāṇa* became an important devotional text in Kerala, the land said to have been created by Paraśurāma. Its political significance seems to originate with the king

Mārtaṇḍavarman (r. 1729–1758), who consulted his family priests—members of the Nambūdiri clan that traces its origins to Paraśurāma's founding of the region—for a ritual to expiate the bloodshed endemic to kingship. They offered up the *bhadradipāpratiṣṭā*, a seven-day private rite of fasting and prayer supposedly performed by the king's legendary ancestor (and Paraśurāma's enemy) Kārtavīrya that included a complete reading of the text at hand (Vielle 2002, 352).

The context is fraught: a king burdened with blood guilt, engaged in a period of asceticism, and identified with a dynasty of foreign origin is hearing his Brahmin priests tell him the story of his own ancestor's destruction at the hands of their progenitor Paraśurāma. There is a similarity here to what Gananath Obeyesekere has observed in his work on the role of parricide and Oedipal myth structures in the dynastic self-understanding of the kings of Sri Lanka—what he calls the "psychic structure of the long run," which "exercises a hold on the imagination of people because it is constitutive of a variety of 'domains' and straddles different, even contradictory, universes of meaning and experience such as those born of psyche, bios, cosmos, and polis" (1990, 202). Figure 3.2 on page 120 illustrates the contextual layers surrounding the *Brahmāṇḍa Purāṇa* narrative told at the *bhadradipāpratiṣṭā* and the dominant struggle in each:

Moving from the *polis* to the *psyche,* we can now turn to the concept of what Freud called the "primal scene" of parental copulation (witnessed or imagined), which he argued was "indispensable to a comprehensive solution of all the conundrums that are set us by the symptoms of the infantile disorder, that all the consequences radiate out from it, just as all the threads of the analysis have led up to it" (1989, 422). Within the matricide micromyth, Reṇukā's encounter at the river functions as a kind of primal scene, spied upon from afar or deduced afterwards by Jamadagni. But it also presents a primal scene within a primal scene, because Reṇukā too is witnessing something she is not meant to see, a man sporting with his wives. In the primal scene at the riverbank, eroticism, voyeurism, and the scopophilic representation of feminine sexual arousal take center stage. But in the primal scene of the two trees or the two *carus,* eroticism and the role of the father are almost entirely eclipsed by symbolic logic and the fantasy of birth from the mother alone, as in the birth of Gaṇeśa.

In the Gaṇeśa story from the *Brahmāṇḍa Purāṇa,* Paraśurāma plays the role of a would-be intruder on the primal scene, imagined to be taking place inside Śiva and Pārvatī's room. This role of the gate-crasher at the chamber door, we should note, is elsewhere performed by the father-figure Śiva, who decapitates Gaṇeśa when the boy tries to stop him from seeing Pārvatī. Paraśurāma performs a symbolic castration upon Gaṇeśa that is a kind of repetition of what Śiva himself does in other myths to Gaṇeśa when the boy (whom she has created from the dead skin of her own body in Śiva's absence) tries to stop him from entering Pārvatī's chamber.

Up until the point of Kṛṣṇa and Rādhā's *dei ex machina*, we have Gaṇeśa, on whose decapitation story this myth is clearly modeled, as the son willing to be castrated to protect his mother's virtue and his father's virility. Paraśurāma, on the other hand, is once again opposed to the mother figure, in this case, Pārvatī. In Gaṇeśa's story, the son is pitted against the father. In Paraśurāma's story, a father-son dyad (and here we should recall Desai's argument that "[Reṇukā's] betrayal affects the sons as much as it does the husband") is pitted against another group of sons with a second father figure present in the form of the bathing prince Reṇukā encounters at the water.

Gaṇeśa and Paraśurāma's story from the *Brahmāṇḍa* pits the two son figures against one another and has Paraśurāma imply that he is Śiva's *nirvikāra*

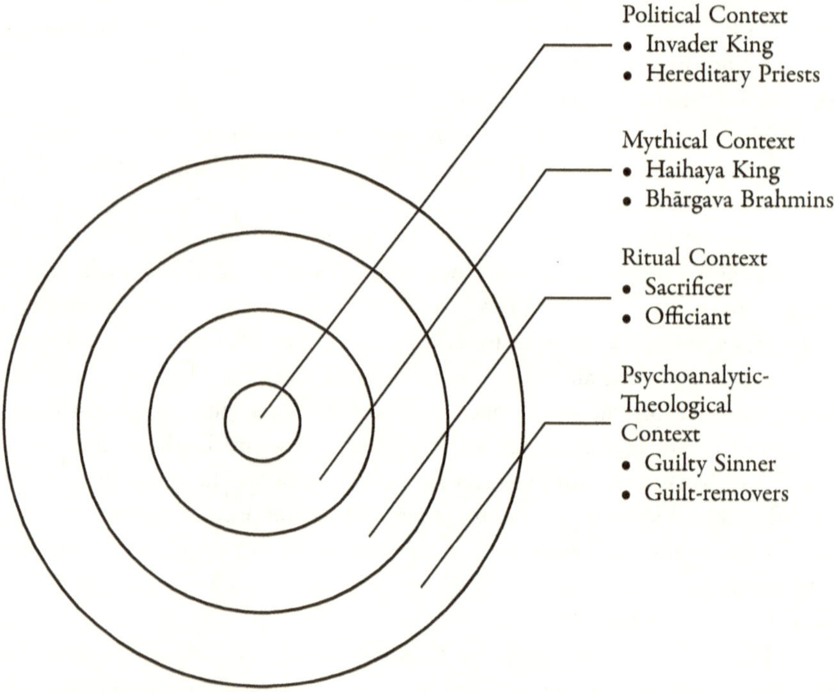


Figure 3.2. The Contextual Layers of the *Brahmāṇḍa Purāṇa* Recitation at the *Bhadradipāpratiṣṭā*.

*śiśu,* unlike Gaṇeśa, who was born solely from Pārvatī's body. *Śiśu* usually refers to a young and innocent child—to put it in modern terms, a son young enough that a mother would feel comfortable taking him into a public women's restroom. *Nirvikāra* usually means stable or changeless (it is used to describe Śiva in the *Skanda Purāṇa*). But Nagar's translation of *BVP* 3.42.17b renders the phrase *nirvikāra śiśu* as "child having a spotless mind" (681) and Tagare's translation of *BḍP* 2.41.48b (the same line verbatim) separates the phrase into two distinct nouns, giving us the meaning, "infant or a person devoid of passionate feelings" (1983, 708). Gail, on the other hand, gives the German translation as "*natürliches Kind*," or "natural-born child" (1977, 127).

Why does Paraśurāma use this phrase to exempt himself from the prohibition against walking in on Śiva and Pārvatī in their private chambers? Is he (falsely) claiming to be Śiva's natural-born son, unlike Gaṇeśa, born from the detritus of his mother's body?[8] One point in support of this reading is that Paraśurāma is often allied with Śiva's other son Skanda, born directly from Śiva's semen.[9] Paraśurāma may also be claiming that he is immovable, not subject to desire, that he is not concerned about Gaṇeśa's warning that anyone who witnesses their parents in this way is separated from his own wife for seven births, since he is a celibate ascetic himself.

| | Intruder | Obstacle | Primal Scene | Result for Child |
|---|---|---|---|---|
| Gaṇeśa's story (*SkP* 3.2.12.15–20) | Śiva (father) | Gaṇeśa (son) | Pārvatī's chamber (mother alone) | Gaṇeśa decapitated (castration) |
| Paraśurāma's story (*MBh* 3.116.5–20) | Jamadagni-Paraśurāma<br><br>(father$_1$ and son) | Paraśurāma's brothers (son) | Reṇukā at the river (mother and father$_2$) | Paraśurāma's brothers cursed (castration) |
| Gaṇeśa and Paraśurāma's story (*BḍP* 2.41.30–2.43.42) | Paraśurāma (son$_1$) | Gaṇeśa (son$_2$) | Pārvatī and Śiva's chamber (mother and father) | Gaṇeśa de-tusked, (castration)<br><br>Paraśurāma rejected by Pārvatī |

Figure 3.3. Comparison of the Gaṇeśa, Paraśurāma, and Gaṇeśa-Paraśurāma Stories.

Taken together, the Gaṇeśa story, the Paraśurāma story, and the Gaṇeśa-Paraśurāma story represent refracted versions of a metanarrative in which the eroticized primal scene becomes a site of conflict where one son or group of sons (Gaṇeśa/Paraśurāma's disobedient brothers) takes the side of the mother (Reṇukā/Pārvātī) and is/are castrated, while the other son (Paraśurāma) takes the side of the father (Jamadagni/Śiva) and is saved.

The metanarrative, following the "Eisenhower principle" of enlarging a problem one cannot solve, then subsumes this narrative into a larger theological framework, mapping it onto the sectarian Vaiṣṇava-Śaiva conflict that is also central to Paraśurāma's identity in the post-epic period, which in turn is mapped onto the dichotomy of *prakṛti* (matter) and *puruṣa* (spirit), allowing the conflict, now enlarged to cosmic proportions, to be resolved on this rarefied plane. Kṛṣṇa and Rādhā, the problem solvers here, represent a higher, more fully realized parental pair whose catholic theology heals the conflict and the wound Paraśurāma has inflicted on Gaṇeśa. The message truly comes from Rādhā, who explains to an angry Pārvatī:

> "The Prakṛti and the Puruṣa—these two are interdependent. In this world they appear as though they are split into two. You and I are one. There is no difference between us. You are Viṣṇu and I am Śiva who has duplicated in form. In the heart of Śiva, Viṣṇu has assumed your form and in the heart of Viṣṇu, Śiva has assumed my form. This [Paraśurāma], O highly fortunate lady, is a Vaiṣṇava (form of Viṣṇu) transformed into a Śaiva (form of Śiva). This Gaṇeśa is Śiva himself transformed into Viṣṇu. No difference is really seen between us both and between the two lords." After saying this, Rādhā placed [Gaṇeśa] on her lap, sniffed at his head and touched his cheeks with her hand. Immediately after being touched, the wound in the cheek healed completely. (Tagare 1983, 714)

The healing of Gaṇeśa's wound also represents a healing of the dualistic universe, of the distinction between Viṣṇu and Śiva, of the conflict between Paraśurāma and Gaṇeśa, and of the split between the maternal side and the paternal side in the Oedipal conflict. Presumably, this kind of resolution would be well received at the *bhadradipāpratiṣṭā* rite at which it was read and may have even served some royal psychotherapeutic purpose. The next narrative we will examine, rather than enlarging and resolving the problem, instead uses parody to point directly to Paraśurāma's problem and then offer a different solution.

## Cooler Heads Prevail While Others Roll: The Story of Cirakāri

First, a digression: On September 28, 1983, in an incident that has become famous belatedly, Stanislav Yevgrafovich Petrov was serving as the duty officer at the bunker Serpukhov-15, monitoring the U.S.S.R.'s new early warning missile detection system. The entire country was on high alert as a result of escalating tensions with the United States following an incident on September 1 in which Korean Air Lines Flight 007 was shot down when it entered Soviet airspace, killing all 269 passengers (including a U.S. congressman). Shortly after midnight, the system installed at Serpukhov-15 detected first one, and then four additional missiles launched from the United States toward the Soviet Union. It was a far cry from the massive first strike the Soviets would have expected based on their understanding of the doctrine of Mutually Assured Destruction, but it was also the first and only chance the Soviets would have to react, since U.S. missiles could reach the U.S.S.R. in a mere twenty-three minutes. Trusting his instincts over his military training, Petrov waited to report the detected missiles, long enough for land radar to disconfirm the new system's flawed reading, and thereby averted a full-scale global thermonuclear war. In not acting, in not following the inflexible protocols on which a successful military is based, in doing *nothing,* Petrov saved millions of lives, if not the world as we know it.

While the stories of Hamlet and Achilles explore the perils of inaction and paralysis, the legendary recounting of Stanislav Petrov's heroism is a celebration of the same. And so is the story of Cirakāri. In either its *Mahābhārata* or its *Skanda Purāṇa* versions, the Cirakāri story takes the form of a digression from the main narrative. It appears in the *Mahābhārata* in the context of a section of Bhīṣma's lengthy deathbed sermon on *dharma* in which he is criticizing the violence of, among other things, the Vedic sacrifice (Fitzgerald 2010, 32). In the *Skanda* it follows a somewhat convoluted story about the consequences of "starting off on the wrong foot" and the perils of receiving gifts.

Cirakāri's story presents a strong critique of the Paraśurāma myth by emphasizing the superiority of dharmically inspired forbearance and consideration over blind obedience. Cirakāri's long internal debate is a parody of the hair-splitting discourse of the *paṇḍitas*, and a pun is even made on his name. The story is also, of course, a rare negative commentary on Paraśurāma's hastiness and lack of discernment. We will begin with the version that appears in the *Mahābhārata*, ably summarized by Fitzgerald:

> 258 (267[6]; 9481). Yudhiṣṭhira asks Bhīṣma whether one should examine one's responsibilities at length or not. Bhīṣma relates The Story of Cirakārin, "Slowpoke." A scion of Gautama named Medhātithi ordered his son Cirakārin to kill his wife, the boy's mother, because she was unfaithful (1–5). Cirakārin accepted his father's command, but the boy then thought the whole matter over carefully. At length he weighed the unhesitating obedience one owes his father against the absolute protection one owes his mother. He concluded the latter is more important than the former (5–30). Turning to the subject of adultery, he judged men, both husbands and paramours, responsible for all the wrong in such incidents (30–40). At the same time, Medhātithi reconsidered the matter and he concluded his wife was innocent of wrongdoing and that he was wrong to have ordered her execution. Shedding copious tears, he fervently hoped his son would live up to his name (40–45). He was relieved to find his son had not yet obeyed his command and the father praised his son and the value of acting with due deliberation (45–65). Bhīṣma repeats the general moral to Yudhiṣṭhira at rather fulsome length (65–75). (2010, 35)

Fitzgerald notes that, although they are not mentioned by name, Cirakāri does seem to have had brothers who refused their father's command since Medhātithi has "passed over his other sons" when he gives the order to Cirakāri in *MBh* 12.258.7.

There is also some further indirect commentary on the Paraśurāma story in the content of Cirakāri's and his father's deliberations. Cirakāri concludes that the mother is the more important member of the parenting pair, and asks rhetorically, "What man with any sense, whose head is not as empty as a gourd, would kill her?" (*MBh* 12.258.31; Fitzgerald 2010, 38). He also concludes that the mother is more important than the father in the conception of the child since it is the mother who knows the child's lineage, or *gotra* (12.258.33). He reasons that his father's command is invalid since only a husband is lord over his wife and no husband would kill his wife, therefore

Medhātithi ceased being a husband when he gave the order and so no longer had any authority to do so. Finally, and most surprisingly, Cirakāri is quite unfazed about his mother's infidelity, reckoning that there is no restriction placed on women's sexual gratification after they have given birth to a son (see Fitzgerald 2010, 45–47). In his own deliberations, Medhātithi decides that no one is at fault in his wife's infidelity with Indra, since the god had misheard her sentence "*paravāti asmi,*" ("I belong to another") as "I am at your disposal" and so all that followed was based on a misunderstanding (Fitzgerald 2010, 48). Addressing matricide, matriliny, the duties of a husband, and female sexuality, Cirakāri's and Medhātithi's ruminations fly in the face of the logic of the Paraśurāma story.

The *Skanda*'s Cirakāri narrative (taking eighty-five lines straight from the epic) appears within a story about the founding of the holy site of Kapila, where all the gods, sages, and celestial beings have assembled. At this assembly, a Brahmin named Hārīta comes forward to have his feet washed and steps first with his left foot. The sage Nārada becomes angry at this impropriety and curses all the Brahmins present, including Hārīta, to be poor and ignorant. Hārīta laughs at this and points out that Nārada has actually cursed himself. Then Hārīta explains why he stepped first with his left foot, saying that he was preoccupied with the perils of receiving gifts; a Brahmin who accepts a gift surrenders his merit to the gift giver and takes on the giver's sins. Because he was engrossed in thought, explains Hārīta, he was inattentive and stepped with the wrong foot. Then he admonishes Nārada for responding too harshly to an honest mistake. Nārada apologizes and agrees that hasty actions are often ill-conceived. It is to illustrate this point that he tells a different story of Cirakāri:

One day, the sage Medhātithi learns that his wife Ahalyā has been watching the demon king Bali bathing with his wives on the banks of the Kauśikī river, causing her to delay in returning to the hermitage. This causes Medhātithi to become angry and he orders his son Cirakāri to kill her. After he has given the order, Medhātithi goes out into the woods and leaves his son alone with his wife, who has no idea that her husband has just pronounced her death sentence. But instead of immediately carrying out his father's order like Paraśurāma does, Cirakāri instead begins to carefully consider the pros and cons of what he has been asked to do, an internal dialogue that takes up some twenty-two verses. Meanwhile, out in the forest, Medhātithi meets Indra disguised as a Brahmin. Indra hails Medhātithi with the verse, "All women are false as the *sutra*-writer has said it. Hence only the fruit must be taken from them. The learned one, the intelligent one, must not keep his eyes on their defects."

By this time, Medhātithi's anger has dissipated and upon hearing Indra's verse he begins to regret ordering his wife's death, considering the punishment unreasonably cruel. He explains what he has done to Indra and the god, making a pun on Cirakāri's name, tells the sage to run back to the hermitage because, if his son really is *cirakāri* ("delaying in action"), it may not be too late. So Medhātithi hurries back to the *āśrama* in grief, expecting to find his wife's lifeless body. Instead he finds her doing chores, unaware of the presence of Cirakāri, who is standing behind her with an axe, still debating what to do. At the arrival of her husband, Medhātithi's wife turns around and sees Cirakāri, weapon in hand, and becomes afraid. By this time, though, Medhātithi has had a complete change of heart and embraces his son, praising the forbearance that saved his wife's life (1.2.6.59–131).

The Cirakāri story as told by Bhīṣma in the *Mahābhārata* and by Nārada in the *Skanda Purāṇa* combine the real infidelity in the story of Gautama and Ahalyā and the element of filial obedience in the story of Paraśurāma's matricide. In both versions, the Kṣatriya exemplar Indra enters the story disguised as a Brahmin, seducing the wife in the *Mahābhārata* and rebuking the husband in the *Skanda*. Figure 3.4 demonstrates the major transformations.

The setting of the sexual misconduct changes from myth to myth. While in the Ahalyā story and the *Mahābhārata*'s Cirakāri story, the seduction takes place at the hermitage while the sage is away, the wife's symbolic infidelity in the Reṇukā story and the *Skanda*'s Cirakāri story takes place when she leaves home and goes to the river. The movement of the action from the center to the periphery also seems to coincide with a decrease in the seriousness of the offense; there is actual sex in the Ahalyā model, but only a kind of voyeuristic lapse in the Reṇukā model. On the other hand, Ahalyā actually seems less culpable than Reṇukā since the man who seduced her was disguised as her husband, although in the version told in the *Kathāsaritsāgara* Ahalyā becomes an accomplice after the fact by trying to help pass off Indra as a cat after her husband comes in the bedroom (Doniger 1999, 99). In the Ahalyā model, the sage himself punishes his unfaithful wife and the guilty seducer while in the Reṇukā model the sage orders his son to do the deed and only targets the wife. Likewise, the agency in the Ahalyā model is with the warrior-seducer himself, who seeks out the sage's wife, while in the Reṇukā model, the sage's wife spies unnoticed on the bathing king and his harem.[10]

There is also an important difference between the Reṇukā story and the Reṇukā-modeled parody version of the Cirakāri story in the *Skanda*: the identity of the king or prince whom the wife watches at the river. In the

| Ahalyā (*Rām* 7.30.17–36) | Reṇukā (*MBh* 3.116.29–41) | Cirakāri$_1$ (*MBh* 12.258.1–75) | Cirakāri$_2$ (*SkP* 1.2.6.59–131) |
|---|---|---|---|
| Husband leaves wife at home alone and warrior-seducer takes the form of the sage and sleeps with her. | Wife/mother goes to the river and watches a warrior bathe, causing her to return late to the hermitage. | Husband/father leaves wife at home alone and warrior-seducer sleeps with her. | Wife/mother goes to the river and watches a warrior bathe, causing her to return late to the hermitage. |
| Husband returns, finds the two and curses them both. | Husband/ father orders son to kill wife/mother. | Husband/father orders son to kill wife/ mother, then leaves them home alone. | Husband/father orders son to kill wife/mother, then leaves them home alone. |
| | Son obeys instantly. | Son hesitates and does not kill wife/mother. | Son hesitates and does not kill wife/ mother. |
| | Husband/father is pleased with son's obedience and resurrects wife/mother. | Husband/father changes his mind and is pleased with his son's disobedience. | Husband/father changes his mind and is pleased with his son's disobedience. |

Figure 3.4. Comparison of the Ahalyā, Reṇukā, and Cirakāri Stories.

Reṇukā story, the bathing prince is the *gandharva* Citraratha, a figure whose ritual and mythological significance we have already explored, linking him to the buffalo demon, the king Kārtavīrya, and the forest being that must be overcome by the hero in Nancy Falk's micromyth. But in the parodic version of the Cirakāri episode, the prince is identified as Bali, a major figure in the *Skanda Purāṇa* and a different sort of character altogether. While Citraratha is a *gandharva,* a fairly innocuous (or at least neutral) species of celestial being, Bali is an *asura,* an enemy of the gods (although frequently "one of the good ones").

The story of Cirakāri is told in the style of comedy and parody, genres that grant texts and speakers a certain amount of license and allow them to more or less openly challenge authority and hegemonic points of view. It makes use of puns that may be read as parodies of the etymologies for different words for mother ("*dhātri* because she holds us in her belly," etc.) that Cirakāri lists when he is deciding whether or not to kill her. In the *Skanda Purāṇa*, the larger story in which Cirakāri's story appears also contains a bizarre play on words in which the accidental utterance of the syllable "ha" by the Brahmins causes Kapila to curse them. The narrative is filled with grotesque imagery: Brahmins cover their eyes with mud in order to see; Nārada shrinks them to the size of ants; they encounter monstrous worms and glowing *siddhas*. Literary scholar Frances Barasch argues that the grotesque structure is subversive in that it "implies a failure of conventional systems to provide rational solutions for human interaction" (1985, 6). This is certainly true of Cirakāri in that his exhaustive and lengthy recollection of all the arguments that the sacred tradition provides for and against obeying his father's command to kill his mother leads to a failure to act which is, ironically, a success. While the Brahminical tradition would have it that learned disputation can solve any problem, this story presents a breakdown in this system that results in the triumph of a buffoon.[11]

So far in this chapter we have been examining the matricide myth through male eyes, belonging to Jamadagni, Paraśurāma, his brothers, and lastly, Cirakāri. It is now time to place Reṇukā at the center of the narrative and examine traditions that posit her agency in the gruesome drama of her decapitation. In the next section, we will look at some versions of the myth connected to Tantric traditions and goddess worship.

## Reṇukā the Headless Goddess

And my head rises
Solitary lookout
In the triumphal flights
Of this scythe
As clean rupture
Rather repels or cuts
Ancient discords
With the body

—Stéphane Mallarmé, "The Canticle of Saint John"

In some goddess-worshipping sects, Reṇukā is identified with one of two nude, headless (or decapitated) goddesses: The first is Chinnamastā, who probably began as a Tantric Buddhist deity around the seventh century. A list of the ten *avatāras* of Viṣṇu paired with the ten *mahāvidyās*, or forms of Devī, names Paraśurāma (called Bhṛgukula, or "Scion of Bhṛgu") as her counterpart/consort (Benard 1994, 5). In her iconography, Chinnamastā holds her head in one hand while blood spurts out of her neck into the mouths of two female attendants on either side. She often stands on top of the divine couple Kāma and Rati, posed in a sexual embrace with the woman on top (12–13). As is often the case with goddess myths, the Chinnamastā-Reṇukā identification takes an orthodox Vaiṣṇava or Śaiva mytheme and reverses its polarity. In this instance, the myth turns the theme of Reṇukā's incontinence on its head (so to speak), changing it from a mortal wound into a life-giving fount.

Concerning her popular depiction, Kinsley asks: "Might not the Chinnamastā image represent the generation of spiritual power in a female, the rising of the *kuṇḍalinī*, by means of the retention of her sexual fluids and the transformation of them into a nourishing fluid?" (1997, 161). This transformation of the decapitated dead mother into the living headless fountain of life recalls the use of the *karakam* pot, symbol of fullness and auspiciousness, to represent Reṇukā-Mariyamman in South Indian goddess festivals.

It also finds expression in some of the literature of twentieth-century Hindu nationalism. In the interest of mitigating the potentially problematic episodes in Paraśurāma's story to more easily render him an acceptable national hero, the Hindi poem *Jay Paraśurām*, authored by Pramad in 1997, folds this Tantric identification of Reṇukā and Chinnamastā into the narrative.[12] Going farther, the author combines the understanding of Reṇukā as the headless goddess with the Bhārgava theme of sacrificial suicide by proxy (as in the story of Aurva in *MBh* 1.170.31–34) to eliminate Paraśurāma's guilt completely and explicitly link the matricide to the destruction of the Kṣatriyas. In the *Jay Paraśurām*:

> Reṇukā explains to Paraśurāma that she has herself wished for and organized everything that has happened because the matricide will be the ultimate test, or even ordeal, to reveal Paraśurāma's capacity to destroy the unjust kings. It means that, if Paraśurāma is able to commit the most difficult deed, it will establish his capacity to accomplish his sacred duty to free the Earth from her burdens and make it a *puṇyabhūmi* [sacred ground]. Even if he is compassion incarnate (*karuṇavatar*), he must become *mahakrodheśvar* [Lord of Terrible Rage] to perform the "matricide theatre play" (*māṃ vadh kā nāṭak*) before killing the bad kings. Having explained her own greatness and her being the Mahāśakti, Reṇukā orders Paraśurāma not to be sad and to cut her head off quickly. (Dejenne 2007, 456)

This Tantric interpretation obviously runs counter to most understandings of the episode and Pramad seems to have cherry-picked it solely to absolve Paraśurāma of the matricide, since nowhere else in the text does the idea that Reṇukā is the *mahāśakti* come up, nor does it affect any other events in the story. "It seems," notes Dejenne, "that the 'Tantric moment' has ended with Reṇukā's beheading" (ibid.).

The second headless goddess connected to Reṇukā is Lajjāgaurī, a name used to refer to an image—found in terracotta and stone sculptures dating from the first to the eighth centuries CE and uncovered in Andhra Pradesh, Uttar Pradesh, Karnataka, and Maharashtra—of a nude headless woman with large prominent breasts and an equally prominent vulva between her splayed legs (Bapat 2008, 79–80). The name and its image create a sense of irony, since *lajjā* is the word used for female modesty. The difference between Chinnamastā and Lajjāgaurī is significant: While the former holds her head in her hands, the latter's head is typically gone. While this is not always the case with Lajjāgaurī, it is the case in the temple in Alampur, Andhra Pradesh where a Lajjāgaurī image is identified with Reṇukā (85–86).

Another example of the Reṇukā-Lajjāgaurī identification is recorded in a Marāṭhī booklet called *Mukapiṭhavāsiṇī Śrī Reṇukā Mahātmya* (*MSRM*), sold at the Śrī Reṇukā Māta temple in Mahur, located in Kinvav Taluka in the Nanded District of Maharashtra.[13] After a familiar narration of Reṇukā's decapitation and resurrection, the text then adds this explanation:

> Reṇukā herself caused this chain of events. While making this happen, she made many free from their sins. For instance, she freed her husband Jamadagni from his anger. Jamadagni knew all along that Reṇukā was a devoted wife. However, extreme anger took over. Reṇukā caused a series of events in which Jamadagni first got enraged, did things that he should not have done and then repented for his wrongdoings, thereby renouncing anger forever. Along with that, the story of Reṇukā Lajjāgaurī gives another message to the world that by moral value man and woman complete each other. The feelings of love arose in Reṇukā's mind by seeing another man, even though she had a husband. This is because Reṇukā was Lajjāgaurī and had more feelings of modesty in her by nature. Where there is the quality of *lajjā,* all other virtues such as strength, valor, brilliance, self-control also reside. Since Reṇukā was also Lajjāgaurī, she had all the above virtues. When the feelings of love arose in Reṇukā's mind, the foundation of *lajjā*

> was shaken. She was involved in committing sin indirectly and she realized her fault. As a consequence, without any complaint she accepted the punishment of death given by her husband at the hands of her brilliant son Paraśurāma. This is how the purest form of Lajjāgaurī is manifested. (*MSRM* 15)

Here Reṇukā is identified as "Lajjāgaurī *sākṣat*" ("Lajjāgaurī herself"), a goddess so modest that she can experience immodesty for the purpose of violently purging it from herself. After her decapitation, Paraśurāma asks Jamadagni to resurrect her and his dead brothers and asks that he erase *their* memories of the event, without saying anything about his own. Later, after Kārtavīrya has killed Jamadagni, Reṇukā enters the pyre with her husband's body but subsequently returns through a crack in the earth at her son's behest. Finally, we should note that while Lajjāguarī is a nude sexualized headless torso, Reṇukā as "Lajjāgaurī *sākṣat*" is represented only as a head.

Yet another image of Reṇukā, popular in the Telugu and Kannada traditions, combines both decapitated body and severed head, making her one half of a pair of goddesses who have switched heads. In a Tamil variant of this story, analyzed in her inimitable fashion by Doniger in *Splitting the Difference*, there is only one mixed-up goddess rather than two. After Paraśurāma has decapitated Reṇukā, Jamadagni gives him the spell to revive her. But Paraśurāma is so distraught that when he goes to rejoin Reṇukā's head to her body he mistakenly joins it to the decapitated body of an Outcaste woman who has been lawfully executed. The resulting monstrosity wreaks havoc on the world in the style of an out-of-control goddess until the gods supplicate her by granting her the power to cure smallpox. Then they once again separate her head from her body, placing her pure Brahmin head inside the temple sanctuary and her impure Outcaste body at the door. Finally, since she is no longer pure enough for Paraśurāma, the gods grant Reṇukā a second son in the form of Kārtavīrya (!) (Doniger 1999, 204–206).

Here is another Tamil variant collected from Tiruverkadu by Srinivasan:

> Born as a princess she was married to a sage Jamadagni. The couple gave birth to four sons. Renuka was such a powerful pativrata that she could make a fresh pot everyday out of the wet sand in the riverbank and bring water to her husband in that pot. One day, when she was drawing water from the river, seeing a Gandharva flying above her, she thought for a moment, "What a man." Immediately the pot of sand dissolved into the river. Jamadagni

> became furious. He called his sons to behead their mother who had erred on the path of dharma. The first three sons refused and Jamadagni cursed them, turning them into plants and rocks. The fourth one, Parasurama, however, complied with his father's command and went seeking his mother. On seeing Parasurama, Renuka started running. Just then, a cobbler woman was coming from the other side, and Renuka hugged her in fear. Parasurama beheaded them both. Before leaving the place, he took an earthen pot with water and kept it near Renuka.
>
> Parasurama went back to his father, who granted Parasurama two boons. Parasurama wished for his brothers coming back to life as his first boon and for the second boon, he asked for his mother to be revived. During the revival of his mother, Parasurama inadvertently joined his mother's head to the cobbler woman's body. Since Renuka's body was transformed, she came to be known as "Mari" or the "transformed one." Jamadagni did not accept her back as his wife, since her body had changed. After Jamadagni's death, Mari entered fire. Siva sent rains and doused the fire. Mari then asked Siva for some means to sustain herself. She got a boon of pearls or poxes from him to rule over this world. (Srinivasan n.d., 3–4)

This variant creates a myth-ritual structure opposing the fluidity of water with the hardening properties of fire, common in South Indian depictions of Reṇukā (see Stark-Wild 1997, 199). Reṇukā is the raw, uncooked pot, able to miraculously hold water without being fired for a time, but ultimately transformed through the funeral pyre and the rains of Śiva into two new beings: the fired clay pot honored by her son Paraśurāma and the smallpox goddess worshipped by the local sect.

<table>
<tr><td>Element</td><td colspan="2">Water</td><td colspan="2">Fire</td></tr>
<tr><td>Goddess</td><td colspan="2">Reṇukā</td><td colspan="2">Mari</td></tr>
<tr><td>Vessel</td><td colspan="2">Wet Sand Pot</td><td colspan="2">Fired Earthen Pot</td></tr>
<tr><td>Ritual/Myth Associations</td><td>River</td><td>Śiva's Rain</td><td>Pyre</td><td>Pox</td></tr>
</table>

Figure 3.5. Structural Comparison of Reṇukā Myths and Rituals in South India.

As both Chinnamastā and Lajjāgaurī, Reṇukā turns her decapitation into a self-sacrifice to illustrate her own virtue and to purge Jamadagni of his excessive anger. Both figures also invert more common understandings of her sexual incontinence, turning it from a sign of weakness into a symbol of her ultimate power. In the story of the switched heads, Reṇukā does not have agency over her death, but is granted a special status and new power upon her imperfect resurrection, which is itself a kind of inversion of Paraśurāma's mixed birth. Going too much farther down this path would turn this into a book about Reṇukā, which is a necessary undertaking but one I will leave to another scholar. The remainder of this chapter, then, will be devoted to using the psychoanalytic models developed by Freud, Lacan, Kristeva, and André Green to interpret the matricide micromyth.

## Further Psychoanalytic Readings of the Matricide Micromyth

As we have already seen, the curse of Paraśurāma's disobedient brothers presents an opportunity to read the myth through a Lacanian psychoanalytic lens. While Paraśurāma's obedience to his father's command to behead Reṇukā represents a successful progression through the Lacanian Oedipus complex, the disobedience of his brothers and their subsequent loss of language, humanity, and life represents a failed transition. We will now continue this psychoanalytic reading of the episode with attention to one of the more specific symbols that come out of the Indian context, the theme of exile in the forest.

### Mapping the Forest

A pattern emerges when we read the matricide micromyth in light of Kristeva's theory of abjection and Kurtz's emphasis on the Indian idea of renunciation. This pattern appears against the background of the erotic and maternal notions of the forest in South Asia that go back to *ṚV* 10.146's mention of the mysterious *araṇyanī* (female forest spirit) and up through the sixteenth-century Telugu *Manucaritamanu* (in which the mother of the first man, Manu, is the Forest Goddess) and modern Bollywood films (See Chattopadhyaya 2018, 59–60; Shulman 1995, 159; Peddana and Rao 2015, 547–49).

Paraśurāma's matricide and its repetition in the destruction of the male Kṣatriyas separates him from the mother's body; it frees him of the forest and makes him an axe-wielding creator of the tilled field, or *kṣetra*. The undifferentiated forest is the mother and the cultivated field is the self's body. This last identification is found throughout Hindu philosophy: "This body is called 'the field'" are the first words spoken by Kṛṣṇa in the famous thirteenth chapter of the *Bhāgavad Gītā* (*MBh* 6.35.1). Paraśurāma's brothers, on the other hand, never leave the forest. They are permanently absorbed into the maternal morass. But, even though Paraśurāma has separated from the maternal forest, the ambivalence of the abjected maternal object continues to work on him and as soon as he creates the Kurukṣetra, Paraśurāma leaves it and goes into an eternal exile (either by the mountains or the sea).

Assayag has collected a Tamil variant that connects the myth to the traditional garb made of tree branches sewn together by devotees of Reṇukā-Yellama in Savadatti:

> After the assassination of his father by Kārtavīrya, Paraśurāma swore to avenge himself by exterminating all the Kṣatriyas. In fulfilling his duty, he spared the women and children. They came to seek shelter in the hermitage of Jamadagni to beg the protection of Yellamma. They reached it in the simplest of garb, destitute of everything. Having regained his composure, Paraśurāma was taken with compassion at this spectacle. He cut branches of *neem* trees so that they could cover their bodies to appear before the goddess. Thus clothed, the devotees prayed to Yellamma to pardon the sins of the Kṣatriyas and to protect them. This she did very willingly in the presence of her son. The joyous crowd began to sing and dance, praising the greatness and magnanimity of the goddess. (1992, 208)

Paraśurāma's brothers are absent here, but, taken as a variant of the Paraśurāma myth, this story of the branch-clad Kṣatriya refugees-turned-devotees looks very much like cursed children returning to the maternal forest. The idea of going into the forest has a long history in South Asia as a journey to a place outside civilization and social order. In the epic tradition, banishment to the forest is a prerequisite for a king to fulfill his destiny. The divine king Rāma's exile from Ayodhya in the *Rāmāyaṇa*, the heroic Pāṇḍavas' twelve years in the forest in the *Mahābhārata*, and the Buddha's renouncing his kingdom to become an ascetic in the *Buddhacarita* all exemplify this theme. The brothers' curse combines the idea of rejection of paternal law with the more specifically Indic theme of exile in the forest, colored by a long-running parallel tradition of the forest as maternal, erotic, and feminine.

In the Paraśurāma cycle, all the action is centered on the forest *āśrama* of Jamadagni, which seems to serve as a bastion of familial order in the chaotic wilderness. As long as the entire family stays within the *āśrama,* things go well. It is when Reṇukā is out getting water and encounters the bathing Citraratha that the trouble begins. Later in the myth cycle, Paraśurāma's trip into the forest to collect firewood for the ritual is the occasion for Kārtavīrya's abduction of Jamadagni's cow and finally, when Paraśurāma has not yet returned from his mission to slay Kārtavīrya, the king's sons raid the hermitage and kill Jamadagni.

On the level of narrative, this back-and-forth movement of the characters is necessary for each event in the story to occur: Reṇukā would have to be away from the *āśrama* to see a strange man bathing and Paraśurāma would have to leave his father unguarded for Jamadagni to be vulnerable to attack. On the level of structure, the movement of the characters translates into a binary sequence of presence and absence. Now I want to pull back and examine the myth cycle in terms of presence in and absence from the *āśrama* and attempt to understand it in Lacanian terms of alienation, separation, and traversing the fantasy.

In Lacan's reading of the Oedipus complex, the child's acquisition of speech coincides with psychological separation from the mother and takes place in three stages. In the first stage, *alienation,* the child acquiesces to the mother's greater power, resulting in his absorption into the maternal identity and the simultaneous opening of a lack, or space, where the child's identity, now absorbed, had been. This initial absence of being and the space that it creates are what makes subjectivity possible in the later stages. Before he enters into language, the child experiences a primordial identification with the mother, sometimes described as an "oceanic feeling." The subsequent introduction of the binary opposition of the mother's alternating presence and absence (exemplified in Freud's description of the *fort-da* game in *Beyond the Pleasure Principle*) reveals to the child that a lack or empty space exists in the mother as well. How else could there be a time when the mother was not present? After this realization, the child attempts to please the mother and to align the lack that is the space opened for his subjectivity in the alienation stage with the lack he now sees in the mother. He wants to become the fulfillment of her desire.

What follows is the stage of *separation.* At this point, a third term enters the picture, the Name of the Father, which Lacan also identifies as the phallus, and the child realizes that the phallus—and not he—can fill the lack in the mother. The phallus stands between the child and the mother, opening up a space for the child to enter into his own subjectivity and also creating a desire in the child that is never to be satisfied—the desire to experience his prior relationship to the mother, the oceanic feeling, which he symbolizes as "*object a.*" The relationship of the child to *object a* then becomes the foundation of all fantasy, and the child has entered into subjectivity through the final stage, *traversing the fantasy,* which I will explain below.

Srinivasan's analysis of the Tamil myth-ritual complex from Tiruverkadu well illustrates the role of *object a* (here embodied in the all-important pot) in Paraśurāma's relationship to Reṇukā and his nostalgia for her "pre-transformed" state:

> [When] a baked pot is placed by Renuka's son Parasurama, the pot prefigures the reconstitution of the fragmented body parts of Renuka into her new form as the goddess Mariyamman. It is kept by Parasurama as "desired" by his mother before her beheading. Why does Renuka desire the pot? Is it because a whole new pot could have saved her from her husband's wrath? Or does the whole new pot represent her desire to regain a whole new body? The new pot operates as a memento of her unfulfilled desire, an emblem of an ideal state of wholeness, which is achieved by Renuka only as Mari, that is, after her body gets "transformed." Renuka is beheaded, but she regains her wholeness in the form of Mariyamman. (Srinivasan 2009, 218)

The mother-child separation precipitated by the introduction of the phallus divides the child into an ego (constituted by subject-position that is the empty space created when he first was subsumed into the maternal) and the unconscious. The phallus also divides the Other (the Mother) into *object a* and the "lacking Other" (stemming from the lack the child first notices in the alternating presence and absence of the mother). In this final stage, the child moves from fantasies revolving around *object a* and the reclamation of oceanic feeling it symbolizes to occupying the space formerly occupied by *object a.* When the phallus, or the Name of the Father, does not completely sever the bond between mother and child, the result is psychosis. The Name of the Father, as the primary signifier, serves as the keystone of language itself, and without it the child will never truly occupy a place in language.

In the part of the story that corresponds to Lacan's separation stage, Reṇukā has left and returned to the *āśrama,* symbolizing the alternating presence and absence of the mother that causes the child to view her as a lacking subject in the Lacanian model. Following this revelation of lack is Jamadagni's far more devastating revelation, delivered under the aegis of the Paternal Law with its omniscient yogic eye, that Reṇukā is incontinent and deserving of death. Consequently, Paraśurāma proves his loyalty to Jamadagni by destroying, and thus separating himself from, his mother.

The fact that in most versions Jamadagni immediately resurrects Reṇukā and erases the incident from everyone's mind complicates the matter. The rest of the myth that follows the moment of separation, corresponding to Lacan's "traversing the fantasy" stage, is likewise complicated. While Paraśurāma does move past the desire to regain the maternal oceanic experience, he does so by exploding into a destructive path of increasingly cold-blooded violence. The extremely violent form that his rejection of the maternal takes predicts a similarly violent manifestation of the erotic drives that are born from this final stage. In more ways than one, Paraśurāma's murder of Reṇukā clearly sets the stage for his subsequent twenty-one-fold destruction of the Kṣatriyas.

## *Ek-Hi* or *Fort-Da*?

Let us now return to Kurtz and his argument that "the psychoanalytic notion of the pro-oedipal phase must be substantially revised when it is applied to the Hindu case" (1992, 92). While he begins with the assumption that Freud's oral, anal, and genital stages of sexuality are universal structures, Kurtz also wants to distinguish "the phases themselves and culturally varied modes of renunciation that propel the child through them" (101–102). Looking at the pre-Oedipal phase in the Hindu idiom, Kurtz does not see movement away from the mother and toward the father, but rather "movement away from the natural mother and toward a more mature immersion in a larger and fundamentally benevolent group of mothers, a group in which all the mothers are, ultimately, 'just-one' " (92–93). The phrase "just-one" is *ek-hi* in Hindi, which gives Kurtz the name for this developmental phase specific to Hindu notions of family.

The basic pattern of the *ek-hi* phase is this: at some point the child is handed by the mother to another female caregiver, causing the child to form a split image of the mother. This split is then reconciled at the group level when the child becomes accustomed to being shared by different mother figures. It is reconciled at the cultural level by a theological model of one Devī (Goddess) who takes a range of forms from benevolent to terrifying (Kurtz 1992, 109–13).

Does the matricide micromyth fit this pattern? In one important sense, it does. After Reṇukā is "split" (at the neck), she is returned to wholeness. And in the goddess-worshipping tradition, she is integrated into the larger Devī continuum. We also see echoes of this process in the introduction of an all-encompassing Rādhāite theology to resolve the bitterness felt by Pārvatī toward Paraśurāma after his struggle with Gaṇeśa in the *Brahmavaivarta Purāṇa*.

But if we focus on Paraśurāma as the one undergoing the transition of the *ek-hi* phase, it is a failed transition. He totally abjects his mother (as the *kṣatra*) in his act of varṇicide and becomes an isolated exile. He seems to be stuck in a regression stemming from failure to resolve what Kurtz calls the "Durga complex," named after the fierce, lion-mounted form of Devī who decapitates the Buffalo Demon. The Durga complex finds expression in ritual and myth as "an identification between the demon decapitated by the goddess and the devotee himself" (135). We can see this identification in the myths of Pōttu Rāja-Pōrmaṉṉaṉ, the "Buffalo King" of South Indian mythology, whose complex story cycles revolve around his identity as the Buffalo Demon slain by Devī, converted into one of her devotees, and who is also sometimes identified with Paraśurāma (Hiltebeitel 1988, 77; 2019, personal communication).

## The Dead Mother Complex

Until now, we have largely been examining the motivations for Reṇukā's murder from the near-cuckold Jamadagni's perspective, since it is he who orders her death. It is just as important though, that Paraśurāma, unlike his brothers, acquiesces to his father's command and decapitates Reṇukā. Attributing his actions to unquestioning obedience to his father or knowledge of the power of his father, the myth gives no indication that Paraśurāma actually wishes to decapitate his mother. The agency of the crime is thus divided between father and son: Jamadagni is enraged but curiously inactive, while Paraśurāma is golem-like, completely unfazed, feeling none of Jamadagni's anger, but acting as the agent of death anyway.

As a side effect, this bifurcation also robs Paraśurāma's actions of internal motivation and makes him harder to comprehend. The narrative's displacement of Paraśurāma's rage onto Jamadagni presents him as little more than a human weapon—free of anger, but also completely lacking compassion or morality. The myth unfolds into a new set of meanings when we see father and son acting as a dyad, with the child's unacceptable feeling of incestuous jealousy toward his mother being projected onto the father figure, leaving Paraśurāma free to possess his mother, exercising the power of life and death over her under the more presentable guise of filial obedience.

In his essay "The Dead Mother," the French (conspicuously non-Lacanian) psychoanalyst André Green argues that the Oedipus complex as a structure has long dominated Freudian and post-Freudian thought to their detriment. In classical psychoanalysis, the Superego (and at least for Freud, religion) derives from the concepts of the dead father and castration anxiety. In Lacanian thought, the Law and the Symbolic replace the Superego, but these concepts also come from the Oedipus complex. When taken as a paradigm rather than a libidinal phase, Green contends, the Oedipus complex has led psychoanalysts down a number of dead ends both in practice and theory.[14] But Green does not wish to abandon the structural function of the Oedipus complex. Instead, he wants to introduce "a structural conception which would be organized not around one centre or paradigm, but around at least two, in accordance with a distinctive characteristic, different from what has been proposed to date" (1986, 145).

The new paradigm that Green introduces is the Dead Mother complex, which, unlike the Oedipus complex, manifests in patients as a "*transference depression*" rather than a "transference neurosis." Green's Dead Mother complex presents a new structure and set of symptoms that are remarkably useful in understanding Paraśurāma's matricide and its aftereffects. So many elements of the Paraśurāma story are suggestive of the Dead Mother complex that one could argue for Paraśurāma as a candidate for Green's Oedipus.[15]

The scenario of the Dead Mother complex is this: The child's mother is depressed (not actually dead) for whatever reason and her depression causes her to lose interest in the child. The child experiences this change as a trauma, but not a separation. "*The essential characteristic of this depression*," writes Green, "*is that it takes place in the presence of the object* [the mother], *which is itself absorbed by a bereavement*" (1986, 149). While still present, the mother has now become the Dead Mother, presenting the child with a "*cold core*" that he interprets as the result of his drives toward her (150). The child's interpretation thus sets up a triangle that resembles that of the Oedipus complex. In its earliest form, the triangle consists of the child, the mother, and the unknown object whose loss is the cause of her bereavement.

From evidence in his clinical work, Green hypothesizes that in the worst cases this lost object is in reality a miscarried pregnancy, which would cause the mother to mourn, though the miscarriage itself would be totally unobservable to the child. But since the lost object is out of sight and the father is not, the triangle soon resolves into the familiar one of the child, the mother, and the father. Toward the father, the child feels either resentment, blaming him for the loss of his mother's love, or intense attachment, looking to him for help to repair or resurrect the dead mother. But the mother's depression or bereavement is also affecting the father, so he too is distant from the child.

Of the defenses the ego deploys in the Dead Mother complex, Green writes:

> The first and most important is a unique movement with two aspects: *the decathexis of the maternal object and the unconscious identification with the dead mother.* The decathexis, which is principally affective, but also representative, constitutes a psychical murder of the object, accomplished without hatred. (151)

Decathexis, the withdrawal of psychic energy or love, is manifest not only in the child's depressed affect but also in the structure of his psyche. His withdrawal of love from the mother is intentional; he decathects or psychically murders the mother out of retaliation for her withdrawal from him. But his identification with her, his "reactive symmetry," is the unintended consequence of the decathexis. As result of this identification, the child's outward personality becomes withdrawn and melancholy to mirror the mother's while inwardly he creates "a hole in the texture of object-relations with the mother" (ibid.). To cope with the situation, the child develops a secondary set of defenses that include a regressive and sadistic impulse to incorporate the lost object into himself, a ruthless search for sensual pleasure sometimes accompanied by sadistic fantasies, and a compulsion to repeat actions that he thinks will repair the hole created by the decathexis.

Before we progress farther into Green's essay, let us look at some of the features of the Paraśurāma story that correspond to the symptoms of the Dead Mother complex. The first triangulation that Green identifies is that of the child, the mother, and the object of bereavement. Well after the matricide episode, Reṇukā becomes a widow, but her dead husband cannot be the object of her mourning in the paradigm of the Dead Mother complex. There is something else. From the time she marries Jamadagni, she has lost part of herself for which she is in mourning: her life as a Kṣatriya, idealized as *kṣatra*.

When Reṇukā marries a forest sage, she leaves the comforts of palace life for life in a hermitage with an ascetic. In some versions of the myth Jamadagni is described as old and ugly while Reṇukā is young and beautiful, further compounding the disparity between what she could have been and what she is. While Reṇukā only infrequently explicitly pines away for the princess's life she has given up, this mourning is at least part of the subtext in the desire aroused by the sight of a prince and his wives bathing and is more pronounced in later myths in which Kārtavīrya is her brother-in-law or her youngest son. There are also traces of this mourning to be found in the mixed birth episode, where she (or her mother on her behalf) consciously or unconsciously takes the *caru* that contains the essence of *kṣatra* instead of the one containing Brahmin-ness that she has been instructed to take. The fact that her mourning for lost *kṣatra* is only implied by a desire she is unable to suppress at the river and by an accidental "slip" with the *carus* corresponds to Green's view that the child cannot directly apprehend the cause of the mother's bereavement. So the triangle stands, with the broken line representing the child's desire for what he cannot see:

Green describes the first ego defense in the Dead Mother complex as a double movement including the decathexis or psychic murder ("accomplished without hatred") of the mother and the identification with the mother. In our myth, the first part of the movement, the psychic murder, is Paraśurāma's actual beheading of Reṇukā. When he swings the axe, Paraśurāma is frequently not only without hatred, but seemingly without feeling of any kind. In contrast to his later killings, the matricide is done on the orders of someone else; Paraśurāma slays Reṇukā not because he is angry about what she has done, but because Jamadagni is.

The second part of the movement, identification with the mother, is evident in Paraśurāma's personality change after the matricide. After he has slain Reṇukā, Paraśurāma is free to act as a Kṣatriya, wielding weapons and driven by bloodlust and the desire for revenge. The matricide episode seems to be the moment in which the *kṣatra* that has been present in Paraśurāma

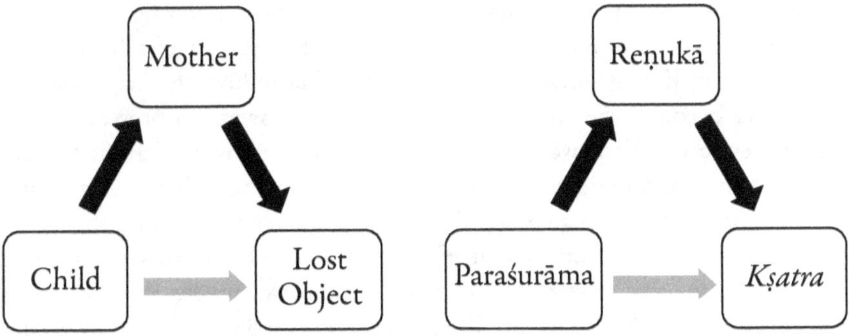


Figure 3.6. The Triangle of the Dead Mother Complex and the Triangle of the Reṇukā Myth.

since the ritual in which he was conceived becomes an active force, making the transition from latent to manifest. The opposite seems to happen to Jamadagni, who is so quick to have his wife killed but is unable to defend his home in the cattle theft episode. One story collected from Belgaum in the Western Ghats explains Jamadagni's post-matricide weakening this way:

> [Seeing] that Jamadagni had been utterly overcome by wrath in the matter of Reṇukā's shame, [Paraśurāma] further begged him to renounce anger forever, on the ground that such mad wrath ill-became him and was likely to prove the source of his destruction. Thereupon Jamadagni expelled Anger from his body,—when lo! it stood incarnate before him and begged him not to reject it as it was capable of achieving difficult tasks, and as there were several matters yet to be brought about with its aid. But Jamadagni paid no heed, and discarding it forever, was purged of all wrath. (Artal 1907, 591)

The image of Anger expelled from the body and turned into a living, speaking being adds a new layer of meaning to the myth. Ironically, the personified Anger acts more rationally than the anger-free Jamadagni, who stubbornly refuses to listen to Anger's reasonable argument about its useful place in the range of emotions. In this story, Jamadagni makes himself incomplete emotionally, which leads to his own decapitation by Kārtavīrya and Paraśurāma's subsequent destruction of the Kṣatriyas.

In Green's theory, the child spends much of his energy trying to imagine the cause of his mother's bereavement, at times linking it to her relationship to the father, at other times to something the child himself has done wrong. At various points of the Paraśurāma story, the mourned *kṣatra* takes the form of other objects in a series of greater and greater losses, all of which reflect some aspect of Kṣatriya-ness. In the cattle theft that follows the matricide, the lost object becomes the cow, the animal that kings swear to protect and by which they reckon their wealth. Where this particular cow is identified as the Kāmadhenu, it also represents the mother's all-giving love in her wish-granting capacity. After Paraśurāma rescues the cow, the lost object becomes the father (obviously not a king, but a source of authority to his son), who is killed in a catastrophe that outstrips that of the cattle theft. Finally, the lost object becomes the earth itself, specifically the earth as sanctified for rule by a king with an act of sacrifice. Since Paraśurāma has just conquered the earth before he is exiled from it, he is in effect losing his kingdom.

Green sums up all the child's defensive mechanisms as various attempts to do three things: Keep the ego alive through hatred of the lost object and the search for pleasure; reanimate the Dead Mother; and "rivalize with the object of her bereavement in the earlier triangulation" (1986, 155). Like Green's analysand, Paraśurāma eventually turns on the lost object with compulsive and violent hatred, rivalizing with and then extirpating the class of people who are the human embodiment of *kṣatra*. He even collects their blood in giant pools, a sadistic incorporation fantasy if ever there was one. As a very helpful reviewer of this manuscript pointed out, it is significant that Paraśurāma only kills the male Kṣatriyas, leaving the mothers and children alive. In this way, he is not only eliminating all potential *varṇa*-appropriate rivals for his mother's love, but also producing innumerable husbandless and fatherless mother-child pairings to mirror his own ideal. Clearly, widows and orphans are also the consequence of real wars (assuming a mostly male army) but the preceding events in the *āśrama,* in which the matricide prefigures the varṇicide, suggest that we should be seeing this war on the Kṣatriya male as connected to Paraśurāma's family situation.

In the same story from Belgaum mentioned above, Paraśurāma also turns Jamadagni's severed head into a stringed instrument and puts his dismembered body in a vessel (Artal 1907, 594). And although Paraśurāma does successfully resurrect the Dead Mother, her resurrection is monstrous and incomplete. In most of the variants we have looked at so far, Reṇukā either disappears from the story after the matricide episode, exists as a monstrous goddess Paraśurāma is bound to serve, or only stays around long enough to set Paraśurāma on his path of revenge by beating her breast twenty-one times and committing *satī*.

Green explains that analysts confronted with a patient's Dead Mother complex will often experience a false sense of security when the depressive power of the Dead Mother seems to have dissipated, only to witness her return again as soon as something goes wrong in the patient's life: "[She] is a thousand-headed hydra whom one believes one has beheaded with each blow; whereas only in fact one of its heads has been struck off. Where then is the beast's neck?" (1986, 158). This image suggests not only Paraśurāma's hacking off the thousand arms of Kārtavīrya, the source of the king's power, but also the subsequent repetitive murdering of the Kṣatriyas.

An analysand unable to resolve the Dead Mother complex, writes Green, "will encounter the inability to love, not only because of ambivalence, but because his love is still mortgaged to the dead mother. The subject is rich but he can give nothing in spite of his generosity, for he does not reap enjoyment from it" (156). Other writers have commented on Paraśurāma's negative personality traits.[16] He is irascible, depressed, quick to anger, slow to forgive, and in almost all myths, without a wife or consort. And unlike the other human *avatāras*, Paraśurāma does not return to Viṣṇu's heaven after his work is over, but wanders on the earth in eternal exile, undying and alone.

Arguing against a Kleinian object-relations interpretation of his theory, Green denies that the Dead Mother complex is a function of the withdrawal of the mother's breast. It is instead a previously unexamined paradigm structurally analogous to, but qualitatively different from, the Oedipus complex. "The solution is to be found," he writes, "in the prototype of the Oedipus complex, in the symbolic matrix which allows for its construction. Then the dead mother complex delivers its secret: it is the fantasy of the primal scene" (158). In Freud's famous analysis of the Wolf Man, he argues that the primal scene is a real event, now distorted, that the patient witnessed at some point. But Green insists that the primal scene is a fantasy, a projection of an event that necessarily happened before the patient was even born.

In the Paraśurāma story, as we have already noted, the fantasy of the primal scene in which the child witnesses the mother participating in a sexual experience of some kind appears in two very different but complementary forms. The first is a totally de-eroticized sex act: Jamadagni's mother's ingestion of the *caru* to conceive Paraśurāma, with Paraśurāma's grandmother representing his mother. The *kṣatra*—Paraśurāma's rival and the object of Reṇukā's mourning—is transformed into a harmless seminal substance, devoid of sexual threat. But the mother nevertheless rejects the idea of Paraśurāma, asking that his birth be deferred—asking not to be his mother, even with him already in her womb.

The second version of the primal scene takes place at the river, where Reṇukā experiences arousal in spite of herself in the presence of an aggressive or sexually powerful male. Here the *kṣatra* has been invested with a large amount of libidinal energy and transformed into a hypermasculine Kṣatriya. As we have already seen, though the *Mahābhārata* distinguishes between the bathing *gandharva* prince Citraratha and Kārtavīrya, the destroyer of the *āśrama,* other versions, under the influence of the myth's internal logic, have collapsed the two figures into one. And as we have already seen, in one Tamil case, Kārtavīrya replaces Paraśurāma as Reṇukā's son after the monstrous resurrection. In her studies of the goddess cults of Tamil Nadu, where the triple connection is made between Kārtavīrya, the Buffalo Demon slain by the goddess, and the seducer at the river, Biardeau observes that "it is not unfitting to recall that the common enemy of Reṇukā and Jamadagni is

Ārjuna Kārtavīrya, king of the marshes in his capital at Māhiṣmatī and that the seducer Buffalo . . . is also fond of water" (2004, 211–12).

The analysand in the midst of the Dead Mother complex is faced with ambivalence: As much as he wants to restore the Dead Mother to life, he knows that if she is alive again, there is a good chance she will go away and leave him. He can choose to have her either present but dead or absent but alive. Here the myth diverges into two traditions, each playing out one of these two imperfect options. The first, having the mother present but dead, runs through the body of myths associated with goddess temples where Reṇukā is worshipped as a goddess and Paraśurāma acts as a guardian deity to his monstrously revived mother with an Outcaste's head. In the goddess-worshipping temples of South India, it is Reṇukā who is the deity that receives worship while Paraśurāma is relegated to a subservient status, sometimes given a smaller shrine outside of the main temple. In the myths and legends associated with these temples, Paraśurāma is allowed to keep his mother alive, but must also pay a price. No longer his loving mother, Reṇukā is now a fearsome and bloodthirsty goddess, or just a pot. In the form of Pōttu Rāja-Pōrmaṉṉaṉ, a temple guardian deity to whom he is connected in Andhra Pradesh, Paraśurāma is a figure of significantly smaller stature than the goddess, and is sometimes represented as a *liṅgam,* which is this case seems to represent castration rather than sexual potency. Though Paraśurāma is made to surrender his sexuality and power to be with her, the mother he knew no longer has even the same face. As we have already seen, Paraśurāma's permanent celibate status leads the epic tradition in Maharashtra to pair him with Reṇukā the same way that Kṛṣṇa is paired with Rādhā and Rāma with Sītā when assigning female consorts or wives to the human *avatāras*, granting the matricidal son his wish to be united with his mother (Karve 1932, 18).

The second option, having the mother absent but alive, is associated with the epic and the Purāṇas, where Paraśurāma lives out the rest of his endless lifespan in seclusion on Mount Mahendra. The *Mahābhārata* does not tell us about Reṇukā's final death or about what she does after Jamadagni is murdered and Paraśurāma goes on his varṇicidal rampage. She may have stayed behind in the forest with her other sons who had refused to kill her (but were mysteriously absent when their father needed protecting), but she is not mentioned again in any of the post-varṇicide stories of Paraśurāma. We must conclude that Paraśurāma, after choosing not to return as a sexually and physically diminished guardian to his mother's living corpse, never sees her again. By renouncing her physical presence, he can maintain the fantasy that she is still living the second life that he (through Jamadagni's power to raise the dead) granted to his mother after decapitating her. In the *Mahābhārata*, he renounces the company of not just his mother but of all women, living a life of taciturn isolation with only his mysterious companion Akṛtavraṇa and the occasional pilgrim for fellowship.

Although it is never mentioned again after the fact and is supposedly undone through Jamadagni's ascetic power, Paraśurāma's decapitation and subsequent resurrection of Reṇukā epitomizes their relationship. We can easily imagine that after he chops her head off, Reṇukā is well and truly dead and that her "resurrection" is a fantasy. After the matricide episode, there is no more meaningful interaction between Paraśurāma and his mother other than her command to go and seek vengeance, but accepting her death and his guilt is outside of the realm of possibility. Faced with the choice between surrendering his masculinity and debasing himself before her grotesquely "living corpse" on the one hand and fleeing into isolation to pretend his mother is alive but far away on the other, the epic Paraśurāma chooses the latter. It is a lonely path, but one that allows him to keep his fantasy and his status as an (erstwhile) *avatāra*.

## Conclusion

In the epigraphs that begin this chapter there are two questions. One (*What shall I ask?*) is posed by the alluring yet innocent daughter of Herodias identified in subsequent traditions as Salome. The other (*What is this I carry in my hands?*) is asked by Agave, the bewildered mother of King Pentheus, her mind gradually clearing after a prolonged state of Dionysian ecstasy. The answer to both of these questions is "a severed human head," that of John the Baptist for Salome and that of her son Pentheus for Agave. John the Baptist's head will come on a silver plate for Herodias to contemplate smilingly in an image immortalized by Titian and later, Aubrey Beardsley. Pentheus's head will be the source of Agave's dawning, horrified realization that she and her fellow maenads have torn her son apart while in the throes of orgiastic ecstasy brought on by Dionysus, fulfilling the god's curse on the family that rejected his worship.

What kind of thing, then, is Reṇukā's severed head? Among other places, it belongs in a category with the enigmatic severed head that figures so prominently in Vedic myth and ritual (see Heesterman 1985, 45–58; Dange 1991–92). But it is also, like the heads of John and Pentheus, the answer to a question posed by the Paraśurāma story. When he chops off his mother's head, is Paraśurāma submitting to the law of Jamadagni as Lacan would have it or renouncing his special relationship with his mother to submit to a polymorphous mother goddess, following Kurtz? Does Paraśurāma lose his place on Mother Earth because he has renounced his earthly mother? Is his raising of the land from the sea to replace the earth from which he has been exiled a repetition of his resurrecting his dead mother? The unspeaking head lies on the ground in mute reply. We might as well add Kristeva's questions to the mix:

> Does decapitation become the emblem of social and historical division? Or rather the brutal admission of our internal fractures, of that intimate instability that prompts movements, but also crises? Self-perception of a fundamental imbalance, of that "dark wood" that is the speaking being, divided and unreconciled? (2012, 105)

Looking at the last three elements of the matricide micromyth, this chapter began with the fate of Paraśurāma's brothers, who resist the order of their father and, if they are not cursed by him either to die or be rendered dumb, choose to become renouncers. Following psychoanalytic understandings of matricide as a developmental moment, we examined variations of the disobedient sons' consequences suffered in Vaiṣṇava *Purāṇas* and South Indian temple legends. Next, we addressed the matricide itself by returning to "The Story of the Axe" and adding comparative material from Śaiva myths of Tibet and Tamil Nadu.

We next examined Paraśurāma's struggle with Śiva's adopted son Gaṇeśa and compared the mythology of the two figures. We then analyzed a critique of Paraśurāma's matricide in the myth of Cirakāri, another son who is also ordered to decapitate his mother, but saves her life by spending so long considering what to do that his father has a chance to change his mind and withdraw the command. After that we turned to traditions from Maharashtra and Tamil Nadu in which Reṇukā is identified with the headless goddesses Chinnamastā and Lajjāgaurī and saw what new readings are possible when the headless mother becomes the focal point of the Paraśurāma myth. Finally, we analyzed the decapitation of Reṇukā through the lens of Green's Dead Mother complex.

As we have seen in this chapter, Reṇukā's head, the axe that frees it from her neck, and the obedient son who swings it are all deeply embedded in the other themes of the Paraśurāma cycle (especially mixed birth and varṇicide), in diachronic tensions of caste and class, in synchronic tensions encoded in ritual, and in the deep psychic structures that comprise the " 'dark wood' that is the speaking being." In the next chapter, we will follow the widening circle of Paraśurāma's violent relation to the world in his genocidal or varṇicidal campaign against the Kṣatriyas.

4

# Varṇicide I

## *The Extermination of the Kṣatriyas and Its Aftermath*

Twenty-one times, Lord, he cleared the earth of Kṣatriyas . . .

—*Mahābhārata* 3.117.9

Kill them all and let God sort them out.

—Unofficial Vietnam-era U.S. military slogan[1]

Paraśurāma's varṇicidal campaign against the Kṣatriyas appears in the *Mahābhārata* thirteen times. The sage Ugraśravas is the first narrator to tell the story in the epic's first book, the Ādi Parvan. After arriving at the Naimiṣa Forest and encountering a group of sages, Ugraśravas begins to recount his travels. When he describes a visit to Samantapañcaka ("Surrounded by Five [Lakes]")—later to be known as Kurukṣetra, the site of the epic's climactic battle—his audience requests more details about these five holy bodies of water.[2] The sage responds with a truncated story that gives a brief (just two couplets) but bloody description of Paraśurāma's varṇicidal annihilation of the Kṣatriyas that serves as prologue for the point at which his story begins in earnest.

To set the scene, he describes the Bhārgava hero, maddened with rage (*krodhamūrcchitaḥ*) and standing in the middle of the five giant pools of royal blood he has created. He offers the blood to his ancestors, who (unnecessarily, since he has quit killing Kṣatriyas by this point) calm him down and decree that these five lakes will be holy sites of pilgrimage. They will also, as Ugraśravas adds, be the site of the war between the Pāṇḍavas and Kauravas, which he places at the turn of the Dvāpara Yuga, a full age after Paraśurāma's varṇicide (*MBh* 1.2.1–12).[3]

The second and third references in the Ādi Parvan are concerned exclusively with the after-effects of the varṇicide rather than the act itself and seem to take for granted the audience's familiarity with Paraśurāma's main story, which has yet to be told. In the second telling Vaiśampāyana tells Janamejaya how the Brahmins repopulated the earth with noble Kṣatriyas after Paraśurāma's varṇicide by having purely procreative intercourse with the Kṣatriya widows (1.58.5–10). And in the third version it is the patriarch Bhīṣma who spins the tale, again skipping to the end and the repopulation of the Kṣatriyas on earth, telling his mother the story of the Brahmins impregnating the Kṣatriya widows in order to justify his own decision to bring in a Brahmin to impregnate his widowed and childless sisters-in-law since he himself has taken a vow of celibacy (1.98.1–5).

In all three tellings, the Ādi Parvan situates the story of Paraśurāma in the legendary past while stressing the connection of those events to the present. The three narrators who mention the story, which they all consider familiar enough not to tell in full, connect it to the origin of the Kṣatriya clans who form the major players in the epic, to the unusual crisis of succession that leads to war between them, and to the battlefield on which the war is fought.

In book two, the Sabhā Parvan, the narrator of the varṇicide story is Paraśurāma's fellow *avatāra* Kṛṣṇa, who, like the previous narrators, is concerned only with the aftermath.[4] His passing mention of Paraśurāma takes place in the course of one of his early Machiavellian political maneuvers, specifically on the occasion of his speech convincing Yudhiṣṭhira to mount an unprovoked attack on the Magadhan king Jarāsaṃdha and thereby establish political and military dominance over the region. Unlike Bhīṣma and Vaiśampāyana, Kṛṣṇa does not ascribe Brahmin origins to the present Kṣatriya population, but instead says they are a remnant (*avaśeṣitam*) of the Kṣatriyas that somehow escaped destruction (2.13.1–5).

In the third book, the Āraṇyaka Parvan, Paraśurāma's disciple Akṛtavraṇa tells the first of the two lengthy versions that serve as bookends to the Pāṇḍava-Kaurava conflict. Akṛtavraṇa tells the story to Yudhiṣṭhira, when the latter is wandering through the forests in search of wisdom to carry into the war to come. After hearing the story of his varṇicide, the future king meets Paraśurāma in person and receives his blessing (*MBh* 3.115–117).[5]

Book twelve, the Śānti Parvan, following the conclusion of the war, contains the second lengthy version of the varṇicide. The context for this telling is much different from the Pāṇḍavas' prewar exile in the forest. After eighteen days of battle and mass casualties on both sides, the Pāṇḍava princes cannot help but see that theirs is a pyrrhic victory and the kingdom they have won is now little more than piles of bones and ashes. It is once more Yudhiṣṭhira who hears the story of Paraśurāma's varṇicide, this time from Kṛṣṇa again. The Śānti Parvan paints Kārtavīrya as a righteous king rather than a violent thief and even blames the abduction of the calf on his evil-minded sons rather than on him. The narrative also somewhat mitigates Paraśurāma's violent actions. While he does make a vow to wipe out the warrior class and he does go on a killing spree to avenge his father's murder, Paraśurāma only slaughters a few thousand Kṣatriyas before retiring to do penance. But after a millennium passes, an arrogant Kṣatriya named Parāvasu, grandson of the warrior-sage Viśvāmitra, begins to proclaim Paraśurāma an idle boaster who never fulfilled his vow to wipe out the Kṣatriyas. Thus provoked, Paraśurāma comes out of retirement and slaughters the Kṣatriyas for twenty-one generations (starting, presumably, with the gadfly Parāvasu himself). He does not even spare the unborn in their mother's wombs, echoing Aśvatthāman's brutal massacre of the Pāṇḍavas in the Sauptika Parvan (12.48.7–12.49).

The first mention of the varṇicide in the Critical Edition uses the phrase "having destroyed the entire *kṣatra*" (1.2.4).[6] The word used for the Kṣatriyas is the collective *kṣatra,* and the verb is *utsada,* "to annihilate." In Akṛtavraṇa's lengthy narration in 3.115–117, he uses the phrase unique to and emblematic of Paraśurāma's story, "thrice-seven times he made the earth devoid of Kṣatriyas."[7] The term "thrice seven" is used in Paraśurāma stories throughout the epic to denote the number twenty-one instead of the standard *ekaviṃśati,* which suggests some significance to the numbers three and seven.[8] It is possible that the epic authors used "thrice seven" for "twenty-one" as a poetic convention like the lofty "four score and seven years ago" that begins Lincoln's Gettysburg Address instead of the more prosaic "eighty-seven years ago." But Dejenne ascribes more importance to the phrase—found throughout the Vedic liturgy of the Horse Sacrifice and the *Atharva Veda,* especially in relation to Śiva's warrior band the Maruts—hypothesizing that the number acts as "a deep symbol, a key of [the] understanding of Rāma Jāmadagnya's myth and perhaps of the whole MBh because it would strengthen its own claim to be seen as the fifth Veda" (2009a, 76). It is suggestive that in the *Baudhāyana Dharma Sutra,* the term "thrice seven" is used to denote the number of times one should scrub articles in order to purify them after they have come into contact with urine, feces, blood, semen, or a corpse (1.8.48).

Outside of the epic, the varṇicide episode is retold again and again, notably in the *Brahmāṇḍa*, *Bhagavāta*, *Viṣṇudharmottara*, *Brahma*, and *Padma Purāṇas*. The actual methods that Paraśurāma employs to dispatch the Kṣatriyas vary. Sometimes he uses the axe (*paraśu*)—now a battle-axe instead of the humble wood-chopping axe he almost certainly must have used to decapitate his mother—that gives him the name "Paraśurāma," a name that never even appears in the *Mahābhārata*.[9] In the *Viṣṇudharmottara* he carries the *cāparatna,* the jewel among bows, which identifies him as a Pāñcarātra adept, since Pāñcarātrins use the metaphor of archery to describe their practice of yoga as "the bow and arrow by which the Pāñcarātra adept reached the target of the transcendent Viṣṇu by piercing through the sun and the moon" (Inden 2000, 57). In the *Srimanmahābhāratam,* based on the South Indian recensions of the epic, the sage Nārada explains that Paraśurāma hangs one thousand Kṣatriyas, drowns another thousand, smashes the teeth of another thousand, cuts off another thousand's noses and ears, and kills another thousand with smoke inhalation (7.70.16; Visweswara 263).

In this chapter, we will trace the theme of Paraśurāma's destruction of the Kṣatriya class as it develops from its beginning in the *Mahābhārata* to the highly theologized and somewhat sanitized forms in takes in the literature of the Pāñcarātra sect. This development is to a large degree the processes of transforming Paraśurāma from a Śaiva figure to a hybrid Vaiṣṇava-Śaiva figure and mitigating the violence of his actions. We will also see that during the same time period in which the Pāñcarātrins are mitigating Paraśurāma's violence, the Jaina tradition is emphasizing it as a warning against indulging one's wrath (*krodha*). Framing this analysis will be a broader discussion about the dialectical relationship of myth and history when it comes to understanding our human capacity for violence, especially insofar as it is aided by today's technology, and how that dialectic shapes our modern readings of myth.

## Scenes from the Bhārgava-Haihaya Feud

When Kārtavīrya shows up at Jamadagni's hermitage demanding hospitality, it is probably not by accident. Kārtavīrya's clan, the Haihayas, already have a long history with the Bhārgava Brahmins before the Paraśurāma cycle even begins.[10] The *Mahābhārata* relates the story of another of Paraśurāma's ancestors, Aurva, which Van Buitenen has argued serves as the model for the

Paraśurāma myth (1975, 194). In the Aurva myth, the Bhārgavas are originally *purohitas*, family priests or chaplains, for the lineage of Kārtavīrya. When the royal family falls on hard times and approaches the Bhārgavas for money, the Brahmins bury their wealth underground and plead poverty.[11] Upon discovering the deception, one of the Kṣatriyas leads a massacre in which all the Bhārgavas are killed except one pregnant woman, from whose thigh Aurva is born. When he emerges from his mother's thigh, Aurva's splendor blinds the Kṣatriyas. After they regain their sight, Aurva vows vengeance and begins generating inner heat in order to destroy the entire world.

To stop him from doing so, the spirits of the murdered Bhārgavas visit Aurva and explain that they had engineered their own slaughter at the hands of the Kṣatriyas because they were tired of life on earth, intentionally burying their wealth where their impoverished patrons would discover it in order to provoke their wrath. The Kṣatriyas, they explain, are not to blame, and the massacre is actually an elaborate staging of some ancient Indian version of "suicide by cop" in which the Brahmins, despite appearances to the contrary, are the true masters of their own lives and deaths, a common Bhārgava theme. After the ghosts of his elders finally convince him not to carry out his plan Aurva casts his pent-up rage into the sea, where it becomes the Submarine Fire (*MBh* 1.169–71).

The mythic Haihaya dynasty, which is said to be descended from the first man Manu, comes up again and again in the Bhārgava myth cycle. In *Jaiminiya Brāḥmaṇa* 3.120–29 the Bhārgava sage Cyavana acts as a priest for the Haihaya patriarch Saryāti (Doniger 1985, 64–66). *Atharva Veda* 5.19 suggests that the Haihaya ancestor Vitāhavya takes Bḥrgu's cow and is punished. The hymn's themes are strikingly reminiscent of the Paraśurāma cycle and the Viśvāmitra story: when she is attacked, the cow becomes "eight-footed, four-eyed, four-eared, four-jawed, two-mouthed, two-tongued [and] dispels the rule of the oppressor of the Brahmin" (5.19.7) The hymn goes on: "That (kingdom) surely she swamps, as water a leaking ship; misfortune strikes that kingdom, in which they injure a Brahmin (5.19.8)." It describes the fate of ninety-nine kings cast off the earth for harming Brahmins (5.19.11) and concludes, "The tears which have rolled from (the eyes of) the oppressed (Brahmin), as he laments, these very ones, Oppressor of Brahmins, the gods did assign to you as your share of water" (5.19.13).[12]

In *Mahābhārata* 13.31 Yudhiṣṭhira asks Bhīṣma to recount the story of how Vitāhavya, like Viśvāmitra, attains Brahmin-hood. While Viśvāmitra becomes a Brahmin through millennia spent in austerities, the Haihaya king Vitāhavya becomes a Brahmin through the power of Bhṛgu's word. When his enemy Pratardana sacks his capital and defeats his army, Vitāhavya comes to Bhṛgu's *āśrama* and asks for sanctuary. Bhṛgu agrees, and when Pratardana tracks Vitāhavya to Bhṛgu's *āśrama* and asks the sage to give up the king, Bhṛgu replies, "There is no Kṣatriya here, only Brahmins" (13.31.49). By the power of Bhṛgu's unerring speech, Vitāhavya is at that moment transformed into a Brahmin. He goes on to become the progenitor of the branch of the Bhārgava line from which comes Śaunaka, the Brahmin whose sacrifice provides the epic's frame story.

There is another Paraśurāma story that picks up on this same narrative structure and also employs the theme of the prince magically adopted by a Brahmin. In the eleventh- or twelfth-century *Mūṣikavaṃśa*, the chronicle of the Mūṣika ("Rat") Dynasty, a queen (possibly the wife of Paraśurāma's archenemy Kārtavīrya) hides in a cave on a holy mountain where she gives birth to a prince during Paraśurāma's varṇicide. Later, Paraśurāma visits the mountain to perform a sacrifice that requires the assistance of a Kṣatriya boy. The spirit of the mountain sends the young prince to help him and after the rite is complete, Paraśurāma installs him on the throne of Kolam, where he refounds the Haihaya dynasty that eventually reconquers Kārtavīrya's old capital of Māhiṣmatī (Vielle 2002, 351).

The Bhārgava-Haihaya relationship is fraught with tension, serving as a synecdoche for the larger Brahmin-Kṣatriya relationship and its internal instantiation in the burning kiln of Paraśurāma's soul. But no amount of background narrative really explains the explosive violence of the twenty-one-fold destruction of the Kṣatriyas. This is an old story, couched in narrative conventions and epic imagery, but it has also always seemed to me that it overflows those conventions and supersaturates those images in a way that seems very modern. And as we shall see, the contemporary uses of Paraśurāma and his near-double Aśvatthāman speak to the attraction they hold for those trying to address genocide and other forms of mass extermination in their own day.

## Varṇicide and Genocide: From Limited to Limitless Violence

Now we can return to a set of questions I formulated in the introduction to address changes in an individual variant—a later version of the myth that we can locate in a time and a place and connect to a community of mythmakers and an audience. The first question to ask is: In the case of a myth whose core narrative remains relatively stable, has the community of readers or hearers changed to the point that they would derive new meanings from it that would have been foreign to its original historical context? By way of an answer, I will note that in the secondary literature, scholars (myself included) have commonly referred to Paraśurāma's actions against the Kṣatriyas with the decidedly negative term "genocide." Goldman alone uses the term eighteen times in *Gods, Priests, and Warriors*, his study of the myths of the Bhārgava clan.[13] None of these scholars feel the need to explain, qualify, or justify their use of the term, raising the question: Why does "genocide," a word not used in any language before 1944 and intended to refer to documented violence perpetrated by human actors, seem, for me and many others, like such an obvious choice to describe a mythical event that also happens to be utterly impossible in human terms?

This was a question I addressed when this work was in its earlier incarnation as my dissertation, "Headless Mothers, Magic Cows, and Lakes of Blood: The Paraśurāma Cycle in the *Mahābhārata* and Beyond." At that time, some of my colleagues and teachers raised objections to bringing the concept of genocide into my textual analysis of Paraśurāma's campaign against the Kṣatriyas. My response then was that connecting Paraśurāma's actions to the modern idea of genocide was important, if only because so many scholars before me had referred to them using this term. I was only somewhat interested in connecting Paraśurāma's story to a historical mass extermination or in establishing that anyone in India had ever used the myth to justify the attempt to eliminate an entire group of people in the way that some argue the legend of Prince Lazar's martyrdom at the Battle of Kosovo in 1389 was used by twentieth-century Serbian nationalists (see Anzulovic 1999; Žižek and Hamza 2013). I was far more interested in understanding what lay behind the repeated and always unexamined use of this loaded and anachronistic term to refer to the twenty-one-fold elimination of the warrior class, which then led me to think about anachronism and the study of ancient narratives of violence in a more general way.

In *Religion, Empire & Torture: The Case of Achaemenian Persia, with a Postscript on Abu Ghraib*, Bruce Lincoln concludes that the ideology of the Achaemenian Empire (550–330 BCE) and the rhetoric surrounding the second Iraq War (2003–2011 CE) share the themes of "ethical dualism, a theology of election, and a sense of soteriological mission." He also acknowledges the near impossibility of analyzing the ancient Persian material without seeing how it provides commentary on current events. "As careful readers will, no doubt, have recognized," he writes, "my anguish and outrage concerning the American imperial adventure in Iraq frequently bubble close to the surface" (2007, 97).

Another relevant case of the question of anachronism in the study of ancient texts can be found among American Virgil scholars in the 1960s, with Adam Parry's "The Two Voices of Virgil's Aeneid" (1963), Wendell Clausen's "An Interpretation of the Aeneid" (1964), and Michael Putnam's *The Poetry of the Aeneid* (1965) representing the so-called Harvard School, which discredited the triumphalist reading of the epic and favored a pessimistic view colored by the growing protest movement against the Vietnam War.[14] Old-guard scholars disdained the scholarship as anachronistic, but Richard F. Thomas argues that the prevailing "optimistic" view of Virgil

> is likewise a political and sociological construction, and is potentially no more exempt from the creative manipulations and transformations of reception than the non-Augustan Virgil. . . . Experiences other than Vietnam, such as French and English imperialism, Prussian expansionism, Italian and German nationalism, fascism and Nazism all play a role in the construction. (2004, xii)

As thought-provoking as the above cases of interpretative anachronism are, in the end I introduced the neologism "varṇicide" to replace "genocide," on the grounds that the latter term actually clouded the waters and obscured the true form of the myth's directed violence. In truth, varṇicide does seem to me to be a more precise way of describing the slaughter of the Kṣatriyas. Since its etymology comes partly from Sanskrit, it better situates the story in the Sanskritic-Brahminical context. It also illustrates the close connection of the motif with the themes of matricide and Paraśurāma's mixed birth, all of which are related to *varṇa* issues. As Brian K. Smith has convincingly demonstrated, the term *varṇa* best represents the central organizing principle of the Vedic cosmos (1994, 7–8). *Varṇa* is the form of group identity that supersedes all others for the Brahmin authors of the epic. And it is *varṇa,* not lineage or "race," that is finally the deciding factor in who finds themselves at the wrong end of Paraśurāma's axe.

That is not to say that mythmakers do not contest the taxonomic supremacy of *varṇa*. The Bhārgavas' relationship with *varṇa* is nothing if not complex and ambiguous, as we have seen. The mythology of the Bhārgavas as a whole frequently seeks to negotiate the competing identities of clan and *varṇa*. Keeping with his argument that the Bhārgavas' customs were at odds with the Brahminical mainstream at a time when they were attempting to become mainstream Brahmins themselves, Goldman goes on to suggest that they therefore had to make major changes in their "family values" to gain acceptance as a true Brahmin clan. "The [Paraśurāma] complex is the end result not of a real war or a campaign of genocide," he writes, "but of a mythic tradition of Bhārgava-kṣatriya tension, centering around a struggle for status and a strong uncertainty as to the proper varṇa of the Bhṛgus" (1977, 143).[15]

One reason I keep returning to the problem of nomenclature is the lingering (and, it must be said, rancorous) controversy occasioned by the publication of Sheldon Pollock's essay "Deep Orientalism? Notes on Sanskrit and Power beyond the Raj."[16] Most salient to the question of scholars' understanding of Paraśurāma's "genocide," especially when considered alongside the related theme of the subsequent reinvigoration of the *kṣatra,* is Pollock's claim in the essay that German Indological thought included "proposals for a eugenics program in India (calling for a revivification through racial planning of the debilitated South Asian Aryan stock)" (1993, 83).

But it was not only the Germans who proposed such a course of action. In the case of British colonialism, argues Joan Leopold, the idea that Indian Āryan culture is a degraded form of the civilizing force that somehow maintained its integrity in Europe "implied that all British attempts at reform in India would be futile unless the racial character of the population were changed, that true reform meant racial reform: the extermination of the non-Aryan population, the reinforcement of the caste system . . . or the encouragement of intermarriage between Indian and European Aryans" (1974, 594–95). This imperial to-do list is striking in its parallels with the actions taken by Paraśurāma in the *Mahābhārata*: Extermination of Kṣatriyas (3.117.60, 12.48.10, etc.), reinstatement of division between classes (12.49.60–61), and intermarriage to reinvigorate the stock (1.58.5, 1.98.4).[17]

The two examples above suggest ways in which readers familiar with contemporary scholarship of postcolonial India may have been subtly pushed to draw the comparison between Paraśurāma's actions and genocide, but they hardly answer the question of whether it is a useful comparison to make.

At this point, it will be useful to look at Scot Straus's 2001 typology of definitions of genocide. After describing the origin of the term in Rafael Lemkin's 1944 project to classify the extraordinary war crimes of the Nazis against Jews, Slavs, and others, Straus argues:

> From its inception, then, genocide has been an empirical, moral, legal, and political concept. To one person, "genocide" means evil and demands preventive or punitive action by a government; to another, "genocide" carries a circumscribed juridical meaning, while to still others it designates a specific type of mass violence. These

> wide-ranging and powerful dimensions—and the relatively small number of terms that connote unspeakable atrocity—ironically have made "genocide" an attractive concept. But these multiple dimensions also have made for a conceptual muddle. (2001, 359)

Straus gives five dimensions as bases for comparing definitions of genocide: "(1) whether intentional group annihilation is a definition's core idea; (2) how intent is conceptualized; (3) how the mode of annihilation is defined; (4) how the agent of annihilation is defined; and (5) how the victim of annihilation is defined" (2001, 361). Since it would be nonsensical to speak of preventing, punishing, or prosecuting Paraśurāma's extermination of the Kṣatriyas, we can safely assume that those who refer to it as "genocide" are doing so to designate "a specific type of mass violence," to wit, the annihilation of a specified group of people. Of the fifteen commonly used definitions Straus analyzes, seven have "intentional group annihilation" as their core idea. Six of them define this targeted group with some form of the word "ethnicity," which presents some difficulty for Paraśurāma's case, since, according to Pollock,

> if we accept the current scholarly opinion on the elements required for constituting an ethnic community—principally, a common proper name, a myth of common ancestry, shared memories of a common past, and a sense of solidarity—we are forced to conclude that ethnicity as the term is presently understood in social science was hardly prevalent in premodern South Asia, if it can be said to have existed at all. (2006, 511)[18]

But if there are no readily identifiable notions of ethnicity in the epic worldview, there certainly is *varṇa.* And while it may be misleading to equate Kṣatriyas with an ethnic group, a number of castes claim descent from the surviving remnant of Paraśurāma's extermination and they would also seem to possess all the elements of an ethnic community listed by Pollock. Among these self-proclaimed degraded Kṣatriyas are the illustrious Kāyasthas of Bengal, the Kalitas of Assam, the Samanthars of Kerala, the Bhavsars, the Khatris, and the Telugu Perike, whose name derives from their claim to be "descendants of coward or runaway [Pirki] kshatriyas in the face of persecution by Paraśurāma" (Choudhary 2010, 299). The Bappura family, also known as the Bali *vaṃśa,* ruled over the western Indian Chalukyan feudatory of Kiṣukāḍ and traced their own ancestry back to the Kṣatriyas who hid out from Paraśurāma's varṇicidal rage in the caves of Mount Kiṣkindhā (Janaki 1966, 71). Apparently, an association with the Paraśurāma myth was worth the stigma of being descended from Kṣatriyas who cowered in fear at a Brahmin's wrath.[19]

Besides the issue of ethnicity and its presence or absence in the world of the epic, another problem to consider is the ambiguous conceptual and historical relationship between genocide and total war. Leading genocide scholar Leo Kuper argues that there is an increasingly blurred boundary between the two phenomena, making the case that "[t]he changing nature of warfare, with a movement toward total warfare, and the technological means for the annihilation of large populations, create a situation conducive to genocidal conflict" (quoted in Flynn and Strozier 1996, 77). However, other historians and sociologists disagree about what kind of kind of distinction we should make between these two categories and how they relate to one another.

Succumbing themselves to this terminological slippage, scholars and interpreters of the *Mahābhārata* have used the term "genocide" not only to refer to Paraśurāma's actions but also to the great battle at Kurukṣetra or other episodes of mass destruction. Meera Uberoi's modern retelling of the epic has Kṛṣṇa announcing to Dhṛtarāṣṭra, "I'm here to prevent genocide and request an amicable settlement," during his embassy to the blind king's court (2005, 277). In Ramesh Menon's novelistic adaptation, Kṛṣṇa tells Dhṛtarāṣṭra's wife Gāndhārī, "You and your husband are responsible for this genocide and you want to shift the blame to me" after the queen curses Kṛṣṇa's clan to destroy itself (2006, 461).[20]

Online commenters on Internet message boards, not known for either methodological rigor or decorum, are even more explicit in their comparisons. And for scholars, these online forums hosting emic debates and discussions about Hinduism are a good way to get a snapshot of the way Hindus are currently thinking about their narrative traditions because it gives us a chance to see members of the community talking to one another from within a shared framework without the editing and code-switching used when explaining one's religion to an outsider. Just as important, they are comparing their own understandings of the myths with those of someone else on a more or less equal footing, which is far more revealing than simply asking a *paṇḍita* to set the record straight.

Take as an example the following question posted on Quora.com in 2015 (though it is unsigned, the inclusion of the title "Lord" and the spelling "Parshuram" indicate a contemporary Hindu understanding of the deity rather than a Sanskritized scholarly one):

> Was Lord Parshuram a racist as he killed the entire Kshatriya clan? If he wanted to avenge his father's death, why didn't he stop after killing the people who were actually responsible for his father's death?

Ten answers, all (except for one anonymous post) from commenters with Indian names and all using recognizable Indian idioms, are posted in response to the question. Here are some of them, with some misspellings corrected but internet typing conventions and alternate spellings left unchanged.[21]

The first (viewed more than eleven thousand times) answers the question by appealing to Paraśurāma's mission as an *avatāra* and the authority of the television version of the *Viṣṇu Purāṇa*, from which it includes a video still of Paraśurāma.

> He did not [have] any enmity with the Kshatriyas but when Khartavirya Arjun tormented his family members, stole cows from the Ashram and Khartavirya Arjun's sons killed his father Rishi Janmadagni he could not tolerate it. During those days other powerful Kshetriyas were present but no one tried to stop this injustice which Lord Parshuram and his family members were facing. It was not only Parshuram but also many Bramhins were facing the similar situations, many Bramhins were being exploited by the Kshatriyas of their regions. Hence Lord Parshuram decided to free the people from the exploitation of the Kshatriyas. But in this act he also killed many innocent Kshatriyas and thus destroying many of the clans.
>
> We should not forget that Lord Parshuram was an incarnation of Lord Vishnu and he was born with a purpose i.e, to punish the egoistic Kshatriyas of his time who exploited the other sects of people of the society during those days. His mother Renuka was a Kshetriya. Parshuram was a disciple of Lord Shiva who never does partiality with any creature on Earth. He was the guru to Bhisma, Drona and Karna and Bhisma was a Kshatriya as well.
>
> He was also the only avataar of Lord Vishnu who had met with other 2 great avataars of Vishnu, Rama and Krishna respectively. Watch Vishnu Puran episodes for further details.

The next author gives a long reply that first recounts Paraśurāma's slaying of Reṇukā before turning to the "riddle" of Paraśurāma, appealing to a tradition that associates Paraśurāma with Rāvaṇa and explains the number twenty-one as the number of sons of Kārtavīrya that are killed, not the number of generations of Kṣatriyas.

> **Understanding Riddle Of Parshuram and his character.**
>
> First question that arise in a mind when it frees itself from the concept of Sanatan is this. Did Renuka deserve death? After all she had just seen one person. Secondly why did Jamadagni ask his sons to kill his wife? Couldn't he do it himself? Also isn't it against hindu tradition that a woman shouldn't be hurt?
>
> Parshuram, on death of his father kills the entire Kshatriya race as the brahmans claims. Why couldn't he just bring back his father to life in the same way his father brought back his mother? Jamadagni was in possession of knowledge to bring the dead back to life. That's what helped him to bring back his dead wife back to life. Now the question is that didn't Jamadagni think his sons especially Parshurama, the incarnation of lord himself, worthy enough to be taught this skill?
>
> Parshuram came back to kill all the Kshatriyas 21 times **(Which in reality is the number of sons of Kartivirya he killed).** Doesn't that mean that he failed at least 20 times? How and why did the incarnation of Lord himself fail 20 times in front of Mortals?
>
> After defeating the Kshatriyas, why did Parshuram choose to donate the land that he won to the Brahmins only especially when Brahmins were not the ruling caste? Why didn't he donate it to Ravan who was his friend and also a king and a great devotee of lord Shiva?
>
> **The more one studies Parshurama the more one gets baffled. The only purpose of such stories is to impose the supremacy of Brahmins over the other castes. Otherwise they serve no purpose at all.** [bold type in original]

The last answer we will look at, unlike the previous two, directly addresses the issue of racism, rephrasing "race" as "verna" [*varṇa*], but is completely contradictory in doing so. The commenter begins by describing Paraśurāma's mixed *varṇa* as if it were the answer to why he does what he does but concludes that it matters not at all.

> Before his birth itself Parushuram was supposed to be born as Kshatriya . . . but his mother did a small mistake by confusingly hugging one tree instead of another. So it was clearly told that though he was born as a Brahmin he will behave like a legendary kshatriya.
>
> His father was murdered without any reason by kshatriyas so he took an oath to kill all kshatriyas and he encircled entire earth 21 times & killed all kshatriyas.
>
> Great people don't have anything to do with verna.

His last statement is so ambiguous that it is hard to tell exactly what he intends. Do great people have nothing to do with *varṇa* in the sense that it does not define them, that they transcend it through their greatness? Or does the author mean that it is beneath them to consider another's *varṇa*, that they are metaphorically "color-blind" to the *varṇa* of those around them?

Before moving on, there is one other question on Quora.com that demands attention. Posted in 2014, it asks, "Is the act of Parshuram killing all the Kshatriya clan valid? If so, why was Hitler wrong if he killed so many Jews?" The spelling of Paraśurāma is the same as in the other question, but it looks less like a real query than a provocation (possibly from within the tradition) against Hindus, forcing them to defend the absurd like Clarence Darrow confronting Biblical literalist William Jennings Bryan with Joshua 10:13 on the witness stand at the Scopes Monkey Trial.[22] It attracts far fewer readers and only three short and dismissive replies.[23]

Why do scholars, novelists, and ordinary Hindus call Paraśurāma's campaign genocide and bring in anachronistic and foreign ideas about race and racism to understand it? Does the absence in premodern India of ethnicity, a central criterion in most definitions of genocide, preclude the use of that term? Is Paraśurāma's violence qualitatively different from the requisite violence of the war? What do we make of the fact the Paraśurāma (with the exception of his mother) only kills male Kṣatriyas, while part of the horrific nature of genocide is its invocation of vulnerable people (the proverbial women and children) being killed? Even with all of these questions made explicit, the issue of genocide in the epic is as difficult as ever. Still, the ease with which the term has slipped into our modern understanding of Paraśurāma (if such a thing can be said to exist) indicates the transformations the text has undergone as a result of being read and retold in the second half of the twentieth century. The negative tone, the condemnation, in the word "genocide" is inescapable. To call Paraśurāma's actions against the Kṣatriyas "genocide" is a subtle and unacknowledged recovery of the voice of dissent in the text, made easier by the ambivalence with which the *Mahābhārata* treats the event.

## The Patron Saint of Total War

It is difficult to read the story of Paraśurāma, a young man who takes bloody and indiscriminate revenge on an entire class of people, without a chill of recognition, anachronistic though that recognition may be. We have seen far too many such wounded and enraged young men armed with guns taking their revenge on crowded theaters, schools, churches, synagogues, and mosques not to perceive a foreshadow in Paraśurāma's pitiless and inexorable extermination of the *kṣatra*. On one hand, it makes no sense to interpret Paraśurāma's actions, which belong to an ancient age even relative to the epic, in modern terms. On the other hand, although he belongs to a prior era with its own dharma, Paraśurāma is not relegated to the past. Besides being an *avatāra,* he is also a *cirañjīvin*. As such, he still sits in meditation on a mountain somewhere, and for many that view him as a form of Viṣṇu he is also always present in his images in temples and shrines throughout India.[24]

Is it cultural myopia to view Paraśurāma through a lens shaped by the Holocaust, by suicide bombers, by mass shootings? It may be more culturally myopic not to do so. On February 1, 2016, in Bihar, against a background of public violence against women, Paraśurāma's fellow *avatāra* Rāma Dāśarathi was the object of a lawsuit for his unfair treatment of his wife Sītā (see Nayar 2016). The case was the object of endless jokes on Indian social media, but there is a serious point to be made: there is not an unbridgeable gulf between the imagined past and the historical present. As Norbert Elias has observed, "the contemporary problems of a group are crucially influenced by their earlier fortunes, by their beginningless development" (1996, 19).

With this in mind, we can read Paraśurāma's story as more than a reflection of certain class anxieties in the early centuries of the first millennium CE, an expression of the conflicts inherent in the Vedic ritual cosmos, an allegory about self-control, or the righteous judgment of divine violence; we can also read it as violent fantasy that is still entertained by many and enacted by a handful in our own time.

Whatever else it may be or have been, the story of Paraśurāma is unquestionably a blueprint for a certain kind of violence that is neither duel nor war nor *crime passionel,* neither personal nor political while being both at the same time. Fulfilling his vow to rid the earth of Kṣatriyas, Paraśurāma steps out of the role of the warrior and becomes a hunter of humans. He hunts warriors, to be sure, but they may as well be unarmed for all the resistance they seem to give him. In fact, it seems less like hunting than herding—slaughtering the bulls after they have impregnated the cows and then waiting for the calves to come of age so he can do it all over again. This goes on for twenty-one generations, the text tells us.

It is also difficult to read the story of Paraśurāma without reflecting on the fact that, unlike the ancient Indian storytellers who composed it, modern readers (Indian and otherwise) live in a world where weapons exist that could easily accomplish in reality what Jamadagni's vengeful son accomplishes in myth. The *Mahābhārata* may be a product of a past era, but in a very real sense, if it has a universal message, that message is only comprehensible in the nuclear age. And if our current post-Holocaust, post-9/11, nuclear-armed worldview opens a new horizon of meaning for ancient myths of cosmic destruction, then the reverse is also true: we moderns (with all due deference to Bruno Latour's thesis that we have never been such people) frequently use ancient mythic ideas to understand the godlike power we have achieved through technology. The first three American space programs were named after Roman gods (Gemini, Mercury, Apollo); the submarine-launched nuclear ICBMs that were designed to be used in a "second strike" (allowing the United States to inflict casualties on the enemy even after its own cities and defenses have been destroyed) are named after Poseidon and his trident; India's nuclear missile is called Agni, after the god of the sacrificial fire and insatiable devourer of the Khāṇḍava forest.[25]

The notion of mythic divine violence as precursor to technologically assisted human violence is as old as the first atomic bomb tests, if we believe the apocryphal story that Robert Oppenheimer recited a verse from the *Gītā* when he witnessed the first mushroom cloud in New Mexico.[26] In ways far more significant than the rather unimaginative theory that Sanskrit descriptions of flying chariots, or *vimānas*, describe some ancient precursors to modern aircraft, mythology (and imaginative literature in general, as Jules Verne demonstrates) allows us to conceptualize things that are not yet possible to enact.[27]

Israel—another modern nation-state whose self-image, like India's, partially derives from a mythical past—takes the name of one of the Hebrew Bible's most popular heroes to denote what it allegedly calls the "Samson Option," a scenario in which Israel, if overrun by invading forces, would launch a massive nuclear strike, destroying itself and taking the rest of the world with it as radiation clouds sweep the globe, just as Samson pulls down the pillars and kills himself along with the gathered Philistines in Judges 13–16 (Hersh

1991). The poet and Holocaust survivor Itamar Yaoz-Kest puts it succinctly in his open letter to former Nazi Günter Grass: "If you force us yet again to descend from the face of the Earth to the depths of the Earth—let the Earth roll toward the Nothingness" (Ronen 2012).

Samson dies with the Philistines after God temporarily grants him the strength to bring down the temple. But Paraśurāma goes on living from age to age. Balamani Amma's *The Story of the Axe* connects Paraśurāma to the violence of the modern era while also granting him the perspective of a *cirañjīvin* who has observed what Sir James G. Frazer called the "long chronicle of folly and crime" that is human history (1922, 325). In this this passage from stanza fifteen of that poem, Paraśurāma is looking down from his isolated home on Mount Mahendra:

From here I see the endless march of epochs
And evolution of souls.
This is the same old world, no doubt;
Yet time has changed its face.
Forests dwindled, cities grew.
Living beings diminished in size,
Feelings grew an edge.
Through the swish of arrows,
The clash of swords,
The boom of guns and the burst of bombs,
The triumphant shouts of war and cruelty
Grow and rise up to me;
And the thought of millions pursuing the wrong path I trod
Makes me restless.
The mental powers of man continue to grow;
Yet the course they take remains the same! (1980, 130)

A similar world-weariness pervades Paraśurāma's character in Shamik Dasgupta's 2008 graphic novel *Vargav,* which shows the Brahmin warrior successively marching with the archetypal Western conquerors Alexander the Great, Julius Caesar, and Napoleon Bonaparte, possibly with the authorial intention of conflating his recurring extermination of the Kṣatriyas with the rise and fall of historical empires. The implication is that Paraśurāma does not personally exterminate twenty-one generations of Kṣatriyas, but—like the narrator in The Rolling Stones' "Sympathy for the Devil" who, during the Hundred Years' War, "watched with glee while your kings and queens fought for ten decades for the gods they made"—rides along incognito with one army after another to watch warriors kill one another *en masse*. These miniature *mahābhāratas* seem to follow one another as inexorably as do Paraśurāma's exterminations of the *kṣatra,* but with an impersonal momentum of their own, like the tides of the ocean or the booms and busts of the stock market. As some god or another (wiser apparently, than anyone in the National Rifle Association) put into Odysseus's head, "of itself the iron draws men to it," meaning that the presence of weapons (not to speak of armies) will eventually create a reason to use them (Homer, Murray, and Dimock 1995, 235). The cyclical buildup of warriors and weaponry that accompany the rise of empires tends to draw annihilation to itself. And, as Dasgupta's graphic novel and Balamani Amma's poem both suggest, Paraśurāma is always there, or at least watching from atop his lonely peak, like a patron saint of total war.

## Aśvatthāman as a Shadow of Paraśurāma

We will now examine the contemporary uses of Paraśurāma alongside those of his near-double Aśvatthāman—another Brahmin warrior whose obsession with avenging his father ends with his being sent into endless lonely exile—and the attraction they hold for those trying to address genocide and other forms of mass extermination in their own day. In an earlier chapter, we looked at Aśvatthāman as one of the *ciranjīvins* and examined his narrative in light of the concept of the "two deaths," with Aśvatthāman's possession by Śiva as a kind of social death that precedes his physical death, which is deferred indefinitely when Kṛṣṇa sends him into exile. Aśvatthāman's undeath is prefigured by the moment in the epic when the Pāṇḍavas kill an elephant that they have named Aśvatthāman so that Yudhiṣṭhira, who is known never to lie, can yell out to Droṇa on the battlefield "Aśvatthāman—the elephant (*sotto voce*)—is dead!" Droṇa is thus fooled into thinking his son has been killed and lays down his arms in despair, allowing the Pāṇḍavas to kill him (7.164). One could argue that Yudhiṣṭhira's calculated lie is not a lie at all but rather an example of "killing words," since from the moment his father dies, Aśvatthāman is metaphorically killed as the man he was and resurrected as a pure instrument of revenge. Aśvatthāman is dead, beware of Aśvatthāman.

Though Aśvatthāman is possessed by Śiva when he attacks the Pāṇḍava camp in the night raid, it is not the kind of possession that takes over the will of the possessed, as is the case when the demon Kali takes over the will of the unfortunate king Nala and forces him to gamble away his kingdom in the Nalopākhyāna story (*MBh* 3.50–78). "Aśvatthāman," Frederick M. Smith observes, "through the most gruesomely violent possession, [becomes] more distinctly himself, his genetic links to Śiva, Death (*antaka*), Lust (*kāma*), and Anger (*krodha*) emerging conspicuously" (2006, 599). In making an "offering of himself" (*atmopahāra*), he is less like Nala and more like the legendary Roman consul Decius Mus, who, according to Livy, became a *devotio* in 340 BCE. After offering himself, his armies, and his enemies to the gods at a battle near Capua early in the Latin War, Decius is transformed.

> [H]e plunged into the thick of the enemy, a conspicuous object from either army and of an aspect more august than a man's, as though sent from heaven to expiate all anger of the gods, and to turn aside destruction from his people and bring it on their adversaries. Thus every terror and dread attended him, and throwing the Latin front into disarray, spread afterwards throughout their entire host. This was most clearly seen in that, wherever he rode, men cowered as though blasted by some baleful star.[28]

Compare Livy's description of Decius above with the imagery associated with Aśvatthāman during the night raid:

> [T]he text tells us that he looks like the very person of Śiva (10.7.66), destroying his victims like Paśupati (10.8.122), roaring like Bhairava (10.8.68). In the camp of his enemies there is confusion: is he human or *rākṣasa* (10.8.30, 34, 43, 116, 119)? He uses the Rudra weapon in his irresistible attack (10.8.31). (Sullivan 2006, 13)

"This nightmare vision of a sacrifice out of control, its violence terminated only by the exhaustion of the supply of oblations," as Sullivan describes the night raid (using terms, I might add, that would be equally applicable to Paraśurāma's varṇicide), "is a representation of Aśvatthāman transgressing the bounds of warrior ethics and brahmanical behavior" (14). There is also a parallel with Paraśurāma (or maybe it is an inversion) in the idea that Aśvatthāman sacrifices with himself as an offering at the beginning of his massacre and is subsequently banished, while Paraśurāma sacrifices with the world as an offering at the end of his massacre and is also banished. The offerings are reversed, but in both cases the self and the world are ritually separated with one being offered up and made sacred and the other left as remainder. The end result for both sacrificers is that they are cursed to remain in the world but no longer of it. When Aśvatthāman sacrifices himself, "because his will to offer up himself up was clear, a golden sacrificial altar sprang up before Great-Souled Aśvatthāman—an altar upon which a blazing fire was lit that spread across the sky and every point in space" (*MBh* 10.7.13–14). Likewise, to offer up the earth, Paraśurāma builds a golden altar "ten fathoms high and nine long" (3.117.12).

In the afterword to his 2002 one-man play *Uttampurush Ekbhachan: Ekta Bhan* ("First Person Singular: A Monologue"), published in English as *The Book of Night,* Sibaji Bandyopadhyay describes Aśvatthāman's expulsion from the human community (or what is left of it after the battle at Kurukṣetra), which begins with Kṛṣṇa depriving him of his divine forehead jewel:

> The Aśvatthāman in the play is dispossessed of his gem, that jewel which had glittered like the (dreaded) third eye of Śiva at the time of *Mahābhārata*'s night-raid. . . . Nevertheless, the impoverished outcaste of *The Book of Night* is untiring in asserting that he is Śiva's incarnation and that his re-materialization has direct bearing upon an unfinished task. Aśvatthāman's "human resentments" had expanded into "divine destructiveness" in the "Sauptikaparvan." And, in parallel to that "expansion," he became more than "just a human rejector of Kṛṣṇa devotion." After his meeting with Śiva, he assumed the role of a god who was an "arch-rival" to Kṛṣṇa. And after much subterfuge, dillydallying and retreat, the reappeared Aśvatthāman declares that he is not just the instrument of *pralaya* or utter devastation but also the most reliable exponent of the metaphysics of *pralaya*. (2012, 497)

In the play itself, the narrator (Aśvatthāman or someone claiming to be Aśvatthāman) contrasts the uniqueness of his character in the Kṛṣṇa-dominated world of the epic with the unimaginative banality of that same character in the human-dominated world of the twenty-first century. He first proclaims, "[Only] I am concealed from Krishna, beyond his reach—dweller in the cavern, secret, free, unique, discrete, independent, *svayamsevak*!"[29] Then he later complains, "My play's degenerating into bathos! Ruined! There it was, my own unique story, proceeding at its own pace—but in a trice it was magnified, so broad that one size fits all, so small that it smells of stale metaphors, refers to nothing" (2008, 67, 73–74). What seems extreme about the violence in the epic has become so unremarkable in the present moment that Aśvatthāman loses all his significance. And at the end of Bandyopadhyay's play the narrator is revealed not to be Aśvatthāman at all, but "an imposter . . . just one more professional solo recitalist recycling the worm-eaten *Mahābhārata*" (2012, 493). Like Paraśurāma's varṇicide, Aśvatthāman's night raid reads differently to a mass media-saturated audience largely numbed to the horrors of weapons of mass destruction and suicide bombers.[30]

Returning to the world of the epic, we can ask: How can Aśvatthāman and Paraśurāma, figures that so embody what the Germanic tradition calls the *friedlos,* or "man without peace," play so central a role in an epic whose overarching aesthetic mood is that of *śāntarasa* or "peacefulness," according to the great ninth-century Kashmiri literary theorist Ānandavardhana?[31] Of course, in asking this question I am (deliberately) confusing the peace of *śāntarasa* with the peace of which the *friedlos* is deprived. The former, as Emily T. Hudson notes, is an aesthetic correlate to a "dispassion for worldly affairs and human ambition" (2013, 58). The latter is the protective peace enforced by a sovereign power, as reflected in the terms "Pax Britannica" and "Pax Americana," or the *Mahābhārata*'s Śānti Parvan, the Book of the Peace. The way in which these two forms of peace most closely resemble each other is that both are bought with sacrifice—the sacrifice of desire and the sacrifice of life, respectively. There is a distinction between these two conceptions of peace, but also a connection. And this connection will become apparent when we follow the transformations of Paraśurāma's varṇicidal extermination campaign as it moves between the poles of theological abstraction and revanchist fantasy.

## The First Theology of Paraśurāma: Mitigating the Myth's Violence in the Pāñcarātra Tradition

For the most part (except for our historically grounded discussion of the *Brahmāṇḍa Purāṇa*), we have so far been dealing with the Paraśurāma macromyth, consisting of all the myth variants read synchronically as a whole. Now, we will turn to a particular variant, the one developed by the Pāñcarātrins, and ask some more of the questions we formulated at the beginning to address to individual variants. Who brought this myth to this new community? Did it resonate with existing cultural values or did it serve to express new imported or developing social forms, either ritual, aesthetic, economic, social, or demographic? And if it exhibits significant differences from other variants, what external circumstances caused the authors to change it from its earlier form?

This line of questioning brings us to the first group to significantly adapt the epic form of the myth to their own purposes. Flourishing between the seventh and eighth centuries CE—but possibly dating back as early as the third century BCE—the Pāñcarātrins represent one of the earliest identifiably Vaiṣṇava religious traditions (Bhandarkar 1913, 39).[32] Bronkhorst notes that the Pāñcarātrins did not often find favor with other Brahmin groups, who doubted their very identity as Brahmins (2016, 133).

The origin of the sect's name is subject to speculation. Pāñcarātra, a compound comprising the elements *pāñca* ("five") and *rātra* ("night") is generally interpreted as a reference to the five nights of the Human Sacrifice described in *Ṛg Veda* 10.90 and *Śatapātha Brāhmaṇa* 13.6.1.1, at the end of which, according to the Pāñcarātrins, Nārāyaṇa achieves ultimate transcendence (van Buitenen 1962, 292–93; De 1931, 417; Schrader 1916, 125).[33] Neevel supplies an interpretation that understands *pāñcarātra* to refer not to five nights, but a "night of five," with "night" meaning something like the metaphorical *Dämmerung* ("twilight") in the German compound *Götterdämmerung* ("Twilight of the Gods") and "five" referring to the five elements—the *pañcabhūta*: earth, water, fire, air, and space—that dissolve and disperse at the time of personal liberation (*mokṣa*) and the dissolution of the universe (*pralaya*) (1977, 8).[34]

In light of the connections between Paraśurāma and Aśvatthāman drawn above, it will also be useful to briefly treat Ruth Katz's intriguing theory that the Pāñcarātrins were the authors of the Sauptika Parvan in which Aśvatthāman carries out his terrible night raid. Relying on Neevel's etymology of *pāñcarātra,* Katz speculates that the Śaiva Brahmin warrior Aśvatthāman's destruction of the five sleeping kinsmen of Draupadī—also called, suggestively, the Pāñcālas—might represent the destruction of the five elements. The raid takes place at night in a kind of literalization of the metaphoric *rātra* and concludes with the resurrection of Parikṣit's slain fetus, which might be "the reflection of a Pāñcarātra initiation" (1985, 116–17).[35]

Whatever the derivation of their name, the Pāñcarātrins laid the foundation for Vaiṣṇavism, combining elements of Tantric ritualism and Sāṃkhya philosophy to build a bridge between late Vedic religion and the devotional temple-based traditions. As H. Daniel Smith puts it in an oft-quoted phrase, the Pāñcarātra traditions "account for and give textual authority for the bulk of the activities undertaken in temples, in public, and in the home of most Viṣṇu-worshippers today" (1975, 173). The oldest and most important of their texts, the *Pauṣkara*, *Sātvata*, and *Jayākha Saṃhitās*, were composed near the end of or soon after the completion of the *Mahābhārata* and their references to the snowy Himālaya and to the birch bark paper used exclusively in

Kashmir place them in that region (Matsubara 1994, 18–19; Schrader 1916, 96). From Kashmir, the traditions of the Pāñcarātrins spread southward, where they gave rise to Śrī Vaiṣṇavism when they were appropriated by Tamil bhakti theologians such as Yāmuna who integrated Pāñcarātra liturgical temple-based practices with the highly developed philosophical systems of Vedānta and Nyāya.

The Pañcarātrins are *ekāntins*, or monotheists. They follow the Upaniṣads in holding the impersonal and ineffable ultimate reality of Brahman as the highest principle and cause of all causes but they also understand Brahman as "the transcendent or nonpersonal *aspect* of the supreme God" (Matsubara 1994, 68). Brahman is both void and infinite, containing within itself the goddess Lakṣmī, who is responsible for creation. But despite its theological necessity, Brahman is "not an integral part of this popular religious system, which centers on the idea of a personal active god" (67).

This personal god Viṣṇu in his transcendent aspect is identified with Brahman, while his immanent aspect is understood to be Vāsudeva, part of a pure creation that precedes the creation of matter. And to resolve the question about whether the supreme godhead is *saguṇa* ("with qualities") or *nirguṇa* ("without qualities"), they ascribe to him six *guṇa*s that are different from the three *guṇa*s associated with created things—namely, *sattvā, rajas,* and *tamas* (lucidity, passion, and dark inertia). The six *guṇa*s of Vāsudeva are knowledge, lordship, power, strength, virility, and splendor. And emanating from Vāsudeva, who embodies these six qualities, are the next three beings to come into existence, the *vyūha*s. The *vyūha*s emanate one from the other as a flame goes from candle to candle, and each of the three embodies two of Vāsudeva's six *guṇa*s. Building on extant stories about the genealogy of Kṛṣṇa (already identified with Vāsudeva in the *Mahābhārata*), the Pāñcarātrins identify each of the three *vyūha*s with a member of Kṛṣṇa's family—his older brother Saṃkarṣaṇa, his son Pradyumna, and his grandson Aniruddha—as well as with one of the Brahminical deities (Śiva, Viṣṇu, and Brahmā). They also give each one a creative and a moral function as well as a goddess for a consort.

The tradition lists Paraśurāma as a manifestation of Saṃkarṣaṇa, the primary *vyūha* of Vāsudeva, identified with the god Śiva, the element of *tamas,* and Kāla, the destroyer form of Viṣṇu (Sanford 2005, 95). The Pāñcarātra tradition is prolific when it comes to producing texts, and the ocean of Pāñcarātra literature contains, unsurprisingly, quite a few inconsistencies and contradictions when it comes to explaining the various emanations of the godhead: *vyūha*s, *avatāra*s, and *vibhava*s. The *Viśvaksena Saṃhitā,* composed around 800 CE (Matsubara 1994, 34) lists Paraśurāma as a secondary *avatāra,* described as a "soul in bondage with a natural body which, however, is possessed (*āviṣṭa*) or pervaded, for some particular function, by the power (*śakti*) of Viṣṇu" (Schrader 1916, 47).[36]

In the *Sātvata Saṃhitā*, Paraśurāma learns the Pāñcarātra system from the "Plower" form of Vāsudeva while living in exile in the southern Malaya Mountains.[37] What is striking about this is the importance of the axe itself to this theology. Describing Paraśurāma's role as the transmitter of teachings from Vāsudeva to the sage Nārada, D. Dennis Hudson writes,

> Parashurama's famous axe (*parashu*) . . . represents "nonclinging" (*asanga*) as the instrumental means to remove the passion that causes one to see Vasudeva as red in color. Krishna refers to this axe in *Bhagavad-gita* 15.1–6, where he tells Arjuna to cut down the cosmic fig tree. The fig tree known as asvattha or pippala is a metaphor for a material body infused with the sap of passion; the body may be Brahma's body of spacetime or the sadhaka's body or both. The fig tree's well-nourished root springs from a seed dropped by a bird up high on a host tree; the root throws out branches in all directions and sends subsidiary roots down to the ground to create a shaded world. Birds restlessly flit from branch to branch to eat its figs. Krishna tells Arjuna to use the axe of nonclinging (*asanga-shastra*) to chop down this tree and then, like a free bird, fly to Krishna's supreme home (*dhama parama*) beyond directional space and chronological time. Vasudeva teaches the details of this "chopping" to the Plower in the *Satvata-samhita*. "Chopping" with nonclinging is the only way to approach and taste the honey of Krishna's lotus feet. (2008, 504)[38]

Also noteworthy about the Pāñcarātrins' conception of Paraśurāma is the way the tradition imbues him and Saṃkarṣaṇa, the *vyūha* whence he emanates, with so many distinctly Śaiva characteristics. The *Viśvaksena Saṃhitā* makes a clear identification of Saṃkarṣaṇa with the destructive Śiva as the one who "by means of the power of his *guṇa* takes away all this," while Pradyumna and Aniruddha use their *guṇa*s to "create" and "support," respectively (Schrader 1916, 38). The Pāñcarātra Saṃhitās' conception of Saṃkarṣaṇa's creative function is also thoroughly Śaiva, employing themes of poison, blackness, and chaos found in the stories of Śiva's role in the churning of the Ocean of Milk and the birth of Kālī from the poison he holds in his throat. Schrader writes,

> With Saṃkarṣaṇa, Non-pure Creation becomes dimly manifest in an embryonic condition, as a chaotic mass without internal

> distinctions. This is expressed in the Saṃhitās by the grotesque but often repeated statement that Saṃkarṣaṇa "carries the whole universe like a *tilakālaka* (dark spot under the skin)," which apparently signifies that the world he carries is still so to speak under the surface, existing only in a germinal condition, as a minute part, as it were, of his body. (1916, 38)

As these passages demonstrate, Pāñcarātrins, following his association with Śiva in the *Mahābhārata*, imbue Paraśurāma with the qualities of a Śaiva figure while absorbing him into a Vaiṣṇava framework.[39] They deify him, but only partially, and his violent behavior can be ascribed to his emanation from the chaotic *vyūha* Saṃkarṣaṇa.

The authority and influence of the Pāñcarātra ritual and philosophical system and Paraśurāma's place in it may go some way toward explaining how Paraśurāma became an *avatāra* in the first place. The first reference to him being one comes in the Nārāyaṇiyā section of the Śānti Parvan (*MBh* 12.321–39), which most scholars consider to be one of the latest additions to the text. It contains the earliest list of the *avatāras,* which includes Paraśurāma and gives as his *raison d'être* to "take birth as Rāma in the race of Bhṛgu, and exterminate the Kṣatriyas who will become proud of their strength and possessions" (*MBh* 12.326.77). Here, Paraśurāma's divine purpose is not distinct from his earthly actions; they are neither mitigated nor theologized. He comes with the purpose of committing varṇicide.

The Pāñcarātrins first introduce the theological mitigation of Paraśurāma's violence in the *Sanatkumāra Saṃhitā*, composed around 800 CE (Matsubara 1994, 27). The text gives a list of eleven *avatāra*s or *vibhava*s of Vasūdeva that include, in order, Varāha the boar, Nṛsiṃha the man-lion, Matsya the fish, Kūrma the tortoise, Tārkṣa (Garuḍa), Vāmana the dwarf, Hayagrīva, Kapila, Paraśurāma (called Jāmadagnya Rāma), Kakutstha (Rāma Dāśarathi), and Kṛṣṇa. According to the text, Saṃkarṣaṇa goes down to earth as Jamadagni's son while at the same time, powerful demons are born on the earth as Kṣatriyas. Then Paraśurāma takes up his axe to kill Haihaya (Kārtavīrya) and destroys all the demon-Kṣatriyas—not because of his knowledge that demons have been born on the earth as Kṣatriyas, but out of a desire to destroy Kārtavīrya—before going away into the south.

Consistent with the nature of the secondary *avatāra,* Paraśurāma is a mortal warrior whose earthly actions (carrying out his revenge) are invested with cosmic significance when he is pervaded by the *vyūha* Saṃkarṣaṇa. By sending Paraśurāma south, the text indexes the body of legends concerning Paraśurāma's afterlife in Malabar without mentioning a sacrifice or an imposed exile due to the sinfulness of his actions. The *Sanatkumāra Saṃhitā* makes no mention at all of the matricide. And though it does mention an axe as Paraśurāma's weapon of choice, it only knows him by his patronymic Jāmadagnya or Jamadagnisuta (6.66–70).

The lengthy Paraśurāma story in the Pāñcarātra *Viṣṇudharmottara Purāṇa* (c. 600–1000 CE), one of the first major Purāṇic accounts of the myth to appear after the redaction of the *Mahābhārata*, further mitigates and theologizes the varṇicide myth. To insulate Paraśurāma and his slaughter of the Kṣatriyas against charges of impropriety, the Pāñcarātra mythmakers have twice removed his story from the realm of human dharma—first by changing his victims from human Kṣatriyas into demons and then by making Paraśurāma an incarnation of Viṣṇu carrying out the orders of Śiva. Here, his enemies are no longer any Kṣatriyas he happens to come across. Nor are they Kṣatriyas that, unknown to him, are demons born as humans. Instead, Paraśurāma's enemies are an army of nonhuman demons who have taken the earth away from the gods. As in other *avatāra* stories, the reason for Viṣṇu's incarnation as Paraśurāma is to rid the earth of demons that have, through obtaining some boon, become invulnerable to the power of the gods and are threatening to destroy cosmic order.

Before looking more closely at the *Viṣṇudharmottara*, it will be helpful to briefly examine the *Nīlamata Purāṇa*, a contemporaneous text also originating from Kashmir (though not part of the Pāñcarātra tradition), which sheds some light on the Śaiva elements of Paraśurāma that were part of the two texts' shared background. The *Nīlamata*, like the *Mahābhārata*, is set within a series of frame stories. The outermost frame, taken directly from the epic, is the conversation between Janamejaya and Vaiśampāyana at the Snake Sacrifice. The next frame is a conversation between the sages Gonanda and Bṛhadaśva after the latter's request for more information about Kashmir. The innermost frame, containing a description of the ceremonies and festivals of the region (presumably the material the authors wanted to link with the epic) is narrated by Nīla, for whom the text is named, in conversation with Candradeva (Kumari 1973, 7–9). While Paraśurāma plays a significant part in the story, he is not listed here as one of the *avatāra*s of Viṣṇu, which he is in the Kashmiri poet Kṣemandra's eleventh century *Daśāvatāracarita* (143).

*Nīlamata Purāṇa* 1.1167–1226 retells the varṇicide story, once again with Paraśurāma wiping out the Kṣatriyas twenty-one times. But on the last round of exterminations, the Kṣatriyas flee to Kashmir where the axe-wielding Brahmin follows them and finishes the job at the Madhumati River. There he erects a statue of a form of Viṣṇu called Keśava. The statue possesses a fierce aspect reflecting the enraged state in which Paraśurāma builds it and visitors offer animal sacrifice to it in contradiction of the Vaiṣṇava custom of vegetarian offerings. Afterward, Paraśurāma returns to Kurukṣetra to complete the sacrifice in the middle of the five lakes of Kṣatriya blood he has created, after which his ancestors tell him that he must go and practice penance to wash the blood off his hands. This command sends him on a tour of the sacred pools of northern India until he arrives at the foot of the famous mountain Gṛdhrakūṭa (Vulture Peak) in central northern India where his father (Bhṛgu, not Jamadagni in this version), or possibly Paraśurāma himself, had installed another statue of Keśava. There he receives a visit from the sage Vasiṣṭha, who complains that the cow he was taking up the mountain to offer to Viṣṇu (in yet another strange animal sacrifice) died on the way because the climb was so difficult. To prevent this from happening again, Paraśurāma propitiates Viṣṇu to move the Keśava image to Kashmir, where it would be more easily accessible. Viṣṇu agrees and that, as Bṛhadaśva explains to Gonanda, is why the Keśava image from Gṛdhrakūṭa is now in Kashmir. In this version of the story, devoid of any attempt to mitigate Paraśurāma's varṇicide, the Brahmin warrior becomes tainted with sin and in need of purification specifically because he kills *palāyamānān,* "those fleeing the battlefield" (1177). Also, his practice of sacrificing animals—apparently even cows—to Viṣṇu underscores his Śaiva nature.

When he appears in the *Viṣṇudharmottara Purāṇa*, Paraśurāma's enemies are once again demons. Paolo Magnone notes that the cattle theft episode is left out of the *Viṣṇudharmottara*, making Paraśurāma's varṇicide solely a matter of relieving the overburdened earth's excessive (demonic) population (2004, 200). And unlike the destruction of the Kṣatriyas in the *Mahābhārata* or the *Nīlamata Purāṇa*, the massacre of the demons does not result in Paraśurāma's exile. He does not accrue the sin of killing heroes that becomes such a problem for him in later myths, but Śiva does tell Paraśurāma twice that he will have to give up his *tejas* and lay down his arms (except to protect women and Brahmins) when he meets Rāma Dāśarathi.

Now, we can begin to answer the question of what external circumstances caused the authors to change this Paraśurāma variant from its earlier form: building on the Pāñcarātrins' existing association of Paraśurāma with Śiva, the authors of the *Viṣṇudharmottara Purāṇa* introduce more of the Śaiva elements that are so common in post-epic stories of Paraśurāma, connecting him to the all-consuming sacrificial fire and its counterpart in the sky, the sun. Paraśurāma's status as a devotee of Śiva is also the occasion for the second of the text's innovations: the insertion of a *gītā,* in this case, the *Śaṅkara Gītā,* to provide Paraśurāma's campaign of violence with a systematic theological justification that emphasizes its dharmic necessity in the cosmic scheme and the fact that only he can carry it out. There is no such justification in the epic version of the myth.

Despite these differences, the *Viṣṇudharmottara*'s version of Paraśurāma's story is very like the *Mahābhārata* version in that it makes use of the fluid motif in the abundance of blood, describing the climactic battle with terms that recall both the five lakes of blood at the Samantapañcaka and Yudhiṣṭhira's descent into Hell at the end of the epic. The text describes Paraśurāma's final assault on the demons with an extended and very graphic landscape metaphor: there is a river formed of the slain demons' blood, the moss and grasses at its banks are hair, the fish that swim in it are arrows, the crocodiles are bows, the fallen umbrellas are swans, and the ocean the river flows into is the realm of ghosts. Also present in the *Viṣṇudharmottara* are the overarching Bhārgava theme of sorcery in Paraśurāma's use of *astras*. And, although the authors remove Paraśurāma's story from the context of the Bhārgava-Haihaya feud when they turn his enemies into demons, they include his kinsman Śukra as the demons' chief priest as well as a reference to the Aurva narrative in *VDhP* 1.32 to remind readers that this is still a Bhārgava myth.

The purpose of combining the Śaiva and Vaiṣṇava aspects of the myth in this way was likely to address the text to the Pāśupata Śaivas who dominated Kashmir when it was composed. On this point, I agree with with Horst Brinkhaus, who disputes Gail's argument that the early Vaiṣṇava theology of Paraśurāma in the *Viṣṇudharmottara* was an example of an "open Viṣṇuism, which is aimed at the incorporation of Śivaism" (Gail 1977, 46 quoted in Brinkhaus 1983, 59). Instead, Brinkhaus argues for a separate Śaiva post-epic Paraśurāma tradition that serves as the source material co-opted by Vaiṣṇavas in order to incorporate and supersede dominant Śaiva ideas (Brinkhaus 1983, 58).

We can also answer the question of whether the community of readers or hearers has changed to the point that they would derive new meanings from the Paraśurāma myth that would have been foreign to its original historical context: The *Sanatkumāra-Saṃhitā*, *Nīlamata Purāṇa,* and the *Viṣṇudharmottara Purāṇa* were composed long after the point at which the *Mahābhārata* was completed and begin a new trajectory in the development of the figure. The theologically informed transition from Rāma Jāmadagnya to Paraśurāma that occurs in these texts seems to presuppose the elevation of Paraśurāma to divine or semi-divine status, the increasingly consistent association of the Kṣatriya-slayer with his emblematic axe, and his incorporation into the

Vaiṣṇava cosmos. The texts also project Śaiva attributes onto the figure while incorporating those elements into a Vaiṣṇava devotional context and connecting local sacred history to pan-Indian religious motifs. Thus, while it is spoken by Śiva, the *Śaṅkara Gītā* is decidedly Vaiṣṇava is its theology. Inden writes:

> Here we have the first major example in the *VDhP* of the deployment of historical narrative as an "illustrative proof" (*pramāṇa*). Viṣṇu was, in Pāñcarātra theology, the master of "deceptive appearances" (*māyā*). The authors of the *VDhP* wanted to show that Śiva was in reality Vāsudeva Kṛṣṇa, and that his preeminent devotee, Bhārgava Rāma, was actually the foremost Pāñcarātrin. (2000, 57)

The Pāñcarātra contributions to the Paraśurāma corpus of myths establish his dual identity as an incarnation of Viṣṇu and a devotee of Śiva and mitigate the harshness of his campaign against the Kṣatriyas by turning them into demons. This transformation was a function both of the intentions of the mythmakers and the shifts in religious attitudes that had occurred since the composition of the epic. In the next section, we will look at a different religious tradition that has no interest in mitigating the violence of the Paraśurāma story, but rather emphasizes its grotesque excess.

## Wrath and Pride: The Jaina Paraśurāma

The story of Subhūma (or Subhauma), the eighth world-ruling *cakravartin* of Jaina mythology, and one of the two who end up in Hell, is found several places in the textual tradition of the Śvetāmbara ("White-Clad") sect. It appears in Śīlāṅkha's ninth-century work, the *Caüpaṇṇamahāpurisacariya* ("The Lives of the Fifty-Four Great Men"); the commentarial literature of Jinadāsa, Haribhadra, and Malayagiri; and in the erotic epic *Vasudevahiṇḍi* ("The Travels of Vasudeva"), composed in Maharashtrian Prakrit by the traveling monks Saṅghadāsagaṇi and Dharmadāsagaṇi in the fifth century (Jaini 1993, 220; Koch 1998, 123–24). Here, we will focus on the latest version, told in the *Triṣaṣṭiśalākāpuruṣacarita* ("The Lives of the Sixty-Three Great Men"), written in twelfth-century Gujarat by the Śvetāmbara Ācārya Hemacandra. In a milieu that mirrors what we will see in Maharashtra and Malabar, Hemacandra was the advisor and preceptor to the Caulukya emperor Kumārapāla, who had succeeded a Śaiva king and was working to impose Jaina social order (Cort 1993, 192–93).

Jainas had little affection for the Hindu Purāṇas, but it was because of their disdain that, in an instance of *dveṣa-bhakti* ("the devotion of the enemy"), they became some of the Purāṇas' most careful and dedicated readers. "[They] knew the Hindu Epics and Purāṇas well," writes Padmanabh Jaini, "studied them with the attention worthy of a board of censors examining the offensive portions of a story, and finally decided to rewrite the script in conformity with their own doctrines and sensibilities" (1993, 207). The popularity of these Hindu Purāṇas among the ruling aristocracy and the mercantile class forced Jaina authors to begrudgingly incorporate them into the new "deep time" narrative of Jaina history and cosmology by composing their own versions. This is the context for the story of Subhūma.

It begins when Vaiśvānara and Dhanvantari, two former sages who had ascended to godhood, begin to argue over whether the religion of the Brahmins is superior to that of the Jainas.[40] To settle the argument, the gods decide to disguise themselves and tempt an exemplar from each religion. First, they try to tempt King Padmaratha, a recent convert to Jainism, to give up his vows, but they are unable to do so. Then the gods move on to Jamadagni, who is celibate and spends his time meditating in the forest. The pair successfully convince Jamadagni that his penance is useless without a son, and the sage gives up his meditations to search for a wife. Jamadagni visits the kingdom of Jitaśatru, who offers him any of his one hundred daughters as a bride. The first ninety-nine flinch at the prospect of marrying the old ascetic, and he curses them to become hunchbacked. But when Jamadagni sees the hundredth daughter, Reṇukā, he tricks her into assenting to marriage by holding out a fruit to her and grabbing her hand when she reaches for it. After Jamadagni restores the good posture of her ninety-nine sisters, he takes Reṇukā to live with him at his hermitage.

In order to receive a son, Jamadagni makes up an oblation for Reṇukā to drink so that she can give birth to a Brahmin boy who will live in the forest like his father. Reṇukā requests anther oblation for her sister, the wife of King Anantavīrya of Hastināpura, so that she can give birth to a great king. Jamadagni obliges and makes another oblation for her sister. But when the time comes to drink them, Reṇukā intentionally switches oblations with her sister, so that her son will not be a forest-dwelling ascetic. As a result, Reṇukā gives birth to Paraśurāma and her sister gives birth to King Kṛtavīrya (Kārtavīrya, who at this point has been the cattle thief, Reṇukā's seducer, Reṇukā's brother-in-law, Reṇukā's son, and now Paraśurāma's cousin).

One day a *vidyādhara* (a celestial magician) comes into the hermitage of Jamadagni after having lost the power of flight due to dysentery. After

Paraśurāma cures him of his ailment, the *vidyādhara* gives him his magic axe in gratitude. Later, Reṇukā goes to visit her sister in Hastināpura and while she is there, she sleeps with her sister's husband Anantavīrya and gives birth to his child.[41] Jamadagni goes to fetch his wife and brings her back along with her bastard son, too blinded by his love for her to condemn her. But Paraśurāma becomes enraged at the sight and kills both his mother and her new son with his axe. When Anantavīrya learns what had happened, he goes to Jamadagni's hermitage and, seeing that Paraśurāma is not there, destroys the place and steals the sage's cattle. But when Paraśurāma hears about the destruction of the *āśrama,* he hunts down Anantavīrya and uses his axe to dismember the king. In turn, Paraśurāma's cousin and counterpart in the oblation-switching, Kṛtavīrya, avenges his father's slaying by killing Jamadagni. At this, Paraśurāma kills Kṛtavīrya and then proceeds to wipe out all the Kṣatriyas of the earth seven (not thrice seven) times.

But Kṛtavīrya's wife manages to escape the slaughter by hiding out in a friendly hermitage. There she gives birth to her son Subhūma. Subhūma grows up in the hermitage, the only Kṣatriya left on earth, and marries the daughter of the *vidyādhara* Meghanāda. After he wipes out all the Kṣatriyas seven times, Paraśurāma begins to grow paranoid about being killed himself and consults astrologers about who his killer will be. The astrologers inform him that his killer will be the one who eats a bowl of rice pudding that Paraśurāma has made out of the teeth of the slain Kṣatriyas. So Paraśurāma constructs a lion throne, sets down the dish of pudding in front of it, and waits to see who will come.

Meanwhile, Subhūma, who has learned from his mother that Paraśurāma is the one who killed his father, goes to take vengeance. Accompanied by his father-in-law Meghanāda, Subhūma attacks Paraśurāma's stronghold and Meghanāda quickly kills the Brahmins who rise to protect it. As soon as he sees the lion throne, Subhūma mounts it and eats the dish of rice pudding made from Kṣatriya-teeth. Seeing this, Paraśurāma hurls his axe at Subhūma, but the weapon has no effect. Then the bowl that had contained the pudding becomes a *cakra,* or discus, and Subhūma throws it at Paraśurāma, cutting off his head. After he kills Paraśurāma, Subhūma then proceeds to wipe out the Brahmins twenty-one times, covering the earth with splintered bones and rivers of blood before moving north to conquer the *mlecchas.* After sixty thousand years of constant killing, Subhūma finally dies and goes to the seventh hell.

In this story, neither Reṇukā nor Paraśurāma nor Jamadagni escapes vilification. Jamadagni foolishly falls for Vaiśvānara and Dhanvantari's ruse to give up his celibacy, then tricks Reṇukā into marrying him. Reṇukā intentionally switches the *carus* to thwart her husband's plans, then willfully sleeps with and has a son by her brother-in-law, a public infidelity for which the cuckolded Jamadagni is uncharacteristically forgiving. Paraśurāma commits matricide uncoerced (significantly, no one bothers to resurrect Reṇukā in this variant) and, after he wipes out the Kṣatriyas, holds on to power himself and behaves like a tyrant. But neither are Subhūma's actions purely heroic, since they ultimately lead to his damnation.

Many of the events in this story are recognizable motifs from the epic versions of the Paraśurāma cycle, but with some variations. The dish of rice pudding made of teeth is a rather startling innovation.[42] This object begins as a product of death and destruction, and then is transformed into an object of generative power for Subhūma, like the seminal rice pudding ingested by Paraśurāma's mother. Then, from a symbol of generation, the rice pudding becomes a symbol of royal power or *kṣatra* when it is placed at the foot of a throne for Paraśurāma's killer to ingest. Its identity as the *kṣatra* is made even more explicit when the dish that held the rice pudding becomes in Subhūma's hand a *cakra,* the royal weapon par excellence, and gives him the means to kill Paraśurāma. The *vidyādharas* in this variant take the place of the *gandharva* in the epic. And while it is Reṇukā who meets a *gandharva* in the *Mahābhārata* and experiences incontinence that leads to her beheading, here it is Paraśurāma who cures an incontinent (in a different and more unpleasant way) *vidyādhara* and receives his axe as a boon.

The earliest layer of the Jaina Paraśurāma tradition only knows him as Rāma, and probably not as an *avatāra* of Viṣṇu (Koch 1998, 127). Perspicacious readers of the Hindu texts that they were, it seems likely that the Jaina authors would make more of an effort to appropriate Paraśurāma to their own religion, as had the Pāñcarātrins, were the notion of his *avatāra*-hood widespread. Instead, the *Vasudevahiṇḍi* does not even put him in the center of the story, but pairs him with Subhūma, one of the two wicked *cakravartins,* as an example of the dangers of *vera* (enmity) to both sides of a conflict.[43] For the Jainas, Paraśurāma appears to have been an excessively violent Śaiva hero whose actions served as a richly illustrative counterexample to the Jaina ideal of *ahiṃsa,* or "non-cruelty," and whose comeuppance would be particularly satisfying to their audience.

## Conclusion

In this chapter, we have focused on Paraśurāma's twenty-one-fold annihilation of the Kṣatriyas, tracing its development from the epic through the transformations it undergoes to become two distinct variants we can situate in their respective contexts. We began the first half of this chapter with a closer look at the varṇicide episode, contextualizing it in the larger Bhārgava-Haihaya cycle, the long-running Brahmin-Kṣatriya blood feud into which both Paraśurāma and Kārtavīrya are born.

Then, after spending the preceding two chapters using psychoanalysis to focus on the ways in which the inner structure of the myth has driven the production of its variants, we examined the ways in which a new historical context could dramatically expand and deepen the import of a myth without actually changing a word of it. Historical and technological developments that have led to new and more broadly destructive forms of violence, I have argued, have led scholars to think about Paraśurāma in terms of genocide and prompted contemporary Hindus to directly question the myth's meaning in those terms. For comparison, we looked at a contemporary literary incarnation of Aśvatthāman, whom I have called Paraśurāma's "shadow" or "near double" because he is also a Śaiva Brahmin warrior whose vengeance for his father's death also leads to violence that the other characters in the epic think of as problematic and ends with him also being sent into an unending exile.

The second half of the chapter, in which we looked at how mythmakers have changed the myth to fit their own needs and authorize new ideas and practices, was dedicated to the Pāñcarātra sanitization (or *sanātan*izantion) of Paraśurāma's varṇicide and the Jaina exacerbation of its more grotesque elements. The transformation of the victims of Paraśurāma's varṇicide from Kṣatriyas into demons may have made some Pāñcarātrins developing their theology of a personal and omnipotent deity more comfortable with the violence of the myth in the same way that some parents today might be more comfortable with their children blowing the heads off of grotesque zombies in a first-person shooter video game than they would be if they were shooting at recognizable (virtual) humans. It also serves the purpose of connecting local and regional sacred history to the great late Vedic mythic structure of the gods warring with the demons in a way that mirrors the connection of the personal deity, physically present in temples and shrines, to the ineffable ultimate reality of Brahman taught by the Upaniṣadic sages of the Vedic tradition.

For the Jainas, Paraśurāma does not become a killer of demons, but a killer of men, and one who grotesquely takes their teeth as trophies so he can mash them up into gruel. His egregious violence and the paranoid period of rule that replaces his exile in the Hindu tradition lead to his own *varṇa,* not that of the Kṣatriyas, being annihilated twenty-one times by Subhūma. In the *Triṣaṣṭiśalākāpuruṣacarita*, Paraśurāma represents the dangers of excessive wrath for a kingdom transitioning from Śaiva to Jaina hegemony.

As we have seen, the authors of the epic are deeply ambivalent about the varṇicide. The innovative Pāñcarātrins, in developing their post-Vedic Vaiṣṇava tradition, make use of the varṇicidal Paraśurāma, already a profoundly Śaiva figure, like Aśvatthāman. Due to the compelling nature of his story for both Kṣatriyas and Brahmins who have used it to elevate their lineage, he has an important role to play in absorbing the transgressive power of Śiva into an expansive Vaiṣṇava framework and connecting local traditions to pan-Indian epic mythology. When his violence becomes problematic, the textual tradition mitigates it by recasting it in the familiar model of theomachy. But, in light of the increased capacity for mass violence in the modern era, readers inside and outside of the tradition—scholars, novelists, average Hindus around the world—cannot help but see the foreshadows of genocide and total war in Paraśurāma's actions and the *Mahābhārata* war as a whole. In the next chapter, we will examine some specific castes and regions in India where Paraśurāma plays the role of a progenitor and culture hero and his varṇicide is seen as an act of creation instead of an act of destruction.

# 5

# Varṇicide II

## *Blood and Soil in Malabar and Maharashtra*

> If Rāma burned the seed of the Kṣatriyas, how did the Kṣatriyas rise up again?
>
> —*Mahābhārata* 12.48.12

> For God's sake, let us sit upon the ground
> And tell sad stories of the death of kings . . .
>
> —*Richard II*, Act 3, Scene 2

As I wrote in the introduction, I understand a myth to be a narrative about events not witnessed by the teller or the audience, existing in more than one variant, that expresses the values, anxieties, and worldview shared by the group of people who receive and reproduce it. We already have a working thesis that the Paraśurāma myth comes out of a time when Brahmins who were anxious about their status in post-Mauryan social life used the story to provide a blueprint for a future privileged position in a Vedic-inspired social hierarchy. This hierarchy, as we have seen, was endorsed and upheld by sectarian kings even though they had mostly abandoned the Vedic religion and it may have contributed to the support Brahmins enjoyed from petty kings in the post-Mauryan centuries. The preexisting material that the Brahmins incorporated into the story of an extremely violent Brahmin warrior contained older mythic motifs that were already overlaid with ritual and anthropological (in the broadest sense) interpretations, acquired from being the subjects of long periods of intense speculation and analysis in the Brahminical tradition, giving rise to emergent metaphysical interpretations that connected the time of the myth's telling to cosmic time.

In the first half of this chapter, we will look at two examples of the way these freighted elements shape our understanding of the myth when we examine the sacrificial remainder submotif and the land creation submotif of the larger varṇicide motif. In the second half of the chapter, we will be looking at two more specific variants of the Paraśurāma myth, both of which accentuate the land creation and sacrificial remainder submotifs. When looking at individual variants in the post-epic literature it is useful to state once again our guiding questions. Who brought the Paraśurāma myth to this new community? What was the geographic, social, economic, and political location of the mythmakers when they deployed the Paraśurāma myth? Did it resonate with existing cultural values or did it serve to express new imported or developing ritual, aesthetic, or economic forms? We will attempt to answer these questions in relation to the Paraśurāma variants deployed in Malabar and Maharashtra before concluding with a broader discussion of "blood and soil" mythology. But first, an introductory discussion of the ways in which past scholars have understood the Paraśurāma myth as pure Brahmin ideology.

## The Uses and Abuses of Paraśurāma

Attempts to reconcile Paraśurāma's extreme violence with the comparatively pure heroism of Viṣṇu's other human incarnations inevitably runs into trouble. Making one such attempt, P. L. Bhargava rejects the very notion of twenty-one generations of dead Kṣatriyas as "an absurd myth which has clouded the glory of this great hero of ancient India" (1992, 28). Taking a semi-euhemerist approach, he argues:

> The credit for this myth also goes to the Mahābhārata and the Bhāgavata Purāṇa. . . . The Padma Purāṇa which gives a long account of Paraśurāma's conflict with Kārtavīrya does say that he killed all the Kṣatriyas, but not twenty-one times. By all the Kṣatriyas the Padma Purāṇa no doubt means all the Kṣatriyas who were on the side of Kārtavīrya . . . (ibid.)

Leaving it to the reader to decide whether one man killing *all* the Kṣatriyas on the side of his enemy is appreciably more plausible than killing twenty-one generations of them, I will move on to a markedly more critical approach to historicizing the myth.

D. D. Kosambi, the godfather of Marxist historians in India, best expresses the historical materialist reading of the myth of Paraśurāma's varṇicide that has been more or less conventional wisdom since V. S. Sukthankar's article on the Bhārgavas in 1937.

> The importance of the fact cannot be overestimated that a clan of the beaten people had full control of the tradition and of the ritual of their conquerors. They used this monopoly for writing in, without troubling themselves about consistency, whatever suited them, either to appease the conquerors or to keep up their own pride. For example, we find in the Mahābhārata that the comparatively insignificant Bhārgava hero Paraśurāma exterminates the *kṣatriyas* no less than twenty-one times in revenge for the destruction of his own people. It is fairly clear that the revenge in this case was taken by the composer of the legend, not by the impotent hero; as such, it naturally betrays the psychological characteristic of overcompensation. A single extermination of the *kṣatriyas* would have sufficed to prevent the Brahmans having to serve them. The foundation of the national trait mentioned, i.e. the lack of a critical attitude, particularly towards historical events, was laid with the foundations of the caste system by the *kṣatriya* conquest. For the rest, the usefulness of an uncritical revision of old legends continued till well on into the historical period, one striking instance being the recasting of the *purāṇas*; the absorption of conquering tribes of invaders followed the same model, as for example in the case of the Scythian Rajputs. (1938–39, 202)

This passage is in line with Pollock's observation about the relationship of Kosambi's critical theory to the contemporaneous critical philological project of editing the *Mahābhārata* (2008, 52–53). It is also a rather unfortunate proof text for Pollock's argument that "Kosambi's general cultural theory and metatheoretical assumptions . . . are derived from the darkest and most undialectical period of Marxist intellectual history" (57).

While Kosambi's extraordinary efforts and erudition deserve much respect, even a superficial reading of his argument shows its problems. How, one wonders, would these myths be transmitted in way that would *not* look to Kosambi like "an uncritical revision of old legends"? If we look in the Sanskrit traditions for something that is critical in the same way as Plato's critique of Hesiod in *The Republic*, no precise analogue will be found. However, as we have already seen, there is a critical attitude within the epic itself from the very start, but it is expressed through other myths.

On one hand, Kosambi is right about the collective fantasy element of the myth, and profoundly so, as I have already argued and will again. On the other hand, this analysis obscures the complexity of the myth, and "Brahmin ideology" does not come close to exhausting its meanings. As anxious about their place in the changing social world about them as they seem to have been, to what extent did Brahmins understand themselves to be "beaten" and see the Kṣatriyas as "conquerors" when the Paraśurāma myth began to circulate? Any Kṣatriya audience hearing the story, even Yudhiṣṭhira in the epic, is de facto the product of a renewed and reinvigorated Kṣatriya line, the very opposite of an invading force. Those prideful and presumptuous Kṣatriyas were part of the "bad old days" before Paraśurāma's purge. In this light, the myth's message reads less like a pure revenge fantasy than the charter of a mutual admiration society for Brahmins and Kṣatriyas alike, with an important caveat that it could all happen again if the Kṣatriyas got out of line. As Choudhary observes, the Paraśurāma myth "was utilised and propagated even by some kshatriyas to justify their new-found status" (2010, 83). It is to questions of utilization and propagation that we turn to in this chapter. But first, we need to examine the simple fact, obvious to the point of invisibility, that Paraśurāma's varṇicide never actually works, ironically because this great mother-killer refrains from killing any Kṣatriya mothers.

## The *Kṣatra* as Sacrificial Remainder

> If even a trace remains of fire, a loan, or an enemy, it will grow back again and again. Therefore you must leave no trace.[1]
>
> —Sanskrit Proverb

In his discussion of the *Mahābhārata*, Goldman identifies the Bhārgavas as the "masters of life and death." "[Non-Bhārgava] Brāhmaṇas are subjected to violent death only sporadically in the epic. In contrast, the Bhṛgu sages are slain or threatened with violence in almost every myth . . ." and "[the] theme is frequently inverted, and Bhārgava sages often attack and kill their enemies, not sparing the unborn" (1977, 75). But Shulman writes that "violent potential is part of the Brahmin's symbolic identity," and that "the Brahmin ideals of detachment, purity, and control exist in relation to a reality of violent engagement in a violent world" (1985, 149). Even without the unique mixed-class status of Paraśurāma, it seems, there is much of the warrior in the Brahmin already, but a warrior whose power is largely ad hoc and bounded by the spatial and temporal confines of the sacrifice.

Whenever a sacrifice is made, there is a remainder or *ucchiṣṭa*: a portion of the offering not consumed or destroyed. As Charles Malamoud notes, "[There] always remains a residue which, while ambiguous, is nevertheless always possessed of an active, rather than an inert character" (1996, 22). Brahminical thinkers view the remainder with a tense ambivalence. On one hand, contact with leftover scraps of a meal, whether one's own or another's, is a source of pollution for Brahmins. On the other hand, both in Vedic mythology and in later temple-based rituals, the remainder takes on a sacred character as the source of creation or as a powerful and auspicious substance in the form of *prasād,* the sacred leftovers of a sacrifice or a temple offering ingested ceremonially by worshippers.

Besides *ucchiṣṭḥa,* there are two other types of sacrificial remainder or residue: *śeṣa* and *vāstu.* In mythology, the *śeṣa* is identified with Anantaśeṣa, the cosmic serpent who serves as Viṣṇu's couch. In the *Śatapatha Brāhmaṇa*, when the gods leave the earth after their great sacrifice, the *vāstu* is the abandoned sacrificial site, the domain of Rudra-Śiva and the source of his epithet Vāstavya (*ŚB* 1.7.3.1). The *ucchiṣṭha* receives special praise in *Atharva Veda* 11.7, which proclaims it as the locus of Name and Form, Indra and Agni, and all the universe.

There are three instances of remainder in the myth of Paraśurāma. The first is the *vāstu,* which is the consecrated sacrificial ground he leaves behind, namely Samantapañcaka, or Kurukṣetra, which becomes the site of the *Mahābhārata* war and the apotheosis of Kṛṣṇa. The second instance of remainder is the piece of land, somehow not technically considered part of the earth at the time he was exiled, on which Paraśurāma has to make his home after his exile.[2] The third remainder is constituted by the remnant of the *kṣatra,* the Kṣatriyas spared during Paraśurāma's varṇicide, either as unborn children in the wombs of Kṣatriya women or hidden away and protected from the massacre, who then become the basis for a new race of kings. We will begin with the *kṣatra.*

In the varṇicide story from the Śānti Parvan, Yudhiṣṭhira first raises the reasonable question of how he, a Kṣatriya, could exist if Paraśurāma had wiped out all the Kṣatriyas on the earth twenty-one times. The sage Akṛtavraṇa explains it this way:

> After [the destruction of the Kṣatriyas] O bull of the Bhāratas, Śūdras and Vaiśyas began acting on their desires with the wives of the Brahmins. When there is no king in the human world, the weaker are oppressed by the stronger, and no one has any control over his own possessions. After some time the Earth entered the Rasātala underworld, for she was not being protected in accordance with prescription, that is, by Kṣatriyas preserving Law. . . . The goddess Earth then propitiated Kaśyapa and made a request of him, asking for Kṣatriyas with brawny arms to be her guardians. (12.49.73)

The earth goddess (Ūrvī) goes on to explain that she has preserved nine Kṣatriyas of the Haihaya clan in various secret places, protected by a list of guardians that includes bears, the sages Parāśara and Gautama, cows in a forest, cows in a pen, monkeys, and the ocean. "These Kṣatriya heirs have been heard of here and there," explains Ūrvī; "let them watch over me right and I will stand without shaking. For my sake their fathers, and their grandfathers too, were killed in a war by the tireless Rāma, who said, 'I will make an end of them, no doubt of it.' I do not want to be always protected by someone who lacks the prowess to wage war" (12.49.75).

At the time Ūrvī is making this request, Paraśurāma has already gone into his final exile, but his absence does not change the fact that this last line clearly refers to him as a Brahmin without the qualities necessary to rule. When Kaśyapa returns the dominion of the Earth to the Kṣatriyas, who have survived as a remainder in the form of the nine hidden Haihayas, he undercuts the thematic thrust of the myth, denying the Brahminical strategy of assuming the political power of the kings. The reversal is doubly antagonistic because the progenitors of the new Kṣatriya class are drawn from the clan whose actions instigated the massacre in the first place. Ironically, Yudhiṣṭhira's response to the story is to exclaim, "My, oh my! The world was fortunate! Men on earth are very lucky that such a righteous [*dharmya*] deed was done by a Brahmin!" (12.50.1).

Another well-known survival story told in the *Bhāgavata*, *Brahmāṇḍa*, *Liṇga*, *Viṣṇu*, and *Vāyu Purāṇa*s, is that of King Bālika, also known as Mulaka because, as the only Kṣatriya to survive the varṇicide, he is the root (*mula*) of the current Kṣatriya line, including the dynasty of Rāma Dāśarathi. In the *Viṣṇu Purāṇa*, Mulaka earns the epithet Nārīkavaca ("He Whose Armor Is Women") because he surrounds himself with a shield of naked women when the extirpation of the Kṣatriyas is underway (*ViP* 4.4.46).[3]

In a Kannada version of the myth from the *Paraśurāmarāmāyaṇa,* a *kāvya* composed by a poet named Babburu Rangappa sometime between the thirteenth and the eighteenth centuries CE, the *kṣatra* remainder is described in this way: After Paraśurāma has killed the Kṣatriyas and given the earth to the Brahmin class, the Brahmins, now in charge of all the kingdoms, become afraid that the remaining Kṣatriyas (presumably unborn at the time of the massacre and now grown to adulthood) will try to overthrow them, and they summon Paraśurāma for help. Paraśurāma hears their plea, but, disgusted by their weakness, "becomes angry and curses them instantaneously that they would become gluttons and lose their self-respect." He then relents and modifies the curse so that Brahmins and Kṣatriyas would thereafter share power, with Brahmins ruling by dint of their learning and Kṣatriyas by their strength (Janaki 1966, 60–61). Stories like this one also echo Vedic myths about the origin of kingship (like the Pṛthu myth) and the ascendancy of Indra as king of the gods.

The figure of Paraśurāma presented in this story is much more consistent with the image of the culture-building progenitor of western Indian myth and temple legends than the apocalyptic destroyer of the *Mahābhārata.* As such, this variant shares much in common with the myths identifying Paraśurāma as the founder of various institutions, temples, clans, and regions. It is also noteworthy that the Brahmins in this myth take on the stereotypical characteristics of weak, decadent parasites that they often embody in medieval dramas.

As we have seen in the previous chapter, some clans saw no shame in claiming descent from those who screamed and ran away and thereby lived to fight another day. The clan history of the Kāyasthas tells of their illustrious and pragmatic ancestor King Candrasena, who preserved his line by readily agreeing to Paraśurāma's condition that he must train his children to write, not fight, if he wanted to live. The Bhavsars (dyers, printmakers, and *dhobis* in the urban centers of Gujarat and Maharashtra) took refuge from Paraśurāma with their patron goddess Hiṅgalā, who stripped them of their sacred threads and gave them needles and thread instead. Their family religious practice centers on Hanumān, Khāṇḍobā, Bālāji, and Hiṅgalā, as well as Paraśurāma, whom they worship in the form of a metal palm and propitiate with the sacrifice of sheep. The silk-weaving Khatris claim not just to have once been Kṣatriyas, but to have been descendants of Paraśurāma's arch-enemy Kārtavīrya Arjuna. Like the Bhavsars, they were protected from the varṇicide by a goddess (Kālī) and they offer monthly goat sacrifices to Paraśurāma's mother, Reṇukāmba (Choudhary 2010, 298–99).

Origin myths of the Fire Clan Rajputs of Rajasthan trace their beginnings to the lawless period after the varṇicide in which demons threatened the sacrifice. In one version, the sacrificial fire is completely extinguished (a catastrophic event) prompting the Brahmins to kindle a second fire and pray to Śiva, who causes three blazing warriors to come out of the fire and attack the demons. When they are unsuccessful, the Brahmins call on Vasiṣṭha, who summons another warrior out of the fire. This fourth fire-born fighter defeats the demons with the help of the lion-mounted goddess and all four become progenitors of the branches of the Fire Clan Rajputs. In another version, Viśvāmitra, not Vasiṣṭha, steps in to help recreate the *kṣatra,* which is accomplished after the gods kindle a "fire-fountain," and throw into it four dolls that reemerge as the four Rajput warriors (Babb 2004, 89–90). This image of the rekindled fire after a polluted sacrifice calls to mind the familiar and foundational Śaiva myth of Dakṣa's sacrifice, echoing Paraśurāma's Śaiva nature.

A distinctive variation on this theme not involving Kṣatriyas is found in the mytho-history of another Rajasthani caste, the mercantile Khaṇḍelvāl Vaiśyas. In the story, Paraśurāma offers Viṣṇu a *yajña* to atone for his varṇicide and one group of officiating priests, the Madhuchandādi sages, at first refuse to accept any part of the sacrificial gift. By the time they relent, there is nothing left but the golden altar itself, which Paraśurāma cuts into forty-nine pieces and distributes among them. Śunaḥśepa, the adopted son of Viśvāmitra, does not take one of the pieces, but uses his wealth to buy one from someone who received it as a sacrificial gift. His descendants then become the Khaṇḍelvāl Vaiśyas.

This story is notable for tying the story of Paraśurāma to the transition from a sacrificial gift-giving economy that forms the background of the Bhārgava-Haihaya feud to a supply-and-demand-based currency economy. It also presents a kind of inversion of the *ucchiṣṭha*—not a remnant, but a lack: if everyone had received an equal portion of the golden *vedi* after the sacrifice, there would be no need to trade. Like a sliding tile puzzle, this sacrifice creates the possibility for movement by leaving an empty square. This empty square is identified, significantly, with Śunaḥśepa, the would-be sacrificial victim who is spared in a paradigmatic act of substitution, or exchange (Babb 2004, 126–27).

Lawrence Babb, who collected this story, emphasizes the lengths to which he had to go to track it down in order to demonstrate "the currently total nascent state, if it can be said to exist at all, of the Khaṇḍelvāl Vaiśyas' quest to rationalize a single mythohistorical construction of their identity" (2004, 125). Clearly, some of the variants discussed here play important roles in the self-understanding of some caste or clan. Some do not. But all of them arise from some aspect of the structure of the Paraśurāma cycle. In this case, that aspect is the nagging, maddening insufficiency of even so monumental and methodical a sacrificial act as Paraśurāma's varṇicide. Lévi-Strauss writes that, in myth, "[the] function of repetition is to render the structure of the myth apparent" (1963, 229). As variants of myth multiply, the mythos becomes richer while, conversely, the structure is increasingly reduced to its simplest form. The form laid bare here is simple indeed: the opposition of static fullness to protean incompleteness. The sliding tile puzzle cannot move if all of its squares are laid in the frame, but if one is removed it can be rearranged to form varied complex patterns.

Despite the finality of the epic's description of Paraśurāma's varṇicidal annihilation of the Kṣatriyas, the deeply held Vedic idea of the sacrifice's necessary incompleteness and the prosaic but undeniable evidence of Kṣatriyas alive and well on the earth today leaves the door open for the *kṣatra* as sacrificial remainder. In the next section, we will look at the land creation motif, a form of the remainder that does not fit as neatly into the Vedic ritual model of the abandoned sacrificial site or the unconsumed offering, but is deeply Śaiva and suggests the presence of deeper (or perhaps wider) Indo-European roots.

## The Land Creation Submotif

> Cuchulain stirred,
> Stared on the horses of the sea, and heard
> The cars of battle and his own name cried;
> And fought with the invulnerable tide.
>
> —William Butler Yeats,
> "Cuchulain's Fight with the Sea."

By way of introduction, let us look first at the Greek myth of Alkmaion as presented by Frazer in *Folklore in the Old Testament.*

> Tradition told how the matricide Alcmaeon, haunted by the ghost of his murdered mother Eriphyle, long wandered restlessly over the world, till at last he repaired to the oracle at Delphi, and the priestess told him that "the only land whither the avenging spirit of Eriphyle would not dog him was the newest land, which the sea had uncovered since the pollution of his mother's blood had been incurred." (1923, 36)

As was his wont, Frazer lays out his treatment of the Greek Alkmaion story alongside examples of man-slayer taboos from various tribes of Africa and the Pacific islands and the biblical story of Cain, arguing that the explanations for the exiles of Cain, a fratricide (and a non-Indic *cirañjīvin*) and Alkmaion, a matricide, are based on a shared idea that the earth is offended when someone sheds the blood of a family member, and so refuses to let a kin-murderer settle or farm on it. If Frazer had been aware of the story of Paraśurāma, he might well have included it in this discussion.

Paraśurāma recapitulates his earlier crime of chopping off his mother's head when he wipes out the Kṣatriyas, "decapitating" society by depriving it of its political leadership. It makes sense, therefore, that both crimes would lead to a state of exile. According to the *Mahābhārata* account, Paraśurāma ends his varṇicide campaign with a sacrifice in which he gives the whole earth to the sages and goes to live on Mount Mahendra. In the account from the *Skanda Purāṇa* and the legend connected to Paraśurāma temple at Pedhe, the situation is somewhat different in that the sages declare that since he has given away the earth in his sacrifice, he can no longer live on its surface. To get around this condition, Paraśurāma has to reclaim some land from the sea, land that was not part of the earth at the time he gave it away, an action that resembles the familiar story of Varāha the boar raising the earth from the bottom of the sea on his tusk, a myth of the "Earth-Diver" type.

Another variant of this submotif appears in the *Brahmāṇḍa Purāṇa*, which conflates an elemental struggle of earth against water with an agonistic sacrifice. Sagara, the god of the ocean, performs a horse sacrifice that gives him dominion over the whole earth. But as the oceans begin to overflow and cover all the land with water, the gods ask Paraśurāma to intercede. Paraśurāma then appeals to Varuṇa to pull back the waters and throws the sacrificial vessel far away, causing the waters to recede and thereby creating the western kingdom of Śūrpāraka (*BḍP* 51–56).[4]

Myths connecting Paraśurāma to the Konkan Coast between Mumbai and Goa sometimes forego the exile (and sometimes the axe as well), focusing on the elemental battle between land and sea, as in the story told in a pamphlet collected by Anne Feldhaus from a temple near Cipḷuṇ in the Ratnāgiri district. In this variant, Paraśurāma is on Mount Mahendra when the ocean begins to pound against the mountainside, prompting the Brahmin warrior to nock an arrow. The ocean quickly surrenders, but once he has taken aim, Paraśurāma cannot withdraw his arrow. Instead, he allows the ocean to retreat past the place where his arrow will land (2003, 12).

In another variant, when he finds himself exiled and in need of a place to live, Paraśurāma prays to Śiva, and the god sends his peacock-mounted son Subrahmaṇya to assist him. Subrahmaṇya then creates a goddess named Kumārī and tells Paraśurāma to spend one year worshipping her. At the end of the year, the god Varuṇa appears and Paraśurāma asks him for some land on which to live. Varuṇa tells him to throw his axe as far into the ocean as he can. As he does this, the water recedes up to Gōkarṇa, the place where his axe finally falls, thus creating the strip of land that stretches from Gōkarṇa in the north to Kanyākumāri in the south (Janaki 1966, 63–64; Veluthat 2009, 135). As Charpentier notes (1937, 12n14), this theme is also found in the Irish myth of Tuirbe Tragmār, who throws his axe into the ocean to create land in the same way:

> Tis from that heritage he, (standing) on Telach Bela ("the Hill of the Axe"), would hurl a cast of his axe in the face of the floodtide, so that he forbade the sea, which then would not come over the axe. And his pedigree is not known, unless he be one of the defectives of the men of art who fled out of Tara before Samildanach, (and whose posterity) is in the secret parts of Bregia. Whence Trdig Tuirbi, "Turbe's Strand." (Stokes 1893, 488–89)

In the *Vādeśvarodaya-kāvya* of Viśvanātha, Paraśurāma's irascible nature comes to the surface and he becomes angry when the ocean refuses to give him dry footing after he has bathed in a sacred stream. In retaliation, he curses the ocean to dry up. But then he lessens the curse, causing the ocean to recede only far enough to create a new strip of coast. Later the demon king Rāvaṇa and his army come to Paraśurāma's new land for sport and sex, incurring the Brahmin's wrath again. After Paraśurāma starts killing demons and threatens to drown Rāvaṇa's kingdom of Lanka, Brahmā intervenes to stop him. Paraśurāma then goes into hiding but swears to come back to aid any Brahmin who calls him. When two boys test him by playing a trick with a corpse and pretending to be in danger, Paraśurāma becomes disgusted and curses them, then goes into hiding permanently (Pusalker 1951, 66–76).

The land reclamation submotif functions as a kind of *point de capiton,* or "quilting point" in the Paraśurāma cycle. It is a repetition of the forest-to-field transformation in the matricide micromyth, with the undifferentiated forest becoming the ocean and the cultivated field becoming the reclaimed and settled land. It is also the intersection of the fluid motif that dominates the matricide stories and the sacrificial remainder motif that is the coda of the varṇicide stories, tied down in geographic space by its inclusion in the mythic self-understanding of multiple communities in Malabar, as told in the Sanskrit *Keralamāhātmya* and its Malayalam counterpart the *Kēraḷōlpatti*.[5]

The submotif arises to solve a conflict in the narrative that at first seems self-evident and logical: Paraśurāma has nowhere to go once he has given up the earth. But a closer look at this problem in the larger context of Hindu mythology reveals its inconsistency. When heroes, or sages, or goddesses-in-disguise are finished with their work upon the earth, they go to another realm, a Devaloka or a Pitṛloka. Whenever the demons lose sovereignty over the earth in the constant back-and-forth war with the gods, they retreat to a hell. Likewise, whenever the gods lose sovereignty, they go up to a heaven to plan their next move. Under what circumstances would an incarnation of Viṣṇu be compelled to stay on earth after his task on it was completed? Why, for Paraśurāma, is the Triple World inexplicably flattened to just one level? The strangeness of Paraśurāma's problem demands our attention and points to a structure that, the reader will notice, closely mirrors the Lacanian process of subjectification described earlier.

The land reclamation motif plays out the contest of "whole versus hole," opposition between stagnant fullness (elsewhere envisioned as a world overburdened by prideful petty kings, a calcified social structure, an unworkable family structure) and malleable incompleteness. Then the land reclamation resolves this opposition: after the sacrifice that concludes the varṇicide, the earth is made whole. But it excludes Paraśurāma, rendering him an excess (a hole in reverse). Transforming the ocean floor into dry land by subtracting its water then creates a new space that the excess can occupy, freeing up space elsewhere. Paraśurāma's act of raising the land from the sea keeps the earth whole, but creates a space like the missing square that allows the sliding tile puzzle to move. This also explains why Paraśurāma cannot go upward to Heaven, since horizontal tension must be worked out horizontally, with the elements of earth and water.

## The Nambudiris: Paraśurāma and the Culture of the Malabar Coast

Lying between the thick green forests of the Western Ghats and the white sand beaches of the Arabian Sea, the Malabar Coast is geologically well suited to Paraśurāma's color palette. The soil is made up of ancient laterite, red with iron oxide that forms a brick-like surface in the hot season. When the monsoon sends down its torrential rainfalls and cracks the ground open, forming seasonal streams that go to the ocean, the rapidly flowing channels dislodge the iron and aluminum from the hardened soil and turn the water the color of rust—or blood.[6] To the south lies gold deposited in subterranean quartz reefs, mined since the beginning of the Christian Era.

Like Saint Thomas, another famous outsider who made an impression on the region, Paraśurāma is revered in southwest India as a bringer of culture. He is the one who not only raises the land from the sea but also imports Brahmins from North India into the Buddhist-dominated landscape, institutes the worship of deities such as Subrahmaṇya and Kālī, introduces Kerala's famed tradition of matrilineal succession,[7] and initiates the era of Paraśurāma, dated to around 1176 BCE, followed by the age of provisional kings called the Perumāls and the age of the Tampurāns, the latter being petty kings ruling after the twelfth century (Veluthat 2009, 134). At one time, the Paraśurāma story was a valuable part of the region's self-understanding, though its stock has sharply declined in recent years.[8] Even low castes such as Valan fishermen and the Pulaya slaves had origin myths based on Paraśurāma's transformative actions (Lemercinier 1984, 119).

The *Mūṣakavaṃśakāvya* describes Cellūr in northern Kerala as being "marked by the sacrificial pillar and never-extinguished sacred fire that commemorate the sacrifice of the Great One with the Battle-ax who extirpated many princes" and Vedic Brahmins from the north served as advisors in the Sangam courts (Narayanan and Veluthat 1983, 256) Both the Nambudiri Brahmins and the martial Nayars have repeatedly deployed the story of "the gift of Paraśurāma," familiar to all throughout the western coastal region known as Paraśurāmakṣetra or Bhārgavakṣetra, to justify their hegemony generally and, in the case of the Nambudiris, their hereditary landholding rights specifically.

In the Keralan myths, water plays an important part in the political use to which the Nambudiri Brahmins put the story of Paraśurāma. The seventeenth-century *Kēraḷōlpatti*, recorded and analyzed by William Logan, the colorful Scotsman who served as a magistrate and colonial administrator in Kerala during the late nineteenth century, stresses the thematic nexus of blood, water, guilt, and possession both in the sacrifice that follows Paraśurāma's slaughter of the Kṣatriyas and in his raising of Kerala from the sea, an event celebrated today with the harvest festival of Onam. After Paraśurāma wiped out the Kṣatriyas, reports Logan, "[at] *Vishvamitra*'s suggestion he then made over all the land within the four seas to Rishis 'with all the blood-guiltiness attached to it by making them drink the water of possession' " (1887, 221).

About blood-guilt and its connection to the "water of possession," Logan writes:

> The deeds of the various dynasties there cited afford the most conclusive proof that in the grants of land conferred on the [Brahmins] in return for their services the act of giving is almost invariably accompanied or preceded by "libations of water" by "pouring of water" by "copious libations of water," "with water in hand," with the pouring of "water out of a beautiful golden water-pot," etc. In twenty-five of these deeds casually observed and extending from about the fifth century A.D. down to the year 1339–40 A.D. the omission to mention a libation of water as accompanying a grant of land to these Vedic [Brahmins] occurs only once. . . . It is hard to resist the conclusions therefore that, as the notes to deeds Nos. 2 and 38 set forth, the customary libation of water in making a hereditary grant of land in Malabar was introduced by the Vedic [Brahmins] about the beginning of the eighth century A.D., and that in parts of the district, where the influence of that caste was but small, this incident in a grant or sale of hereditary land did not obtain currency down to quite recent years. (600)

The connection Logan draws between the emphasis on the property-transferring nature of water in the Nambudiri ("Vedic") Brahmins' version of the Paraśurāma myth and the importance of water libations in the places where they attained cultural and economic hegemony is instructive and points toward the large role the myth had in propping up Brahminical power in South India.

Besides marking the connection of water libations to Nambudiri hegemony, Logan is also tactless enough to point out the rather transparent ideology (in this variant, it can hardly be seen as anything less) contained in the various versions of the *Kēraḷōlpatti* with this cutting assessment of the Brahminical histories:

> What is substituted for the real history of this period in these traditions is a farrago of legendary nonsense, having for definite aim the securing to the Brāhmaṇa caste of unbounded power and influence in the country. The land was miraculously reclaimed for their benefit; the whole of it was made over to them with the "blood-guilty water of possession"; they were the first inhabitants; the kings were appointed and the land was governed by them;

> and the only allusion to prior occupants is an obscure reference to "serpents," from fear of which the first immigrants fled back to the country whence they came. (1887, 244)

Logan gives several suggestions of who he thinks these "serpents" really were. He conjectures that the text may be referring to the early Christian settlers of the region, or more likely, to a Persian Manichean sect, since the Manicheans saw Christ as a serpent (201, 222). Further in the text, he writes that "[this] allusion to the serpents, who 'protected' the land, contains perhaps an allusion to Jaina immigrants, worshippers of the twenty-third Jaina *Tirtham Kara*, *Parsva* or *Parsvanatha*, whose symbol was a hooded snake" (244). But it also seems likely that the text refers to real snakes, given Paraśurāma's solution to the problem: in a move that would have been unpopular with his ophidiophobic kinsman Ruru, Paraśurāma orders the Brahmin colonists to adopt the native snakes as family deities and establishes preserves for the snakes to live in undisturbed (Menon 2003, 2).

Paraśurāma's expertise in social engineering also apparently extends to agricultural practices. In the Malayalam *Kṛṣi Gītā,* Paraśurāma perceives unhappiness among his Keralan Brahmins and comes to see what the trouble is. After they assure him they are properly performing the Vedic rites and dutifully praise him for his destruction of Kārtavīrya, they make this request:

> In the interminable space Your Highness has given in this universe, you have self-willingly instructed us solely on what is just and unjust. Be kind enough also to command on the names of different grain crops, the tubers and fruits for the blessed, with their optimal time of sowing and planting, besides the techniques for proper cultivation. What other means of subsistence do we have? (*KG* 1.40–50)

Paraśurāma obliges and instructs them on the relative yields of different seed varieties (1.69–297), the five uncertainties faced by the plowman (3.251–260), and the proper days on which to sow dry sesame (4.23–40).

In one respect, Paraśurāma's consecration of his newly created land bears a striking resemblance to other stories from the Bhārgava corpus. After Paraśurāma installed the serpent deities and built his martial arts academies, according to the *Kēraḷōlpatti,* "[on] the earth was sprinkled gold dust and firmly fixed water in which gold had been immersed, and gold coins incorporated in the soil as treasure; thus was the quaking of the earth stopped" (Menon

2003, 28–29). Of course, this could be pure imagination, or it could be a reference to the actual gold mines in the region. But if we see the stories of Aurva and Paraśurāma as the bookends of the great Bhārgava-Kṣatriya conflict, it is pleasingly symmetrical that the feud, which begins when the Bhārgava Brahmins bury their gold in the ground, thereby deliberately provoking their patrons the Haihaya kings into exterminating them and causing the surviving Bhārgava Aurva to seek equally violent retribution (*MBh* 1.169–71), should end with gold being buried into the ground once more, to stop "the quaking of the earth" once and for all.[9]

Even if we limit our analysis to the cycle as it appears in the *Mahābhārata*, the conflict ends there too, with gold being put back in the ground; Paraśurāma performs his final sacrifice at Kurukṣetra on a golden altar ten *vyāma*s wide and nine *vyāma*s high that he then gives to Kaśyapa. In the *Kēraḷōlpatti* version of events, Paraśurāma's great sacrifice at Kurukṣetra is replaced by his creation of the Paraśurāmakṣetra, which he then consecrates as the Karmabhūmi. That both events return to the motif of gold in the ground from the Aurva story is more evidence of the high degree of thematic continuity that runs through the Bhārgava cycle.

After Paraśurāma initially reclaims the land from the sea with his axe, makes it habitable, and imports his population, he is left with the most unwelcome task facing any conqueror: setting up an administration. Since, to his knowledge, there are no Kṣatriyas left on the earth after his massacre (and even if there were, he would be unlikely to invite his sworn foes into his new home), Paraśurāma recruits Brahmins from other parts of India to settle the land, organizing them into sixty-four villages, most of which were probably understood to be located in present day Cochin, Malabar, and North Travancore. T. Madhava Menon, translator of the *Gundert Kēraḷōlpatti*, writes:

> There is difference regarding the source from which the [Brahmins] were recruited; according to one version, it was from the banks of the Krishna; Logan's version indicated that it was one sole individual, a poor Brāhmaṇa who had eight sons. According to our version, Parasuraman "created" (*uṇḍākki*) [Brahmins] and gathered them from several locations. It might have been this version that became responsible, later on, for the myth that Parasuraman actually recruited local fisher folk, and conferred Brahminhood on them, before bringing them in to populate the new lands. (2003, 2)

But a society run by Brahmins and not Kṣatriyas is bound to run up against the conventions of dharma, necessitating that Brahmins use violence or at least the threat of it to keep order. As we have already seen, in the version told in the Ādi Parvan of the *Mahābhārata*, Paraśurāma has to repopulate the earth with kings by having the Brahmin males impregnate the Kṣatriya widows and give birth to a race of righteous rulers. It is out of this stock that the dharmic Pāṇḍavas come, along with (oddly enough) their evil Kaurava cousins (*MBh* 1.98.1–10).

But in Kerala, either because he has massacred the Kṣatriya women along with the men or because he has too little faith in the purifying power of an injection of Brahmin blood, Paraśurāma uses only Brahmins to build his new society. He establishes thirty-two villages around Gokarnam in the north and thirty-two south of Payyanur. Then, to prevent the Brahmins from leaving their new homes, he institutes new customs, such as tonsure and matrilineal succession (the latter custom, according to one *Kēraḷōlpatti* tradition, is one that Paraśurāma has instituted because of his own *varṇa* connection to his mother, and only the Brahmins of the village of Peiyanur have adopted it) that would mark them forever as different from the Brahmin communities they left behind and therefore make them unlikely to be readmitted. He also establishes certain Brahmin clans as militias and trains them in combat. As a result, these Brahmins fall from their positions of purity and are no longer worthy to perform sacrifice. Meanwhile, the immigrants who ran from the snakes are received as half-Brahmins when they come crawling back and Śūdra groups like the Nayars—who also adopt matrilineal succession on Paraśurāma's orders (Logan 1887, 223)—are promoted to be the new military caste and "the eye, the hand, and the command" of the Brahmin leadership (Menon 2003, 5).

To keep order, Paraśurāma invests governing power in just four of the sixty-four villages: Peiyanur, Perinchellur, Parappur, and Chenganiyur. But when the power of the four villages proves insufficient to arbitrate all the disputes that arise, the Brahmins appoint, presumably from among themselves, a protector for each village who will serve for three years in return for one-sixth of the yield from the land. Even this is not enough to keep the inhabitants of Kerala happy, and when the utopian society of Kerala begins to struggle under the weight of oppressive and greedy Brahmin landlords, the inhabitants decide to appoint a foreigner as a provisional king called the Perumāl. The Perumāl would serve at the pleasure of the Brahmins for a period of twelve years and receive only a place of residence at the capital in Kodungallur as compensation. Logan writes,

> Thus runs the Kēraḷōlpatti:—"When the Brahmans first appointed a king they made an agreement on oath with him to this effect—'Do that which is beyond our power to do and protect. When complaints happen to arise, we will settle them by ourselves. You are not to question us on that point. For formality's sake you may ask why we deal with affairs ourselves after making you a king.' At this day even when complaints arise the king says:—'Why do you deal with them? Why did you not make your complaint to me?' This is owing to the former oath. (1887, 224)

Unsurprisingly, kings had a tough row to hoe in the region founded by their relentless exterminator. Menon reports that, in the legends of Kerala, "[many] Perumāls did not survive the full term, but died, deserted, or resigned well before the expiry of it" (2003, 5). Logan identifies the first three Perumāls with the three warring dynasties of southern India: the Cēra, the Chola, and the Pāṇḍya. The first Perumāl, identified with the Cēra kingdom, dies eight years and four months into his twelve-year reign. His successor Chola Perumāl leaves after ten years and two months, and the third Perumāl, Paṇḍi, leaves after nine years.

The fourth Perumāl secures the aid of two demons to protect him from the Brahmins' sorcery and proceeds to overstep his bounds. The story of this king's defeat as it appears in the Sanskrit *Keralamahātmya* and the Malayalam *Kēraḷōlpatti* demonstrates a politically motivated manipulation of the themes of the Paraśurāma story. In the Sanskrit version, the fourth Perumāl, Bhūtarāya Pāṇḍya (his epithet, associated with Śiva, means "King of the Ghosts"), is a king who invades the land with a demon army and establishes a temple and a trade center called Bhūtanāth, only to be driven out of the kingdom by Paraśurāma.

But the version in the *Kēraḷōlpatti* does not involve Paraśurāma at all and it is useful to see how the elements associated with him are woven into the epic after he has been removed.

> One Bhattatiri vowed that he would remove the demons and kill [Bhūtarāya]; he challenged the Perumal to a game of chess and defeated him; then, playing for stakes, he again defeated Perumal and won from him his demon attendants. He ordered them to go to the seashore and count the waves; as there was no end to the waves, the demons had to stay there, and could not return. He notified the other Brahmins that the Perumal should be murdered

> that evening; so from 10 villages, they assembled, armed, went to the palace, and then, the same Bhattatiri killed the king. Then, conscious that he had committed the sin of violence, he voluntarily sat on the doorstep and he (and the members of his lineage) were known as "Nambidi" ever since. This, let it be known, is the Nambidi who is the Kakkad Karanavappad. (Menon 2003, 38)

The first motif one recognizes is the dicing match, unrelated to Paraśurāma but significant in the *Mahābhārata* as the weakness that the Kauravas exploit in Yudhiṣṭhira to send him and his brothers into exile. Here it takes the form of a chess game in which a gullible king is tricked out of his kingdom by one who takes advantage of his vice. And, like the winner of the dicing match in the *Mahābhārata*, the victor claims the stakes only to set up a devious assassination plot. In the epic, Duryodhana is unable to find the exiled Yudhiṣṭhira and his brothers and murder them before they can muster an army to replace the one they had lost. But Bhattatiri and his Brahmin co-conspirators attack their king en masse and murder him when he is unprotected, his demon army presumably still absorbed in counting the waves.

The name that Bhattatiri assumes after the regicide, Kakkad Karanavappad, Menon relates in a footnote, is the name of "the eldest member of the combined lineage comprising four 'royal' families, viz., Manakkulam, Cheralayam, Ayinkkuru, and Punnasseri. They fall in between the Brahmins and the Kṣatriyas in ritual and status" (38). The Nambidi, we learn from Logan, belong to a group of castes called the Ambalavasis who "form a sort of intermediate class between the Nambudiris and the Nayars" (1887, 130). He goes on to explain that one subdivision of the caste, which is permitted to wear the Brahmin thread, call themselves Nambudiris and follow the law of matrilineal succession.

Anthropologist L. K. Ananthakrishnan Iyer dismisses out of hand the folk etymology of Nambidi as deriving from the phrase *nam padiyil* ("we on the step") suggested by the story (Menon 2003, 38). But it is clear what underlies it. The Nambidis are being identified, either from the inside or, more likely, from the outside, as a liminal caste. After he kills the Perumāl Bhūtarāya, Bhattatiri realizes that he has lost his Brahmin purity by shedding blood, exiles himself to the doorstep (a liminal space familiar from its association with the story of the Narasiṃha *avatāra* in the *Bhāgavata Purāṇa*), and becomes the progenitor of a new caste that is neither Kṣatriya nor Brahmin.

With its elements of regicide, impurity, exile, and culture creation, Bhattatiri's story clearly draws upon the themes of Paraśurāma's slaughter of the

Kṣatriyas and subsequent founding of Kerala even if the axe-wielding Brahmin himself is missing. One reason for this may be that, while the *Kēraḷōlpatti* is ambivalent about Bhattatiri's actions, it is frequently openly critical of Paraśurāma's legacy as a whole, pointing out the disastrous violations of *varṇa* and dharma that come out of his attempts to found an all-Brahmin society, which quickly begins to fall apart at the seams like the nameless South Indian Brahmin village in U. R. Anantha Murthy's novel *Samskara*.

As soon as Paraśurāma founds his holy land in Kerala, the Brahmins he imports begin to be lowered and debased by the actions (taking up arms) and customs (matrilineal succession) that he forces on them. The first wave of immigrants, according to the text, flee from the snakes and are accepted as degraded Brahmins only when they return. Other Brahmin clans are summarily downgraded in status when Paraśurāma appoints them armed protectors of the land. Menon's translation reads:

> Thereafter, [Paraśurāma] ordained that the land should be protected (from attacks); "you require to use arms and weapons; you take these from me," so addressing all the 64 villages, they thought together and decided: "if we take to arms, then we will become involved in the governance, and will lose our commitment to penance; it is not consistent with the recital of the Vedas; it will vitiate several of our rites and rituals." (27)

But Paraśurāma invests some thirty-six thousand of them with arms anyway, and grants them the right to kill anyone without permission, possibly as a tradeoff for their loss of ritual purity. The inherent dangers for members of Paraśurāma's Brahmin army are even more explicit in his recruitment of the Bharadvāja clan (Droṇa's clan, as we recall):

> Then Sri Parasurama enquired: "Who will take over my sin in having killed heroes?" In response, some belonging to Bharadvaja gotra undertook to bear that sin. (Menon 2003, 30)

Along with lowering the status of some Brahmins by charging them with the duties of Kṣatriyas, Paraśurāma compromises the ritual purity of his entire menagerie of Brahmins when he elevates the lowest and least pure *varṇa,* the Śūdras, to Nayars and puts them in constant contact with their Brahmin masters. However fraught their relations with them had been, at least the Kṣatriyas were twice-born. And in the absence of oppressive kings, the

Brahmins quickly begin to oppress each other, necessitating first the failed experiment of Brahmin protectors, and then the institution of the Perumāls, a development right out of George Orwell's *Animal Farm*.

The *varṇa* breakdowns continue with the reign of Ceramāṉ Perumāl, whom the Brahmins allow to rule for three times the prescribed terms of twelve years, despite his propensity for bowing down to washermen who happen to resemble Śiva and his attempt to give away his kingdom to an itinerant singer whose songs pleased him (Shulman 1985, 247–48). As a result of this descent into monarchy, the Brahmins abandon Paraśurāma's custom of matrilineal succession and the unity of the Brahmin communities evaporates.

While, in this mythical version of the history of Kerala, "coincidences in the narration with actual historical facts [are] only a matter of chance," the stories take on a new life with the arrival of European colonizers (Menon 2003, 16). Powerful Brahmins, especially the deeply orthodox Nambudiri Brahmins, use the oft-repeated story of "Paraśurāma's gift" to protect the property rights to their gifted lands. The many versions of the *Kēraḷōlpatti* that are current by the eighteenth century sometimes throw in actual, and often wildly anachronistic, historical names to lend themselves authenticity. The Keralan historian E. K. Pillai writes, somewhat cynically,

> The aim of all these was the same—to impress on the people the story of Parasurama's gift and induce them to accept it as truth. The central theme of all the [*Kēraḷōlpattis*] is that the land was entrusted to the kings by the Nambudiris and, therefore, it was the duty of the kings to obey implicitly the directions of the Nambudiris. (1970, 192)

As Logan's stated opinions on the matter indicate, British colonial administrators were unimpressed by the Nambudiris' claims. But the Muslim and Portuguese dynasties that preceded them had been happy to accept and enforce the extensive Nambudiri privileges outlined in the *Kēraḷōlpatti* tradition, with its emphasis on the unequivocal nature of Paraśurāma's gift.

> One feature that comes through with great impact is that [the *Kēraḷōlpatti*] sufficed as a moral and cultural force, in a region marked by a cultural identity, but without cultural leadership. This enabled the few Brahmins to establish a monopoly over cultural sources, which they used to silence other traditions. (Menon 2003, 17)

Some of these other traditions are found in temple inscriptions in the region from the ninth through the thirteenth centuries. These inscriptions demonstrate that Nambudiris, who were most closely identified with the legacy of the Paraśurāma story, were not the majority landholders during that period, but were receiving land gifts from other wealthier groups (Pillai 1970, 325). The story of Paraśurāma's gift was also circulated in Tulu Nadu (South Canara) in the Kannada *Grāmapaddhati*, but it never gained an ideological foothold there as it did in Kerala.[10] Brahmins never became landholders in Tulu Nadu, where the tradition has Paraśurāma cursing the Brahmins he has brought in for their ingratitude and turning them into outcastes (Veluthat 2009, 136–37).

While the story of Paraśurāma from the *Kēraḷōlpatti* agrees with the epic on the basic points of Paraśurāma's varṇicide and expiatory sacrifice, everything that follows is a departure from the *Mahābhārata* narrative. And even regarding the massacre and the sacrifice, there are some differences. The *Kēraḷōlpatti* says that Paraśurāma, whom it regards as an *avatāra* of Viṣṇu, killed all of the Kṣatriyas twenty-one times over and then, in an episode that conflates the sacrifice at Kurukṣetra, the penance on Mount Mahendra, and the reclaiming of earth from the ocean,

> decided that the sin of killing heroes should be got rid of, and to perform the required rites, proceeded to Gokarnam [in Karnataka], sat on the great mountain there, worshipped and did penance to Varuna, had the waters pushed back; bowed to Goddess Earth, created 110 *kātam*-s of land; and for the Malayalam land (thus created), deciding that protection was needed, installed 108 deities. (Menon 2003, 26)

Although it has moved the site of Paraśurāma's sacrifice a fair distance south and west, this version does include the *vāstu* that is Kurukṣetra, naming it as the home of the Brahmins that Paraśurāma imports into his new land.

## Paraśurāma and the Keralan Martial Arts Traditions

Along with Brahmins, practitioners of the martial art of *kalaripayattu* also trace their tradition back to the instruction of Paraśurāma. Even though the practice as it is known today does not predate the middle of the twentieth century, those who want to see *kalaripayattu* recognized as an authentic South Indian tradition are glad to be able to trace their lineage back to the region's mythical founder and the *dhanurveda* teachings associated with him. Although the term *kalaripayattu* has only been in use for less than a century, the tradition to which it refers is a mixture of Tamil martial traditions from the Sangam era (early centuries CE) and the dhanurvedic practice of the north Indian Brahmins who began setting up schools called *salai* or *ghatika* during the seventh century CE (Zarrilli 1998, 24–35).

To put this in historical perspective, we should note that toward the end of the twelfth century, the Tamil armies of the Chola dynasty had been largely driven out of Kerala after centuries of warfare with the Cēra kings. One of the factors that turned the tide in the Cēras' favor was the deployment of suicide squads made up of Chavers, warriors sworn to triumph in battle or die trying. Another factor was the Nambudiri Brahmins' use of their translocal ties of lineage to organize rural armed resistance movements based in temples. Over the course of the fighting, the central authority of the Cēra kings weakened and the Brahminical military-religious power structures grew stronger.

*Kalaripayattu* scholar and practitioner Phillip B. Zarrilli describes the Kerala of the Sangam Era, marked by strife between the Cēra, Chola, and Paṇḍya kingdoms, as a time when "a warlike martial spirit predominated across southern India" and "[war] was considered a sacrifice of honour" (Zarrilli 1998, 29). In the introduction to his translation of four hundred Tamil poems called the *Puṟanāṉūṟu*, dating from the first through the third centuries of the common era, George Hart identifies three features of the society that produced the often war-themed poems: a powerful king imbued with magical abilities; an emphasis on the purity of women; and an indigenous caste system (Hart and Heifetz 1999, *xvii*). Hart writes:

> It is impossible to overstate the importance of the king in ancient Tamil society. He is the main figure that makes possible the creation of an ordered condition of the world, and he does this by tapping the disorder, chaos, and death endemic to it. . . . Because of the king, the rains come, enemies are kept at bay, and the fields are fertile. . . . [The] king is considered to be a sort of machine designed to metamorphose dangerous power—the killing on the battlefield—into its auspicious analogue—the production and harvesting of grain. (*xix*)

While the martial and connected literary traditions of the Sangam Era are based on the centrality of kingship and the linked cycles of war and agriculture, the *dhanurveda* traditions brought by North Indian Brahmins in the seventh century and passed on to their students were meant to be used to defend their schools from attack. But between the founding of a new Cēra capital at Makotai in the ninth century and its collapse in the eleventh century, the cultural landscape of Kerala changed dramatically from the rest of South India, and by the end of that period, an armed subcaste of the Nambudiri Brahmins called the Cattar established dominance in the absence of a centrally controlled kingdom. Their practice of bearing arms and giving instruction in the martial arts continued even to the period of Portuguese colonialism, when, according to Zarrilli, "the Edapalli Nambiadiri (a special designation for a Namboodiri leader) [served] as commander of the Zamorin of Calicut's army and navy in the early wars with the Portuguese" (33).

The techniques of *kalaripayattu* include kicks, throws, punches, blocks, pressure points, healing techniques, and the use of various weapons, including the "*otta*, a curved wooden elephant-tusk-shaped weapon meant to attack the body's vital spots, three-span stick, long staff, dagger, sword and shield, and . . . the flexible double-edged sword (*urumi*)" (Zarrilli 1998, 12). Instruction takes place in a rectangular, often sunken room called a *kalari,* surrounded by deities installed on the walls and used as a center for training, worship, and traditional medical care. The *kalaripayattu* master is referred to with the plural *gurukkal* because he is the living embodiment of the guru lineage that stretches back to Paraśurāma himself and the original twenty-one students he trained (72). Many gurus have manuscripts that recount the legendary history of the martial arts in Kerala, including Paraśurāma's causing the ocean to recede, his consecration of one hundred and eight images, his establishment of the original forty-three *kalari,* his recruitment of learned Brahmins from the north, and his training of the first twenty-one students—maybe a number drawn from the number of Kṣatriya generations he destroyed (32).

In medieval Kerala, beginning around the twelfth century and continuing to the nineteenth, it was the Nayars (previously of the Śūdra *varṇa*), as well as Cattar Brahmins and even some Muslims who were receiving training in *kalaripayattu* so that they could enter into the services of landholding rulers. And these rulers were usually the Nambudiri Brahmins, who held the land by the same birthright reified by the *Kēraḷōlpatti* version of history. Along with their masters, the fighters also pledged to defend Brahmins and cows.[11]

Legends of Kerala are replete with warriors initiating blood feuds:

> [*Kalaripayattu*] was also used in two other forms of duel—to resolve blood feuds (*kutipakka*) between households and to resolve

> interpersonal disputes through duel (*poyttu*) without having to inform local authorities. . . . It was in these non-legislated forms of conflict that more unconstrained forms of violence could be exercised as a means of social protest. (Zarrilli 1998, 43)

It goes without saying that the phrases "blood feuds," "non-legislated forms of conflict," "unconstrained forms of violence," and "social protest" all call to mind Paraśurāma's varṇicidal vendetta against the Kṣatriyas.

But practitioners of historical *kalaripayattu* also engaged in a kind of combat that seems at odds with the themes of the Paraśurāma story. A special kind of fighter called a *chekor* was engaged to duel another *chekor* on behalf of two opposing high-caste parties to prevent the explosion of a blood feud. When one of the *chekors* defeated or killed the other in the public duel called the *ankam,* the two parties considered the matter closed without either having spilled any of their own blood. It is as if the violence of the sacrifice, fanned to a conflagration in the Paraśurāma story, is brought under control once more in the *ankam.*

Along the southern west coast of the Indian subcontinent, the land creation submotif of the Paraśurāma mythos takes center stage, transforming his exile into a civilizing moment. The mixed-birth element of his story is well suited to the unique levels of economic and military power achieved by Brahmins in the region. And Paraśurāma's struggles against the sea play well in a coastal economy. As Choudhary notes, some scholars have argued the Paraśurāma's reclamation of the land from the sea is a mythologized memory of a real geological event, like the sea receding (presumably as a result of global cooling) or a deep historical one, such as humans using primitive axes to clear the land for farming (2010, 185). For "geographical reasons," Gail concludes that the land reclamation episode is the original ending of the Paraśurāma myth, suggesting that the story may in fact have originated on the Western Ghats (1977, 221). Charpentier too, gives priority to the tradition of Paraśurāma going west and dates the story to at least the time of Aśoka (1937, 12–13).

Reserving judgment on whether these claims about the coastal origins of the myth are true, we will now attempt to answer our guiding questions in the case of Malabar. As to who brought the myth to this new community or at least popularized it, we can say that it was most likely the Brahmin caste who benefited from the "gift of Paraśurāma," the Nambudiri. Although we have evidence of Vedic Brahmins attached to area kings from the Sangam Era, the large-scale migration of Nambudiris seems to have happened between the seventh and ninth centuries and their hegemony was established under the Cēra dynasty beginning at the end of that three hundred-year period, when they received huge land grants and developed a separate translocal culture.

As to whether the Paraśurāma myth resonated with existing cultural values or served to express new imported or developing ritual or economic forms, we can be fairly confident that it was the latter. Under the Cēras, Nambudiris became major landholders and acquired great wealth while at the same time their ritual services were increasingly limited to temple duties as the practice of the sacrifice declined. This major change was followed by still more radical shifts in the post-Cēra era, when Brahmins became chieftains and even fought skirmishes among themselves, as in the Śukapuram-Panniyūr feud of the early thirteenth century (Narayanan and Veluthat 1983, 271). For Brahmins facing these kinds of developments, the figure of Paraśurāma must have seemed tailor-made to reflect their new collective identity as landholders and sometime-warriors.

## The Citpāvans: "Paraśarāma" [*sic*] Among the Marāṭhās

The political, religious, and economic rearrangements that occurred in medieval Kerala set the stage for the Paraśurāma myth's popularity and the reshaping of the social world to which it was addressed. Likewise, Marāṭhā identity as it developed in the period following Ala-ud-Din-Khilji's incursions into the Deccan Plateau at the beginning of the fourteenth century was based on the privileged status that the new Muslim rulers granted to clans who participated in military service. Castes such as the Lohar, Kunbi, Thakar, and Sutar received hereditary land grants and collectively developed into a new martial caste with its own distinctive dress, customs, and marriage rules. But since the Deccan was ruled by five Muslim kingdoms and not a single conqueror, prominent families developed independently, and were not hesitant to fight each other or their Muslim rulers, as the seventeenth-century Marāṭhā ruler Śivājī famously did during the reign of Aurangzeb (Gordon 1993, 13–17). As this new military class emerged, the role of Brahmins changed in Maharashtra.

Specifically, I am referring to the Citpāvans, or Koṅkaṇasthas, a group of Brahmins who claim to have been imported by Paraśurāma. Indeed, one account of the origin of the clan's name from the eighteenth-century Marāṭhī rescension of the *Skanda Purāṇa* claims that Paraśurāma was so polluted by blood-guilt after he slaughtered the Kṣatriyas that no Brahmin would perform rites for him. So, he found fourteen dead bodies washed up on shore and put them on an altar where he burned, purified, and resurrected them. He then taught the fourteen revived men the Veda and they became the ancestors of the Citpāvans, which means "purified on an altar" (Choudhary 2010, 295). Dorothy Figueira notes that the Citpāvan community has produced some of the most influential shapers of modern India, including the nationalist leader B. G. Tilak and Gandhi's assassin Nathuram Godse, and that when "modern Mahārāshtrians think of the Aryans, they associate them with the Chitpavans, who pride themselves on their fair complexions and greenish gray eyes" (2002, 121).

The rise of the Citpāvans begins with the Marāṭhā prince Śāhūjī (the grandson of Śivājī and son of Śaṃbhūjī, the latter of whom was tortured and executed by Aurangzeb in 1688), who grew up well cared for as a hostage in the Mughal court, but left upon the death of Aurangzeb in 1707 to reclaim his throne. In 1713 he appointed a Citpāvan Brahmin named Bāḷājī as his Peśwā, or prime minister. Due to factional infighting and Mughal expansion, the land controlled by Śāhūjī had been reduced to Pune and its immediate surroundings. And it was his Citpāvan Peśwā Bāḷājī who, through military force and diplomatic pressure, forced the Mughal emperor to formally recognize Śāhūjī's legitimacy and sovereignty (Gordon 1993, 110–13).

The Peśwā died in 1720 and Śāhūjī appointed Bāḷājī's son Bājīrao to his father's post. Bājīrao saw an opportunity to expand the Marāṭhās' borders as the power of the Mughals was declining and so he pushed into Gujarat and Malwa. He even briefly took the emperor hostage in Delhi in 1737. During these military campaigns, Bājīrao consolidated de facto power in the office of the Peśwā, gaining control over the military, banking, and land granting, financially supporting Brahmins, and bringing in fellow Citpāvan Brahmins to fill out his bureaucracy (127–30).

The *Paraśarāma Caritra,* a semihistorical account of the rule of the Brahmin Peśwās in Maharashtra, was composed in Marāṭhī around 1772 by an author called Vallabha, who has no other surviving works to his name. A man named Durlabh, a banker at the Peśwā ruler Mādharāva's mint in Pune, commissioned the work, possibly as a tribute to Mādharāva after his death and probably to improve his standing with the Peśwā who succeeded him (Vallabhācārya 1976, *x*). It belongs to a literary genre called *bakhar,* a kind of cross between a Purāṇa and a historical biography, popular between the reign of Śivājī in the late seventeenth century and the British conquest of the Marāṭhā state, which became official when they removed the last Peśwā in 1818.

The first chapter contains a Purāṇic account of history, starting from the incarnation of Paraśurāma and his destruction of the Kṣatriyas. The matricide is left out completely and Paraśurāma destroys Kārtavīrya and his army after they steal his father's cow in a raid that leaves his father unharmed. Later, other Kṣatriyas send an assassin who decapitates Jamadagni and shows his head to Reṇukā. Instead of the erotic sight of a prince bathing with his wives, it is the disturbing and violent image of her husband's severed head that distracts Reṇukā in this variant. This prompts Paraśurāma to make an oath with water to wipe out the Kṣatriyas and use their blood to perform his father's funeral rites. Then he goes to Kurukṣetra, plants in the ground what the text calls a "*staṃbha rovila*," and proceeds to kill Kṣatriyas. After a time, the sage Nārada steps in and stops the bloodshed, telling Paraśurāma that the surviving Kṣatriyas will surrender. Paraśurāma ceases the killing, gives the earth to the Brahmins after completing his father's funeral rites, and goes off to settle the Konkan Coast with Brahmins from the Deśasth, Karhāde, and Citpāvan clans.

The rest of the first book includes a greatly truncated telling of the *Rāmāyaṇa*, which places Rāma in the Dvāpara Yuga and (in a reversal of the order of incarnation from the Pāñcarātra tradition) asserts that the Kṣatriyas Paraśurāma had killed were reborn as demons in Rāvaṇa's army and absolved of their sins by dying at the hands of Rāma. This is followed by a brief mention of Kṛṣṇa (whom the text places in the Kali Yuga), his adventures first in Vraja and later with the Pāṇḍavas, and the destruction of the Yādava clan by a Brahmin curse (20–23, 145–50).

The second book takes the reader via a path of anachronism and chronological error from the reign of the last true Kṣatriyas (Yudhiṣṭhira's line) up to the Mughal sultans of Delhi. In true Purāṇic fashion, the influence of Kaḷī, the male demonic figure who is an embodiment of the adharmic forces of the *yuga*, exerts more and more influence over the rulers, until the *mleccha*s and Yavanas are in control of the holy Karmabhūmi. And though early Yavana rulers such as Bābar tend to respect the Brahmins and uphold dharma, Kaḷī's power soon turns them against the Hindus and they begin to persecute them and defile their sacred sites. This disastrous turn of events sets the stage for Paraśurāma's return to earth (23–39, 151–57).

But before we look at the rest of text, it will be worthwhile to look closely at some elements of the Paraśurāma story as it appears in book one. First, the text leaves out the matricide episode, eliminating a potential problem for an audience who wants to see Paraśurāma as a patron deity. Second, the episode of Reṇukā's decapitation becomes transformed into an episode in which a Kṣatriya decapitates Jamadagni and shows his head to Reṇukā, causing her to faint. Third, the fluid motif appears in the water Paraśurāma takes in his hand to swear his oath to kill the Kṣatriyas (*gheunī jaḷā śabdh bolilā*). Fourth, there is the *staṃbha rovila* that he plants at the Kurukṣetra when he challenges the Kṣatriyas to battle. The word *staṃbha* must refer to the Vedic sacrificial post (which we also see in the Kerala myth and the cults of Reṇukā described by Biardeau), and the word *rovila* appears to be from the Arabic *ro'b,* which enters Hindustani as an adjective that means "causing fear" (McGregor 1993, 873). Finally, Paraśurāma is linked explicitly with another dominant Brahmin group, the Citpāvans (with whom the Bene Israel Jews of India also identify themselves).

Next, we move to the fourth book, which opens by extolling the wisdom of the Mughal emperor Shāhjahān, then tells how Kaḷī enters the body of his son Aurangzeb, who is already known for his anger. Aurangzeb then begins oppressing Brahmins, killing cows, and otherwise undoing dharma. This causes the divine king Vikrama to come to earth as Śivājī to fight the *mleccha*s and Yavanas. But after the deaths of Śivājī and his son, the gods decide they have to step in again. Viṣṇu (who is here distinguished from Paraśurāma), when he was incarnated as the Buddha, had decreed that no more gods could go to earth. So, Indra turns to Paraśurāma, who, like Vikrama, is apparently not included among the gods (since he is unaffected by Viṣṇu's ban), and asks him to go down to earth and rescue dharma. Paraśurāma agrees to send his *aṃśa* in human form down to earth, but informs the gods that it is improper to bear weapons (i.e., to be a Kṣatriya) in the current *yuga.* So Paraśurāma decides to take birth in the Brahmin lineage of Bāḷājī to destroy the *mleccha*s. Meanwhile, Śiva takes birth in the form of Śāhūjī, the Marāṭhā prince who appoints Bāḷājī as the first Peśwā (Vallabhācārya 1976, 39–43, 59–67).

When Paraśurāma sends his *aṃśa* into Bāḷājī's body, he faces a dilemma. He has already given the earth to the Brahmins in his great sacrifice and thereby has permanently renounced sovereignty over it. So, as Bāḷājī, Paraśurāma decides to give nominal power to someone else and accomplish his ends from behind the scenes. After becoming the Peśwā serving under Śāhūjī, Bāḷājī begins to expand the kingdom and even marches on Jaipur. And when he dies, as all humans must in the Kali Yuga, Paraśurāma places his *aṃśa* into his son Bājīrao. The rest of the text concerns the deeds of the Peśwās (consistently referring to them as *aṃśadhārī*s), and especially the career of the recently deceased Mādharāva.

After this brief discussion, we can come to some conclusions. Who brought the Paraśurāma myth to this new community? The Citpāvans are the obvious candidates, but the deployment of the Paraśurāma myth in the Deccan Plateau in the centuries before the *Paraśarama Caritra* paints a more complicated picture. The Citpāvans are generally considered to be a southern Brahmin group, according to the classification scheme (about one thousand years old) of Indian Brahmins into five Gauḍa or Bengali clans and five Draviḍa or Tamil clans, with the Gauḍas located north of the Vindhya mountans and the Draviḍas located to their south (Deshpande 2010, 29). The Draviḍas were said to be the superior branch because they maintained the Vedic tradition and practiced vegetarianism while the Gauḍas had stopped performing the sacrifice and begun eating fish.

Deshpande traces this list to the *Sahyādrikhaṇḍa*, a Kannada and Sanskrit tradition from the Konkan region that purports to be part of the *Skanda Purāṇa*. Significantly, the specific delineation of the Brahmin clans does not include the Citpāvans at all, suggesting they were either not a noteworthy presence or beneath consideration. But the *Sahyādrikhaṇḍa* also contains significant Paraśurāma material in its *Reṇukāmahātmya* (Glorification of Reṇukā) and its *Citpāvanabrāhmaṇotpattiḥ* (Origin of the Citpāvan Brahmins), both added after the thirteenth century, which do identify the Citpāvans as Draviḍa. The *Citpāvanabrāhmaṇotpattiḥ* section begins after Paraśurāma has raised the Konkan Coast from the sea:

> In the newly recovered land of Konkan, there are no traditional brahmins, either of the Gauḍa or Draviḍa persuasion, to be found. Paraśurāma invites all the brahmins for carrying out ancestral offerings (*śrāddha-pakṣa*), and yet no one showed up (Chapter 1, verse 31). The angry brahmin Paraśurāma decided to produce new brahmins (*brāhmaṇā nūtanāḥ kāryāḥ*, Chapter 1, verse 33). As he was wandering along the bank of the ocean, he saw some men gathered around a funeral pyre and asked them about their caste and dharma. These were fishermen, and Paraśurāma purified their sixty families and offered them brahminhood (*brāhmaṇyaṁ ca tato dattvā*, Chapter 1, verse 37). Since these fishermen were purified at the location of a funeral pyre (*citā*), they received the designation of *citapāvana* (ibid.). These "newly created" brahmins soon engaged in unrighteous works (*akāryaṁ kurvate karma*, Chapter 1, verse 42). Observing this, Paraśurāma cursed them to become despised and poor (*śāpaś ca prāpyate tasmāt kutsitāś ca daridriṇaḥ*, Chapter 1, verse 44), and settled them in the town of Cittapolana (= modern Chiplun), Chapter 1, verses 46–47. (Deshpande 2010, 37)

We should here note that the identification of the Citpāvans with fishermen seems to connect them to the degraded fish-eating Gauḍa Brahmins rather than the orthodox Draviḍa branch to which they claimed membership. Deshpande concludes from the sad fate of the Citpāvans "to become despised and poor" that the myth was created by a different group who wanted to denigrate them rather than the Citpāvans themselves (38). And it is true that Gajanan Gaitonde, a recent translator of the text, has omitted these sections to avoid offending Citpāvan audiences (37–38). However, in light of the self-effacing narratives of the degraded Kṣatriyas whose ancestors ran and hid from Paraśurāma and the ambivalent elements in the Bhārgava cycle, it seems entirely possible that the Citpāvans actually were the ones who created this myth.

Turning to the specific variant found in the *Paraśarāma Caritra*, which is certainly a pro-Citpāvan document, we can now ask about the social and political location of the mythmakers when they deployed it. In the early eighteenth century, the Citpāvans found themselves in hereditary positions of political power, having experienced a much more rapid rise than did the Nambudiris. They were also in need of a myth to legitimate some developing cultural forms, specifically the rule of the Peśwās. The author of the *Paraśarāma Caritra*, whose identity we know, had a vested interest in presenting something that would please his patron Durlabh, who in turn would have wanted to sing the praises of the Peśwā ruler Mādharāva, in whose employ he worked. To do so, the author drew on the Paraśurāma tradition, already popular in Maharashtra through its connections to the cults of Reṇukā and Dattātreya, and already associated with the Citpāvans.

Like the *Kēraḷōlpatti* narrative tradition, the *Paraśarāma Caritra* lends authority to a social institution in need of same by tying it to the divine figure of Paraśurāma, already significant as a cultural hero in the region. But while Paraśurāma myths in Kerala paint his story with the broad strokes of elemental struggle, the Marāṭhi versions have a more granular historical narrative that lends itself to theological niceties about the power and nature of the gods, like those we have already seen in the writings of the Pāñcarātrins. With respect to sectarian sensibilities, the *Paraśarāma Caritra* seems to differentiate Paraśurāma from Viṣṇu and the rest of the gods and uses the term *aṃśadhārī* instead of *avatāra* to describe him.[12] It also puts Paraśurāma in a superior position to Śiva (who has somehow broken the ban on gods coming to earth to be born as Śāhūjī), since Śiva's Kṣatriya incarnation is only a figurehead while Paraśurāma's Brahmin *aṃśadhārī*s hold all the real power.

## Conclusion

We began this chapter with Kosambi's brusque dismissal of Paraśurāma's varṇicide campaign against twenty-one generations of Kṣatriyas. After all, "a single extermination of the *kṣatriyas* would have sufficed to prevent the Brahmans having to serve them" (1938–39, 202). This is rather a crude version of historical materialist criticism of the Marxist variety. And, considering all the violence that such hasty false unmasking can do to a text, it would perhaps be better to leapfrog over Marx, back to Nietzsche's more ruminative observations in *On the Use and Abuse of History for Life*:

> [S]ince we are now the products of earlier generations, we are also the products of their aberrations, passions, mistakes, even crimes. It is impossible to loose oneself from this chain entirely. When we condemn those mistakes and consider ourselves released from them, then we have not overcome the fact that we are derived from them. In the best case, we bring the matter to a conflict between our inherited customary nature and our knowledge, in fact, even to a war between a new strict discipline and how we have been brought up and what has been congenital to us from time immemorial. We cultivate a new habit, a new instinct, a second nature, so that the first nature atrophies. It is an attempt to give oneself, as it were, a past *a posteriori*, out of which we may be descended in opposition to the one from which we are descended, always a dangerous attempt, because it is so difficult to find a borderline to the denial of the past and because the second natures usually are weaker than the first. (2010, 3)

As a result of changing political and economic fortunes, the Nambudiri Brahmins in Malabar and the Citpāvan Brahmins in Maharashtra saw worldly power and Brahmin-ness overlap in ways that seemed unprecedented. Both groups turned to the Paraśurāma myth and the sacrificial categories it employs to work out their new situations. In coastal Malabar, the deep structure of the land reclamation motif appealed to a culture long influenced by migration and trade. In Maharashtra, the Citpāvans saw themselves as a purified sacrificial remainder, insulated from the blood guilt that comes with political power. All used the Paraśurāma story to narrate a "second nature" that enabled them to adapt to their new circumstances.

Following Nietzsche's insights, we can get a much more nuanced and complex picture of the relationship between author and audience in the case of the Paraśurāma myth than we would if we were to treat it as vulgar propaganda. Rather than imagining the victorious-in-defeat mythmakers rescuing their pride, as Kosambi would have it, is more useful to think in terms of Nietzsche's curious consolation: "[Our] first nature was at one time or another once a second nature and . . . every victorious second nature becomes a first nature" (2010, 3). The collective fantasy is not ultimately concerned with whether Brahmins or Kṣatriyas were on top of the social hierarchy *in illo tempore*. It is a fantasy of mastering the conflict inherent in being a Brahmin and controlling how the Brahmin's inwardly violent nature will transform or explode when exposed to the world.

It is worth noting that Paraśurāma's fortunes as a culture hero have been mixed in recent years. In April 2017, the "Hindutva firebrand" Yogi Adityanath, responsible for reconverting 6,800 Christians in a "purification drive" in 2005, was barely more than a month into his term as chief minister of Uttar Pradesh when he courted controversy by cancelling fifteen school holidays. Predictably, one of them was Mawli, the birthday of the Prophet. But Paraśurāma Jayanti, celebrated on the third day of the bright fortnight of Vaishākha, also got the axe, so to speak.[13] On the other hand, Facebook groups populated by young Brahmin males sympathetic to the Hindutva cause have turned to Paraśurāma as the paradigmatic "intellectual Kṣatriya," going so far as to decorate their bodies with elaborate tattoos of his *paraśu*.[14]

In my own homeland, the American South, there is a mythology that surrounds the Confederacy defeated in the Civil War and its semidivine heroes Stonewall Jackson, Jefferson Davis, and Robert E. Lee, elevating them hopefully with its strident refrain of "The South will rise again." On August 11, 2017, a few hours after I finished writing the first draft of this chapter, a collection of White Nationalists descended on the campus of the University of Virginia to protest the planned removal of a monument to Lee. They were carrying Tiki torches and chanting, "Blood and Soil!" The next day, after a scheduled "Unite the Right" rally was broken up by police, one of their number drove a car into a crowd of counterprotestors, killing a thirty-two-year-old woman named Heather Heyer.

The Charlottesville protest was the result of a confluence of forces that cannot be fully understood outside of the context of the historically significant American elections of 2008 and 2016 and the rise of internet message board culture. But it also draws authority from an imagined Third Reich as well as a mythology and set of rituals, including human sacrifice in the form of lynchings, shared in the American South (See Wilson 1980 and Patterson 1998). Lloyd A. Hunter describes it as the "Lost Cause Religion":

> Conceived in the ashes of a defeated and broken Dixie, this powerful, pervasive idea claimed the devotion of countless Confederates and their female counterparts. When it reached fruition in the 1880s its votaries not only pledged their allegiance to the Lost Cause, but they also elevated it above the realm of common, patriotic impulse, making it perform a clearly religious function. At annual meetings and other gatherings of veterans' groups and their women's auxiliaries, Southerners gave sacred status to the symbols of their Confederate past, dramatized them in formalized ritual, and expressed their meaning in mythic terms. They not only mythologized, but they also made sacred the Southern way of life, laying the foundation for a Southern culture religion, a regional faith based upon Dixie's wartime experience. (2000, 186)

The differences with the Paraśurāma story are many and profound, but as we saw in the last chapter, the story of Paraśurāma's varṇicidal campaign against the Kṣatriyas has provoked reflexive comparisons to twentieth-century acts of genocide by scholars of Hinduism as well as by Hindus themselves, so it seems perverse not to try to think about how the concept of blood and soil has been and is being deployed around the world.

In this chapter, we have seen how Paraśurāma's act of violence became an act of creation and culture building in places where new stories were needed to undergird new power structures. Paraśurāma's axe kills Kṣatriyas but it also clears land for cultivation, and *kṣetra* (as in the blood-soaked battlefield of Kurukṣetra) can simply mean "field." But swords can become plowshares and then become swords again, as the stories of Paraśurāma's vengeful returns from exile illustrate. In the foundation myth of the Hebrew Bible, it is the agriculturalist Cain who commits the first murder by killing his pastoralist brother and is sent into permanent exile. As Karen Armstrong has demonstrated, in agrarian myths from Syria, Greece, Egypt, and Mesopotamia, violence plays a central role, reflecting the "institutional or structural violence in which a society compels people to live in such wretchedness and subjection that they are unable to better their lot" (2015, 13). The shift from a small-scale society to a large agricultural one requiring a large labor force comes with a level of structural violence. Similar but less dramatic shifts resulting in a hierarchical reorganization of society are reflected in the ascent of the Peśwās in Maharashtra and of the Nambudiris and Nayars in Malabar, and are also imagined in violent terms.

Taken as a whole, there is nothing really triumphalist about the Paraśurāma myth. The foundation of the land of Malabar and the political order of Maharashtra, like the *Mahābhārata* war, is a consequence and a repetition of the sacrificial preparation of the Kurukṣetra. As Carl Schmitt understood, every attempt to wall off the world requires someone to shut the door from the outside, and Paraśurāma is that outsider. Where is the triumph in that? The website *Prokeria.com* puts it this way: "Unlike Lord Rama and Krishna, Parashurama is believed to be still living on Earth and is not worshipped." This simple sentence demonstrates an understanding of what the myth is about: Paraśurāma's castelessness, rootlessness, and connection to the deep past make him an ideal culture hero for groups trying to understand and to make understood their new political and social locations. But they also permanently defer his full apotheosis.

# Conclusion

## *Introducing Paraśurāma*

I salute that Rāma with an axe,
Who is being saluted by devas,
Who is the consort of Lakṣmī,
Who is expert in fighting in war,
Who shines due to his crown,
Who holds Kodaṇḍa in his right hand,
And arrows in his left hand,
Which are capable of saving the oppressed,
Who is armed with the terrible white axe,
Who is effulgent with light,
And who has a well-proportioned heavenly body.

Victory to that Bhārgava Rāma,
Who has a laughing face of Brahmin as well as Kṣatriya,
Who is the great fire which destroyed the clan of kings,
Who held the terrible axe in his hand,
Who shined like the rising sun,
Who had very electrifying matted locks,
Who dressed himself using the bark of trees,
And who was famous as the one
Who knows the holy chants of the sacrifice.

—*Paraśurāma Stotra*

What but strife can emerge from the conflux of the powers of [the] Brahmin and the Kshatriya?

—Balamani Amma, "*Maluvinte Katha*" ("The Story of the Axe")

As we approach the end of this book, I am compelled to point out the lacunae in it and explain why they are there. To keep *The Other Rāma* to a reasonable size, I had to excise a lot of the material that dealt specifically with Paraśurāma in the *Mahābhārata.* I took out my discussion of his duel with Bhīṣma over Ambā, the princess kidnapped by Bhīṣma in a cattle raid–like episode and then sent into a kind of liminal existence (she is unable to marry either the celibate Bhīṣma who has claimed her or the man to whom she was originally betrothed but whom she is now unworthy to wed), only to return as the male warrior Śikhaṇḍin to bring Bhīṣma his death. I likewise removed the section on his brief but consequential time with Karṇa, the Brahmin-supporting Kṣatriya adopted by and raised as a member of the Sūta caste (listed in *The Laws of Manu* as the offspring of a Kṣatriya father and a Brahmin mother) because he was rejected at birth by his own Kṣatriya mother. Paraśurāma takes Karṇa on as a student but then, upon learning of his true *varṇa,* effectively curses him to die on Kurukṣetra.

As these brief descriptions show, there is a lot of material to be mined in both of these minor episodes. But they are also mostly confined to the epic and do not really make it into the Purāṇic versions of the myth or temple legends. Therefore, I decided to spin them off into a separate article and use the time and space I have for this book to trace the development of the major motifs across an array of variants so that in this conclusion I could say something about the deep structure of the Paraśurāma myth, which we are only now ready to tackle.

## Summary of Contents

In chapter 1, "The Brahmin Warrior: Paraśurāma *in Extremis,*" we began with a trope originated by Žižek to explore the Paraśurāma myth on three levels: the universal-ontological, the particular-sexual, and the singular-subjective. At the broadest level, we examined the cosmic implications of Paraśurāma's paradoxical identity as both an *avatāra,* characterized by Lutgendorf as a "'compression' of infinitude into a mortal frame" and a *cirañjīvin,* which he describes as "just the reverse: an endless extension of corporeal life" (2007, 279). We observed that this paradox also illuminates Paraśurāma's Śaiva-Vaiṣṇava identity through the Śaiva theme of *coincidentia oppositorum* and the Vaiṣṇava theme of the infinite contained within the finite and is mythically resolved in an episode in which Paraśurāma gives up his *avatāra* status to Rāma Dāśarathi.

We next analyzed myths of Paraśurāma's conception in which his mother figure either hugs the wrong tree or eats the wrong *caru* and rejects him as a monstrous hybrid when she learns what she has done, a favor that Paraśurāma will repay when he chops his birth mother's head off. I also argued that the seminal *caru* (which reappears in the form of a bowl of crushed teeth in the Jain "countermyth" of Subhūma) is the first instantiation of the fluid theme in the myth, and that it establishes the *kṣatra* as a separable object, a theme that plays out in both the matricide and the varṇicide motifs.

To understand Paraśurāma's singular-subjective aspect, we examined how his character is represented in the late–twentieth-century Malayalam poem *Maḻuvinṯe Katha* ("The Story of the Axe") which establishes him as a unique figure with the power of a Brahmin and the temper of a Kṣatriya. To wrap up the first half of the chapter, we situated Paraśurāma's story in the myth cycle of the Bhārgavas, a clan that includes Aurva and Śukra and is known for having a contentious relationship with its Kṣatriya patrons.

Next, we looked at the concept of the *varṇa* system, both in terms of the normative concepts expressed in the Sanskrit texts and the far different picture described by historians, by whose accounts the "Vedic restoration" of Puṣyamitra Śunga after the fall of the last Maurya was probably as mythical as Paraśurāma was. Then, based on Sanderson's epigraphical findings that Indian kings who had converted to Vaiṣṇavism and Śaivism between the fifth and the eighth centuries commonly proclaimed their commitment to upholding the *varṇa* system that put Brahmins on top, along with Bronkhorst's argument that Sanskritic myth provided a model for a new Kṣatriya-Brahmin relationship in the post-Vedic era, we concluded that the Brahmin mythmakers who originated the Paraśurāma story had a specific agenda to advance—securing their political and social position against the forces of change.

We explored the Paraśurāma myth's elaboration of the concepts of dislocation, excess, and becoming by reading it alongside the myths of Droṇa, Dattātreya, and Viśvāmitra, respectively. Droṇa's story, we concluded, illuminates Paraśurāma's temporal and spatial exceptionalism, while Dattātreya's story illuminates his embodiment of Śaiva excess and Viśvāmitra's story shows us how the figure of Paraśurāma acts as a spinning thaumotrope, embodying the vanishing mediator of "becoming." To see how Paraśurāma exemplifies both the sovereign above the law and the *homo sacer* outside the law, we looked at the myth of the first king Vena and his lynching by a Brahmin mob as well as theoretical models of the state of exception developed by Carl Schmitt and Giorgio Agamben. We also employed another Western philosophical concept, that of the double negation, to analyze Paraśurāma's resemblance to that paradigmatic Western exile, the Wandering Jew.

In the second chapter, "Matricide I: The Broken Pot," we focused on the first element of what I called the matricide "micromyth," which is as follows.

1. A married woman sees an attractive man, becomes sexually aroused involuntarily and loses control, after which her husband sees evidence of her arousal and perceived infidelity.

2. The sons refuse their father's command to kill their mother and are cursed to become animals or idiots as a result, losing the power of speech.

3. The youngest son obeys his father's command to behead his mother.

4. The father/husband restores and resurrects the mother/wife, and the youngest son asks for the whole incident to be forgotten.

We saw how ancient Indian values and anxieties inherent in notions of the fluidity of female sexual desire informed the episode of Reṇukā's "leakage" at the river. We next analyzed Reṇukā's wet clothing through the lenses of the Aristotelian concept of *akrasia,* the folkloric motif of the woman waylaid at the well, stories about *gandharva*s and other water spirits, Sanskrit sexological literature, and the symbolic significance of the pot in the wider culture. Finally, we brought in two rituals for purposes of comparison: the Vedic *varuṇapraghāsa* rite, and a contemporary Tamil exorcism performed for a woman possessed by a *pēy.*

In chapter 3, "Matricide II: The Severed Head," we used a psychoanalytic model drawing from the work of Jacques Lacan, Julia Kristeva, Stanley M. Kurtz, and André Green to interpret the other elements of the matricide micromyth: the cursing of the disobedient sons, the matricide itself, and the subsequent resurrection and repression of the mother. We observed that the sons who refuse Jamadagni's command are cursed either to die, be rendered dumb "like animals," or else become renouncers, which corresponds to their being stuck in a pre-Oedipal phase as a result of failing to reject the mother and submit to the law of the father. Next, we looked at the matricide itself as it appears in "The Story of the Axe" along with some parallels and inversions from the Śaiva tradition in Tibet and Tamil Nadu. We also explored the cultic and psychoanalytic ramifications of Paraśurāma's conflict with Śiva's adopted son Gaṇeśa.

Following that was a digression in which we looked at a critique of Paraśurāma's matricide in the myth of Cirakāri, another son who is also ordered to decapitate his mother by his father, but spends so long thinking about what to do that it gives his father a chance to take back his command.

Next we analyzed myths of Reṇukā as a headless goddess (often identified with Chinnamastā and Lajjāgauri) from Maharashtra and Tamil Nadu. Finally, we analyzed the decapitation of Reṇukā through the lens of Green's Dead Mother complex.

In the fourth chapter, "Varṇicide I: The Extermination of the Kṣatriyas and Its Aftermath," we began by contextualizing the episode in the larger myth cycle of the rivalry between the Bhārgavas and the Haihaya kings. Then we tackled the complex subject of how modern notions of race, genocide, total war, and terrorism relate to Paraśurāma's story by looking at how it has been viewed by Indologists and contemporary Hindus. We also returned to the figure of Aśvatthāman, this time in the form in which he appears in a twentieth-century Bengali play. We next turned to the sanitization and theologization of Paraśurāma's varṇicide by the Pāñcarātrins, who turned his human Kṣatriya victims into inhuman demons (not unlike the enemies of Rāma Dāśarathi). We concluded the chapter with a look at the Jaina "countermyth" of Subhūma, who annihilates the Brahmins, rather than the Kṣatriyas, twenty-one times over.

In the last chapter, "Varṇicide II: Blood and Soil in Malabar and Maharashtra," we started with a critique of D. D. Kosambi's Marxist reading of the Paraśurāma myth and then turned to the Vedic idea of the sacrificial remainder in order to understand the explanations mythmakers constructed of how a remnant of Kṣatriyas survived the varṇicide campaign in order to rise again, including the origin stories of the Fire Clan Rajputs and the Khaṇḍelvāl Vaiśyas. Continuing the theme of Paraśurāma as a progenitor, we next looked at the land creation submotif that is part of his exile story as it develops on the western coast, concluding that it serves as a *point de capiton,* bringing together the fluid motif from the matricide stories and the sacrificial remainder motif from the varṇicide stories. We followed this thread to the Sanskrit *Keralamahātmya* and the Malayalam *Kēraḷōlpatti* traditions of Kerala, a region identified as the strip of land Paraśurāma reclaimed from the sea with his axe and where his myth has been used to legitimize the land rights of the Nambudiri Brahmins. We also noted that Paraśurāma is credited with originating some of Kerala's most distinctive cultural features: matrilineal succession; the rule of the Perumāls, and the practice of *kalaripayattu*—three institutions that address, respectively, inherited identity, kingship, and martial violence. We next turned from Kerala to Maharashtra, where a late–eighteenth-century semihistorical account of the rule of the Peśwās was used to lend legitimacy to the Brahmins of the Citpāvan clan who achieved a level of hegemony during this period. Finally, we concluded with a brief comparison of the ideology of these Paraśurāma myths with other "blood and soil" mythologies recently deployed by white supremacists in the United States.

## Tying It All Together: Structure and Transformation in the Myth Core

In the introduction, I described a myth as a narrative about events not witnessed by the teller or the audience, existing in more than one variant, that expresses the values, anxieties, and worldview shared by the group of people who receive and reproduce it. But, as has been demonstrated in our creative redescriptions of the Paraśurāma cycle, "values, anxieties, and worldviews" are not just three boxes a myth has to tick off in order to do its job. Instead, they are dynamically integrated functions that alternately reshape, obscure, clarify, invert, warp, and magnify each other as more and more variants are added to the mythos: anxieties undermine worldviews, worldviews authorize values, values become entrenched in the face of anxieties, and so on.

To use a planetary metaphor (with no claims to scientific accuracy), values, anxieties, and worldviews are the wind, rain, and upwelling magma that drive the constant changes in geomorphology. But none of these forces would be in operation without the energy derived from—and the magnetic field exerted by—the planet's spinning molten core, which in the case of Paraśurāma, consists of three elements: his split identity as a Brahmin warrior, his matricide, and his annihilation of the Kṣatriyas.

Now, in the interest of tying together all the observations, comparisons, analyses, and creative redescriptions we have made in the previous chapters, I will put forward a set of new, summative arguments. First, I argue that the "doubling" of Paraśurāma's conception narrative in the Critical Edition (first appearing in the story of the ritual mistake, then in the story of Jamadagni and Reṇukā's Brahmin-Kṣatriya marriage) is intentional. And, I might add, Paraśurāma's birth is not just doubled, it is doubly redoubled! There are two versions of the ritual mistake that creates his dual nature, one with *carus* and one with trees. And there are also two stories of his birth from mixed parentage: first the Brahmin-Kṣatriya marriage of Ṛcika and Satyavatī that should—but does not—result in Paraśurāma's birth, and then the exactly parallel Brahmin-Kṣatriya marriage of Jamadagni and Reṇukā, which does ultimately result in his birth. By presenting the story of Paraśurāma's birth from a ritual mixup of Brahmin-producing and Kṣatriya-producing *carus* and trees and then mooting it by giving Paraśurāma mixed parentage (just as

Jamadagni had), the mythmakers are conflating the categories of paternal and maternal with Brahmin and Kṣatriya.[1] All of the repetition is here to focus our attention on this analogical relation, which we are to use to interpret the rest of the myth—*Paternal : Maternal :: Brahmin : Kṣatriya*.

Second, I argue for the existence of four subcycles within the Paraśurāma myth that serve to establish themes, demonstrate the interconnectedness of its elements, and develop the profound mythmaking possibilities of superimposing the most intimate relationship of a child's life—the one he has with his mother and father—on top of what the Brahmin mythmakers imagined as the competing domains of power of the Kṣatriya and the Brahmin. The first of these cycles is that of the primal scenes, which encompasses the two stories of Paraśurāma's birth along with Reṇuka's encounter at the river. The second is the Kārtavīrya cycle, which begins with the river episode and ends with the death of Arjuna Kārtavīrya at Paraśurāma's hands. This cycle is predicated on identifying the bathing *gandharva* prince with the protean figure of Kārtavīrya, an identification that our psychoanalytic readings support. It is also enacted, as Biardeau observes, in rituals of the South Indian cults of Reṇukā, which oppose the figures of Jamadagni and Kārtavīrya (who is associated with the swampy kingdom of Māhiṣmatī just as *gandharvas* are linked to water) to one another, leaving out Citraratha:

> [Reṇukā] is caught between two men, a Brahman whose anger is great enough to torture his wife, and a prince who above all has a grudge against her husband, but for whom she incarnates the power of this irascible Brahman. . . . The two adharmic personages are rigorously complementary and they confront each other around the cow: princess and cow are the two equally complementary aspects of the same victim, the Earth. When the cow is wronged, brahmanic power is violated and Jamadagni is killed; only a warrior Brahman can then rid the Earth of this bane, a delinquent kṣatra. (2004, 188–89)

The overlapping cycles of the primal scenes and Kārtavīrya are then contained within the *kṣatra* cycle, which begins with the *kṣatra* (in the sense of "Kṣatriya-ness") that Satyavatī accidentally ingests in the ritual mistake episode and concludes with Paraśurāma's twenty-one-fold annihilation of the *kṣatra* (in the sense of "the Kṣatriya class") in order to purge from himself this original *kṣatra* (now with a double meaning) and thereby become a Brahmin renouncer.

Finally, the entire myth up to Paraśurāma's exile is contained in the *avatāra* cycle, which covers his entrance into the world, the completion of his assigned task, and his exit, or "first" (social) death in the form of exile. However, because a second birth requires a second death, the myth extends beyond this narrative arc. This lack of an ending and the structural tensions it leaves unresolved are the intramythic source of Paraśurāma's dual nature as an *avatāra* and a *cirañjīvin* and lie behind the subsequent developments of his mythos outside the epic.

This brings me to my third and final argument: the open-ended structure of the Paraśurāma cycle is a mythogenetic element that results in the rich and textured elaborations and inversions that we find in the wide variety of variants we have seen so far. Of course, many other mythic characters have Purāṇic and folkloric afterlives in India without a structure like the one I have described, so I do not claim that an open-ended structure is necessary for mythogenesis. I only argue that the specific way that the Paraśurāma myth has developed in the post-epic literature has been as much guided by tensions within the myth itself as by tensions in the communities that adopted it in Kerala, Maharashtra, and elsewhere.

## THE ANALOGIC KEY: FATHER, MOTHER, BRAHMIN, KṢATRIYA

Once we have looked at the doubled birth and drawn from it the analogy of Paternal : Maternal :: Brahmin : Kṣatriya (which is of limited use to us outside this myth, but is, I think, well enough established *within* the myth), the structure of the Paraśurāma myth cycle becomes clearer, reinforcing the procreative/sexual overtones of Reṇukā's encounter at the river and making the eventual identification of Kārtavīrya (who, we may recall, is sometimes Reṇukā's brother-in-law and sometimes her youngest son) with the bathing *gandharva* prince almost inevitable. This structure plays out across three parallel conflicts framed by a double birth at one end and a double death at the other with the second death left untold, like an open cadence in a musical composition that, by pausing on the dominant harmony without resolving the tonic harmony, creates tension and the feeling in the listener of needing to continue (Greenberg 2006, 283). With B as birth, C as conflict, R as resolution, and D as death, we can represent the myth with this formula:

$$[B_1, B_2]; [C_1, R_1]; [C_2, R_2]; [C_3, R_3]; [B_3]; [D_1 \ldots]$$

To keep us from getting lost in the argument that follows, I will restate the macromyth with which we began in a truncated form, marking the relevant portions with their corresponding symbols and substituting Kārtavīrya for Citraratha:

## DOUBLE BIRTH

[$B_1$]: Satyavatī asks Bhṛgu to help her give birth to a Brahmin son and to help her mother give birth to a Kṣatriya son. Bhṛgu agrees and infuses a *caru* with *brahman* for Satyavatī and another with *kṣatra* for her mother (or tells them to embrace two trees). But the women accidentally mix up the ritual and Bhṛgu predicts that Satyavatī will give birth to a Brahmin who will act like a Kṣatriya and her mother will give birth to a Kṣatriya who will act like a Brahmin. Satyavatī convinces Bhṛgu to defer the prediction for one generation, to her grandson Jamadagni.

[$B_2$]: The Brahmin Jamadagni marries the Kṣatriya princess Reṇukā and gives birth to five sons, of which Paraśurāma, inheritor of the mixed nature intended for his father, is the youngest.

## EPISODE ONE (CONFLICT AND RESOLUTION)

[$C_1$]: One day Reṇukā goes out to the stream to collect some water, and as she is filling her pot, sees a prince named Kārtavīrya bathing in the water and engaging in erotic play with his concubines a little farther downstream. Distracted by her momentary attraction to Kārtavīrya, Reṇukā spills the water she was collecting and leaves a wet stain on the front of her clothes.

[$R_1$]: When Reṇukā returns to the hermitage, Jamadagni sees the stain on his wife's clothes and orders Paraśurāma to cut off his mother's head. Paraśurāma obeys his father's command without hesitation and decapitates Reṇukā with his axe. Pleased with his son's obedience, Jamadagni then resurrects Reṇukā and takes away all memory of the event.

## EPISODE TWO (CONFLICT AND RESOLUTION)

[$C_2$]: Kārtavīrya comes to the hermitage of Jamadagni while on a hunting trip and demands hospitality from Reṇukā. With the help of her husband's divine "Wishing Cow" Reṇukā is able to provide the king and his hunting party with an elaborate feast. Impressed with her abilities, Kārtavīrya steals it from the hermitage.

[$R_2$]: Paraśurāma returns to find the cow missing and goes after Kārtavīrya to avenge the theft. When he catches up to him, Paraśurāma cuts off Kārtavīrya's thousand arms with his arrows before killing him.

### Episode Three (Conflict and Resolution)

[$C_3$]: While Paraśurāma is still away and the hermitage is unprotected, Kārtavīrya's sons sneak in and kill Jamadagni in retaliation.

[$R_3$]: When Paraśurāma returns to find his father dead, he swears revenge on all Kṣatriyas, and wipes them out twenty-one times over.

### Regeneration

[$B_3$]: Brahmins impregnate the Kṣatriya widows to repopulate the earth, which has been suffering with no warriors left to protect it.

### First Death

[$D_1$]: Paraśurāma gives away the earth that he has conquered and goes into exile to spend the rest of his days in meditation.

[$D_2$]: OPEN

The formulaic rendering of [$B_1$, $B_2$]; [$C_1$, $R_1$]; [$C_2$, $R_2$]; [$C_3$, $R_3$]; [$B_3$]; [$D_1$ . . .] is useful for representing the three parallel episodes between the paired births and deaths and gives us an opportunity to think through the way they relate to each other in terms of the Paternal : Maternal :: Brahmin : Kṣatriya analogy, which tells us that a male figure should be read as Paternal and Brahmin and a female figure should be read as Maternal and Kṣatriya.

[$C_1$, $R_1$] is the scene of Reṇukā's incontinence at the river. Using the analogical key, we would read Reṇukā as a personification of the Maternal Kṣatriya, which seems obvious, but then we would also have to read Citraratha (from the Critical Edition) as the Paternal Brahmin figure, which seems quite wrong. Later mythmakers building on this structure were surely right to identify Kārtavīrya as the bathing prince at the river, and to understand that figure as a Kṣatriya. However, he is not a Paternal Brahmin, but a Paternal Kṣatriya, which does not fit. But, if we read the [$C_1$, $R_1$] episode as an inversion of the analogy, in which Paternal : Maternal :: *Kṣatriya* : *Brahmin*, then it starts to make sense. Defined against Citraratha/Kārtavīrya, we would see Reṇukā as Brahmin, which makes good sense because her identity as a Brahmin's wife and mother is front and center in this episode. Whether we see Reṇukā as distracted by lust or by nostalgia, her forest-dwelling ascetic life is the source of her discontent in either case. This makes Citraratha/Kārtavīrya a kind of paternal figure, as I have already argued in my readings of the incontinence episode as a secondary primal scene, analogous with the Bharadvāja myth. The "action" in the scene, the energy that animates the static analogy, is Reṇukā's intrusion on the bathing prince at the river.

The inverted analogy that we now see in the first conflict [$C_1$] creates an imbalance, which translates into momentum leading to the next conflict. A Maternal Brahmin has intruded upon a Paternal Kṣatriya. However, in the resolution [$R_1$], we see the analogic key briefly reestablished—but as a formula of death rather than a formula to create life—when a Paternal Brahmin (Paraśurāma *acting on Jamadagni's orders*) kills a Maternal Kṣatriya, as Reṇukā has become again when she returns to the *āśrama*. At the river, her Brahmin-ness defines her role in the conflict, while back at the *āśrama*, her Kṣatriya-ness defines her role in the conflict. Likewise, when I moved from North Carolina to Chicago in 2001, people in Chicago always noticed my Southern accent. But when I returned home to visit, people in North Carolina thought I had lost it. In North Carolina I was a Chicagoan, and in Chicago I was a North Carolinian.

[$C_2$, $R_2$] is the cattle theft scene, which continues the inverted relation of Paternal : Maternal :: Kṣatriya : Brahmin with Kārtavīrya (again) as the Paternal Kṣatriya and Reṇukā as the Maternal Brahmin. This latter identification is reinforced by the presence of Jamadagni's cow. As we have already seen in the Viśvāmitra and Vasiṣṭha story to which this episode is a clear reference, "a king on this earth is not supposed to seize two kinds of jewels belonging to a Brahmin: the cow used for his *agnihotra* rituals or his incomparable wife, the mother of his children" (Sathaye 2015, 7n4 website). A second inversion occurs in [$C_2$, $R_2$] with the action animating the structure: This time it is the Paternal Kṣatriya who is intruding upon the Maternal Brahmin. This double inversion finally breaks the analogy apart in a kind of structural rupture. This rupture is reflected in the narrative content of [$C_2$], in which a king and his hunting party enter the *āśrama,* overrun it, and explode it in a chaotic scene.

Meanwhile, the thematic content of the cattle raid that overlays the second episode sets up the transformation that will happen in the third and final episode. In [$C_2$], the first half of the cattle raid, we see the expected model of a Kṣatriya performing the raid, but in the second half [$R_2$], we find the unexpected and inverted model of the Brahmin performing the raid to get the cow back. [$R_2$], in which Paraśurāma kills the cattle thief, also calls back to [$C_1$], in which Reṇukā intrudes upon the bathing prince, since Kārtavīrya, whom we have to identify in the context of the macromyth structure as both the bathing prince and the cattle thief, is the Paternal Kṣatriya figure in both.

Rather than expressing some structural iteration of the analogical key like the previous two episodes, [$C_3$, $R_3$], the twenty-one-fold extermination of the Kṣatriyas, is an episode of restoration. It is a compulsively repetitive act of extreme violence that arrests our attention and tells us that something big is changing, but it almost hides what that something is. The systematic destruction of all the Kṣatriya males is so dramatic that it distracts us from what Paraśurāma is *creating*, namely twenty-one generations of fatherless children with Kṣatriya mothers. Over and over and over again, he is eliminating the Paternal Kṣatriya figure that crept into the structure with the first inversion of the analogical key in episode [$C_1$, $R_1$] (Reṇukā's encounter at the river). This movement concludes in [$B_3$] when a new generation of Kṣatriyas are sired with Brahmin fathers and Kṣatriya mothers. It is here, finally, that the Paternal : Maternal :: Brahmin : Kṣatriya analogy set up in the double birth story is reestablished with its original life-giving sense, as Figure C.1 on the opposite page illustrates.

Reading the myth with the analogic key and extending this analysis into the post-epic traditions gives us a whole new set of associations, in light of which the relationships of these four terms (Paternal, Maternal, Brahmin, and Kṣatriya) creates a new image of the structure for the myth, laid out in Figure C.2 on page 232.

Figure C.2 represents a kind of quantum macromyth, showing us all the divergent paths myth can take simultaneously. Here, we see all of Paraśurāma's timelines laid out synchronically on the same plane to show how the competing identities of Mother, Father, Brahmin, and Kṣatriya create a base out of which all of the myth's variants, inversions, and elaborations arise.

Reading left to right along the row of elements marked by Roman numerals, we move through the stages of Paraśurāma's shifting identity. We begin with the stage of Brahmin-Kṣatriya stasis, in which Paraśurāma's two sides are in balance. Then we move to the stage of the internal Brahmin-Kṣatriya conflict suspended under the law of the father (with Paraśurāma acting primarily as an obedient son rather than either a Brahmin or a Kṣatriya). Next comes the stage in which Paraśurāma's Kṣatriya nature is ascendant over his Brahmin nature, a condition that accompanies his varṇicide. Then, finally, we end with the stage of his Brahmin nature's ascendance over his Kṣatriya nature when he becomes a renouncer after his exile.

| Double Birth | Episode One (River) | Episode Two (Cattle Theft) | Episode Three (Varṇicide) | Regeneration |
|---|---|---|---|---|
| $B_1$, $B_2$ | $C_1$, $R_1$ | $C_2$, $R_2$ | $C_3$, $R_3$ | $B_3$ |
| Analogy Established | Inversion | Double Inversion | Restoration | Analogy Re-established |
| Paternal : Maternal :: Brahmin : Kṣatriya | Paternal : Maternal :: Kṣatriya : Brahmin | Paternal : Maternal :: Kṣatriya : Brahmin | ~~Paternal~~ : Maternal :: ~~Kṣatriya~~ : Brahmin | Paternal : Maternal :: Brahmin : Kṣatriya |

Figure C.1. The Inversion and Re-establishment of the Analogic Key.

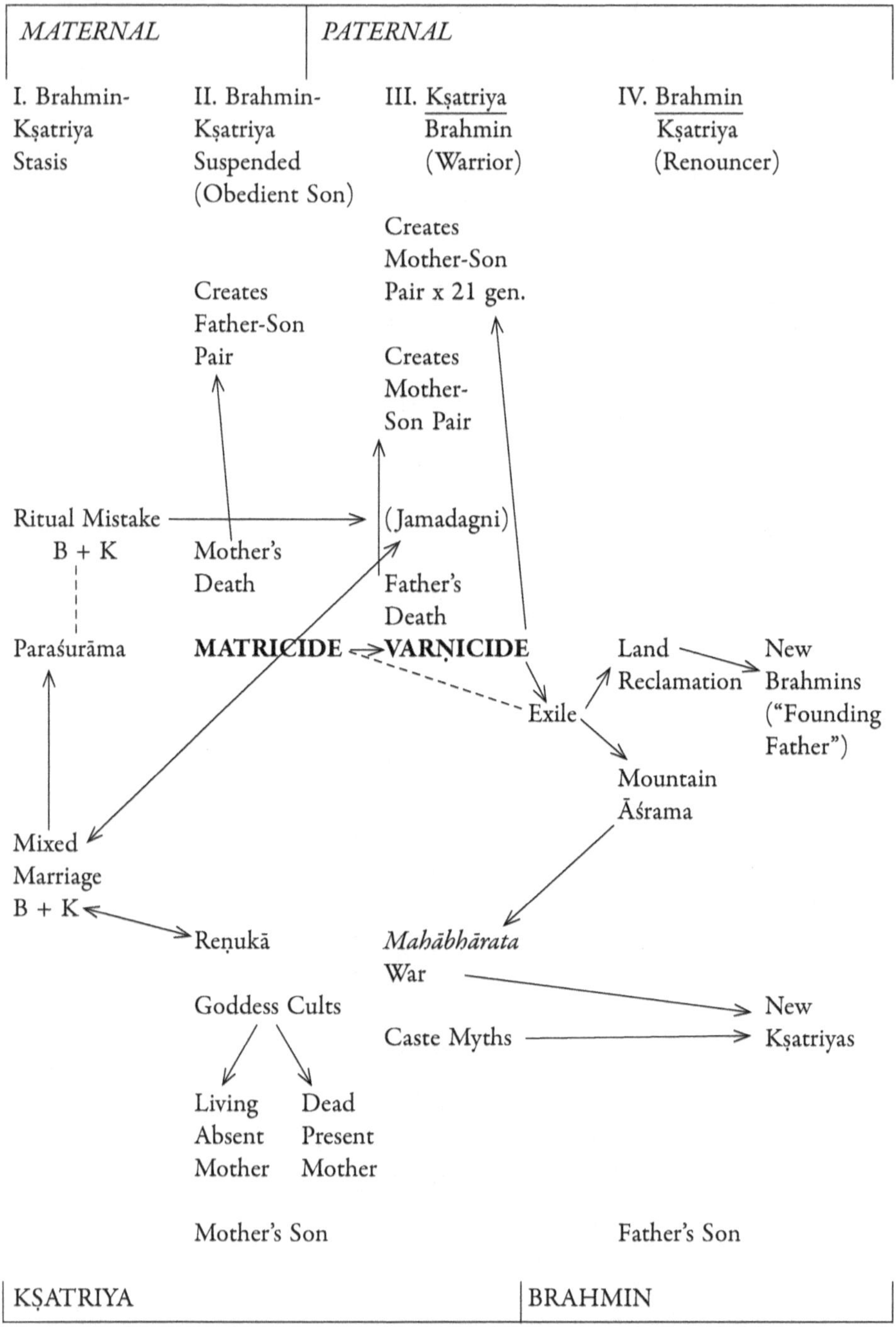


Figure C.2. A Synchronic Representation of the Paraśurāma Myth as an Expression of the Relationship between Mother and Father and Kṣatriya and Brahmin.

These four stages head up four columns into which the elements below them are arranged. Looking down column one, the stage of Brahmin-Kṣatriya stasis, we first see the ritual mistake mytheme, which we have called Paraśurāma's "first birth." There is a dotted line connecting the ritual mistake to Paraśurāma because it happens in the previous generation and, because of Satyavatī's wish, does not produce Paraśurāma directly. Instead, it results in the birth of Jamadagni, and so a solid line connects the ritual mistake to Jamadagni's name in column three. Below Paraśurāma's name is the proximate cause of his mixed nature, what we have called his "second birth," the marriage of Reṇukā and Jamadagni, which is connected by solid arrows to Reṇukā's name in column two and Jamadagni's name in column three.

In columns two and three, respectively, the words "matricide" and "varṇicide" are rendered in bold capital letters because the relationship between these two elements is the key for understanding the events in both columns. We will therefore start in the middle of these columns and work our way out, first going up and then going down. The matricide element is instantiated in the myth as the mother's death, which is directly above the central term in column two. An arrow then links this element to the creation of a father-son pair, which exists in the brief period between Reṇukā's death and her resurrection. Moving down from the center, we find Reṇukā's name and the goddess cults of South India in which she appears. As we have seen in chapter 3, the psychoanalytic reading of these goddess myths alongside the epic and Purāṇic ones suggests that after her resurrection Paraśurāma either chooses to leave her forever and always remember her as alive or he chooses to stay with her disembodied head or decapitated body as a devotee of her corpse. Reading down from these two alternatives, we find the term "Mother's Son," which I supplied to connect the elements in the bottom half of the column to the pre-Oedipal phase of attachment to the mother.

To move to column three, we first return to the middle of column two where the word "matricide" is connected by a solid arrow to the term in the middle of column three, "varṇicide." Once more going first up and then down, the term "father's death" appears as the direct cause of the varṇicide. It is also paired with "mother's death" in column two. Likewise, we see the mother-son pair created by Jamadagni's death directly opposite the father-son pair created by the matricide. The direct parallels end here, though, because the varṇicide is not a mere analogue to the matricide but a transformation (in terms of the gender of the victims) and an intensification of it. Therefore, at the top of column three, in which Paraśurāma's Kṣatriya nature is ascendant over his Brahmin nature, is the multiplication of the mother-son pair, which is repeated for every Kṣatriya family for twenty-one generations. Looked at this way, Paraśurāma is not merely killing Kṣatriyas, but transforming families, which points to the deep connection between the sets of events that surround the matricide and the varṇicide and also connect to the metaphorically paternal elements in column four.

Below the term "varṇicide" we see the *Mahābhārata* war, the second destruction of the Kṣatriyas that takes place on the field Paraśurāma prepares for that purpose and in which he participates. Finally, at the bottom of the column are the mythic histories of groups who trace their origin to the varṇicide, such as the Kāyasthas, Kalitas, Perikes, and Rajputs. Two arrows connect these terms to "New Kṣatriyas" at the far right of column four, indicating that both the Kurukṣetra battle and these caste myths refer to a new type of Kṣatriyas rising from the ashes. Comparing the bottom halves of column two and three, we also notice that the subsequent development of the matricide and the varṇicide themes takes place in two different contexts. The matricide theme plays out in goddess mythology and ritual, while the varṇicide is connected to the epic and to genealogical myths.

To move from column three to column four, we return again to the middle and follow the arrow that leads from "varṇicide" to "exile." Note that a dotted line also leads from "matricide" to "exile," because occasionally it is Paraśurāma's decapitation of Reṇukā that results in his being cast out, as in the *Kālikā Purāṇa*. The exile theme then branches off to the right along two paths, indicating the fact that some versions of the exile story send Paraśurāma to the mountains while others send him to the coast. The top branch, "land reclamation," then leads to the creation of new Brahmins, as we saw in the stories of the Citpāvans in Maharashtra and the Nambudiris in Kerala. In addition, these stories turn Paraśurāma himself into something of a father, in the sense of "founding father," which establishes him as the Paternal Brahmin of the analogic key we examined above. The bottom branch, "mountain *āśrama*," leads back to the *Mahābhārata* war in column three, since it is in the version of events in which Paraśurāma retires to the mountains that he is enlisted to intervene in the narrative of the epic. And if we continue following the arrows, we see that it also leads back to column four and the creation of new Kṣatriyas, completing the complementary relationship of the two parallel exile trajectories. Finally, at the bottom of column four, headed up by the ascendance of Paraśurāma's Brahmin nature over his Kṣatriya nature, I have written, "father's son," since all of these elements are post-Oedipal, not only identifying Paraśurāma as a Paternal Brahmin, but also representing a return to his father's asceticism.

At the very top and bottom of Figure C.2 are two divisions corresponding to the two halves of the genealogic key: Maternal-Paternal and Kṣatriya-Brahmin. They do not line up exactly, since a textured presentation of the material necessarily complicates the picture. Nevertheless, we can see the elements in the figure more or less occupy one or the other domain in the case of each pairing. The maternal, pre-Oedipal material in which attachment to Reṇukā is paramount covers most of the first two columns, but we should also note that the switch to the Paternal side in which obedience to Jamadagni is paramount actually occurs in the middle of column two, for which reason in sits on top of the line of division. At the bottom of the figure, the Kṣatriya domain covers the first three columns, transitioning into the Brahmin domain with the exile episode. The lack of strict parallelism between the Maternal-Paternal and Kṣatriya-Brahmin divisions in the figure is a result of the post-epic developments in the myth having filled out the structure and completed the open-ended nonconclusion created by Paraśurāma's lack of a second death, thereby complicating the analogy established in the original epic myth.

## INTERLOCKING AND ENCOMPASSING NARRATIVES: CYCLES WITHIN CYCLES

As Figure C.3 demonstrates, internal connections abound throughout the myth cycle, further emphasizing the coherence of the narrative. We will begin with the cycle of the primal scenes, which goes from [$B_1$] to [$C_1$]. As our psychoanalytic readings have suggested, [$C_1$] (Reṇukā intrudes upon the bathing prince), calls back to [$B_1$] (the ritual mistake) with [$C_1$] functioning as a second primal scene in which the seminal *caru* is transformed into the female sexual fluid Reṇukā releases involuntarily at the river. [$B_2$] (the actual marriage of Jamadagni and Reṇukā) is thus bookended by these two

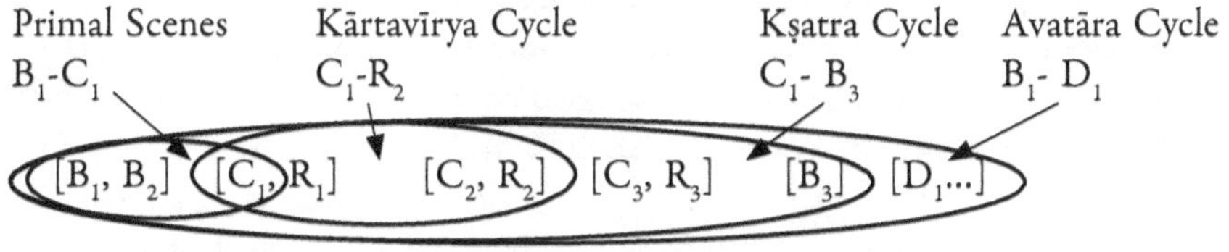


Figure C.3. The Four Cycles within the Paraśurāma Myth.

problematic primal scenes, one in which Paraśurāma's "first mother" Satyavatī rejects his birth and the other in which his "second mother" Reṇukā has an illicit contact with a Kṣatriya. [$B_3$], which picks up the mixed birth theme with the new generation of Kṣatriyas sired by Brahmin fathers, is not a primal scene in that it does not constitute the fantasy of witnessing something one should not see.

The second cycle-within-a-cycle overlaps with the first, in that [$R_2$] (Paraśurāma kills the cattle thief) calls back to [$C_1$] since Kārtavīrya—at least in the context of the macromyth structure—is the Paternal Kṣatriya figure in both. [$C_1$] through [$R_2$] thus comprises the Kārtavīrya cycle, which begins with Reṇukā's intrusion and incontinence at the river and ends with the death of the cattle thief. It is here that we see the inversion of Paternal : Maternal :: Kṣatriya : Brahmin. The Mother/Cow and Brahmin's Wife/Brahmin's Cow associations are also an important part of this cycle, constructing a mirror-image relationship between the two halves in which Reṇukā and the cow are aspects of a single symbolic nexus that is both maternal and erotic. In the first half, Reṇukā intrudes upon Kārtavīrya and lusts for him, while in the second half Kārtavīrya intrudes upon Reṇukā and lusts, not for her, but for the "desire cow," to which she is closely connected in all the ways we have already seen.

Encompassing the interlocking cycles of the primal scenes and of Kārtavīrya is what I have termed the *kṣatra* cycle, after the phrase in *MBh* 1.2.4, *"sarvaṃ kṣatram utsādya* [having destroyed the entire *kṣatra*]," used to refer to Paraśurāma's varṇicide for the first time. The word *kṣatra* does not occur either in the oft-repeated "*triḥsaptakṛtvaḥ pṛthivīṃ kṛtvā niḥkṣatriyāṃ prabhuḥ*" or "*triḥsaptakṛtvaḥ pṛthivī kṛtā niḥkṣatriyā purā,*" which are used to describe his annihilation of the Kṣatriyas, or in the story of the mixed-up *carus*. Nonetheless, the double sense of *kṣatra* as both Kṣatriya-ness and the Kṣatriya "race" as a whole creates the boundaries of this cycle.

Something very interesting happens when we retell the story contained in the *kṣatra* cycle with the *kṣatra* itself as the main character. First it is the essence of Kṣatriya-ness, created by the Brahmin Bhṛgu to put a Kṣatriya child in a Kṣatriya womb (that of Satyavatī's mother). But it enters into the wrong womb and is effectively aborted or destroyed for one generation before reappearing in Paraśurāma. Then, through Paraśurāma, it comes face-to-face with its other sense, the collective *kṣatra,* and compels its host Paraśurāma to wipe the collective *kṣatra* out completely for twenty-one generations. The essence of the thing has encountered the multiplicity of its instantiations in the world and eliminated them to remake them in its own image: the new collective *kṣatra* that arises in the world after the varṇicide is put by Brahmins into Kṣatriya wombs, just as the *kṣatra* essence itself was at the beginning of the cycle.

Finally, there is the *avatāra* cycle, which encompasses all three previous cycles and stretches from [$B_1$] (Paraśurāma's first birth) to [$D_1$] (his first death); from his incarnation until the fulfillment of his purpose on earth. It is the familiar arc of an *avatāra*'s story, with the significant difference that it ends before his life does. It is true that the popular human *avatāra*s Rāma and especially Kṛṣṇa have stories told about them outside their respective epics, but all of these stories are inserted within what mythmakers understand to be the normal lifespan of the *avatāra*s. The stories of Kṛṣṇa in the *Harivaṃśa* and the *Bhagavāta Purāṇa*, for example, take place in Kṛṣṇa's childhood and youth. Only Paraśurāma outlives his *avatāra*-hood, giving rise to the metaphysical puzzles we looked at in the first chapter. His second birth requires a second death, which he does not get. Going back to our structure and the musical metaphor, we can observe that the "open cadence" of [$D_1$ . . .] makes possible and renders meaningful all the controlled improvisations of the post-epic variants.

But first, some observations derived from examining the cycle structure in light of the analogic key. In Figure C.4 on page 238, I have laid out the four cycles within the myth summarizing the relation between Maternal and Paternal and Kṣatriya and Brahmin that characterize each event. Some very telling patterns emerge as a result. First, looking at the cycle of the primal scenes, we see a progression of eroticism and a breaking down of screen memories. The first episode is totally de-eroticized, with the *brahmaṇ* in the *caru* mixing with the *kṣatra* in Satyavatī through totally nonsexual means.[2] The next episode involves a marriage and presumed sexual intercourse, but still within the bounds of propriety. But in the last episode the cycle builds to a climax (as it were) when propriety is violated and frank eroticism takes center stage, with voyeurism, adulterous thoughts, and involuntary female ejaculation.

The second cycle, focused on Kārtavīrya, contains a binary structure which I have already described above. To me it seems significant that the point at which it intersects with the primal scenes is the most highly sexualized episode of the latter, but only truly appears so if we see this episode as the climax (as it were, again) of a three-stage progression. In other words, the river episode was mildly erotic before, but in context the primal scene cycle, it seems positively pornographic.

| $B_1$ | $B_2$ | $C_1$ | $R_1$ | $C_2$ | $R_2$ | $C_3$ | $R_3$ | $B_3$ | $D_1$ |
|---|---|---|---|---|---|---|---|---|---|
| *Brahman* | Paternal Brahmin | Maternal Brahmin | Paternal Brahmin | Paternal Kṣatriya | Brahmin | Kṣatriyas | Brahmin | Paternal Brahmins | *Brahman* |
| Couples With | Impregnates | Intrudes Upon | Kills | Intrudes Upon | Kills | Kill | Kills | Impregnate | Decouples From |
| *Kṣatra* | Maternal Kṣatriya | Paternal Kṣatriya | Maternal Kṣatriya | Maternal Brahmin (Reṇukā/ Cow) | Paternal Kṣatriya | Paternal Brahmin | Paternal Kṣatriya(s) =*Kṣatra* | Maternal Kṣatriyas | *Kṣatra* |
| Primal Scenes | | | | | | | | | |
| | | Kārtavīrya Cycle | | | | | | | |
| *Kṣatra* Cycle | | | | | | | | | |
| *Avatāra* Cycle | | | | | | | | | |

Figure C.4. The Four Cycles Interpreted with the Analogic Key.

When we then read the Kārtavīrya cycle as beginning with this highly sexualized episode, it shows the cattle theft episode in a new light. We now notice that Kārtavīrya, identified as the bathing prince for reasons discussed above, is bursting in upon the same woman who became aroused watching him bathe and he is doing so at a time in which she is at home alone with no men to protect *or chaperone* her. His taking of the maternal cow is now not just a reference to Indo-European second function mythology, but also reminiscent of the proverbial cow from that old sexist chestnut, "He's not going to buy the cow if he can get the milk for free." This sexual reading of the cattle theft theme is found in another part of the mythos, namely, Bhīṣma's "theft" of Ambā (whose name literally means "Mother"), leading Paraśurāma to intervene on her behalf. There is ambiguity as to whether or not we believe Reṇukā actually *wants* the bathing man she has spied upon at the river to visit her at home when her husband is out. But, if we continue with this sexual interpretation of the Kārtavīrya cycle and see his arrival at the *āśrama* as his coming to give Reṇukā what she was lusting after at the river, its two halves fit together in a new way. In the first conflict, Paraśurāma kills the adulterous wife; in the second, he kills the cuckolding seducer. This reading also makes Paraśurāma's violent rage and his killing of the "cattle thief" much more understandable.

As we continue reading the cycles through the new interpretive lens established by the overlapping of the primal scenes and the Kārtavīrya cycle, the *kṣatra* cycle takes on new meaning as well. It becomes a movement from increasingly explicit sexual overtones in [$B_1$-$C_1$] to escalating violence in [$R_1$-$R_3$], ending with what now looks like a very gruesome act of sexual violence and violation indeed: the forced impregnation of the Kṣatriya widows.

Further expanding this new reading of the myth to the all-encompassing *avatāra* cycle, we now see some vague but intriguing parallels between Paraśurāma's cycle and that of Rāma himself (i.e., Rāma unqualified, Rāma Dāśarathi). Simply put, if we read the cattle raid as having something to do with Reṇukā, the thousand-armed Arjuna Kārtavīrya now comes to resemble the ten-headed Rāvaṇa abducting Sītā from her forest hermitage, and Paraśurāma's annihilation of the Kṣatriyas looks like Rāma's destruction of the demon army of Lanka.

There is some evidence to support this connection. First is Kārtavīrya's relationship to Rāvaṇa, whom he defeats and holds captive, then releases in the *Vāyu Purāṇa* (Tripathi 1979, 41). Second, Kārtavīrya's guest appearance in the *Rāmayāṇa* expresses a strong thematic resonance with the Reṇukā-Citraratha encounter. In *Rām* 7.33, Rāvaṇa (a Brahmin, we should recall) is praying to Śiva at a river when he notices that the water has stopped flowing. Rāvana looks to see what has happened and sees Kārtavīrya holding back the water with his hands in order to create an artificial lake in which to frolic with his wives. A battle ensues in which Kārtavīrya defeats, binds, and then releases Rāvaṇa. The third piece of evidence is the contentious meeting of Paraśurāma and Rāma that we examined in chapter 1 and the subsequent determination that there is only room for one *avatāra* on earth. Why, we might ask, did Kṛṣṇa not make the same demand that Paraśurāma give up his power in the epic? It seems to point to a special relationship between the two Rāmas. Fourth and finally (and most tenuous), is the later conversion of Kṣatriyas into demons under the Pāñcarātrins. As we have already seen, the Pāñcarātrins' theological sanitization of the myth is overdetermined by various historical circumstances, but it seems likely that some preexisting associations with the *Rāmayāṇa* may have played a part.

## MYTHOGENESIS IN ACTION: FILLING OUT THE STRUCTURE WITH THE POST-EPIC VARIANTS

In this section, I will attempt to visually represent the significance of all the controlled transformations in the larger macromyth. Earlier, I used a planetary metaphor to describe values, anxieties, and worldviews as the wind, rain, and upwelling magma that drive the constant changes in the geomorphology of a myth. But I also argued that these forces are driven and constrained by the energy and the magnetic field exerted by the spinning molten core of the myth, containing Paraśurāma's split identity as a Brahmin warrior, his matricide, and his annihilation of the Kṣatriyas. Now it is time to review what we have observed about the larger corpus of Paraśurāma literature and think about the role that values, anxieties, and worldviews have had in shaping it.

To elucidate this interpretation, at which I have arrived through the self-conscious acts of critically informed creative redescription that make up this book, I now present Figures C.5–C.7, which render this dynamic process into two dimensions. I do this in order to represent the major motifs and submotifs; the thematic connections between them; their parallels in Bhārgava, other Indic, and non-Indic myths; their regional variants; the rituals that help to explain them; and a brief survey of my readings using the comparative toolbox that is the History of Religions.

| Motif | Brahmin Warrior (Chapter One) | | |
|---|---|---|---|
| Submotifs | Switched *Carus* or Trees | *Avatāra-Cirañjīvin* | Cattle Theft |
| Bhārgava Parallels | | | Bhārgava-Haihaya Feud |
| Other Indic Parallels | *Śālabhañjikā*<br>Droṇa<br>Mitra and Varuṇa<br>Crushed teeth in Subhūma story (*caru*) | Aśvatthāman<br>Struggle with Rāma Dāśarathi | Viśvāmitra and Vasiṣṭha<br>Indra and Vṛtra |
| Non-Indic Parallels | Indo-European Trifunctionalism (Dumézil) | Wandering Jew (medieval European legend) | Indo-European cattle raid (Lincoln) |
| Connecting Themes Across Motifs | 1. Fluid (*caru*)<br>2. Kṣatriya-Brahmin relations (Kārtavīrya as cattle thief)<br>3. *Kṣatra* as a separable object (*caru*) | | |
| Regional Traditions | Dattātreya (Deccan Folk God) | | |
| Ritual Resemblances | *Audambarī* rite (trees) | | Vedic ritual cattle raid |
| Theoretical Approaches and Creative Redescriptions | Universal-Particular-Singular (Žižek)<br>Śaiva-Vaiṣṇava nature<br>Enforcement of *varṇa* hierarchy under sectarian kings in medieval period (Sanderson and Bronkhorst)<br>Paraśurāma as vanishing mediator of Being and Becoming (Hegel)<br>Paraśurāma as sovereign and *Homo Sacer* (Schmitt and Agamben)<br>The two deaths (Lacan and Žižek)<br>The sacred executioner (Theme of Exile) | | |

Figure C.5. The Brahmin Warrior Motif.

| Motif | Matricide (Chapters Two and Three) | | | |
|---|---|---|---|---|
| Submotifs | Reṇukā's encounter at the river | Curse of disobedient sons | Decapitation | Resurrection |
| Bhārgava Parallels | | | | Śukra<br>*mṛtasaṃjīvinī vidyā* |
| Other Indic Parallels | Cirakāri (countermyth) | | | |
| | Ahalyā<br>*paṇaghaṭa-līlā*<br>Symbolism of the pot | | Chinnamastā<br>Lajjāgaurī | Parikṣit (Resurrected embryo) |
| Non-Indic Parallels | | | | Norman Bates |
| Connecting Themes Across Motifs | 1. Fluid (female ejaculation, river, *gandharvas*)<br>2. Kṣatriya-Brahmin relations (Kārtavīrya as man at river "cuckolding" Jamadagni)<br>3. Matricide as destruction of *kṣatra* (female) | | | |
| Regional Traditions | South Indian goddess cults (Yellama, Māriyamma<u>n</u>, Pōttu Rāja)<br>Dattātreya (performs funeral rites for Reṇukā)<br>Chinnamastā and Lajjāgaurī (headless goddesses) | | | |
| Ritual Resemblances | *Pēy* exorcism<br>*Varuṇa-praghāsa* | Jogappas | *Pēy* exorcism | |
| Theoretical Approaches and Creative Redescriptions | Misogynistic images of the female body as a leaky vessel<br>*Akrasia* (Greek) and defilement (Ricoeur)<br>The Dead Mother complex (Green)<br>Pre-Oedipal stage and language (Lacan)<br>Matricide as necessity (Kristeva)<br>Durga complex (Kurtz) | | | |

Figure C.6. The Matricide Motif.

| Motifs | Varṇicide (Chapters Four and Five) | | |
|---|---|---|---|
| Submotifs | Destruction of Kṣatriyas | Remainder | Land reclamation |
| Bhārgava Parallels | Aurva | Submarine Fire | |
| Other Indic Parallels | *MBh* War<br>Subhūma<br>Puśyamitra<br>Snake sacrifice in *MBh* | *ucchiṣṭha*<br>*śeṣa*<br>*vāstu*<br>*prasād*<br>Parikṣit | Myths of creation from waters of chaos<br>Varāha rescuing earth from the ocean |
| Non-Indic Parallels | | | Tuirbe Tragmār (Irish)<br>Alkmaion (Greek) |
| Connecting Themes Across Motifs | 1. Fluid (pools of blood, driving back the sea)<br>2. Kṣatriya-Brahmin relations (Kṣatriyas sired by Brahmins)<br>3. Varṇicide as compulsively repetitive destruction of *kṣatra* (male) | | |
| Regional Traditions | All clan origin myths tracing their origin to destruction of the Kṣatriyas<br>Pāñcarātra theology | Nambudiri Brahmins (Malabar)<br>Citpāvan Brahmins (Maharashtra) | |
| | | Degraded Kṣatriya castes | |
| Ritual Resemblances | Myth of sacrifice gone out of control (Śaiva) | | |
| Theoretical Approaches and Creative Redescriptions | Destruction of Kṣatriyas as revenge for murder of Jamadagni<br>Destruction of Kṣatriyas as repetition of matricide with genders switched<br>Destruction of Kṣatriyas as compulsive reproduction of fatherless mother-child couples<br>Sanitizing myth by changing Paraśurāma's victims into demons (Pāñcarātra, *VDhP*)<br>Scholars' and Hindus' willingness to describe Paraśurāma's actions as genocide<br>Varṇicide as blueprint for mass destruction ("Blood and Soil") | | |

Figure C.7. The Varṇicide Motif.

## Killing the Mother, Killing the Other: Thoughts on Gendered and Genocidal Violence

As we conclude, we are now ready to look at what insights the Paraśurāma myth gives us about the complexity of Indian attitudes toward women's bodies and retributive violence and then, through some speculative associations, try to make some more general observations about the relationship between matricide and mass killing. On the question of women's bodies, expressed in the matricide motif of the myth, we must first acknowledge that we are really talking about high-caste men's attitudes toward women's bodies. The Paraśurāma myth is embedded in and permeated by a patriarchal and often misogynistic worldview that places high value on female submissiveness and expresses deep anxiety about the idea of women exercising control over their own bodies. This is most aptly summed up in Nīlakaṇṭha's crude explanation (which surely would be called a "man-splanation" if it were issued today) that, "when she sees a handsome man, whether it be her brother, father, or even a son, a woman's vagina grows wet."

It is also important to note that the specific point of view through which the incontinent Reṇukā is presented is that of a son looking at his mother. Reading it through our analogic key, we can see that the myth is projecting a worldview in which the father is superior to the mother as the Brahmin is superior to the Kṣatriya. The superimposition of attitudes derived from a child's primary relationships onto an idealized larger social order has profound effects that are felt deeply on both conscious and unconscious levels. This is apparent in the preoccupation with legitimacy, either genealogical or political, that has accompanied the reception of the Paraśurāma story. We can see this preoccupation with the Citpāvans, the Nambudiris, and the various "degraded" Kṣatriya castes, most of whom have masochistically cast themselves in passive or victimized roles in their connections to the mythos.

When a myth anchors the political anxieties of the historical moment into the depths of the most profound and often suppressed anxieties, wishes, and traumas of the early developmental years, it throws the libidinal floodgates open, encouraging violent and erotic imagery to flow freely. This nexus of meanings accounts for the presence throughout the Paraśurāma cycle of blood, seminal substances, and female sexual fluid amid scenes of sacrificial killing, eroticism, and mind-bending distortions of time and space, all of which are recognized to varying degrees as paths to transcendence in the Indian traditions.

The maternal body on which the myth focuses our attention is the site of peaceful absorption, but also of fantasies and of horrors. As Kristeva has told us, matricidal horror toward and rejection of the vessel of the mother's body is "our vital necessity" (1989, 28). In the case of Reṇukā, the vessel is a leaky one, but that is not an unusual image. Looking past the myth into Indian popular culture we have seen similar ideas of the permeable female form in the cases of *pēy* possession in the South. But Reṇukā is more than permeable, she is flowing (or trying not to be). Compare Reṇukā's incontinence to Freud's case study from 1893's "The Neuro-Psychoses of Defence":

> [A] girl suffered from the dread of being overcome by the need to urinate, and of being unable to avoid wetting herself, ever since a need of this kind had in fact once obliged her to leave a concert hall during the performance. By degrees this phobia had made her completely incapable of enjoying herself or of going into society. She only felt well if she knew that there was a W. C. near at hand which she could reach unobtrusively. There was no question of any organic complaint which might justify this mistrust in her power to control her bladder; when she was at home, in quiet conditions, or at night, the need to urinate did not arise. A detailed examination showed that the need had occurred first in the following circumstances. In the concert hall a gentleman to whom she was not indifferent had taken a seat not far from her. She began to think about him and to imagine herself sitting beside him as his wife. During this erotic reverie she had the bodily sensation which is to be compared with an erection in a man, and which in her case—I do not know if this is always so—ended with a slight need to urinate. She now became greatly frightened by the sexual sensation (to which she was normally accustomed) because she had resolved within herself to combat this particular liking, as well as any other she might feel; and next moment the affect had become transferred on to the accompanying need to urinate and compelled her after an agonizing struggle to leave the hall. In her ordinary life she was so prudish that she had an intense horror of everything to do with sex and could not contemplate the thought of ever marrying. On the other hand, she was so hyperaesthetic sexually that during every erotic reverie, in which she readily indulged, the same voluptuous sensation appeared. The erection was each time accompanied by the need to urinate, though without its making any impression on her until the scene in the concert hall. (2001a, 56)

Turning to contemporary Indian popular culture, Aditi Sen gives some examples of the role of sexual and spiritual vulnerability during urination and bathing in a low-budget Hindi horror film that seem especially relevant to the case of Reṇukā.

> In *Sar Kati Laash* (The Headless Corpse), a woman badly needs to urinate during a long drive through the woods, and she keeps telling her husband how bad her situation is. He tries to dissuade her, saying, "Let the rest house come." He then scolds her for drinking a lot of water, and there is a long discussion on the subject. She finally manages to persuade him to stop the car, and as she goes to urinate, the headless corpse possesses her. In other films, such as *Maut ka Badla* (Revenge for Death) and *Adamkhor Hasina* (Man-Eating Beauty), people are possessed during the discharge of bodily wastes. The act is not seen with abhorrence, but these acts open people to susceptibility and spirits take advantage of that. These acts form a major part of the narrative, not something gross, laughable, or unnatural. The vulnerability of a person in their bath is a common occurrence in horror films. Similarly, these acts make people susceptible, exposed, and helpless, providing a perfect opportunity for evil spirits to strike. (2011, 86)

It is useful here to take up Perundevi Srinivasan's argument about the construction of heteronormativity in the rituals surrounding Māriyamman̲, in which female "frugal sexual economy" functions as "an articulation falling within the 'juridical' (regulative and prohibitive) as well as 'productive' heteronormative power and discourse" (2009, 20–21) and read it alongside Sen's argument about the deconstruction of heteronormativity in the representation of urination and eroticized male bathing scenes in low-budget Indian horror movies where "incest is digestible, women's sexual desires are acknowledged, and gender categories are transgressed" (2011, 86). Both contemporary ritual and low-budget genre cinema point us to a fixation on the female body with its secretions as a site for defining and regulating the identities and roles available in the social world out of which it speaks, just as the Brahmin warrior Paraśurāma's body is a site for regulating and defining *varṇa* and caste identities.

In the Paraśurāma myth, the maternal body is also connected to the forest, as we have seen in the fate of Paraśurāma's brothers who remain in the pre-Oedipal forest and the Reṇukā devotees profiled by Assayag who wear traditional garb made of tree branches (1992, 208). Combining the forest with the idea of incontinence, David Haberman reports that on the

Ban-Yatra pilgrimage through the twelve sacred forests of Braj, "jungle" is used as a euphemism for "toilet" (1994, 81). Taken on their own, bits of cultural trivia like this may not add up to much, but they take on meaning in light of Freud's observation that fantasies of the primal scene draw heavily from cultural scripts, such as stereotypical notions of the Witches' Sabbath that came up in the "Satanic Panic" of the 1980s, in which innocent people made confessions based on invented memories of themselves worshipping the Devil and committing incest (see Wright 1995).

In the case of Paraśurāma, we also observe the connection of a dense network of cultural associations and pre-Oedipal fantasy material to a collective rage for political order—for the enforcement of *varṇāśramadharma* and *maryāda,* the latter term having been used recently to refer to the hierarchical gender relationships in Indian society sanctioned by the ever more powerful Hindutva movement (see Janaky 1992; Poonacha 1993; and Jain and Sharma 2002). The word *maryāda,* which refers to a boundary or a limit, is a Hindi word drawn from Sanskrit where its derivation is doubtful. As is frequently the case, the completely invented folk etymology listed by Monier-Williams elucidates the word wonderfully. According to his entry, the word is "fancifully said to be [from] *marya* + *ada* 'devouring young men' who are killed in defining boundaries" (2009, 791).

Connecting the fluidity of the female body to struggles over political violence and social order is not confined to India. In his monumental study of fascism, *Male Fantasies, Volume I: Women, Bodies, Floods, Histories,* Klaus Theweleit observes that since the Enlightenment, European thought has engaged in

> an intensified form of the struggle against an increasingly impregnable body armor, against an increasingly marked atomization of individuals in the early days of market competition. The writers applied the name "woman" to anything that flowed, anything limitless; in the place of God, the dead transcendence, they set the female sex as a new transcendence that finally abolishes lack. The earth became a limitless woman: life, thy name is woman; woman, thy name is vagina; vagina, thy name is ocean, infinity. In other words, they used, or misused, the fluidity—the greater malleability and as yet unspent Utopian potential of femaleness, a desiring production that is fallow, undirected, not yet socially defined, and thus remains in closer proximity to the unconscious; a life of emotion, rather than of intellect (that cruel, demarcating product of the constraints that beset men's bodies)—to encode

> their own desire, their own Utopias, their own yearning to be free of boundaries, with the notion of an "endlessly flowing woman." (2007, 380)[3]

The Paraśurāma story, in its full macromyth form, actually expresses a less condemnatory and more ambivalent attitude toward female fluidity than its Brahmin- and male-centered earlier versions, as we have already seen in the use of the *karakam* pot to represent Reṇukā in South India and Kinsley's suggestion that the headless, blood-spurting figure of Chinnamastā with whom she is sometimes identified might "represent the generation of spiritual power in a female . . . by means of the retention of her sexual fluids and the transformation of them into a nourishing fluid" (1997, 161).

Even with its episodes of creation (of new Brahmins, new Kṣatriyas, new land), the prevailing mood of the myth is still one of violence, taking the form of impersonal and dispassionate execution in the matricide and bloody-minded berserker rage gradually cooling into cold-blooded repetition-compulsion in the varṇicide. The decapitation of Reṇukā, as we have already seen, connects directly to the extermination campaign against the Kṣatriyas. We have likewise already discussed the intractable problems with—and the inescapability of—using the genocide model in understanding this myth. But, given the connection of the two acts of violence, there is another, more individualistic form of repetitive killing that we should therefore consider as a framework for interpreting the figure of Paraśurāma.

## Paraśurāma the Serial Killer

In the index to *Splitting the Difference*, Doniger describes Paraśurāma as a "Hindu serial killer" (1999, 371). What first appears to be a bit of casual cleverness hidden in the paratext is actually quite a perspicacious observation. It leads us down another popular culture detour, this time into American so-called "slasher" films such as *Halloween* (1978) and *Friday the 13th* (1980), in which the (usually masked) serial killer, completely without affect or visible emotion but possessing an unstoppable will to violence, is an archetypal figure. In the *Halloween* films, Michael Myers, the killer, wears a "Captain Kirk" mask painted white to give it a completely blank expression. The masked killer is represented in the *Friday the 13th* franchise by Jason Voorhees, whose face is covered first by a pillowcase and in later films by an iconic hockey mask. In the first film, however, it is Jason's mother who is the killer. That is, until she is decapitated with an oar, which Jason responds to by preserving her severed head in a makeshift shrine and murdering every sex-crazed teenager he sees while her command to "kill, kill" echoes in his head.

In the vocabulary of slasher films, a child's vision of the mother's sexuality and simultaneously of her moral turpitude (these are in many ways the same thing at the level of this particular myth and fantasy) is frequently the "breaking point" at which the child becomes a killer, often at the very moment of that vision. In *Halloween*, six-year-old Michael Myers calmly stabs his older sister and her boyfriend to death when he finds them embracing. The protagonist of John McNaughton's *Henry: Portrait of a Serial Killer* (1986), loosely based on the confessions of convicted multiple murderer Henry Lee Lucas, begins his career by killing his prostitute mother, who had abused him and forced him to watch her have sex with her clients. And in Alfred Hitchcock's genre-defining *Psycho* (1960), young Norman Bates murders his mother and her lover after finding them in bed together.

In most of these transformative moments, the child's incestuous desire and jealous rage are awakened simultaneously, with violent results. This potent mix also plays an important role in the matricide episode of the Paraśurāma cycle, where conflicting emotions are divided between Paraśurāma and Jamadagni. The killer's jealous rage is projected on the father, while desire for the mother—desire enough to wish her back to life (through the power of the father)—is attributed to the son. Together, the two form a dyad: the impulsive and murderous father and the dutiful, mother-loving son. In the first half of the myth, Jamadagni is the source of the negative and violent emotions and Paraśurāma is merely the instrument of his will. In the second half, when Paraśurāma asks for his mother to be revived, the terms of their relationship are inverted: Paraśurāma has become the source of positive emotion in the form of love and devotion, while Jamadagni is the instrument, carrying out his son's will in bringing Reṇukā back to life. Significantly, this dyad collapses into the single, but always internally divided, figure of Paraśurāma when his father is killed. It is the death of his father and the subsequent collapse of the dyad that transforms Paraśurāma into a figure of what is often called "genocidal" rage, but which we will here identify with the emergence of the mythical serial killer. The first killing is without emotion but acts as a catalyst for the emotions released in the massacre to follow.

The same kind of sequence occurs in *Psycho*, or is at least explained as having already happened by the psychiatrist character at the film's conclusion. Upon learning that his mother is sleeping with a married man, Norman Bates reacts not with a spontaneous act of violence committed with some ready-at-hand weapon but with a methodical murder by poison. There is also premeditation in his subsequent theft and preservation of his mother's corpse: Norman does not run out to the graveyard in the middle of the night with a shovel in a fit of remorse and loneliness. Instead, demonstrating cool logic and planning, he fills the coffin with rocks and does not even allow his mother to be buried at all. After he has killed her, Norman resurrects his mother in himself, "becoming" her when he begins to murder the attractive young women at the motel for whom he feels sexual desire. While his actions as "Mother" (or "Norma," which is her actual name as well as a feminized version of his own) are frenzied and involve repeated penetrations of the woman's body with a butcher knife, the only crime he commits *as* Norman Bates (poisoning his mother and her lover) is essentially bloodless.

The *modus operandi* of the pre-trauma Norman stands in stark contrast to his crimes as Mother, which are, with the exception of the private investigator s/he kills in self-preservation, aimed at women of a particular type (the psychiatrist who examines Norman at the film's end tells the sheriff to look for more bodies of young girls in the lake) and, in the paradigmatic shower scene in which the nude Marion Crane is stabbed to death, highly eroticized. This increase in violence coincides with an inversion of the love triangle that is the setting of his act of matricide. In Figure C.8, the triangle on the right represents the matricide he commits as Norman and the one on the left represents the shower murder he commits as Norma (wearing her wig and dress). The black arrows represent libidinal energy while the gray arrows represent violence.

An analogous process occurs in the Paraśurāma cycle with respect to intensity. In the murder of Reṇukā, when the feelings of jealous rage and incestuous desire underlying the matricide are still divided between Jamadagni

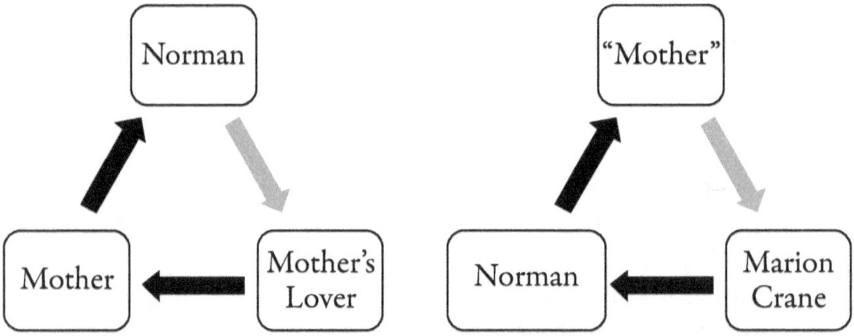


Figure C.8. The Libidinal Triangles Representing the Two Murders of *Psycho*, with the Pre-Matricide Murder on the Left and the Post-Matricide Murder on the Right.

and Paraśurāma, the killing is followed by remorse and expiation. The killing of the Kṣatriyas, after the death of Jamadagni, is a virtually ceaseless campaign of annihilation in which each mass extermination is followed, not by remorse, but by more killing, until twenty-one generations of Kṣatriyas are wiped out. Paraśurāma's ambivalence has been replaced by focused fury. To continue the comparison to *Psycho*, both the matricide (left) and the subsequent killing (right) can be represented as love triangles.

The first triangle has at its apex a dyad of rage-filled parent and dutiful son (what I have described as the stage of Brahmin-Kṣatriya suspended under the law of the father), while the second triangle is topped by the single figure of the ultimate dutiful son, a figure who has internalized the transgressive tendencies of a murdered parent and whom those tendencies have come to dominate.

Whereas in *Psycho* Norman has internalized or introjected "Mother," who represents both the object of his desire and the vehicle for his violent impulses, Paraśurāma has, in a sense, internalized both parents. While his father is clearly associated with jealous rage, he is also impotent in that he is unable to commit violence himself and must depend on his son to carry out the murder of his wife. Later, when he is murdered in the attack on the hermitage that precipitates the mass-killing episode, he lays down his arms and dies crying out for Paraśurāma. Jamadagni's wrath is harmless until it meets the Kṣatriya nature within Paraśurāma, lying dormant until it is awakened by his act of matricide and the partial internalization of his mother in the form of the *kṣatra*.

It is the dual nature of Paraśurāma that allows him to carry out the murder that Jamadagni—a full Brahmin whose mother has spared him from the mixed nature that afflicts his son—cannot. While the matricide

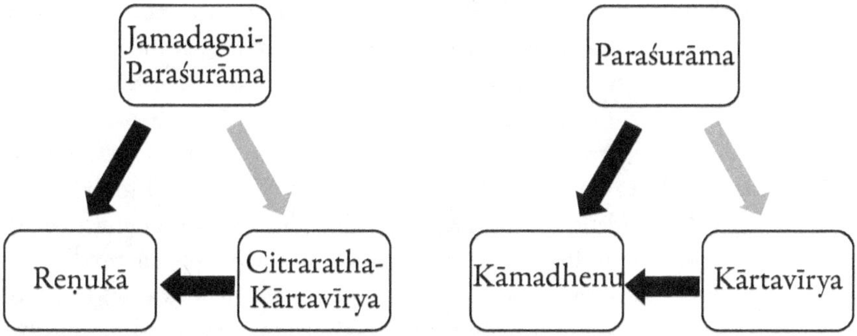


Figure C.9. The Libidinal Triangles Representing Paraśurāma's Matricide on the Left and the Cattle Theft on the Right.

is effectively "undone" at the end by a magic resurrection, it still involves a partial internalization of the dead mother, whose nature is Kṣatriya by birth. It is Paraśurāma's inner Kṣatriya nature that takes control during the mass killing (the stage of Kṣatriya over Brahmin). His father's impotent rage and his mother's martial heritage are fused into one enormously destructive and unbalanced figure. Just as Norman uses "Mother" to punish himself by killing the women he desires and who threaten to disintegrate his carefully constructed personality complex, so Paraśurāma's campaign to eradicate the Kṣatriya class can be read as a desire to eradicate (successfully, in the end) the Kṣatriya in himself, even as it continues to overpower his more pacific Brahmin nature.

Unlike Norman Bates, though, Paraśurāma has no object of sexual desire to complete the second love triangle in the place occupied by Norman's potential lovers in the *Psycho* model. Instead, this place is occupied by the Kāmadhenu, which represents desire itself and its instant gratification. The cow has the power to give her owners whatever they desire, which makes the evil king Kārtavīrya desire to possess her. As the instant gratification of all wishes, the Kāmadhenu is the symbol of that imaginary solution to the Oedipus complex, complete maternal envelopment and the self-sufficiency of the mother-son unit. As an animal commonly associated with maternity and domesticity, she represents the desired mother drained of all eroticism, neutralizing Paraśurāma's attraction by removing its incestuous component. Like the resurrection and induced amnesia of Reṇukā, the Kāmadhenu allays the anxieties associated with separation from the mother.

The post-matricide murders committed by Norman Bates are highly sexual; his victims are those who are a threat to "Mother," mostly attractive young women who might tempt Norman away from her. In Paraśurāma's post-matricide killings, the sexual element is radically transformed; his victims are exclusively male, as he allows the women to live so that they can bear a new generation of victims. Sexuality is present, nonetheless, in its absence, expressed in the desexualized object of desire represented by the Kāmadhenu.

In reality, the so-called profiling of serial killers, which has become such a staple of modern serial killer films such as *The Silence of the Lambs* (1991), has proven to be ineffective in actually providing useful information that would help to identify a suspect (see Godwin 2002). But quite apart from its questionable utility as an investigative tool, the implicit mythology of profiling provides some very useful insights into widely held and largely unexamined attitudes about the connection between matricide and compulsive serial murder. Consider this article from 1985, titled, "Psychologists Say Serial Killers Have Victims in Mind":

> Killers like the Night Stalker, who has been linked to 14 murders in California, often choose their victims because they symbolize someone else, a psychologist told a conference. "Of all violent individuals, the serial murderer engages in the most horrific behavior and finds himself the focus of popular media attention when captured," Dr. J. Reid Meloy said Friday at the 93rd annual American Psychological Association convention. Meloy, director of the psychiatric security unit at the San Diego Central Detention Facility, said serial killers usually have a deep-seated sexual component to their violence. In some cases, he said, the serial killer suffers from displaced matricide—a desire to kill their mother that becomes targeted on victims that resemble her. People who actually do kill their mothers "are at low risk for future violence in the community despite the sensational nature of the crime," Meloy said. "The potential target pool (in matricide) is one, and there is zero probability that the killer will encounter his mother again." But the serial killer does not kill his mother and therefore, seeks out victims because they symbolize her.[4]

Sweeping generalizations aside, some prominent serial killers or mass murderers do indeed kill their mothers, sometimes as a prelude to their later crimes, including the previously mentioned Henry Lee Lucas, as well as Ed Kemper and the University of Texas sniper Charles Whitman (technically a mass murderer). The point of this observation is that a connection between matricide and repeated, compulsive acts of killing—between killing the Mother and killing the Other—resonates far beyond Ancient India. Displaced matricide as a motive for mass killing *makes sense* (i.e., functions as a kind of myth) to contemporary audiences and even to experienced FBI investigators.

Paraśurāma's internal contradictions, reflecting anxieties situated in a specific time and place, provide fertile ground not only for metaphysical speculation but also for psychological symbolism, the latter giving expression to the same kind of impulses and anxieties that inform our own attempts to comprehend incomprehensible acts of violence. The question remains: Why is Paraśurāma, whose mythology bears such uncomfortable similarities to that of our own myths of genocidal maniacs and serial killers, an *avatāra*?

## The Harvest Festival

The following lines conclude "The Story of the Axe."

Beneath the blue, like a green plantain leaf,
Lies my land where my eye runs ever and anon,
There I see, as elsewhere too,
Tears, pain, revenge, hatred and strife
And realize that earthly winds
Dim the sparkle of any noble ideal;
Any virtue man can sharpen
Turning it into a tool of torture.
To find fault is futile;
How long should a man live to realize his mistakes!
With moist eyes I look at my countrymen,
Their hearts stamped with my axe's tip,
Who are violently furious
Surly, cross and distraught
But brave,
Who are tossed in the cradle of passions . . .
This consolation I have—
This land adorns itself, these people revel,
Not for me;
Nor for this warrior ever haunted by memories of past crimes,
But, for Mahabali, who found strength in humility
And saw the Lord in the foot that pressed him down. (1980, 130–31)

We know now, at the end of the poem, that Paraśurāma has been narrating his story as he watches the Keralan harvest festival of Onam, which commemorates not only his destruction of the Kṣatriyas, but also the dwarf *avatāra* Vāmana's bloodless victory over the demon king (and *cirañjīvin*) Bali. That story begins as the righteous Bali is distributing gifts to the guests at his royal sacrifice. When Viṣṇu appears as the Brahmin dwarf Vāmana, he makes the humble request for only for as much land as he can cover in three steps. When Bali agrees, Viṣṇu assumes his giant cosmic form with the first stride. With his second stride, he covers the entire triple world. Seeing this, Bali falls to his knees and asks Viṣṇu to take the third step on his head so that the demon king can experience the god's grace. As a reward for his humility, Bali is allowed to return to Kerala once a year to celebrate the Onam festival with his people (Rinehart 2004, 146–47). Paraśurāma, as the poem makes clear, can only watch from afar.

By way of a conclusion, I will try and work out what I think the poet means by putting these myths together and having Paraśurāma express his gratitude that Bali, and not he, is the culture hero Kerala is celebrating at the moment. Both Bali and Paraśurāma are *homines sacri,* exiled from the world as the result of a sacrifice. But Bali is not alone; he exists in his own parallel heaven and is able to be reunited with his delighted worshippers when it comes time to celebrate the harvest each year. Paraśurāma is alone, exiled even within the corner of the world he created himself by force of will as a place to which he could escape.

Why? Bali "found strength in humility" and "saw the Lord in the foot that pressed him down." There is more than triumphalist self-serving ideology at work here. In the poem, Viṣṇu's foot represents cosmic finitude, not earthly hegemony. Bali sees and accepts what Paraśurāma cannot—the meaning of human mortality. Paraśurāma, always out of place and out of time, is stuck in a jerking and flickering freeze frame, embodying our profound inability to let go of what we have determined is our place in the world and all the destructive and isolating consequences of that inability. Bali, though, has realized that the only way to be connected to life and the world is to understand the transience of existence and imagine oneself as part of the future only insofar as one has contributed to its onward flow.

In the end, the Paraśurāma myth does what I think every myth does. It expresses, in all of their dynamic and mutually constitutive interrelatedness, values (such as women's continence, filial obedience, and *varṇāśramadharma*), anxieties (about women's incontinence, the breakdown of the *varṇa* system, and the end of the Vedic sacrifice), and a worldview (centered, in this case, on the figure of the male Brahmin). But it also addresses a specific set of historically grounded concerns about identity, violence, and the maternal body in a way that reaches downward into widely shared developmental psychic traumas and is thus uncannily and uncomfortably familiar to us.

Like the Bhārgava himself, driving back the water to create a new land, when theologians made Paraśurāma an *avatāra* they pushed his human violence back into the realm of divine violence and doubly exiled him as a deified *homo sacer*, creating enough distance to dull the shock of recognition while also birthing a powerful symbol that could be used to conceptualize existential loneliness, neurosis, and the contradictions of sovereignty while also serving as a warning against the violent conflagration that awaits those who put vast knowledge in the service of coercive power.

# Notes

## Preface

1. Marcion understood the Old Testament demiurge as "a being who united in himself the whole gradations of attributes from justice to malevolence, from obstinacy to inconsistency" (Harnack 1905, 271).

2. Vālmīki, author of the Rāmāyaṇa, was saved from a life of sin by saying his name unintentionally while chanting "māra māra māra" ("death, death, death") until it became "ma/rā ma/rā ma/rā." On the Ramnami sect who repeats his name as the core of their practice, see Lamb 2002.

3. Although when a very independent-minded Rajput woman of my acquaintance received this compliment, her response was, "Ugh!"

## Introduction

1. My further thoughts on this work can be found in my afterword for the Italian translation, "Un pezzo troppo quadrato: la vita e l'opera di Robert Eisler," in Robert Eisler, *Uomo diventa lupo: un'interpretazione antropologica di sadism, masochismo e licantropia.* Traduzione di Raul Montanari (Milan: Adelphi Edizioni, 2019).

2. It need not have turned out this way, of course. In Ancient China there were "virtually no traces of chaos or cosmogonies," and so, "given that it never was constituted on a mythical basis, Chinese thought never needed to construct itself philosophically (in the mode of logos)" (Jullien 2002, 806).

3. To my mind, this is still an enormously useful formulation.

4. Bruce Lincoln has demonstrated this in essays such as "Sacrificial Ideology and Indo-European Society" (1991, 167–75) and "Competing Uses of the Future in the Present" (2014, 36–49).

5. This understanding of sight is not unique to Sanskrit. In English, "vision" and "sight" alike refer both to the sense faculty and the thing it apprehends.

6. I use "receive" and "reproduce" to include both "hear and retell" and "read and recreate." But the latter sense is the most salient for us here, since all of the Paraśurāma myths we will look at exist in written form, even if that form is simply an anthropologist's or colonial administrator's field notes.

## Chapter 1

Epigraph, from *Avadhūta Gītā* 1.25: *neti neti śruṭir brūyāt anṛtaṁ pāñca-bhautikam*

1. Paraśurāma's problematic (even if not unique) nature as a Brahmin warrior, the result of a ritual mistake, is central to his identity. Or so one would think. But, in his introduction to the English translation of the *Brahmāṇḍa Purāṇa*, Ganesh Tagare claims (untenably, in my view) that we should regard Paraśurāma as a pure Kṣatriya:

> [In *MBh* 1.58.5–6], we are told that when all Ksattriyas were slaughtered by Paraśurāma, Ksattriya ladies went to Brāhmanas and the children born from them were the Ksattriyas of the new generation. If this matriarchical [he must mean "matrilineal"] system was then the accepted custom, Jamadagni, the son of a Ksattriya Princess must be regarded as a Ksattriya. He married Renukā, a Ksattriya Princess of Ayodhyā and Paraśurāma is a full-blooded Ksattriya and not a Brāhmana at all. (1983, *lxii*)

He further claims, without presenting any evidence of a pre-epic tradition, that the *Mahābhārata* authors, wrongly taking their patrilineal genealogies for granted as timeless custom, introduced the notion of Paraśurāma as a Brahmin. Unable to comprehend matriliny, they interpolated the entire story of the mixed-up *carus* to explain his martial character. Tagare does not explain why in the Malayalam tradition Paraśurāma is credited with inventing matrilineal succession, which is seen as an innovation, and a bizarre one at that. In fact, the sixteenth- or seventeenth-century Keralan *Laghudharmaprakāśikā* is a text dedicated to integrating that local custom of matriliny into a dharma framework (see Davis 2013, 147–64 in Lindquist). One could counter that the matrilineal succession Paraśurāma institutes in Kerala is actually a reintroduction of an older practice associated with his clan in the past, which would strengthen Tagare's argument. The problem with this hypothesis is that Paraśurāma's Brahmin identity is central in these stories and this makes it unlikely that the traditions that connect him to matrilineal succession could also see him as Tagare does, that is, as a pure Kṣatriya descended through his mother's and grandmother's lines.

2. Dejenne explains:

> Indeed, the other conceivable terms all had important disadvantages by insisting on one aspect of Paraśurāma's personality or by revealing themselves, on reflection, to be inadequate: He is an *avatāra* of Viṣṇu

> but this element does not seem decisive in many of the representations studied here, particularly in the stories of creation of social groups by Paraśurāma. The term god seems excessive to the extent that, despite his interactions and encounters with the gods, the divine status of Paraśurāma is far from obvious—and the rarity of his temples in India is undoubtedly a clue. The term *cirañjīvin* is both too technical and too focused on the longevity of Paraśurāma, and only takes its meaning and produces its effects as a function of more fundamental qualities. Despite the asceticism of Paraśurāma and his attachment to spiritual values, the extreme violence and physical nature of his actions prevent him from being designated as a saint, a sage, or a *muni*. (2007, 12)

3. Hazariprasad Dvivedi, the great scholar of the devotional (*bhakti*) movements, said that the poet Kabir, who straddled and muddled Muslim and Hindu identities, came to earth like Narasiṃha, "at the point of contradiction in settings that seemed irreconcilable" (quoted in Hawley 2015, 251). Narasiṃha is also a favorite image for the International Society for Krishna Consciousness (ISKCON) and is represented prominently at their famous temple in New Vrindaban, West Virginia.

4. Before moving on, we should note that the story in the seventeenth-century "vulgate" edition from Varanasi features both the *carus* and the trees, as does the subsequent *Viṣṇudharmottara Purāṇa*.

5. The word in question. "*ugrakarma*," could as easily be "mighty deeds," but since the word occurs in apposition to the explicitly negative term "*krūrakarma*," it makes sense to translate it with a negative valence.

6. This valence is especially clear in the myth of Pippalāda ("he who eats fruit from the *pippala* [another name for the *aśvattha* tree]") that occurs in the *Skanda Purāṇa*. When he is born, Pippalāda learns that his father Dadhīci was killed by the gods. Enraged, Pippalāda churns his left thigh with his left hand and summons the destructive power of a fiery mare called the submarine mare or Aurva (because of its connection to another Bhārgava myth) to exact his revenge. He is then unable to control the mare and the gods trick her into going down to the bottom of the ocean (see Doniger 1971, 24 and 1980, 228–29). This added shade of meaning makes the inclusion of the *aśvattha* tree in the conception of Paraśurāma doubly appropriate, as it serves both to inform his inner Kṣatriya nature and to foreshadow his vengeful obsessions.

7. Gail argues that the two trees version of the mixed birth episode in the Āraṇyaka Parvan was composed later than the version from the Śānti Parvan, which attributes Paraśurāma's dual nature to a mixup with consecrated *carus* rather than trees. But Goldman takes the opposite position, arguing that the two trees narrative, belonging to what he identifies as the "Brahmin" version of the cycle recounted by the mysterious and long-lived Akṛtavraṇa, is older than the "Kṣatriya" tradition narrated by Kṛṣṇa in the Śānti, which paints a less favorable picture of its protagonist. Along

with substituting bowls of rice pudding for trees, the second telling also leaves out the matricide episode entirely. On the seminal nature of the *caru,* see Gonda 1987, 149.

8. As Sathaye notes, this version becomes the model for subsequent Purāṇic accounts (2010, 204n58).

9. Here the child is truly father to the man!

10. The perspective of the matricide Paraśurāma seems an unusual voice for the author of *Amma* ("Mother") and *Mutaśśi* ("Grandmother") to assume.

11. Looking forward to chapter 4 of this book, we can draw a parallel between the matricidal axe as a bloodthirsty personification of Paraśurāma's dead mother, egging him on, to the desiccated corpse of Norma Bates in *Psycho.*

12. By "metamyths," Goldman means "mythological material of a decidedly secondary character when compared with the primary material that they restructure and explain" (1971, 8).

13. Perhaps this explains why the Brahmin Paraśurāma has to renounce the world after he conquers it through violence, while his counselor Kṛṣṇa prevents the Kṣatriya Yudhiṣṭhira from renouncing his kingdom after the *Mahābhārata* war.

14. Another thing to note here about this "second Paraśurāma" born from a Śudra's womb is that, "after him, the world's kings will be Śudras" (*ViP* 4.24.3).

15. Elst writes that "we have seen how a 20th-century Hindu-born scholar will twist and turn the literary data in order to uphold a sectarian and miracle-based calumny against the Hindu ruler Pushyamitra, and to explain away a sobring [*sic*] testimony about the fanaticism of Ashoka, that great secularist avant la lettre. Such is the quality of the 'scholarship' deployed to undermine the solid consensus that among the world religions, Hinduism has always been the most tolerant by far" (http://koenraadelst.bharatvani.org/articles/ayodhya/pushyamitra.html).

16. I must depart from Bagchee again, though, when he comes to the conclusion that we must interpret Paraśurāma not as "a mere sign: either for a proto-historical conflict between brāhmaṇas and kṣatriyas, or for brāhmaṇa frustration at kṣatriya incompetence" but as a symbol whose "core meaning . . . must be sought rather in the way that the symbol is sufficient unto itself" (ibid.). Part of his argument builds on the etymology of the original Greek word from which we derive "symbol." The Greek *symbolon* does mean "thrown together" as Bagchee writes. But the sense of the word is not primarily its self-sufficiency or its coherence, but its broken-ness and its role as a mediator between two parties who have no reason to trust each other. As Anthony Stevens notes:

> The Greek noun *symbolon* referred to a token or tally which could be used as a verification of identity. An object, such as a bone, would be broken in half and each given separately between two people . . . who could then identify each other by producing both halves and checking that they fitted together. Each tally-holder knew his own half to be

> genuine; when contact was made, "goodness of fit" between the two halves of the *symbolon* was the criterion which satisfied the other's *bona fides*. (2001, 12)

In other words, a symbol cannot mean anything until it is broken, and people whose relationship is one of mutual dependence and complementarity would have no reason to use one.

17. Choudhary notes that the first inscription that mentions Paraśurāma, attributed to the Gaṇga king Durvinīta Koṅguṇivṛddha around 522 CE, calls the king an incarnation of Paraśurāma in his knowledge of *astra*s and *upāstra*s—that is, magic weapons (2010, 22).

18. Vielle notes that a "later Konkan tradition about Paraśurāma is found in the Sahyādrikhaṇḍa [of the *SkP*] . . . according to which the brahmins firstly established in the region of Gokarṇa and Baṇavallī [*sic*] were finally cursed and degraded by the Bhārgava because of their bad behaviour, and were later replaced by king Mayūravarman with Northern brahmins coming from Ahicchatra . . ." and that "[the] arrival of brahmins from Ahicchatra in the North Kanara region of Banavasi is an historical fact assignable from inscriptions to the 9th–10th centuries . . ." (2002, 350n39).

19. Paraśurāma himself is also connected to the worship of Tripurā through the ritual texts the *Paraśurāma-kalpa-sūtras*.

20. Karṇa's ability to endure the pain of the worm boring through his leg without waking his guru Paraśurāma, who is sleeping with his head in Karṇa's lap, is what convinces the Bhārgava that he has been tricked into training a Kṣatriya, the only kind of man who would stupidly withstand such pain.

21. Griffin-Kremer notes a similar role for cattle raiding in Ireland, past and present:

> Outside the punctilious world of legal technicalities, we might recall that the injury or death of men in their prime was often closely bound up with the politically correct and violent acquisition of wealth through cattle rustling, even if there was a frequent aura of ritual about it. . . . It held the prestige of a royal pastime (and requirement), and the custom had been superseded by gentrified manners only a generation or two before Thomas Pennant . . . visited the Highlands in the mid-eighteenth century, where riding on a *creach*, the local name for a cattle raid, had been a young man's best recommendation to his sweetheart, so that it also figured among the rites of passage in the life cycle. (2001, 171)

22. Examples of this include the *Brahmāṇḍa* and *Brahmavaivarta Purāṇa*s. See Choudhary 2010, 135–37.

23. The idea of king as bandit is an important one in ancient India. Describing the symbolic roles of bandit, Brahmin, and king, respectively, Shulman writes,

> The interaction of these three types also reveals the underlying fragmentation of the political universe: power adheres naturally to the least legitimate figure, who can only use it to achieve his own limited, tragic transfiguration, not to impinge upon the center; the most authoritative figure, the Brahmin, is largely paralyzed by self-exclusion; the center itself, or what's left of it, discharges its power and resources through the king's public consumption (*bhoga*), distribution (*dāna, tyāga*), and, above all, his self-subversive games (*līlā*). (1985, 373)

When he slaughters the Kṣatriyas and makes the earth a sacrificial gift, Paraśurāma rapidly brings the "underlying fragmentation of the political universe" under the authority of *brahman*. Central to Paraśurāma's importance is his willingness to abandon Brahminical detachment and get his hands dirty with the polluting work of bloodshed, becoming a "bandit," in the sense that he is one who is under the ban (the literal meaning of the Italian and Spanish *bandito*) of the Brahmins who have exiled him.

24. http://global.oup.com/us/companion.websites/fdscontent/uscompanion/us/static/companion.websites/9780199341115/chapter_2.pdf.

25. It is worth noting, however, that both the *Pañcaviṃśa* and the *Taittirīya Brāhmaṇas* pair Viśvāmitra with Paraśurāma's father Jamadagni as the two allied opponents of Vasiṣṭha (Panda 1984, 25).

26. For more on this topic see Collins 2014, 2017a, and 2017b.

27. I am grateful to my colleague Myrna Pérez Sheldon for pointing this out to me.

28. This sovereign would turn out to be *der Führer*, Adolf Hitler.

29. "In thinking about Hanuman's immortality," Lutgendorf continues, "devotees have often considered such related matters as the locales in which he might reside and the physical forms in which he might appear; they have also recognized him as temporarily or partially embodied in other human beings" (2007, 279). Although he is not nearly as beloved or worshipped as his fellow *cirañjīvin* Hanumān, there are some examples of worshippers making the same kinds of considerations for Paraśurāma. For instance, in 2008 the *Sakaal Times* reported a Brahmin gangster in eastern Maharashtra "revered among the Brahmins as an incarnation of Parashurama" (Salunkhe 2009, 14).

30. The *avatāra-cirañjīvin* juxtaposition functions as a mythical analogue to the disorienting "dolly zoom" effect used in Alfred Hitchcock's *Vertigo*: the camera simultaneously moves closer to the subject along a fixed straight trajectory while zooming out, making the object in focus appear to stay the same size while the background seems to rush toward the viewer.

31. We should distinguish here between the paradoxes or dichotomies that are diachronic and those that are synchronic with respect to the myth. The diachronic paradoxes are proper to and constitutive of Paraśurāma's personality as he moves through his narrative. The best example of this is the Brahmin-Kṣatriya identity. Within his own

story, he has this mixed nature from birth. Synchronic paradoxes, on the other hand, attach to Paraśurāma's myth cycle rather than Paraśurāma himself. The best example of this is the *cirañjīvin-avatāra* paradox, because at no time is Paraśurāma himself an *avatāra* and a *cirañjīvin* simultaneously. Rather, he becomes a *cirañjīvin* only after his *avatāra*-hood is passed on to Rāma Dāśarathi. The *cirañjīvin-avatāra* paradox thus only applies to Paraśurāma as a figure who metonymically represents his own myth cycle. The dynamism of the Paraśurāma myth derives partially from its tendency to take synchronic paradoxes that result from sectarian receptions of the story and absorb them into the narrative in diachronic form. We will see this clearly in the *Viṣṇudharmottara Purāṇa*, where the conflict of Paraśurāma's devotion to Śiva and identity as a form of Viṣṇu (obviously more of a conflict among readers than within the myth itself) are a major part of the story. To take another example and, hopefully, clarify my argument, we could say that there is a diachronic conflict between Huckleberry Finn and the escaped slave Jim over the issue of slavery in Mark Twain's 1884 classic *The Adventures of Huckleberry Finn*. That conflict takes place and is resolved inside the narrative. But their conflict takes on a synchronic dimension when it is analyzed as a narrative whole in light of race relations in America. Interpreters of the book can then read that conflict about the place of Tom and Jim's fictional relationship in the larger and very real conflicts surrounding the issue of race in America back into the diachronically unfolding conflict in the novel.

32. I am reminded here of the line from the *Satyricon* about the Sybil cursed with eternal life without eternal youth, famously used by T. S. Eliot as an epigraph for *The Waste Land:* "For on one occasion I myself saw, with my own eyes, the Cumaean Sibyl hanging in a cage, and when some boys said to her, 'Sibyl, what do you want?' she replied, 'I want to die' " (Eliot and Rainey 2006, 75).

33. Far-fetched as it may seem at first glance, the Wandering Jew as the peripatetic Buddha is not out of the question. Buddhist literature did in fact spread through medieval Europe, as Gui de Cambrai's thirteenth-century Old French poem *Barlaam and Josaphat* attests (see Lopez and McCracken 2014).

34. 3.16–17 describes the last visit of Paraśurāma to Kalki after the latter has completed his destruction of Kali and conquest of the world. In his final act, Paraśurāma instructs Kalki's wife Ramā to observe the Rukmiṇī vow to obtain a son and tells the story of Devayānī and Śarmiṣṭhā (see Collins 2014, 108–109).

35. To demonstrate the way that this kind of negation is understood in Hegelian dialectic, Žižek frequently refers to a joke from the 1939 Ernst Lubitsch film *Ninotchka*: "The hero visits a cafeteria and orders coffee without cream; the waiter replies: 'Sorry, but we've run out of cream. Can I bring you coffee without milk?' " (2012, 765). In dialectical terms, there is a distinction to be made between coffee without cream and coffee without milk. And neither one of them is just plain coffee.

36. For more instances, see Nagar 2006, 40–100 and Choudhary 2010, 142–48.

37. Long after his first, terrestrial death, the mythic king Indrayumna falls out of heaven because his fame on earth has faded. To avoid the second death, he

has to go back to earth to find an ancient tortoise who remembers his name so that he can be let back in (*MBh* 3.191). Today, this notion is still very present in Western culture, from the 2017 Disney Pixar film *Coco* (in which people live on in the world of the dead as skeletons until they are forgotten on earth, at which point they disappear completely) to retired Marine Colonel and Alabama Senate hopeful Lee Busby's remark in a 2017 interview with *Southern Living* that "[in] the military, we say a warrior dies twice. The first time is when he draws his last breath, and the second time is when someone speaks his name for the last time" ("This Retired Marine Colonel Is an Incredible Sculptor | Southern Living." https://www.youtube.com/watch?v=rk_f8aE2T0s; last accessed November 29, 2017).

## Chapter 2

1. Theweleit 1987, 230.

2. A more general statement of the motif of the sons' curse utilized in the Paraśurāma story appears in a myth recounted in *Aitereya Brāhmaṇa* 7.13–18, in which Viśvāmitra saves Śunaḥśepa from being sacrificed by his greedy father and adopts him as his own eldest son, placing him before the hundred other sons he already has. Śunaḥśepa agrees, but the older fifty of Viśvāmitra's sons complain about the unfairness of this new development. As a result, Viśvāmitra curses them to lose caste and inherit the least desirable lands of the earth. The younger fifty, who accept his word, he blesses in turn with promises of cattle and heroic sons (see Collins 2014, 127–32).

3. Samuel Beckett, *Ill Seen, Ill Said* (London: John Calder 1979), 39.

4. The line of Nīlakaṇṭha that Goldman cites is from a seventeenth-century commentarial text called the *Bhāratabhāvadīpa* ("Light on the Nature of the *Bhārata*"). In full, it reads, "'In water' means 'in the pond' and 'soaked' means 'flowing.' Thus it is said, 'When she sees a handsome man, whether it be her brother, father, or even a son, a woman's vagina grows wet. This is the truth, the truth, Janārdana' [*ambhasi sarasya iva klinnā drutā/ tathā ca uktam/ sundaraṃ puruṣaṃ dṛṣtvā bhrātaram pitaraṃ sutam/ yonir dravati nārīṇāṃ satyaṃ satyaṃ janārdana/*]" (Poona Ed, 184).

5. The symbolism of the woman's stained clothes also suggests the famous story of Indra's curse, a myth of Brahmin-Kṣatriya tension among the gods. Not wanting to share power with him, Indra beheads the divine priest Viśvarūpa. Then when he is punished for the act, he makes women share his sin of Brahminicide by causing their clothes to be stained with menstrual blood once a month (*TS* 2.5.1).

6. Here is one of those tangential connections that are relegated to the footnotes, but that pop into one's mind when one is considering the fundamental unity of the epic as proposed by Hiltebeitel: In the Pāṇḍavas' palace, Duryodhana slips into a pool of water and wets himself, necessitating a gift of clean clothes and provoking mocking laughter from his hosts (*MBh* 2.43.5–10). In the B. R. Chopra television serial, Draupadī even calls him blind like his father, which Freud sees as

a displacement of castration, an interpretation made more convincing by connecting blindness to his weak and impotent father, Dhṛtarāṣṭra. Later, during the disrobing scene, Duryodhana mocks Draupadī by showing her his thigh ("a thunderbolt and elephant's trunk in one" in 2.63.11), disproving her taunt. But after that same thigh is smashed by Bhīma in duel with clubs, Duryodhana retreats back into a pool of water and seals himself in (demonstrating his own power to make water solid) and refuses to come out just as he did when he spent two years in the iron ball of his mother's womb (1.107). In light of all this castration imagery, is Duryodhana accidentally wetting himself and being publicly shamed for his visibly soaked clothes a kind of "unmanning" meant to foreshadow Reṇukā's incontinence?

7. MBh 3.116.8a-b: *vyabhicārāt tu sā tasmāt klinnāmbhasi vicetanā; MBh 3.116.11: tān ānupūrvyād bhagavān vadhe mātur acodayat/ na ca te jātasaṃmohāḥ kiṃ cid ūcur vicetasaḥ.*

8. Rahul Peter Das, frustrated with what he sees as the lack of depth in the work of scholars like such as Doniger (and presumably the present author as well) has taken it upon himself to compile a meticulously researched work on Indian sexological literature. Although he admits that some will probably find his conclusions at the end of nearly five hundred pages "rather banal, and maybe also a bit frustrating as the end-product of such a lengthy and intricate discussion" (2003, 494) they are necessarily so, since when it comes to the subject of Indian sexological ideas, "we still have not passed the very preliminary stage of dogged, minute and maybe boring probing, frustrating as this may be for the individual scholar concerned" (10).

9. Some online commentators, such as Deborah Sundahl, see images of female ejaculation in the *ḍākinī* sculptures of Khajuraho (http://isismedia.org/sacred-liquid-tantra/). However, they could as easily be images of menstruation.

10. David Gordon White explains a closely related idea:

> The notion of *chidra*—as a person's "weak point," a "chink" in one's bodily defences, or simply a "gap" or "discontinuity" in one's psychosomatic Gestalt—is widespread and relatively ancient in India, going back to at least the time of the *Harivaṃśa* (HV), a work dating from the first centuries of the common era. There, we are told that following the gods' victory over the demon Kālanemi, Brahmā warned them to never let down their guard because "the despicable Dānavas always force their way into the openings (*chidreṣu*)" (HV 38.77b–78a). (2012, 151)

11. Gurumurthy interprets this myth symbolically, identifying the pot as the mind (fragile and easily shattered) and the coiled snake as passion, which must be kept subdued by the mind.

12. Here we should recall the declaration of Georges Bataille's sacrificer: "*Intimately,* I belong to the sovereign world of the gods and myths, to the world of violent and uncalculated generosity, just as my wife belongs to my desires" (1989,

44) as well as Charles Taylor's observation that the aristocratic heroes of the seventeenth-century French plays penned by Pierre Corneille "are always declaring their 'générosité' as the reason for the striking, courageous and often gruesome acts they are about to commit" (2018, 134).

13. In modern parlance, "Champagne for my real friends, real pain for my sham friends."

14. *ūrdhvám̐ bhárantam udakám̐ kumbhénevodahāryàm/páśyanti sárve cákṣuṣā ná sárve mánasā viduḥ//*. See also Jurewicz 2016, 291–92.

15. We can also see variants of the motif in Gilgamesh's defeat of Humbaba, the Khmer *pañcuḥ sīmā* rite (see Davis 2016, 126–27), the defeat of *jinn* by legendary warriors in the Gambia (see Sarr 2016, 96–98 and *passim*.), and in any number of stories of Green Men from the British Isles recounted in Simon Schama's wonderful *Landscape and Memory* (1995, 37–245 *passim*).

16. *Padma Purāṇa* 2.5.60–65 has Vāsudeva telling Aditi that he will be born from her womb as Paraśurāma, then Rāma, then Kṛṣṇa, making Aditi the mother of all the human incarnations.

17. In the movie, Reṇukā uses a coiled cobra to balance the pot of water on her head as in the myth from Savadatti and also has the power to form a pot magically out of sand, which she does the first time she accidentally breaks the pot and is late bringing water for her husband's ritual anointing (*abhiṣekha*). She then finds that she is not only unable to reform the pot from sand, she has also lost her beauty and been disfigured by blotches and boils on her face. Later in the film, her beauty is restored when she prays to Śiva and bathes in the stream of water flowing from the top of a statue of the god's head (after the manner of the iconographic convention that depicts the Gangā bouncing off of Śiva's dreadlocks in a waterfall). However, when she returns home she is still unable to make a sand-pot and Jamadagni's wrath has not abated: the axe swings, the head falls, and so on. For a partial list of film adaptations of the Paraśurāma story, see Dejenne 2007, 380–91.

18. *ṚV* 8.3.16 also compares the Bhārgavas to the sun, along with another group, the Kaṇvas.

19. We should note here the connection between this activity and Paraśurāma's driving the sea out with his axe or his arrows in the coastal myths as well as the Marāṭhī tradition in which Paraśurāma shoots his arrow into the air and Dattātreya creates all of the *tirtha*s at the place where it lands (Rigopoulus 1998, 93).

20. There may be a parallel here to the Vedic Svarbhānu myth treated in Jamison 1991, 133–303, especially given the prevalence of the theme of Reṇukā being cursed with a facial disfigurement in South India. The pox element in the Tamil myth-ritual complex analyzed by Srinivasan 2009 also points in this direction.

21. V. C. Srivastava argues that the association of the sun with shoes and an umbrella is an Iranian innovation in the practice of sun worship whose incorporation into the Indian tradition is the subject of the Jamadagni myth (1972, 186).

22. BhP 9.16.4: *kalaśaṃ tasthau purodhāya kṛtāñjaliḥ*

23. There may be a sort of a mild version of a curse in *MBh* 3.115.9 when Jamadagni exclaims the Sanskrit curse word *dhik* (often translated with the utterly inadequate "fie!" which sounds like something one might say while wringing one's hands and hopping from foot to foot) when he "sees" what Reṇukā has done.

24. "The Goddess who decapitates the buffalo-demon has by implication offered herself for decapitation. Her warrior's sacrifice is what saves the world. Reṇukā is first sacrificed by her son in a sacrifice that would be more monstrous than self-sacrifice. She is then replaced by substitute victims, the Kṣatriyas who proved to be dangerous to the well-being of the cosmic order, dharma. The theme of the beheaded Goddess thus explained could account for the mysterious affinities that seem to draw the Goddess close to the demon that she kills" (Biardeau 1993, 83–84).

25. Asko Parpola's contention that the image of a tumescent water buffalo mounting a prostrate woman on an Indus seal excavated at Chanhu-daro reflects a pre-Vedic ritual model adopted by the Aryans for their horse sacrifice points to a deeper possible connection between the *aśvamedha* and the goddess cult (2015, 239).

26. In one Tamil *Mahābhārata* cult described by Hiltebeitel, an incarnation of Duryodhana named Periyantavar has dominion over the *pēys* for one day because it was granted to him by Draupadī (2011, 340).

## Chapter 3

1. As a term that refers to Kṣatriya-ness as well as the collectivity of the Kṣatriyas; it is the analogue to the term *brahman,* but never became part of an elevated discourse on the nature of reality and thereby avoided encrustation with metaphysical and theological accretions.

2. Rarely, as in the *BhP*, Paraśurāma himself kills his brothers, again at his father's command.

3. A great feud arose between the gods and the demons over the sovereignty of the universe and every creature in it, moving and standing. To ensure victory, the gods selected Angiras's son the ascetic [Bṛhaspati] as their sacrificial priest, the [demons] chose Uśanas Kāvya [Śukra]. These two Brahmins were long-time bitter rivals. The gods killed the demons who had gathered for the battle, but Uśanas drew on the power of his knowledge to bring them back to life and they rose again to make war on the gods. The demons in turn cut down the gods in the heat of battle but the wise Bṛhaspati could not resurrect them because he did not have the *mṛtasaṃjīvinī vidyā* possessed by Uśanas (*MBh* 1.71.5–10).

4. This pattern is prevalent in southern variants of the myth.

5. This part of the story suggests the Vedic *pravargya* rite in which milk is heated in a clay pot. I have written elsewhere: "The myth connected with the Pravargya ritual is found, among other places, in the *Śatapatha Brāhmaṇa*. It contains allusions to the story of Indra beheading Makha in *ṚV* 10.171.2 and the beheading and then

re-heading (with a horse's head) of Dadhyañc, two popular variants of the 'beheaded sacrifice' motif" (Collins 2014, 193–94).

6. It is worth noting that in the *Rāmāyaṇa*, when Rāma Dāśarathi's mother tries to prevent him from going into exile in the forest as his father has instructed, he responds with a thinly veiled threat—telling the story of Paraśurāma's killing of Reṇukā and the sage Kaṇḍu's killing of a cow, both at their father's command (*Rām.* 2.18.26–30; Hiltebeitel 2018, 58n11).

7. Compare this to the story of the Bhārgava sage Śukra and his pupil Kaca, who explodes out of his guru's stomach after being accidentally ingested and then resurrects him (Collins 2014, 106–107).

8. The same detritus Gaṇeśa's mother uses to create him—waxy balls of dead skin cells produced by vigorously rubbing the skin—is used by Freud's mother to demonstrate a different point:

> When I was six years old and was given my first lessons by my mother, I was expected to believe that we were all made of earth and must therefore return to earth. This did not suit me and I expressed doubts of the doctrine. My mother thereupon rubbed the palms of her hands together—just as she did in making dumplings, except that there was no dough between them—and showed me the blackish scales of *epidermis* produced by the friction as a proof that we were made of earth. My astonishment at this ocular demonstration knew no bounds and I acquiesced in the belief which I was later to hear expressed in the words: "*Du bist der Natur einen Tod schuldig.*" (2010, 226)

This too, is a screen memory protecting the primal scene.

9. As Choudhary observes, Skanda is present at the Paraśurāma-Gaṇeśa conflict but does not take Gaṇeśa's side, and in the regional epic of Kerala drawn from the *Brahmāṇḍa* tradition, Skanda helps Paraśurāma to settle the newly formed land (2010, 141).

10. We should also note here that in the version of the Ahalyā story that appears in the *Godāvarī Māhātmya*, another example of the fluid motif appears when the unfaithful wife is cursed to become a river (Feldhaus 1995, 175).

11. The Cirakāri narrative fits into the motif classification index devised by Aarne and Thompson under the headings of L115 (successful foolish son) and L121 (stupid hero), variants of the "unlikely hero" motifs denoted by L100–L199.

12. Dejenne describes the poem as an "example of a contemporary and modernist reinterpretation of an epic and Purāṇic character [that] bears testimony to the capacity of Hindu myths to acquire new meanings and new relevance in various historical contexts" (2009, 466).

13. In India there are one hundred and eight Śākta Pīṭhas, pilgrimage sites at which some part of the goddess Satī's body is said to have fallen as Śiva carried

her corpse across the sky (Sircar 1973; Kinsley 1997, 178–87). Three and one-half of these are in Maharashtra. The Śrī Reṇukā Māta is known as a "half" Sākta Pīṭha because only the goddess's head is there.

14. Green continues:

> On the one hand, reference to castration as a model has obliged authors to "castratize," if I may express myself thus, all other forms of anxiety; one speaks of anal or narcissistic castration, for example. On the other hand, by giving an anthropological reading of Freudian theory, one relates all the varieties of anxiety to the concept of Lack in Lacanian theory. Now, I believe that, in both cases, one is doing violence as much to experience as to theory to save the unity of a concept. (1986, 145)

15. See also Hiltebeitel's extremely productive rereading of the epic through the Dead Mother complex in 2018, 33–79.

16. Swedish scholar Jarl Charpentier describes Paraśurāma as "singularly unsympathetic . . . vainglorious, self-seeking, and cruel . . . a puzzle and, besides, a dark and ominous one" (1937, 9). For Gail he is "a rather pale figure" marked by his "rigid obedience and cruel heroism" (1977, 229). Magnone calls him "the bizarre *brāhmaṇa* warrior famed for his gruesome feat of the 21-fold extermination of the warrior (*kṣatriya*) caste" (2002, 196).

## Chapter 4

1. Adapted from the Latin "*Caedite eos. Novit enim Dominus qui sunt eius,*" attributed to Arnaud Amalric, a Cistercian monk at the siege of Béziers in 1209.

2. Oddly, the *Bhāgavata Purāṇa* describes Paraśurāma making *nine* lakes of blood at Samantapañcika (9.16.19).

3. The epics and Purāṇas are inconsistent or do not specify when in the cosmic cycle Paraśurāma's varṇicide takes place. Citing Lawrence Babb's (1975, 141) report that the *akti or* Akṣaya Tṛtīya festival in Madhya Pradesh marks the end of the Tretā Yuga as well as Paraśurāma's birth, and the Marāṭhī *Mahābhārata*'s placement of Reṇukā at the turning (*yugānta*) of the Tretā Yuga as Sītā is placed at the Dvāpara and Draupadī at the Kali (Karve 1932, 138), Lynn Thomas notes that "there is evidence from the regional variants to suggest that [Paraśurāma] came to be associated more precisely with the *kṛta/tretā yugānta*" (1996, 84). She concludes: "The logic of his presence in the *Mahābhārata*, therefore, becomes clearer: he stands there as one of the many *yugānta* 'motifs' that supply the epic with the eschatological context for the human tragedy unfolding" (85).

4. For an argument for the priority of the Sabhā Parvan's version see Goldman 1973.

5. Missing from the version in the Critical Edition but included in the Citraśāla Press Edition is a prelude that tells the story of Arjuna Kārtavīrya. In the Citraśāla version, Kārtavīrya upsets the cosmic balance with the excessive power he has gained through his austerities, and the chaos he wreaks on earth disturbs Indra's chariot, causing Indra and Viṣṇu to hatch a plan, presumably for Viṣṇu to incarnate himself on earth as Paraśurāma to defeat the demonic king. This variant also says that Viṣṇu engineers the improperly executed ritual that results in Paraśurāma's (that is, his own) mixed birth (see Biardeau 1970).

6. *Sarvaṃ kṣatram utsādya* ("having destroyed the entire *kṣatra*"), with the variant reading *kṣatram utsāditaṃ*.

7. As Dejenne and others have noted, the phrase *triḥsaptakṛtvaḥ pṛthivīṃ kṛtvā niḥkṣatriyāṃ* occurs in two variants in the *Mahābhārata*. In 1.58.4, 3.117.9, and 12.49.56, the phrase is *triḥsaptakṛtvaḥ pṛthivīṃ kṛtvā niḥkṣatriyāṃ prabhuḥ*. Twice as popular is the variation *triḥsaptakṛtvaḥ pṛthivī kṛtā niḥkṣatriyā purā*. The only notable difference between the two variants of the phrase is the substitution of *purā* ("long ago") for *prabhuḥ* ("lord") in the second version, which is not surprising considering that the varṇicide is consistently portrayed as ancient history.

8. Veṭṭam Māṇi reports that, in a departure from the *Mahābharata*, the number of times Paraśurāma destroys the Kṣatriyas in the Purāṇas is eighteen (1975, 569). However, we do find *triḥsapta* in *Bhagavata Purāṇa* 9.16.18, *Brahmāṇḍa Purāṇa* 2.30.28, and *Viṣṇudharmottara Purāṇa* 3.351.45.

9. As Goldman has observed, "Nowhere in the endless references to this figure which find their way into the most remote corners of this most massive and comprehensive of epics is he called by a name which refers to what is generally thought to be his most characteristic attribute; the mighty and fearful *paraśu*, the dreaded battle-axe" (1972, 155). He is not called Paraśurāma in the *VDhP* but the name does appear in an *avatāra* list in another Pāñcarātra text, the *Agni Purāṇa* (*AP* 4.12). He is also called Paraśurāma in the *Narasiṃha Purāṇa*.

10. Gaya-Charan Tripathi connects the Haihayas with a historical kingdom in north central India: "The Haihayas were an historical race who not only find mention in the Purāṇic genealogies but are known to have existed till almost the end of the 12th century (i.e. A.D. 1181) when their descendants, the Kalacuris of Cedi, ruled over large tracts of Mahākośala and central India with their capital at Tīvar, some eight miles west of the city of Jabalpur and not far from the ancient Mahīṣmatī, the capital of Kārtavīrya on the bank of the Narmadā" (1979, 37).

11. In the *Padma Purāṇa* version of the Paraśurāma story, Jamadagni's cow is originally a gift from the king of the gods, Indra, a Kṣatriya deity. This motif of a Kṣatriya trying to take back the payments he has made to Brahmins recalls the story of Aurva, since the Bhārgavas' gold was almost certainly a previous gift from their Kṣatriya patrons, given in return for carrying out their ritual duties (*PP* 6.241.1–8 and see Choudhary 2010, 59).

12. Translation is based on Bloomfield 2001, 74.

13. The other extermination campaigns associated with the Bhṛgus are also frequently described as "genocides." Below are three representative examples from the first decade of the twenty-first century. The first comes from Dejenne: "[M]aybe for the epic heroes of the main plot of the MBh and for its listeners, the genocidal destruction of the Kṣatriyas by Rāma, followed by the regeneration of the *kṣatra,* could be seen as a rehearsal and a model of the great battle of the MBh, it may teach that destruction can be the necessary condition for a genuine rebirth" (2009, 74–75). In the second example, James L. Fitzgerald explains the role of Janamejaya's Snake Sacrifice and the war between the gods and the demons in the epic's frame stories: "These two framings of the telling of the Bhārata war with first a genocide and then a never-ending war between two different types of being are, each of them, bonded with an allusion to the brahmin Rāma Jāmadagnya's repeated genocidal slaughters of the kṣatriyas" (2006, 273–74). Finally, Adheesh Sathaye, building on Goldman's work, describes Paraśurāma as "the *kṣattravṛttir brāhmaṇaḥ* whose infamous genocidal rampage against the Kṣatriyas has left the fringes of the *Mahābhārata* indelibly stained in blood" (2010, 185). Zia Abbas, a less traditional scholar, goes as far as calling Paraśurāma's campaign "a massive global genocide" in his provocatively (not to mention triply) titled *Atlantis: The Final Solution: A Scientific History of Humanity Over the Last 10,000 Years* (2002, 67).

14. If the "Harvard School" represents classical scholars of the Vietnam generation who read Virgil in a new way shaped by their experience of a war widely regarded as illegitimate and unwinnable, then psychiatrist Jonathan Shay's *Achilles in Vietnam: Combat Trauma and the Undoing of Character* represents a more dialectical approach. For Shay, a close reading of the *Iliad* yields crucial insights for understanding PTSD as suffered by combat veterans. For our purposes, one of the most noteworthy of these insights derives from Shay's use of Homer's description of Achilles mistreating the corpse of Hektor. Shay refers to this episode in order to understand a soldier's recollections of going into a "berserk state" after being shot in the cheek by a North Vietnamese combatant whom he was trying to take prisoner:

> Then I saw blood dripping on the back of my hand and I just went crazy. I pulled him out onto the paddy and carved him up with my knife. . . . Even then, I wasn't satisfied. . . . I felt betrayed by trying to give the guy a chance and then I got blasted. I lost all my mercy. I felt a drastic change after that. I just couldn't get enough. I built up such hate, I couldn't do enough damage. . . . Got worse as time went by. I really loved fucking killing, couldn't get enough. For every one I killed I felt better. Made some of the hurt went away [*sic*]. Every time you lost a friend it seemed like part of you was gone. Get some of them to compensate what they had done to me. I got very hard, cold, merciless. I lost all my mercy. (1995, 77–78; underlining and capitalization removed)

15. But *varṇa* is not the only criterion that Bhārgava heroes use to launch extermination campaigns. Paraśurāma's family history is full of stories of excessively violent retributive killing sprees that are *not* varṇicidal. Aurva undertakes a vow to destroy the whole world (not just the Kṣatriyas) when the Haihayas slaughter the Bhārgavas and steal their gold. In another non-varṇicidal extermination campaign, Aurva's nephew Ruru sets out to exterminate all snakes after a snake bites and kills (temporarily) his new bride (*MBh* 1.8–10). But even in the light of these stories, the seemingly hereditary Bhārgava tendency to overreact violently still does not completely account for the out-of-control retribution of the Paraśurāma story or its centrality in the epic.

16. For a rundown of the controversy between 1993 and 2011, see Adluri 2011, 257–60.

17. Equally striking, and exemplifying a reversal of the Indo-German gaze, is India's continuing fascination with Adolf Hitler, as understood through his autobiography (a best-seller in India). Hitler is widely regarded as a model of strength, patriotism and leadership. See the following sources documenting the phenomenon in the second decade of the twenty-first century: D'Souza 2012; Shaftel 2012; Scheinert 2014.

18. Even in the age of genetic science, no kind of pseudo-scientific theories of ethnicity developed in South Asia to replace the ideas we see expressed in the Paraśurāma myth. Writing on the history of eugenics in India, Sarah Hodges writes that "eugenicists in India were unconcerned with understanding the specific workings of heredity" (2010, 231). She continues:

> Researchers failed to reach consensus regarding which groups should be singled out for eugenic study. While most experts in the early twentieth century agreed that "race" did not satisfactorily distinguish among Indians, there was no agreement regarding how caste might stand in for race as *the* taxonomy within which to understand eugenic analysis. (232)

19. There is an essay to be written on the element of bathos in a group tracing their lineage to a great mythic war only to claim descent from those who fled or cowered in caves. This seems quite distinct from the "glorious defeat" so beloved of the British and best exemplified by the death of Charles Gordon in Khartoum in 1885.

20. On a related note, this event—the extinction of the Vṛṣṇīs and the Andhakas described in the Mausāla Parvan—has itself been the occasion for not only overlapping conceptions of war and genocide, but also myth and history. Writing on the 2002 "genocide" in Gujarat ("It is pointless quibbling about whether this conforms to the criteria of genocide in international law, which itself provides a highly limited definition and needs to be interrogated"), Siddharth Varadarajan invokes Ramachandra Gandhi's analysis of the violence "as a recurrence of the Mahabharata, when the Yadava clan suffered the curse of Gandhari" (2002, 406).

21. It is too large a question to treat here, but one wonders how these forums, which get thousands of views and are populated by both experts and dilettantes, used

by advocates of Hindutva, Marxism, and liberalism, and often informed by Indian television serials, are reshaping the understandings of Hindu mythology both in India and the Diaspora.

22. The verse in the King James Bible reads, "And the sun stood still, and the moon stayed, until the people had avenged themselves upon their enemies. *Is* not this written in the book of Jasher? So the sun stood still in the midst of heaven, and hasted not to go down about a whole day." Darrow's examination of Bryan goes as follows:

> Q. The Bible says Joshua commanded the sun to stand still for the purpose of lengthening the day, doesn't it, and you believe it?
>
> A. I do.
>
> Q. Do you believe at that time the entire sun went around the earth?
>
> A. No, I believe that the earth goes around the sun.
>
> Q. Do you believe that the men who wrote it thought that the day could be lengthened or that the sun could be stopped?
>
> A. I don't know what they thought.
>
> Q. You don't know?
>
> A. I think they wrote the fact without expressing their own thoughts. (Darrow 2008, 124)

23. The views for the three replies number 202, 42, and 382 respectively. In contrast, the views for the replies to the question about Paraśurāma's racism are between 1,700 and 11,100, even though the Hitler question has been up for one year longer. The first reply is a straightforward dismissal of the question.

> This question proves that you can't differentiate between History and Mythology. Hitler was real but Parshu ram is a mythological character. Hence you can't compare the two situations mentioned by you.

The second begins by responding to the first reply rather than the question itself, then makes an unexpectedly positive comparison of Paraśurāma's varṇicide to *jihad*. The poster claims to be a researcher for the Discovery Channel and also makes reference to Sanātana Dharma, although it is unclear whether the "or" in the first sentence is meant to differentiate "Hinduism" from "Sanatanism" or denote that they are two terms for the same thing.

> If anybody thinks Hinduism or Sanatanism is mythological then I am sure that person has no knowledge about the Hindu scriptures. They would never know who created Hindu religion and how it started. To find real Hinduism, we Hindu must go back to our scriptures and holy books. 1st of all Parushram was not just any human, he was an incarnation of lord Vishnu . . . He was sent by God for 1 sole purpose only & that is to end bad deed of bad people not just khatriyas. But khatriyas as their breed was one of warriors, they loved fighting, they didn't have a lot of emotions as that is of know use of on the battlefield. When khatriyas dint have anything to do they fought as they were meant to do that. So lord Parushram had to put end to this tyranny. God sends great souls to earth in order to bring peace. Now in order to stop Hitler the American, Britisher and Russian Soviets had to kill equal amount of people to stop this bloodshed which the delusional Hitler started. He wasn't send by God, was mere human with no purpose. Even prophet Muhammad had to start jihad at the order of Lord God to save his religion, in other to save the right way to follow God & God himself ordered Muhammad to start a way to resist the oppression. So it's simply simple that lord Parushram did something similar. So I would humbly request you to please stop comparing great souls to people such as Hitler.

The final answer comes from a professed Christian convert (though probably *not* Robert Downey Jr., as the profile picture indicates) and ends with what must be read as sarcasm.

> I am Hindu by birth but follow Christianity. So this guy Parshuram killing Kshatriya clan means nothing to me. And hence going by the known reality and horror of mass genocide/holocaust I strongly believe Hitler was wrong.
>
> However thanks for keeping quora lit with this type of WONDERFUL assertions and logic. wow

24. A consecrated image, according, at least, to Śrī Vaiṣṇava theology, is "an actual and real manifestation of the deity, neither lesser than nor a symbol of other forms" (Narayan 1985, 54) Of course, no Hindu would expect to get an audience with Paraśurāma at his place of exile like the one Yudhiṣṭhira gets in the *Mahābhārata*, but he is no more a figure from some unreachable past than Jesus is to a Catholic fervently engaged in prayer.

25. The Agni VI, under development as I write, has a range of ten thousand kilometers, making it capable of striking targets on six continents.

26. See Hijiya 2000. We should note though, that Oppenheimer, inspired by John Donne, named the bomb itself after a deity closer to home: Trinity.

27. For an appraisal of a supposed ancient Sanskrit aeronautical treatise, see Mukunda, et al. 1974.

28. Titus Livius (Livy), *The History of Rome,* Book 8., trans, Benjamin Oliver Foster, PhD, Ed, 39. See Versnel 1976.

29. The term *svayamsevak* (which can mean "self-reliant" or "volunteer") here is likely a reference to the Rashtriya Swayamsevak Sangh, right-wing Hindu nationalist group in India.

30. Anirban Das argues that in reading Aśvatthāman's story, "one may have a glimpse of a certain training in the reorganization of desires and imaginations that might, and it pretty well might not, render one's self a little responsive—if not responsible—to the mundane excesses of a terrified world" (2017, 217).

31. On the peacefulness of the epic and the Kashmiri reading, see Tubb 1985. Hiltebeitel 2020 persuasively argues instead that the rasa of the epic is *adbhuta* or "wonder."

32. The other group is the Bhāgavatas. "The relation of the Pāñcarātrikas and the Bhāgavatas is obscure," writes Mitsunori Matsubara, who distinguishes the two early Vaiṣṇava groups based on his readings of *MBh* 12.332.13–17 and 12.336.1–4 and 7 (1994, 3–4). But, based on *Padma Tantra* 4.2.88, Govindacarya Svamin concludes that, "it is evident that *Pāñcarātra* = Bhāgavata = Sātvata = Ekāntika" (1911, 935). S. K. De leaves out the Bhāgavatas, but takes the rest of this equation for granted, leaving room, however, for separate origins for the sects (1931, 417n1). Bhandarkar titles his chapter on the subject(s), "The Pāñcarātra or Bhāgavata System," and writes, "The authorities on which the Bhāgavata system was based are the Pañcarātra Saṃhitās" (1913, 39). Schrader seems to accept this identification as well (1916, 3).

33. S. K. De relegates to apocrypha the etymologies of the name that refer to the five types of knowledge in the system (with *rātra* given an idiosyncratic gloss unattested elsewhere) or the "five-fold manifestation of the supreme deity" and speculates that *pāñcarātra* may refer to a five-night ritual undergone by initiates into the sect (1931, 417–18). Raghavan uses the organizational scheme of the *Sanatkumāra Saṃhitā* (about which more below) to argue that the name must "be based on the five nights during which five discourses were given, associated with five persons, Siva, Brahman, Indra, Ṛṣis and Bṛhaspati" (1965, 76).

34. Given that the non-Pāñcarātra literature that mentions the sect focuses on their status as mendicants rather than their ritual or philosophical systems, van Buitenen concludes that the term more likely derives from a "five-night rule" that ensured that the peripatetic Pāñcarātrins did not stay too long in one town before moving on (1962, 299). Bhaṭobās makes the same recommendation to the wandering ascetics of the heterodox Mahānubhāv sect that reveres Dattātreya and Reṇukā in Maharashtra (Feldhaus and Tuḷapuḷe 1992, 138).

35. More fodder for Katz's speculation is found in a line (10.18.5) spoken by Vāsudeva referring to "the fivefold sacrifice, whose fifth part is the sacrifice to be offered to men [*pañcabhūtamayo yajño nṛyajñaś caiva pañcamaḥ*]." Johnson notes that

"the text here is uncertain and difficult to interpret (this verse is missing from some manuscripts altogether)" (1998, 133).

36. The same text has all the *avatāras* emanating from Aniruddha, but the earlier *Padma Tantra* maintains that Paraśurāma is a manifestation of Saṃkarṣaṇa while assigning Balarāma to Pradyumna and Kṛṣṇa to Aniruddha.

37. Hudson argues that along with this story, the theological interpretation of Paraśurāma had made it south to Tamil Nadu by the eighth century, when it acted as a formative influence on the iconography of the Vaikuṇṭha Perumal Temple built by the Pallava king Nandivarman II.

38. The vulgate and a few others included in the appendices to the Critical Edition of the *Mahābhārata* mention Paraśurāma's axe, but Goldman suggests that they belong to an emerging Purāṇic tradition that sees Paraśurāma as an *avatāra* and gives him an axe to distinguish him from Rāma Dāśarathi (1972, 165). An inscription from Karnataka dated to 522 CE in which a king named Durvinīta Konguṇivṛddha declares himself an incarnation of Paraśurāma is further evidence that there existed at that time the veneration of an axe-wielding Rāma (Saletore in Gail 1977, 54).

39. Respecting iconography, a chief concern of the Pāñcarātrins, we can see a place where Paraśurāma's Vaiṣṇava adoption hits a snag. The tradition is consistent that Paraśurāma must have matted hair and an axe, clearly Śaiva imagery, but that he can be shown with four arms to assist in his identification with Viṣṇu (Smith, Venkatachari, and Ganapathi 1969, 146–47). However, except for possibly in Tamil Nadu, the two-armed image proved far more popular, minimizing the chances for artists to provide him with Vaiṣṇava implements (Donaldson 1995, 178–80; Choudhary 2010, 236–42).

40. In the commentarial tradition, Dhanvantari is a Hindu and Vaiśvānara is a Jaina, but in the *Vasudevahiṇḍi*, it is the other way around (Koch 1998, 130).

41. This happens in the commentarial tradition, but there is no mention of adultery or Reṇukā's death in the *Vasudevahiṇḍi*. Instead, Anantavīrya kidnaps Reṇukā and the cow at the same time (Koch 1998, 131).

42. Paraśurāma's removal of his defeated enemies' teeth (canines in the *Vasudevahiṇḍi*) has a parallel in his smashing of Kṣatriya teeth in the southern *Srimanmahābhāratam*.

43. This idea of Paraśurāma and Subhūma as a feuding pair that represents one common sin is abandoned by the time of the *Triṣaṣtiśalākāpuruṣacarita*, which uses them to demonstrate the sins of *krodha* (wrath) and *māna* (pride), respectively (Koch 1998, 134).

## Chapter 5

1. *Agniḥ śeṣaṃ ṛṇaḥ śeṣaṃ śatruḥ śeṣaṃ tathaiva ca/ Punaḥ punaḥ pravardheta tasmāt śeṣaṃ na kārayet//* See Collins 2017b, 313–16.

2. In *Rāmāyaṇa* 1.75.14, Paraśurāma explains that after he gave the earth in sacrifice, "I promised that I would not spend a night on earth."

3. *Yo 'sau niḥkṣatre kṣmātale 'smin kriyamāṇe strībhir vivastrābhiḥ parivārya rakṣitaḥ tatas taṃ nārīkavacam udāharanti.* (One also cannot help but think of Moamar Gaddafi's famous Amazon Guard). *Vivastra* ("naked") is the same word used in the famous attempted disrobing of Draupadī and appears again in the version of this story in the *Brahmāṇḍa Purāṇa* (2.63.179). In the *Liṅga Purāṇa*, however, the women that surround the king are not described as unclothed (1.66.29). The implication that Paraśurāma will not attack women, naked or otherwise, is an odd one given the treatment Reṇukā receives from him.

4. But not all versions of the myth require Paraśurāma to go into permanent exile. In the *Śiva Purāṇa*, Paraśurāma atones for the slaughter of the Kṣatriyas by performing a *tulapuruṣavrata*, a vow to sacrifice something equal to the number of people he has killed.

5. Malabar, like Tranvancore and Cochin, is now part of the modern state of Kerala.

6. This image is evoked in *MBh* 12.49.47 in which Paraśurāma makes "the earth muddy with the blood of kings" (*cakāra bhārgavo rājan mahīṃ śoṇitakardamām*).

7. The Sātavāhanas, whose empire was in the Deccan plateau, introduced the use of matronyms as opposed to patronyms, creating a form of matrineal succession.

8. Thanks to Keralan filmmaker Jayan Cherian for this observation.

9. Twelfth-century inscriptions memorializing the Chola king Rajendra II's campaigns of conquest record that Paraśurāma owned a magnificent golden crown "worthy of Lakṣmi" that he deposited in the fortress-like island of Śāndimat after the Kṣatriya slaughter. The inscriptions also claim that Rajendra II captured the crown himself when he conquered Tiruvanchikkolam. We can interpret this golden crown as a Kṣatriya counterpart to the golden altar of the *Mahābhārata* and attribute this transformation to the fact that the story appears in an inscription meant to glorify a king.

10. Still, there is some connection there. Janaki points out that the city of Uḍipi is supposed to be founded by Paraśurāma and that there are Tulu inscriptions at Paraśurāmapura in Karnataka (1969, 69).

11. Although this is also a formulaic description of warrior duties, found in *MBh* 13.118.21, among other places.

12. In another Marāṭhi text, A. H. Salunke uses the term *aṃśavatāra* (2001, 12).

13. "Adityanath Scraps 15 Holidays, Some Muslims Unhappy Prophet's Birthday on List," *Hindustan Times*, April 26, 2017.

14. My thanks to Borayin Larios for this observation.

## Conclusion

1. I say "paternal and maternal" rather than "male and female," because these terms are defined not just in relation to each other but in relation to the son, Paraśurāma.

2. This brings up a puzzling point. Satyavatī (a Kṣatriya) drinks the *kṣatra*-infused *caru* and gives birth to a Brahmin who acts like a Kṣatriya. But since she is

a Kṣatriya and the *caru* is Kṣatriya, whence comes the Brahmin nature? From the father? If patriliny were determinative in this way, the whole ritual seems pointless—if the father is already a Brahmin and his son will therefore be a Brahmin, why is she so concerned to do all this extra work to get a Brahmin son? Added to that, later in the myth the Brahmins impregnate the Kṣatriya widows, who give birth to the new Kṣatriya race (not Brahmins). The ritual only really makes sense if it is there to establish the analogic key, as I propose.

3. Compare with admitted haemophobe and personification of adharma Donald Trump's oft quoted dismissal of Fox News personality Megyn Kelly during the 2016 American presidential election debates: "There was blood coming out of her eyes, blood coming out of her wherever" (Chavez and Stracqualursi 2016).

4. UPI Archives. "Psychologists Say Serial Killers Have Victims in Mind." Aug. 24, 1985.

# Works Cited

## Primary Texts


Allasāni Peddana, Velcheru Narayana Rao, and David Shulman. 2015. *The Story of Manu*. Murty Classical Library of India: 4. Cambridge: Harvard University Press.

American Bible Society. 2010. *Holy Bible: Containing the Old and New Testaments: King James Version.*

Ananthakrishna Sastry, R. 1942. *The Aitareya Brāhmaṇa.* Trivandrum: University of Travancore.

Aristóteles and H. Rackham. 1999. *The Nicomachean Ethics*. Cambridge: Harvard University Press.

*Atharva Veda, Saunaka Recension*. Input by Vladimir Petr and Petr Vavrousek, in cooperation with Jost Gippert, Arlo Griffiths and Philipp Kubisch. http://www.sub.uni-goettingen.de/ebene_1/fiindolo/gretil.htm#Samh. Last accessed May 4, 2019.

Atulakavi, and K. P. A. Menon. 1999. *Atulakavikṛtaṃ muṣikavaṃśamahākāvyam = Atulakavi's Mūṣikavaṃśamahākāvyam: Text with Introduction and English Translation*. Delhi: Nag.

Balamani Amma, N., and N. K. Seshan. 1980. "The Story of the Axe." *Journal of South Asian Literature*, 15, no. 2. Malayalam Anthology Part 2: Poetry, Drama, Criticism, 124–131.

Bandyopadhyay, Sibaji. 2008. *The Book of Night: A Moment from the* Mahabharata. Calcutta: Seagull Books.

Beckett, Samuel. 1979. *Ill Seen, Ill Said.* London: John Calder.

*Bhāgavata-Purāṇa*. With the Commentary of Śrīdhara. Benares: Pandita Pustakalaya, 1972.

Bhavabhuti, and Ramchandra Mishra. 1968. *Mahaviracarita.* [Varanasi]: [Chowkhamba Vidyabhawan].

Bloomfield, Maurice. 2001. *Hymns of the Atharva-Veda: Together with Extracts from the Ritual Books and the Commentaries.* Richmond: Curzon.

*Brahma Purāṇa*. 2001. Delhi: Motilal Banarsidass.

*Brahmāṇda-Purāṇa.* 1857. Bombay: Venkateshvara Sagara Press.

*Brahmavaivarta Purana*. 1981. Sammelan, Allahabad: Hindi Sahitya.

*The Brahma-vaivarta Puranam. Translated into English by Rajendra Nath Sen*. 1920. Allahabad: Panini Office.

Croly, David G. 1995. *Miscegenation: The Theory of the Blending of the Races, Applied to the American White Man and Negro*. Unionville, NY: Royal Fireworks Press.

Dasgupta, Shamik. 2008. *Vargav*. New York: Virgin Comics.

Dattātreya, and Sudhanshu Chaitanya. 2012. *Avadhūta Gītā*. Bhopal: Indra Pub. House.

Deshpande, N. A. 1988. *The Padma Purāṇa*. Delhi: Motilal Banarsidass.

Doniger, Wendy. 1981. *The Rig Veda: An Anthology: One Hundred and Eight Hymns, Selected, Translated and Annotated*. New York: Penguin Books.

Edgerton, Franklin. 1965. *The Beginnings of Indian Philosophy: Selections from the Rig Veda, Atharva Veda, Upaniṣads, and Mahābhārata*. Cambridge: Harvard University Press.

Eliot, Thomas Stearns, and Lawrence S. Rainey. 2006. *The Annotated Waste Land, with Eliot's Contemporary Prose*. New Haven: Yale University Press.

Feldhaus, Anne, and Śā. Go Tuḷapuḷe. 1992. *In the Absence of God: The Early Years of an Indian Sect: A Translation of Smṛtisthaḷ, with an Introduction*. Honolulu: University of Hawaii Press.

Gangadharan, N. 1985. *Agni Purāṇa*. Delhi: Motilal Banarsidass.

*The Garuda Purāṇa*. 1978. Delhi: Motilal Banarsidass.

*The Garuda Purāṇa*. Based on Bombay: Venkatesvara Steam Press. Input by members of the SANSKNET-project. http://gretil.sub.uni-goettingen.de/gretil/1_sanskr/3_purana/garup1_u.htm. Last accessed May 4, 2019.

Gundert, Hermann. 2003. *Kēraḷōlpatti*. Thiruvananthapuram: International School of Dravidian Linguistics.

Guptā, Pushpā. 2014. *Śrīkalkipurāṇam = Śrī Kalki Purāṇam: Original Sanskrit Text, English Translation and Relevant Notes, Index of Ślokas*. New Delhi: Eastern Book Linkers.

Hardy, Adam. 2015. *Theory and Practice of Temple Architecture in Medieval India: Bhoja's Samaranganasutradhara and the Bhojpur Line Drawings*. New Delhi: Dev Books.

Hart, George L., and Hank Heifetz. 2010. *The Four Hundred Songs of War and Wisdom: An Anthology of Poems from Classical Tamil, the Purananuru*. New York: Columbia University Press.

Hemacandra, and Helen Moore Johnson. 1931. *Triṣaṣṭiśalākāpuruṣacarita*. Baroda: Oriental Institute.

Hemacandra, and R. C. C. Fynnes. 1998. *The Lives of the Jain Elders*. Oxford: Oxford University Press.

Homer, George E. Dimock, and A. T. Murray. 1995. *The Odyssey*. Cambridge: Harvard University Press.

Jain, Jagdishchandra. 1977. *The Vasudevahindi: An Authentic Jain version of the Brhatkatha: with Selected Translations Compared to the Brhatkathaslokasangraha*

*Kathasaritsagara, Brhatkathamañjari and Some Important Jaina Works, Including the Unpublished Majjhimakhanda and with Extensive Notes, Introduction and Appendices.* Ahmedabad: L.D. Institute of Indology.

Jamison, Stephanie W. 2014. *The Rigveda.* Oxford: Oxford University Press.

Jośī, Kanhaiyālāla. 2003. *Narasiṃhapurāṇam = Narasiṃha-Purāṇam: Sanskrit Text, English Translation, and Index of Verses.* Delhi: Parimal.

Jośī, Kanhaiyālāla, and Shanti Lal Nagar. 2007. *Matsya Mahāpurāṇa: An Exhaustive Introduction, Sanskrit Text, English Translation, Scholarly Notes and Index of Verses.* Delhi: Parimal.

Krishnamacharya, Pandit V. 1975. *Laksmi-tantra: A Pāñcarātra Āgama.* Adyar: Adyar Library and Research Centre.

Kṛṣṇadāsa Kavirāja Gosvāmi, Edward C. Dimock, and Tony K. Stewart. 1999. *Caitanya Caritāmṛta of Kṛṣṇadāsa Kavirāja: A Translation and Commentary.* Cambridge: Dept. of Sanskrit and Indian Studies, Harvard University: Distributed by Harvard University Press.

Kṛttibāsa, Shanti Lal Nagar, and Suriti Nagar. 1997. *Kṛttivāsa Rāmāyaṇa.* Delhi: Eastern Book Linkers.

Kṣemendra, Paṇḍita Durgāprasāda, and Kāśīnātha Pāṇḍuraṅga Paraba. 1983. *Śrīkṣemendrapraṇītaṃ Daśāvatāracaritam.* New Delhi: Munśīrāma Monoharalāla.

Kumar, B. Mohan, and P. K. Ramachandran Nair. 2008. *Krishi gita = Agricultural Verses: A Treatise on Indigenous Farming Practices of the Malayalam Desam (Kerala).* Secunderabad: Asian Agri-History Foundation.

Kumari, Ved. 1973. *The Nīlamata Purāṇa.* Srinagar: J & K Academy of Art, Culture and Languages.

Lakṣmī Narasiṃha Bhaṭṭa. 1972. *Viṣvaksena Saṁhitā.* Tirupati: Kendriya Sanskrit Vidyapeetha.

*The Liṅga-purāṇa.* 1982. Delhi: Motilal Banarsidass.

*The Mahābhārata: Text as Constituted in Its Critical Edition.* 1976. Poona: Bhandarkar Oriental Research Institute.

*The Mahābhārata.* 1973–78. Translated by J. A. B. van Buitenen. 3 volumes. Chicago: University of Chicago Press.

*The Mahābhārata, Volume 7.* 2004. Book 11: The Book of the Women; Book 12: The Book of the Peace, Part One. Translated by James L. Fitzgerald. Chicago: University of Chicago Press.

*The Mahabharata in Sanskrit: Parallel Devanagari and Romanization.* Edited by Muneo Tokunaga, John D. Smith. http://www.sacred-texts.com/hin/mbs/index.htm. Last accessed May 4, 2019.

*Mahābhārata.* Edited by Rāmchandra Śāstri. Poona: Citraśāla Press, 1930.

Manu, Wendy Doniger, and Brian K. Smith. 1991. *The Laws of Manu.* London; New York: Penguin Books.

*Markandeya-Purana (Input by Members of the Sansknet Project)* http://www.sub.uni-goettingen.de/ebene_1/fiindolo/gretil.htm#Samh.

Menon, Ramesh. 2006. *The Mahabharata: A Modern Rendering*. New York: iUniverse, Inc.

Menon, T. Madhava. 2003. *Gundert: Keralolpatti*. Thiruvananthapuram: International School of Dravidian Linguistics.

*Mukapiṭhavāsiṇī Śrī Reṇukā Mahātmya*. Pamphlet.

Munshi, K.M. 1965 [1946]. *Bhagawan Parashurama*. Chaupatty: Bharatiya Vidya Bhavan.

Murthy, U. R. Anantha, and A. K. Ramanujan. 1976. *Samskara: A Rite for a Dead man*. Delhi: Oxford University Press.

Nagar, Shantilal. 2001. *Brahmavaivarta Purāṇa. Text with English Translation*. Delhi: Parimal.

Olivelle, Patrick. 2000. *Dharmasūtras: The Law Codes of Āpastamba, Gautama, Baudhāyana, and Vasiṣṭha*. Delhi: Motilal Banarsidass.

"Parashurama Jayanti." *Prokeria.com*. https://www.prokerala.com/festivals/parashurama-jayanti.html. Last accessed April 29, 2019.

Pereira, José. 1976. *Hindu Theology: A Reader*. Garden City, NY: Image Books.

Plato. 1991. *The Republic: The Complete and Unabridged Jowett Translation*. New York: Vintage Books.

*Rāmāyaṇa. Critical Edition*. 1960–75. Baroda: Oriental Institute.

*Ṛg Veda*. Input by H. S. Ananthanarayana and W. P. Lehman. http://www.sub.uni-goettingen.de/ebene_1/fiindolo/gretil.htm#Samh. Last accessed May 4, 2019.

Śarmā, Oṅkarlāl ("Pramad"). 1998. *Jay Paraśurām (Mahākāvyam)*. Guna, Madhya Pradesh: Srī Balajī.

Sastri Haraprasad. 1974. *Bṛhaddharma Purāṇam*. Varanasi: Chowkhamba Amarbharathi Prakashan.

*Śatapatha-Brāhmana, Mādhyandina Śākha*. 1971. Encoded by H. S. Ananthanarayana and W. P. Lehmann. Input by John Robert Garner, 1996–2010. http://vedavid.org/index-sutra.html. Last accessed August 3, 2012.

Shah, Priyabala. 1999. *Vishnudharmottara-purāṇa: Pauranic Legends and Rebirths*. Delhi: Parimal.

Sharma, Rajendra Nath. 1984. *The Bhaviṣyamahāpurāṇam*. Delhi: Nag.

Shastri, Biswanarayan. 1991. *Kālikā Purāna: Text, Introduction and Translation in English*. Delhi: Nag.

Śīlāṅka, and Amritlal Mohanlal Bhojak. 1961. *Cauppannamahāpurisacariaṃ*. Ahmedabad: Prakrit Text Series.

*Śiva-purāṇa*. 1964. Benares: Pandita Pustakalaya.

Somadeva Bhaṭṭa, and J. L. Shastri. 1977. *Kathāsaritsāgara*. Delhi: [publisher not identified].

Strong, John S. 1989. *The Legend of King Aśoka: A Study and Translation of the* Aśokāvadāna. Delhi: Motilal Banarsidass.

Suśruta, G. D. Singhal, L. V. Guru, L. M. Singh, Kuṃvarapālasiṃha, and K. R. Sharma. 1972. *Suśruta-saṃhitā*. Allahabad: G.D. Singhal.

Tagare, Ganesh Vasudeo. 2003. *The Vayu Purāṇa*. Delhi: Motilal Banarsidass.

———. 1999. *The Skanda Purāṇa*. Delhi: Motilal Banarsidass.
———. 1983. *The Brahmāṇḍa Purāṇa*. Delhi: Motilal Banarsidass.
Titus Livius (Livy). 2018. *The History of Rome,* Book 8. Translated by Benjamin Oliver Foster. Cambridge: Harvard University Press.
Twain, Mark. 1884. *The Adventures of Huckleberry Finn*. London: Chatto and Windus.
Uberoi, Meera. 2005. *The Mahabharata*. New Delhi: Penguin Books.
Vaidya, Parashuram Lakshman. 1971. *The Harivāṃśa, Vol. II. Mahābhārata*. Poona: Bhandarkar Oriental Research Institute.
Vallabhācārya, N. K., N. Wagle, and Anant Ramchandra Kulkarni. 1976. *Vallabha's Paraśarāma Caritra: An Eighteenth Century Marāthā History of the Peśwās*. Bombay: Popular Prakashan.
*The Veda of the Black Yajus School Entitled Taittirīya Sanhitā*. 1914. Translated by A. B. Keith. Harvard Oriental Series 18. Cambridge: Harvard University Press.
*The Viṣṇudharmottara Purāṇa*. 1912. [Bombay]: [Veṅkaṭeśvara Steam Press].
*Viṣṇu-purāṇa. With the Commentary of Śrīdhara*. 1972. Calcutta: Sanatana Sastra.
Visweswara, G. H. *Mahabharatha Spectroscope*. http://www.ghvisweswara.com/mahabharata-2/mahabharata-spectroscope-a-unique-resource/. Last accessed May 4, 2019.

## Films

*Adamkhor Haseena*.["The Man-Eating Beatuy"] 1997. Directed by Joginder Shelly.
*Coco*. 2017. Directed by Lee Unkrich and Adrian Molina.
*Friday the 13th*. 1980. Directed by Sean Cunningham.
*Friday the 13th Part 2*. 1981. Directed by Steve Miner.
*Halloween*. 1978. Directed by John Carpenter.
*Henry: Portrait of a Serial Killer*. 1986. Directed by John McNaughton.
*Maut ka Badla* ["Revenge for Death"]. 2011. Directed by Suresh Jain.
*Psycho*.1960. Directed by Alfred Hitchcock.
*Renuka Devi Mahatyam*. 1960. Directed by K. S. Prakash Rao.
*Sar Kati Laash* ["The Headless Corpse"]. 1999. Directed by Teerat Singh.
*The Silence of the Lambs*.1991. Directed by Jonathan Demme.
*Vertigo*. 1958. Directed by Alfred Hitchcock.

## Secondary Texts

Aarne, Antti, and Stith Thompson. 1928. *The Types of the Folk-tale: A Classification and Bibliography*. Helsinki: Suomalainen Tiedeakatemia, Academia Scientarum Fennica.
Abbas, Zia. 2002. *Atlantis: The Final Solution: A Scientific History of Humanity Over the Last 10,000 Years*. New York: iUniverse.

Adluri, Vishwa P. 2011. "Pride and Prejudice: Orientalism and German Indology." *International Journal of Hindu Studies* 15, no. 3: 253–92.

Agamben, Giorgio. 2005. *State of Exception*. Chicago: University of Chicago Press.

———. 1998. *Homo Sacer: Sovereign Power and Bare Life*. Stanford: Stanford University Press.

Anderson, G. K. "Popular Survivals of the Wandering Jew in England." In *The Wandering Jew: Essays in the Interpretation of a Christian Legend*, edited by Galit Hasan-Rokem and Alan Dundes, 76–104. Bloomington: Indiana University Press.

Anzulovic, Branimir. 2000. *Heavenly Serbia: From Myth to Genocide*. Annandale, N.S.W.: Pluto Press.

Apte, Prabhakar. 1972. "Claim of Pāñcarātra on Bhagavadgītā." *Annals of the Bhandarkar Oriental Research Institute* 53, no. 1/4: 200–203.

Arabagian, Ruth Katz. 1984. "The Goddess in Indo-European Heroic Literature." *Religion* 14, no. 2: 107–42.

Armstrong, Karen. 2015. *Fields of Blood: Religion and the History of Violence*. New York: Alfred A. Knopf.

Artal, Rao Bahadur R. C. 1907. "A Theoretical History of the Goddess Yellama." *Journal of the Anthropological Society of Bombay* 7: 591–602.

Assayag, Jackie. 1992. *La colere de la deesse decapitee: Traditions, cultes, et pouvoir dans le Sud de l'Inde*. Paris: Presses du CNRS.

Axelrod, Paul, and Michelle A. Fuerch. 1996. "Flight of the Deities: Hindu Resistance in Goa." *Modern Asian Studies* 30, no. 2: 387–421.

Babb, Lawrence A. 2004. *Alchemies of Violence: Myths of Identity and the Life of Trade in Western India*. New Delhi: Sage.

Bagchee, Joydeep. 2018. "Yoking the Brāhmaṇa to the Kṣatriya." In *The Churning of the Epics and the Purāṇas*, edited by Simon Brodbeck, Adam Bowles, and Alf Hiltebeitel, 96–126. Delhi: Dev.

Bailey, G. M. 1981. "Brahmā, Pṛthu, and the Theme of the Earth-milker in Hindu Mythology." *Indo-Iranian Journal* 23: 105–16.

Bālakṛṣṇan, Pi. 1995. *Kalarippayattu: The Ancient Martial Art of Kerala*. Trivandrum: C. V. Govindankutty Nair Gurukkal.

Ball, Phillip. 2018. *Beyond Weird: Why Everything You Thought You Knew about Quantum Physics Is Different*. Chicago: University of Chicago Press.

Bandyopādhyāya, Śibājī. 2012. *Sibaji Bandyopadhyay Reader: An Anthology of Essays*. Delhi: Worldview.

Bapat, Jayant Balchandra. 2009. "The Lajjāgaurī: Mother, Wife, or *Yoginī*." In *The Iconic Female: Goddesses of India, Nepal, and Tibet*, edited by Jayant Bhalchandra Bapat and Ian Mabbett, 79–111. Clayton, Victoria, Australia: Monash University Press.

Barasch, Frances K. 1985. "The Grotesque as a Comic Genre." *Modern Language Studies* 15, no. 1 (Winter): 3–11.

Barnett, Lionel D. 1977. *Hindu Gods and Heroes: Studies in the History of the Religion of India*. Delhi: Ess Ess.

Basham, A. L. 1963. *The Wonder That Was India: A Study of the History and Culture of the Indian Sub-continent before the Coming of the Muslims*. New York: Hawthorn Books.

Bataille, Georges. 1989. *The Accursed Share: Essays on General Economy*. New York: Zone Books.

Beck, Guy L. 2008. *Sonic Theology: Hinduism and Sacred Sound*. Columbia: University of South Carolina Press.

Behera, M. C. 1998. *Pilgrim Centre Parashuram Kund: Articulation of Indian Society, Culture, and Economic Dimension*. New Delhi: Commonwealth.

Benard, Elisabeth Anne. 1994. *Chinnamastā, the Aweful Buddhist and Hindu Tantric Goddess*. Delhi: Motilal Banarsidass.

Bhandare, Shailendra. 2006. "Numismatics and History: The Maurya-Gupta Interlude in the Gangetic Plain." In *Between the Empires: Society in India 300 BCE to 400 CE*, edited by Patrick Olivelle, 67–112. New York: Oxford University Press.

Bhandarkar, R. G. 1913. "The Pāñcarātra or Bhāgavata System." In *Encyclopedia of Indo-Aryan Research*, edited by Jacob Wackernagel. Strassburg: K. J. Trübner.

———. 1913. *Vaiṣṇavism, Śaivism and Minor Religious Systems*. Strassburg: Verlag von Karl J. Trübner.

Biardeau, Madeleine. 2004. *Stories About Posts: Vedic Variations Around the Hindu Goddess*. Chicago: University of Chicago Press.

———. 2002. *Hinduism: The Anthropology of a Civilization*. New Delhi: Oxford University Press.

———. 1970. "The Story of Arjuna Kārtavīrya without Reconstruction." *Purāṇa* 12, no. 2: 286–303.

———. 1969. "La Décapitation de Reṇukā dans le mythe de Paraśurāma." In *Pratidānam*, edited by J. C. Heesterman, 563–72. Mouton: La Haye.

Black, Brian. 2007. *The Character of the Self in Ancient India: Priests, Kings, and Women in the Early Upaniṣads*. Albany: State University of New York Press.

Blanshard, Alastair. 2005. *Hercules: A Heroic Life*. London: Granta Books.

Blind, Karl. 1986. "Wodan, the Wild Huntsman, and the Wandering Jew." In *The Wandering Jew: Essays in the Interpretation of a Christian Legend*, edited by Galit Hasan-Rokem and Alan Dundes, 169–89. Bloomington: Indiana University Press.

Blumenburg, Hans. 1985. *Work on Myth*. Translated by Robert M. Wallace. Cambridge: MIT Press.

Bonnefoy, Yves, Wendy Doniger, and Gerald Honigsblum. 1991. *Mythologies*. Chicago: University of Chicago Press.

Booth, Wayne C. 1987. *The Rhetoric of Fiction*. Chicago: University of Chicago Press.

Borofsky, Robert. 1997. "Cook, Lono, Obeyesekere, and Sahlins." *Current Anthropology* 38, no. 2: 255–82.

Bourdieu, Pierre. 1977. *Outline of a Theory of Practice*. Cambridge: Cambridge University Press.
Brinkhaus, Horst. 1983. "Zur Paraśurāma-Monographie von Adalbert Gail." *Wiener Zeitschrift für die Kunde Südasiens* 27: 43–63.
Brodbeck, Simon. 2006. "Ekalavya and *Mahābhārata* 1.121–28." *Hindu Studies* 10: 1–34.
Bronkhorst, Johannes. 2017. "Brahmanism: Its Place in Ancient Indian Society." *Contributions to Indian Sociology* 51, no. 3: 361–69.
———. 2016. *How the Brahmins Won: From Alexander to the Guptas*. Leiden and Boston: Brill.
Brubaker, Richard Lee. 1978. *The Ambivalent Mistress: A Study of South Indian Village Goddesses and Their Religious Meaning*. PhD dissertation, University of Chicago.
Buitenen, J. A. B. van. 1962. "The Name 'Pāñcarātra.'" *History of Religions* 1, no. 2: 291–99.
Calasso, Roberto. 2016. *Ardor*. New York: Farrar, Straus and Giroux.
———. 1998. *Ka*. New York: Alfred A. Knopf.
Cassirer, Ernst. 1955. *Philosophy of Symbolic Forms*. Volume II: Mythical Thought. New Haven: Yale University Press.
Charpentier, Jarl. 1936. "Paraśurāma: The Main Outlines of His Legend." *Mahamahopadhyaya Kuppuswami Sastri Commemoration Volume*, 9–16. Madras: G. S. Press.
Chattopadhyaya, Brajadulal. 2018. *The Concept of Bharatavarsha and Other Essays*. Albany: State University of New York Press.
Chavez, Paola, and Veronica Stracqualursi. 2016. "The History of the Donald Trump–Megyn Kelly Feud." Abcnews.go.com. May 17. https://abcnews.go.com/Politics/history-donald-trump-megyn-kelly-feud/story?id=39151987. Last accessed April 29, 2019.
Choudhary, Pradeep Kant. 2010. *Rāma with an Axe: Myth and Cult of Paraśurāma Avatāra*. Delhi: Aakar Books.
Ciolfi, Sabrina. 2010. "Movies, Romance, and the Forest: An Indian Cultural Stereotype." In *The City and the Forest in Indian Literature and Art*, edited by Danuta Stasik and Anna Trynkowska, 163–82. Warsaw: Elipsa.
Clausen, Wendell. 1964. "An Interpretation of the *Aeneid*." *Harvard Studies in Classical Philology* 68: 139–47.
Collins, Brian. 2017a. "The Eastern Revolution: From the Vedas to Buddhism, Jainism, and the Upanishads." In *The Handbook of Mimetic Theory and* Religion, edited by James Alison and Wolfgang Palaver, 111–17. London: Palgrave MacMillan.
———. 2017b. "Burning Desires, Burning Corpses: Girardian Reflections on Fire in Hinduism and Buddhism." In *René Girard and World Religions*, edited by Wolfgang Palaver and Richard Schenk, 303–17. East Lansing: Michigan State University Press.
———. 2014. *The Head Beneath the Altar: Hindu Mythology and the Critique of Sacrifice*. East Lansing: Michigan State University Press.

———. 2012. "Avatāra or Cirajīvin? Paraśurāma and His Problems." *Journal of Vaishnava Studies* 21, no. 1: 187–97.

———. 2010. *Headless Mothers, Magic Cows, and Lakes of Blood: The Paraśurāma Cycle in the* Mahābhārata *and Beyond.* PhD Dissertation, University of Chicago.

Cort, John. 1993. "An Overview of the Jaina Purāṇas." In *Purāṇa Perennis: Reciprocity and Transformation in Hindu and Jaina texts*, edited by Wendy Doniger, 185–206. Albany: State University of New York Press.

Courtright, Paul B. 1985. *Gaṇeśa: Lord of Obstacles, Lord of Beginnings.* New York: Oxford University Press.

Creuzer, Georg Friedrich. 1819–1821. *Symbolik und Mythologie der alten Volker, besonders der Griechen.* 2nd Edition, 4 vols. Leipzig: Darmstadt.

Dange, Sadashiv Ambadas. 1974. "Cosmo-Sexualism in Vedic Ritual." In *Charudeva Shastri Felicitation Volume, Volume 1*, edited by Sunit Kumar Chatterji, 23–44. Delhi: Charu Deva Shastri Felicitation Committee.

Dange, Sindhu S. 1991–92. "The Severed Head in Myth and Ritual." *Annals of the Bhandarkar Oriental Research Institute* 72/73, no. 1/4: 487–96.

Darrow, Clarence. 2007. *The Essential Words and Writings of Clarence Darrow.* Edited and with an introduction by Edward J. Larson and Jack Marshall. New York: Modern Library.

Das, Anirban. 2017. "Of Sleep and Violence: Reading the Sauptikaparvan in Times of Terror." In *Mahābhārata Now: Narration, Aesthetics, Ethics*, edited by Śibājī Bandyopādhyāy̑a and Arindam Chakrabarti, 203–18. New Delhi: Routledge India

Das, Rahul Peter. 2003. *The Origin of the Life of a Human Being: Conception and the Female According to Ancient Indian Medical and Sexological Literature.* Delhi: Motilal Banarsidass.

Davis, Erik W. 2016. *Deathpower: Buddhism's Ritual Imagination in Cambodia.* New York: Columbia University Press.

Dawkins, Richard. 2006. *The God Delusion.* New York: Houghton Mifflin.

De, Sushil Kumar. 1961. *Early History of the Vaiṣṇava Faith and Movement in Bengal, from Sanskrit and Bengali Sources.* Calcutta: Firma K.L. Mukhopadhya.

———. 1931. "A Note on Pañca-Kāla in Connection with Pañcarātra." *Journal of the Royal Asiatic Society of Great Britain and Ireland* 2: 415–18.

Dębicka-Borek, Ewa. 2015. "Why Did Narasiṃha Descend to the Earth? Some Cases from Andhra." In *The Volatile World Of Sovereignty: The Vratya Problem and Kingship in South Asia*, edited by Tiziana Pontillo, Cristina Bignami, Moreno Dore, and Elena Mucciarelli, 254–74. Delhi: DK Printworld.

Dejenne, Nicholas. 2009a. "*Triḥsaptakṛtvaḥ*: The Significance of the Number 'Thrice Seven' in the Rāma Jāmadagnya myth of the Mahābhārata." In *Epic Undertakings: Proceedings of the 12th World Sanskrit Conference (Helsinki, July 2003)*, edited by Robert P. Goldman and Muneo Tokunaga, 65–78. New Delhi: Motilal Banarsidass.

———. 2009b. "Paraśurāma as Torchbearer of a Regenerated Bhārat in a Contemporary Rewriting of His Narratives." In *Parallels and Comparisons: Proceedings of the Fourth Dubrovnik International Conference on the Sanskrit Epics and Purāṇas, September 2005*, edited by Petteri Koskikallio, 447–68. Zagreb: Croatian Academy of Sciences and Arts.

———. 2007. *Du Rama Jamadagnya épique au Parasurama contemporain: Représentations d'un héros en Inde*. PhD Dissertation, Universite Sorbonne Nouvelle-Paris 3.

Desai, Rashmi. 2008. "When Reṇukā Was Not a Goddess." In *The Iconic Female: Goddesses of India, Nepal, and Tibet*, edited by Jayant Bhalchandra Bapat and Ian Mabbett, 65–78. Clayton, Victoria, Australia: Monash University Press.

Deshpande, Madhav M. 2010. "Pañca Gauḍa and Pañca Drāviḍa: Contested Borders of a Traditional Classification." *Studia Orientalia* 10: 29–58.

Devereux, George. 1951. "The Oedipal Situation and Its Consequences in the Epics of Ancient India." *Samiksa, Journal of the Indian Psychoanalytical Society* 5, no. 1: 5–13.

Donaldson, Thomas Eugene. 1995. "The Cult of Paraśurāma and Its Popularity in Orissa." In *Studies of Jaina Art and Iconography and Allied Subjects*, edited By R. T. Vyas, 159–92. New Delhi: Abhinav.

Doniger, Wendy. 2014. "The History of Ekalavya." In *On Hinduism*, 547–55. New York: Oxford University Press.

———. 2009. *The Hindus: An Alternative History*. New York: Penguin Press.

———. 1999. *Splitting the Difference: Gender and Myth in Ancient Greece and India*. Chicago: University of Chicago Press.

———. 1998. *The Implied Spider: Politics and Theology in Myth*. New York: Columbia University Press.

———. 1985. *Tales of Sex and Violence: Folklore, Sacrifice, and Danger in the* Jaiminīya Brāhmaṇa. Chicago: University of Chicago Press.

———. 1980. *Women, Androgynes, and Other Mythical Beasts*. Chicago: University of Chicago Press.

———. 1976. *The Origins of Evil in Hindu Mythology*. Berkeley: University of California Press.

———. 1973. *Śiva: The Erotic Ascetic*. New York: Oxford University Press.

D'Souza, Dilip. 2012. "Hitler's Strange Afterlife in India." *The Daily Beast*. November 30. *https://www.thedailybeast.com/hitlers-strange-afterlife-in-india*.

Dumèzil, Georges. 1988. *Mitra-Varuna: An Essay on Two Indo-European Representations of Sovereignty*. New York: Zone Books.

———. 1973. *The Destiny of a King*. Chicago: University of Chicago Press.

———. 1970. *The Destiny of the Warrior*. Chicago: University of Chicago Press.

Dumont, Louis. 1980. *Homo Hierarchicus: The Caste System and Its Implications*. Oxford: Oxford University Press.

Edmunds, Albert J. 1913. "The Wandering Jew: His Probable Buddhist Origin." *Notes & Queries* 7, no. 160: 47.

Eisler, Robert. 1978 [1949]. *Man into Wolf: An Anthropological Interpretation of Sadism, Masochism, and Lycanthropy.* Santa Barbara: Ross-Erickson.
Elias, Norbert. 1996. *The Germans: Studies of Power Struggles and the Development of Habitus in the 19th and 20th Centuries.* Cambridge: Polity Press.
Elmore, W. T. 1915. *Dravidian Gods in Modern Hinduism: A Study of the Local and Village Deities of Southern India.* Hamilton, NY: The Author.
Elst, Koneraad. N.D. "Why Pushyamitra Was More 'Secular' than Ashoka." koenraadelst.bharatvani.org/articles/ayodhya/pushyamitra.html. Last accessed May 5, 2019.
Falk, Nancy E. 1973. "Wilderness and Kingship in Ancient South Asia." *History of Religions* 13, no. 1: 1–15.
Feldhaus, Anne. 2006. *Connected Places: Region, Pilgrimage, and Geographical Imagination in India.* New York: Palgrave Macmillan.
———. 1995. *Water and Womanhood: Religious Meanings of Rivers in Maharashtra.* New York: Oxford University Press.
Feldman, Burton, and Robert D. Richardson Jr. 1972. *The Rise of Modern Mythology, 1680–1860.* Bloomington: Indiana University Press.
Feller, Danielle. 2014. "The Epic Hero: Between Brahmin and Warrior." *Indologica Taurinensia: The Journal of the International Association of Sanskrit Studies* 11: 97–113.
Figueira, Dorothy M. 2002. *Aryans, Jews, Brahmins: Theorizing Authority through Myths of Identity.* Albany: State University of New York Press.
Fink, Bruce. 1995. *The Lacanian Subject: Between Language and Jouissance.* Princeton: Princeton University Press.
Fitzgerald, James L. 2010. " 'Slowpoke' as Deep Thinker: In Defense of 'Straying' Wives against Father's Uxoricidal Rage." In *Epic and Argument in Sanskrit Literary History*, edited by Sheldon I. Pollock, 31–59. Delhi: Manohar.
———. 2002. "The Rāma Jāmadagnya Thread of the *Mahābhārata*: A New Survey of Rāma Jāmadagnya in the Pune Text." In *Stages and Transitions: Temporal and Historical Frameworks in Epic and Purāṇic Literature, Proceedings of the Second Dubrovnik International Conference on the Sanskrit Epics and Purāṇas, August, 1999*, edited by Mary Brockington, 89–132. Zagreb: Croatian Academy of Sciences and Arts.
———. 1983. "The Great Epic of India as Religious Rhetoric: A Fresh Look at the *Mahābhārata*." *Journal of the American Academy of Religion* 51, no. 4: 611–30.
Flynn, Michael, and Charles B. Strozier. 1996. *Genocide, War, and Human Survival.* Lanham, MD: Rowman and Littlefield.
Foulston, Lynn. 2002. *At the Feet of the Goddess: The Divine Feminine in Local Hindu Religion.* Brighton, UK; Portland, OR: Sussex Academic Press.
Frazer, James George. 1927. *Folk-lore in the Old Testament: Studies in Comparative Religion, Legend, and Law.* New York: Macmillan.
———. 1922. *The Golden Bough: A Study in Magic and Religion.* New York: Macmillan.

Frazier, Jessica. 2017. *Hindu Worldviews: Theories of Self, Ritual, and Divinity*. London: Bloomsbury.

Frese, Pamela R., and S. J. M. Gray. 2005 [1987]. "Trees." In *Encyclopedia of Religion*, Vol. 14, Transcendental Meditation-Zwingli, Hurldrych, edited by Lindsey Jones, 9333–40. Detroit: MacMillan Reference USA.

Freud, Sigmund. 2010. *The Interpretation of Dreams: The Complete and Definitive Text.* New York: Basic Books.

———. 1975. *Beyond the Pleasure Principle*. New York: Norton.

Freud, Sigmund, and Peter Gay. 1995. *The Freud Reader*. London: Vintage.

Freud, Sigmund, James Strachey, Anna Freud, Alix Strachey, and Alan Tyson. 2001a. *The Standard Edition of the Complete Psychological Works of Sigmund Freud. Vol. III (1893–1899)*. London: Vintage.

———. 2001b. *The Standard Edition of the Complete Psychological works of Sigmund Freud. Vol. IV (1900)*. London: Vintage.

Furui, Ryosuke. 2013. "Finding Tensions in the Social Order: A Reading of the Varṇasaṃkara Section of the *Bṛhaddharmapurāṇa*." In *Revisiting Early India: Essays in Honor of D. C. Sircar*, edited by Suchandra Ghosh, Sudipa Ray Bandyopadhyay, Susmita Basu Majumdar, and Sayantard Pal, 203–18. Kolkata: R. N. Bhattacharya.

Gail, Adalbert J. 1978. "Paraśurāma: Brahmin and Warrior." *Indologica Taurinensia: The Journal of the International Association of Sanskrit Studies* 6: 151–54.

———. 1977. *Paraśurāma, Brahmane und Krieger: Untersuchung über Ursprung und Entwicklung eines Avatara Visnus und Bhakta Sivas in der indischen Literatur*. Wiesbaden: Harrassowitz.

*Gazetteer of the Bombay Presidency, vol. X (Ratnagiri District)*. 1885.

Gelders, Raf, and Willem Derde. 2003. "Mantras of Anti-Brahmanism: Colonial Experience of Indian Intellectuals." *Economic and Political Weekly* 38, no. 43: 4611–17.

Gerrety, Finnian. 2016. "Tree Hugger: The Sāmavedic Rite of the *Audumbarī*." *In Roots of Wisdom, Branches of Devotion: Plant Life in South Asian Religions and Culture*, edited by Fabrizio Ferrari and Thomas Dänhardt, 165–90. Sheffield, UK: Equinox.

Girard, René. 1977. *Violence and the Sacred*. Baltimore: Johns Hopkins University Press.

Glucklich, Ariel. 1994. *The Sense of* Adharma. New York: Oxford University Press.

———. 1988. "The Royal Sceptre (Daṇḍa) as Legal Punishment and Sacred Symbol." *History of Religions* 28, no. 2: 97–122.

Godwin, Maurice. 2002. "Reliability, Validity, and Utility of Criminal Profiling Typologies." *Journal of Police and Criminal Psychology* 17, no 1: 1–18.

Goldman, Robert P. 1979. "A Reply to Biardeau." *The Journal of Asian Studies* 38, no. 2: 439–40.

———. 1978. "Fathers, Sons and Gurus: Oedipal Conflict in the Sanskrit Epics." *Journal of Indian Philosophy* 6, no. 4: 325–92.

———. 1977. *Gods, Priests, and Warriors: The Bhṛgus of the* Mahābhārata. New York: Columbia University Press.

———. 1976. "Vālmīki and Bhṛgu Connection." *Journal of the American Oriental Society* 96, no. 1: 97–101.

———. 1973. "Akṛtavraṇa vs. Śrīkṛśṇa as Narrators of the Legend of Bhārgava Rāma: Apropos some Observations of Dr. V. S. Sukthankar." *Annals of the Bhandarkar Oriental Research Institute* 53: 161–73.

———. 1972. "Some Observations on the *Paraśu* of Paraśurāma." *Journal of the Oriental Institute* 21, no. 3: 321–30.

Gonda, Jan. 1987. *Rice and Barley Offerings in the Veda.* Leiden: E. J. Brill.

———. 1966. *Ancient Indian Kingship from the Religious Point of View.* Leiden: E. J. Brill.

Gordon, Stewart. 1993. *The Marathas 1600–1818.* New York: Cambridge University Press.

Green, André. 1986. *On Private Madness.* London: Hogarth.

Greenberg, Robert. 2007. *How to Listen to and Understand Great Music.* Chantilly, VA: Teaching Company.

Griffin-Kremer, Cozette. 2001. "Bovine Bodies and the Domestication of the Human Mind." In *Imagined States: Nationalism, Utopia, and Longing in Oral Cultures*, edited by Luisa Del Giudice and Gerald Porter, 167–92. Logan, UT: University Press of Colorado.

Griswold, H. D. 1971. *The Religion of the Ṛgveda.* Delhi: Motilal Banarsidass.

Gurumurthy, K. G. 2005. *Religion and Politics: A Cultural Study of the Sacred Complex of Reṇukā-Yellamma.* Athani: Vimochana Prakashana.

Haberman, David L. 1994. *Journey through the Twelve Forests: An Encounter with Krishna.* New York: Oxford University Press.

Von Harnak, Adolph. 1905. *History of Dogma, Vol. I.* Boston: Little.

Hawley, John Stratton. 2015. *A Storm of Songs: India and the Idea of the Bhakti Movement.* Cambridge: Harvard University Press.

Hazra, Rajendra Chandra. 1958. *Studies in the Upapurāṇas, Vol I.* Calcutta: Calcutta Sanskrit College Research Series.

Heesterman, J. C. 1993. *The Broken World of Sacrifice: An Essay in Ancient Indian Ritual.* Chicago: University of Chicago Press.

———. 1985. *The Inner Conflict of Tradition: Essays in Indian Ritual, Kingship, and Society.* Chicago: University of Chicago Press.

Hegarty, James. 2012. *Religion, Narrative, and Public Imagination in South Asia: Past and Place in the Sanskrit* Mahābhārata. London and New York: Routledge.

Hegel, G. W. F. 2010. *Science of Logic.* Cambridge: Cambridge University Press.

Hersh, Seymour M. 1991. *The Samson Option: Israel's Nuclear Arsenal and American Foreign Policy.* New York: Random House.

Hijiya, James A. 2000. "The 'Gita' of J. Robert Oppenheimer." *Proceedings of the American Philosophical Society* 144, no. 2: 123–67.

Hiltebeitel, Alf. Forthcoming. *World of Wonders:* Adbhuta Rasa *in the* Mahābhārata. New York: Oxford University Press.

———. 2018. *Freud's Mahābhārata*. New York: Oxford University Press.

———. 2000. "The Primary Process of the Hindu Epics." *International Journal of Hindu Studies* 4, no. 3: 269–88.

———. 1999. *Rethinking India's Oral and Classical Epics: Draupadī among Rajputs, Muslims, and Dalits*. Chicago: University of Chicago Press.

———. 1988. *The Cult of Draupadī 1: Mythologies: From Gingee to Kurukṣetra*. Chicago: University of Chicago Press.

———. 1976. *The Ritual of Battle: Krishna in the* Mahābhārata. Ithaca: Cornell University Press.

*Hindustan Times*. 2017 "Adityanath Scraps 15 Holidays, Some Muslims Unhappy Prophet's Birthday on List." April 26. https://www.hindustantimes.com/india-news/yogi-adityanath-scraps-15-holidays-in-up-muslims-unhappy-prophet-s-birthday-features-in-list/story-C6Ioncmg7JOvmjudDH0bRL.html. Last accessed May 5, 2019.

Hodges, Sarah. 2010. "South Asia's Eugenic Past." In *The Oxford Handbook of the History of* Eugenics, edited by Alison Bashford and Philippa Levine, 228–42. Oxford: Oxford University Press.

Hudson, D. Dennis. 2008. *The Body of God: An Emperor's Palace for Krishna in Eighth-Century Kanchipuram*. Oxford: Oxford University Press.

Hudson, Emily T. 2013. *Disorienting Dharma: Ethics and the Aesthetics of Suffering in the* Mahabharata. New York: Oxford University Press.

Hughes, Aaron W. 2017. *Comparison: A Critical Primer*. Sheffield, UK: Equinox.

Hunter, Lloyd A. 2000. "The Immortal Confederacy: Another Look at Lost Cause Religion." In *The Myth of the Lost Cause and Civil War history*, edited by Gary W. Gallagher and Alan T. Nolan, 185–218. Bloomington: Indiana University Press.

Inden, Ronald B., Jonathan S. Walters, and Daud Ali. 2000. *Querying the Medieval: Texts and the History of Practices in South Asia*. New York: Oxford University Press.

Jabr, Farris. 2018. "This Is Where Your Childhood Memories Went: Your Brain Needs to Forget in Order to Grow." *Nautilus*. March 8. http://nautil.us/issue/58/self/this-is-where-your-childhood-memories-went-rp. Last accessed May 5, 2019.

Jain, Pratibha, and Sangeeta Sharma 2002. "Honour, Gender, and the Legend of Meera Bai." *Economic and Political Weekly* 37, vol. 46 (Nov. 16–22): 4646–50.

Jaini, Padmanabh S. 1993. "A Purāṇic Counter Tradition." In *Purāṇa Perennis: Reciprocity and Transformation in Hindu and Jaina texts*, edited by Wendy Doniger, 207–49. Albany: State University of New York Press.

Jamison, Stephanie W. 1996. *Sacrificed Wife/Sacrificer's Wife: Women, Ritual, and Hospitality in Ancient India*. New York: Oxford University Press.

———. 1991. *The Ravenous Hyenas and the Wounded Sun: Myth and Ritual in Ancient India*. Ithaca: Cornell University Press.

Janaki, K. S. S. 1966. "Paraśurāma." *Purāṇa* 8, no. 1: 52–82.

Janaky. 1992. "On the Trail of the *Mahabharata*: A Response." *Economic and Political Weekly* 27, no. 37 (Sept. 12): 1997–99.

Johnston, Sarah Iles. 2018. *The Story of Myth*. Cambridge: Harvard University Press.

Jonte-Pace, Diane. 2001. *Speaking the Unspeakable: Religion, Misogyny, and the Uncanny Mother in Freud's Cultural Texts*. Berkeley: University of California Press.

Joshi, Sarasvati. 2000. "La femme et l'eau." In *Le Rajasthan: Ses dieux, ses héros, son people*, edited by Annie Montaut, 63–80. Paris: INALCO.

Jouveau-Dubreuil, G., and A. C. Martin. 1937. *Iconography of Southern India*. Paris: P. Geuthner.

Jullien, François, and Janet Lloyd. 2002. "Did Philosophers Have to Become Fixated on Truth?" *Critical Inquiry* 28, no. 4: 803–24.

Jurewicz, Joanna. 2016. *Fire, Death and Philosophy: A History of Ancient Indian Thinking*. Warsaw: Elipsa.

Kaelber, Walter O. 1989. *Tapta Mārga: Asceticism and Initiation in Vedic India*. Albany: State University of New York Press.

Karve, Irawati. 1932. "The Paraśurāma Myth." *Journal of the University of Bombay* I: 115–39.

Katz, Ruth. 1985. "The Sauptika Episode in the Structure of the *Mahābhārata*." *Journal of South Asian Literature* 20, no. 1: 109–24.

Kershaw, Priscilla K. 2000. *The One-eyed God: Odin and the (Indo)germanic Männerbünde*. Washington, DC: Journal of Indo-European Studies.

Kinsley, David R. 1997. *Hindu Goddesses: Visions of the Divine Feminine in the Hindu Religious Tradition*. Berkeley: University of California Press.

Koch, Rolf Heinrich. 1998. "Subhūma in den Jaina-Versionen der Paraśurāma-Erzählung." *Berliner Indologische Studien* 11/12: 123–58.

Kolhatkar, Madhavi. N.D. "The Vedic Myth behind the Purāṇic Paraśurāma Story." Unpublished.

Kraut, Richard. "Aristotle's Ethics." *The Stanford Encyclopedia of Philosophy* (Summer 2018), ed. Edward N. Zalta; plato.stanford.edu/archives/sum2018/entries/aristotle-ethics. Last accessed May 5, 2019.

Kristeva, Julia. 2012. *The Severed Head: Capital Visions*. New York: Columbia University Press.

———. 1989. *Black Sun: Depression and Melancholia*. New York: Columbia University Press.

Kumari, Ved. 1968. *The Nilamata Purana: A Cultural and Literary Study of a Kasmiri Purana*. Srinagar: J & K Academy of Art, Culture and Languages.

Kuper, Leo. 1982. *Genocide: Its Political Use in the Twentieth Century*. New Haven: Yale University Press.

Lacan, Jacques. 2016. *The Ethics of Psychoanalysis 1959–1960. Book VII*. London: Taylor and Francis.

———. 2006. *Ecrits: The First Complete Edition in English*. New York: W. W. Norton.

Lamb, Ramdas. 2002. *Rapt in the Name: The Ramnamis, Ramnam, and Untouchable Religion in Central India.* Albany: State University of New York Press.

Latour, Bruno. 2000. *We Have Never Been Modern*. Harlow, Essex: Pearson Education

Lemercinier, Geneviève. 1984. *Religion and Ideology in Kerala*. New Delhi: D. K. Agencies.

Leopold, Joan. 1974. "British Applications of the Aryan Theory of Race to India, 1850–1870." *The English Historical Review* 89, no. 352: 578–603.

Levine, Emily J. 2013. *Dreamland of Humanists: Warburg, Cassirer, Panofsky, and the Hamburg School.* Chicago: The University of Chicago Press.

Lévi-Strauss, Claude. 1966. *The Savage Mind.* Chicago: The University of Chicago Press.

———. 1963. *Totemism.* Boston: Beacon Press.

Levitt, Stephan Hillyer. 2017. "Reflections on the *Sahyādrikhaṇḍa*'s *Uttarārdha*." *Studia Orientalia Electronica* 5: 151–61. DOI 10.23993/store.65156.

Lincoln, Bruce. 2018. *Apples and Oranges: Explorations in, on, and with Comparison.* Chicago: University of Chicago Press.

———. 2012. *Gods and Demons, Priests and Scholars: Critical Explorations in the History of Religions.* Chicago: University of Chicago Press.

———. 2007. *Religion, Empire, and Torture: The Case of Achaemenian Persia, with a Postscript on Abu Ghraib*. Chicago: University of Chicago Press.

———. 1999. *Theorizing Myth: Narrative, Ideology, and Scholarship*. Chicago: University of Chicago Press.

———. 1991. *Death, War, and Sacrifice: Studies in Ideology and Practice*. Chicago: University of Chicago Press.

———. 1981. *Priests, Warriors and Cattle: A Comparative Study of East African and Indo-Iranian Religious Systems*. Berkeley: University of California Press.

———. 1976. "The Indo-European Cattle-Raiding Myth." *History of Religions* 16, no. 1: 42–65.

Logan, William. 2000. [1887]. *Malabar Manual.* New Delhi: Asian Educational Services.

Lopez, Donald S., and Peggy McCracken. 2014. *In Search of the Christian Buddha: How an Asian Sage Became a Medieval Saint*. New York: W. W. Norton.

Lutgendorf, Phillip. 2007. *Hanuman's Tale: The Messages of a Divine Monkey.* Oxford: Oxford University Press.

Macauley, Thomas Babbington. 1910. *The Complete Works of Thomas Babbington Macauley*. Fireside Edition. Volume 10, Miscellanies, Poems, and Letters. Boston and New York: Houghton Mifflin.

———. 1835. Minute by the Hon'ble T. B. Macaulay, dated the 2nd February 1835.

Maccoby, Hyam. 1986. "The Wandering Jew as Sacred Executioner." In *The Wandering Jew: Essays in the Interpretation of a Christian Legend*, edited by Galit Hasan-Rokem and Alan Dundes, 236–60. Bloomington: Indiana University Press.

Magnone, Paolo. 2002. "Paraśurāma's Rise to Avatārahood: A Glimpse of Early Avatāra-Theology." *Rendiconti: Classe di letter e scienze morali e storichi* 136: 195–210.

Malabou, Catherine. 2008. *What Should We Do with Our Brain?* New York: Fordham University Press.

Malamoud, Charles. 1996. *Cooking the World: Ritual and Thought in Ancient India.* New York: Oxford University Press.

Mallinson, James. 2018. "Yoga and Sex: What Is the Purpose of *Vajrolīmudrā*?" In *Yoga in Transformation: Historical and Contemporary Perspectives,* edited by Karl Baier, Philipp A. Maas, and Karin Preisendanz, 183–222. Vienna: Vienna University Press.

Mate, M. S. 2001. *Temples and Legends of Maharashtra.* Mumbai: Bharatiya Vidya Bhavan.

Matsubara, Mitsunori. 1994. Pāñcarātra Saṃhitās *and Early Vaiṣṇava Theology, with a Translation and Critical Notes from Chapters on Theology in the* Ahirbudhnya Saṃhitā. Delhi: Motilal Banarsidass.

Minkowski, Christopher. 2002. "Nīlakaṇṭha Caturdhara's *Mantrakāśīkhaṇḍa*." *Journal of the American Oriental Society* 122: 329–44.

Mirashi, Vasudev Vishnu. 1974. *Bhavabhūti: His Date, Life, and Works.* Delhi: Motilal Banarsidass.

Monier-Williams, Monier. 2009. *An English-Sanskrit Dictionary.* New Delhi: Asian Educational Services.

Mukunda, H. S., S. M. Deshpande, H. R. Nagendra, A. Prabhu, and S. P. Govindraju. 1974. "A Critical Study of the Work 'Vyamanika Shastra.'" *Scientific Opinion*: 5–12.

Nabokov, Isabelle. 1997. "Expel the Lover, Recover the Wife: Symbolic Analysis of a South Indian Exorcism." *The Journal of the Royal Anthropological Institute* 3, no. 2: 297–316.

Nagar, Shantilal. 2006. *Paraśurāma (An Incarnation of Viṣṇu).* Delhi: B. R.

Narayan, Vasudha. 1985. "*Arcāvatāra*: On Earth as He Is in Heaven." In *Gods of Flesh, Gods of Stone: The Embodiment of Divinity in India*, edited by Joanne Punzo Waghorne and Norman Cutler, 53–67. New York: Columbia University Press.

Narayanan, M. G. S., and Kesavan Veluthat. 2010 [1983]. "A History of the Nambudiri Community of Kerala." In *Agni: The Vedic Ritual of the Fire Altar*, edited by Frits Staal, 256–78. 2 vols. Delhi: Motilal Banarsidass.

Nayar, Ashmita. 2016. "Man Sues Lord Rama for Cruelty Towards Wife Sita." *The Huffington Post.* http://www.huffingtonpost.in/2016/02/01/lord-rama-complaint-case-_n_9128872.html. Last accessed August 21, 2017.

Neevel, Walter G. 1977. *Yāmuna's Vedānta and Pāñcarātra: Integrating the Classical and the Popular.* Missoula, MT: Scholars Press.

Neuhouser, Frederick. 2009. "Desire, Recognition, and the Relation between Bondsman and Lord." In *The Blackwell Guide to Hegel's* Phenomenology of Spirit, edited by Kenneth R. Westphal, 37–54. Chichester: Wiley-Blackwell.

Nietzsche, Friedrich Wilhelm. 2010. *On the Use and Abuse of History for Life.* Revised Edition. Translated by Ian Johnston, Vancouver Island University. Nanaimo,

British Columbia, Canada. http://johnstoniatexts.x10host.com/nietzsche/historyhtml.html. Last accessed May 5, 2019.

Obeyesekere, Gananath. 1990. *The Work of Culture: Symbolic Transformation in Psychoanalysis and Anthropology*. Chicago: University of Chicago Press.

———. 1977. "The Impact of Āyurvedic Ideas on the Culture and the Individual in Sri Lanka." In *Asian Medical Systems: A Comparative Study*, edited by Charles Leslie, 201–26. Berkeley: University of California Press.

Omvedt, Gail. 2006. *Dalit Visions: The Anti-Caste Movement and the Construction of an Indian Identity*. Hyderabad: Orient Longman.

Panda, Jayanti. 1984. *Bhṛgus, a Study*. New Delhi: B.R.

Parampanthi, Swami Bangovinda. 1987. *Bhagawan Parashuram and Evolution of Culture in North-East India*. Delhi: Daya.

Parry, Adam. 1963. "The Two Voices of Virgil's 'Aeneid.' " *Arion: A Journal of Humanities and the Classics* 2, no. 4: 66–80.

Pattanaik, Devdutt. 2002. *The Man Who Was a Woman and Other Queer Tales of Hindu Lore*. New York: Harrington Park Press.

Patterson, Orlando. 1998. *Rituals of Blood: The Consequences of Slavery in Two American Centuries*. New York: Basic Civitas.

Paul, Robert. 1982. *The Tibetan Symbolic World*. Chicago: The University of Chicago Press.

Pauwels, Heidi. 2010. '"The Woman Waylaid at the Well' or *Paṇaghaṭa-līlā:* An Indian Folk Theme Appropriated in Myth and Movies." *Asian Ethnology* 69, no. 1: 1–33.

Piḷḷai, E. K. 1970. *Studies in Kerala History*. Trivandrum: National Book Stall, Kottayam.

Pollock, Sheldon I. 2008. "Towards a Political Philology: D. D. Kosambi and Sanskrit." *Economic and Political Weekly* 43, no. 30: 52–59.

———. 2006. *The Language of the Gods in the World of Men: Sanskrit, Culture, and Power in Premodern India*. Berkeley: University of California Press.

———. 1993. "Deep Orientalism? Notes on Sanskrit and Power beyond the Raj." In *Orientalism and the Postcolonial Predicament: Perspectives on South Asia*, edited by Carol A. Breckenridge and Peter van der Veer, 76–133. Philadelphia: University of Pennsylvania Press.

Poonacha, Veena. 1993. "Hindutva's Hidden Agenda: Why Women Fear Religious Fundamentalism." *Economic and Political Weekly* 28, no. 11: 438–39.

Pusalker, A. D. 1951. "*Vādeśvarodaya-kāvya* of Viśvanātha." *Journal of the Bombay Branch of the Royal Asiatic Society* 26: 66–76.

Putnam, Michael C. J. 1965. *The Poetry of the Aeneid: Four Studies in Imaginative Unity and Design*. Cambridge: Harvard University Press.

Raghavan, V. 1965. "The Name Pāñcarātra: With an Analysis of the *Sanatkumāra-Saṃhitā* in Manuscript." *Journal of the American Oriental Society* 85, no. 1: 73–79.

Ramanujan, A. K. 1984. "The Indian Oedipus." In *Oedipus: A Folklore Casebook*, edited by Lowell Edmunds and Alan Dundes, 234–61. New York: Garland.

Rappaport, David C. 2012. "Fear and Trembling: Terrorism in Three Religious Traditions." In *Terrorism Studies: A Reader*, edited by John Horgan and Kurt Braddock, 3–26. London and New York: Routledge.

Ray, Himanshu Prabha. 1986. *Monastery and Guild: Commerce under the Satavahanas*. Delhi: Oxford University Press.

Ricoeur, Paul. 1972. *The Symbolism of Evil*. Boston: Beacon Press.

Rigopoulos, Antonio. 1998. *Dattātreya: The Immortal Guru, Yogin, and Avatāra: A Study of the Tranformative and Inclusive Character of a Multi-faceted Hindu Deity*. Albany: State University of New York Press.

Rinehart, Robin. 2004. *Contemporary Hinduism: Ritual, Culture, and Practice*. Santa Barbara: ABC-CLIO.

Rocher, Ludo. 1986. *The Purāṇas*. A History of Indian Literature Vol. II. Edited by Jan Gonda. Wiesbaden: Otto Harrassowitz.

Ronen, Gil. 2012. "Letter-poem to Grass: If We Go, Everyone Goes." August 4. http://www.israelnationalnews.com/News/News.aspx/154608. Last accessed May 5, 2019.

Rosella, Daniela. 2010. "The Indian Forest: Nobody's Land or Everybody's?" In *The City and the Forest in Indian Literature and Art*, edited by Danuta Stasik and Anna Trynkowska, 147–62. Warsaw: Elipsa.

Roy, Udai Narain. 1979. Śālabhañjika *in Art, Philosophy, and Literature*. Allahabad: Lokabharti.

Rushby, Kevin. 2003. *Children of Kali: Through India in Search of Bandits, the Thug Cult, and the British Raj*. New York: Walker.

Russon, John. 2011. "The Project of Hegel's *Phenomenology of Spirit*." In *A Companion to Hegel*, edited by Stephen Houlgate and Michael Baur, 47–67. Chichester: Wiley-Blackwell.

Sahlins, Marshall. 1981. *Historical Metaphors and Mythical Realities: Structure in the Early History of the Sandwich Island Kingdom*. Ann Arbor: University of Michigan Press.

Salunkhe, A. H. 2001. *Paraśurāma: Joḍṇyāce Pratīk, kī Toḍṇyāce?* Satara, MH: Lokāyat Prakāśan.

Sanderson, Alexis. 2009. "The Śaiva Age: The Rise and Dominance of Śaivism during the Early Medieval Period." In *Genesis and Development of Tantrism*, edited by Shingo Einoo, 41–349. Tokyo: Institute of Oriental Culture.

Sanford, A. Whitney. 2005. "Holi through Dauji's Eyes: Alternate Views of Krishna and Balarama in Dauji." In *Alternative Krishnas: Regional and Vernacular Variations on a Hindu Deity*, edited by Guy Beck, 91–112. Albany: State University of New York Press.

Sarr, Assan. 2016. *Islam, Power, and Dependency in the Gambia River Basin: The Politics of Land Control, 1790–1940*. Rochester: University of Rochester Press.

Sathaye, Adheesh. 2015. *Crossing the Lines of Caste: Viśvāmitra and the Construction of Brahmin Power in Hindu Mythology*. Oxford: Oxford University Press.

———. 2010. "The Other Kind of Brahman: Rāma Jāmadagnya and the Psychosocial Construction of Brahman Power in the *Mahābhārata*." In *Epic and Argument in Sanskrit Literary History Essays in Honor of Robert P. Goldman*, edited by Sheldon Pollock, 185–204. Delhi: Manohar.

Schaftel, David. 2012. "Hitler Has a Following in India." *Bloomberg*. December 6. https://www.bloomberg.com/news/articles/2012-12-06/hitler-has-a-following-in-india. Last accessed May 5, 2019.

Schama, Simon. 1995. *Landscape and Memory*. New York: Knopf.

Scharfe, Hartmut. 1989. *The State in Indian Tradition*. Leiden: Brill.

Scheinert, Josh. 2014. "Why Is Adolf Hitler Popular in India?" *The Jerusalem Post*. September 29. https://www.jpost.com/Opinion/Why-is-Adolf-Hitler-popular-in-India-376622. Last accessed May 5, 2019.

Schmitt, Carl. 1985. *Political Theology: Four Chapters on the Concept of Sovereignty*. Cambridge: MIT Press.

Schrader, Friedrich Otto. 1916. *Introduction to the Pāñcarātra and the Ahirbudhnya Saṃhitā*. Madras: Adyar Library.

Sen, Aditi. 2011. " 'I Wasn't Born with Enough Middle Fingers': How Low-budget Horror Films Defy Sexual Morality and Heteronormativity in Bollywood." *Acta Orientalia Vilnensia* 12, no. 2: 75–90.

Shay, Jonathan. 1995. *Achilles in Vietnam*. New York: Simon and Schuster.

Shulman, David Dean. 1995. "First Man, Forest Mother: Telugu Humanism in the Age of Kṛṣṇadevarāya." In *Syllables of Sky: Studies in South Indian Civilization in Honor of Velcheru Narayana Rao*, edited by David Shulman, 133–64. Delhi: Oxford University Press.

———. 1993. *The Hungry God: Hindu Tales of Filicide and Devotion*. Chicago: University of Chicago Press.

———. 1985. *The King and the Clown in South Indian Myth and Poetry*. Princeton: Princeton University Press.

Siegel, Lee. 1987. *Laughing Matters: Comic Tradition in India*. Chicago: University of Chicago Press.

Sinhabu, Supriya. 2008. "Interview with J. Z. Smith." *The Chicago Maroon*. June 2. https://www.chicagomaroon.com/2008/06/02/interview-with-j-z-smith/. Last accessed May 5, 2019.

Sircar, Dinesh Chandra. 1973. *The Śakti Pīṭhas*. New Delhi: Motilal Banarsidass.

Sleutels, Jan. 2008. "Greek Zombies: On the Alleged Absurdity of Substantially Unconscious Greek Minds." In *Reflections on the Dawn of Consciousness: Julian Jaynes's Bicameral Mind Theory Revisited*, edited by Marcel Kuijsten, 303–17. Henderson, NV: Julian Jaynes Society.

Smith, Brian K. 1994. *Classifying the Universe: The Ancient Indian Varṇa System and the Origins of Caste*. New York: Oxford University Press.

Smith, Frederick M. 2012. *The Self Possessed: Deity and Spirit Possession in South Asian Literature and Civilization*. New York: Columbia University Press.

Smith, H. Daniel. 1975, *A Descriptive Bibliography of the Printed Texts of the Pāñcarātrāgama*. Baroda: University of Baroda Press.

Smith, H. Daniel, K. K. A. Venkatachari, and V. Ganapathi. 1969. *A Sourcebook of Vaiṣṇava Iconography According to Pāñcarātrāgama Texts*. Madras: Pāñcarātra Pariśodhana Pariṣad.

Smith, Jonathan Z. 1987. *To Take Place: Toward Theory in Ritual*. Chicago: University of Chicago Press.

Soifer, Deborah A. 1991. *The Myths of Narasiṃha and Vāmana: Two Avatars in Cosmological Perspective*. Albany: State University of New York Press.

Sørensen, Søren, Pratāpacandra Rāya, Elof Olesen, and Dines Andersen. 1978. *An Index to the Names in the* Mahābhārata*: With Short Explanations and a Concordance to the Bombay and Calcutta Editions and P. C. Roy's Translation*. Delhi: Motilal Banarsidass.

*Southern Living*. 2018. "This Retired Marine Colonel Is an Incredible Sculptor." https://www.youtube.com/watch?v=rk_f8aE2T0s. Last accessed May 5, 2019.

Sprengnether, Madelon. 1990. *The Spectral Mother: Freud, Feminism, and Psychoanalysis*. Ithaca: Cornell University Press.

Srinivasan, Perundevi. 2009. "Stories of the Flesh: Colonial and Anthropological Discourses on the South Indian Goddess Mariyamman." PhD Dissertation, George Washington University.

Srivastava, V. C. 1972. *Sun-Worship in Ancient India*. Allahabad: Indological Publications.

Stark-Wild, Sonja. 1997. *Die Göttin Reṇukā in Mythos und Kultus: Eine Analyse ihrer sakralen Präsenz unter besonderer Berücksichtigung ihrer Verbreitung in Maharashtra*. Inauguraldissertation zur Erlangung des Doktorgrades der Fakultät für Orientalistik und Altertumswissenschaft der Universität Heidelberg.

Stevens, Anthony. 2001. *Ariadne's Clue: A Guide to the Symbols of Humankind*. Princeton: Princeton University Press.

Stokes, Whitley. 1893. "The Edinburgh Dinnschenchas." *Folklore* 4: 471–97.

Stone, Michael E. 2002. *Adam's Contract with Satan: The Legend of the Cheirograph of Adam*. Bloomington: Indiana University Press.

Straus, Scott. 2001. "Contested Meanings and Conflicting Imperatives: A Conceptual Analysis of Genocide." *Journal of Genocide Research* 3, no. 3: 349–75.

Strenski, Ivan. 2016. "Actually, You Can Compare Apples to Oranges: Secrets of Successful Comparison of Myths." In *Religion: Narrating Religion*, edited by Sarah Iles-Johnston, 49–64. Farmington Hills, MI: Macmillan Reference USA.

Stutley, Margaret, and James Stutley. 2019. *A Dictionary of Hinduism: Its Mythology, Folklore, and Development 1500 BC–AD 1500*. London: Routledge.

Subramanian, Shreerekha. 2016. "Women Writers, India." In *Pop Culture in Asia and Oceania*, edited by Jeremy A. Murray and Kathleen M. Nadeau, 117–21. Santa Barbara: ABC-CLIO.

Sukthankar, V. S. 1936. "Epic Studies VI: The Bhṛgus and the Bhārata." *Annals of the Bhandarkar Oriental Research Institute* 18: 1–76.

Sullivan, Bruce. 2006. "The Ideology of Self-Willed Death in the Epic *Mahābhārata*." *Journal of Vaishnava Studies* 14, no. 2: 61–80.

Sundahl, Deborah. "Sacred Liquid/Tantra." https://isismedia.org/sacred-liquid-tantra/. Last accessed April 27, 2019.

Svamin, A. Govindacarya. 1911. "The Pancaratras or Bhagavat-Sastra." *The Journal of the Royal Asiatic Society of Great Britain and Ireland* 1, no. 1–2: 935–61.

Taylor, Charles. 2018. *A Secular Age*. Cambridge: The Belknap Press of Harvard University Press.

Thapar, Romila. 2000. *Cultural Pasts: Essays in Early Indian History*. New Delhi: Oxford University Press.

Theweleit, Klaus, and Barbara Ehrenreich. 2007. *Male Fantasies, Volume I: Women, Bodies, Floods, Histories*. Minneapolis: University of Minnesota Press.

Thomas, Lynn. 1996. "Paraśurāma and Time." In *Myth and Mythmaking: Continuous Evolution in Indian Tradition*, edited by Julia Leslie, 63–86. Richmond, Surrey: Curzon Press.

Thomas, Richard F. 2006. *Virgil and the Augustan Reception*. Cambridge: Cambridge University Press.

Tripathi, Gaya-Charan. 1979. "The Worship of Kārtavīrya-Arjuna: On the Deification of a Royal Personage in India." *Journal of the Royal Asiatic Society of Great Britain and Ireland* 111, no. 1: 37–52.

Tubb, Gary A. 1985. "Śāntarasa in the *Mahābhārata*." *Journal of South Asian Literature* 20, no. 1: 141–68.

UPI Archives. 1985. "Psychologists Say Serial Killers Have Victims in Mind." Aug. 24. https://www.upi.com/Archives/1985/08/24/Psychologists-say-serial-killers-have-victims-in-mind/3197493704000/. Last accessed March 3, 2020.

Varadarajan, Siddharth. 2002. *Gujarat, The Making of a Tragedy*. New Delhi: Penguin Books.

Veluthat, Kesavan. 2009. *The Early Medieval in South India*. New Delhi: Oxford University Press.

Versnel, H. S. 1976. "Two Types of Roman *Devotio*." *Mnemosyne*, Fourth Series, vol. 29, fasc. 4: 365–410.

Veṭṭammāṇi. 2015. *Purāṇic Encyclopaedia: A Comprehensive Work with Special Reference to the Epic and Purānic Literature*. Delhi: Motilal Banarsidass.

Vielle, Christopher. 2005. "From the *Vāyuprokta* to the *Vāyu* and *Brahmāṇḍa Purāṇas*: Preliminary Remarks Towards a Critical Edition of the *Vāyuprokta Brahmāṇḍapurāṇa*." In *Epics, Khilas, and Purāṇas: Continuities and Ruptures. Proceedings of the Third Dubrovnik International Conference on the Sanskrit Epics and Purāṇas, September 2002*, edited by P. Koskikallio, 535–60. Zagreb: Croatian Academy of Sciences and Arts.

———. 2002. "An Introduction to the *Jaiminīyasaṃhitā* of the *Brahmāṇḍapurāṇa*." In *Stages and Transitions: Temporal and Historical Frameworks in Epic and Purāṇic Literature, Proceedings of the Second Dubrovnik International Conference on the Sanskrit Epics and Purāṇas, August, 1999*, edited by Mary Brockington, 337–57. Zagreb: Croatian Academy of Sciences and Arts.

Wickett, Elizabeth. 2010. *The Epic Of* Pabuji Ki Par *In Performance*. Cambridge, UK: World Oral Literature Project.

White, David Gordon. 2012. "*Netra Tantra*, at the Crossroads of the Demonological Cosmopolis," *Journal of Hindu Studies* 5, no. 2: 145–71.

———. 1991. *Myths of the Dog-Man*. Chicago: University Of Chicago Press.

Whitaker, Jarrod. 2011. *Strong Arms and Drinking Strength: Masculinity, Violence, and the Body in Ancient India*. Oxford: Oxford University Press.

Wilson, Charles. 1980. *Baptized in Blood: The Religion of the Lost Cause, 1865–1920*. Athens: University of Georgia Press.

Winternitz, M. 1981. *A History of Indian Literature*. Delhi: Motilal Banarsidass.

Wright, Lawrence. 1995. *Remembering Satan*. New York: Vintage Books.

Zarrilli, Phillip B. 1998. *When the Body Becomes All Eyes: Paradigms, Discourses, and Practices of Power in Kalarippayattu, a South Indian Martial Art*. New Delhi: Oxford University Press.

Žižek, Slavoj. 2017. *Incontinence of the Void: Economico-Philosophical Spandrels*. Cambridge: The MIT Press.

———. 2012. *Less Than Nothing: Hegel and the Shadow of Dialectical Materialism*. London: Verso.

Žižek, Slavoj, and Agon Hamza. 2013. *From Myth to Symptom: The Case of Kosovo*. Prishtinë: Autorët.

Žižek, Slavoj, and Rex Butler. 2014. *The Universal Exception*. London: Bloomsbury.

# Index

*Note: Page numbers followed by "n" denotes notes*


Abbas, Zia, 271*n*13
abjection (Julia Kristeva), 107, 133
acculturation, through embodied practices, 21
*adharma*, 69–70
Ādi Parvan (*Mahābhārata*), 149–150, 199
Adityā (solar god), 93–94
Adityanath, Yogi, 215
Adluri, Vishwa, 50
Agamben, Giorgio, 8, 69, 77, 221
*agrahāras* (income-earning estates), 48
Ahalyā, 125–126
  comparing Reṇukā and, 127
  and Indra, 10
*Aitereya Brāhmaṇa*, 264*n*2
*akrasia* (self-control), 9, 102
  defilement of Reṇukā, 83–88, 96, 222
Akṛtavraṇa (sage), 118, 146, 151, 187–188
  and Yudhiṣṭhira, 35, 150
Akṣaya Tṛtīya festival, in Madhya Pradesh, 269*n*3
Ala-ud-Din-Khilji (Sultan of Delhi), 208
alienation stage, in mother-child relationship, 135
Alkmaion (Greek myth), 191–192
Ambā (princess)
  and Bhīṣma, 220, 239
Anantavīrya, and Reṇukā, 178–179, 276*n*41
Anantha Murthy, U. R., 202
Ananthakrishnan Iyer, L. K., 201
annihilation, of Kṣatriyas. *See* varṇicide
anxieties, and myths, 24–25, 223
Aquinas, Thomas, xv
Āraṇyaka Parvan (*Mahābhārata*), 150, 259*n*7
Aristotle, 9, 83
Arjuna (king). *See* Kārtavīrya Arjuna
Arjuna (Pāṇḍavas), 24, 72
Armstrong, Karen, 216
Āryans, 157, 209
  Horse Sacrifice, 267*n*25
Aśoka (Mauryan emperor), 43, 45, 47
*Aśokāvadāna*, 45
*āśramas* (hermitages), 48, 135
Assayag, Jackie, 134, 246
*astrāṇi* (spells/offensive magic), 53–54
*aśvamedha* (Horse Sacrifice), 97–98, 267*n*25
*aśvattha* (tree), 37–38, 52, 172, 259*n*6
Aśvatthāman (Droṇa's son), 10, 52–54, 223
  massacre of Pāṇḍavas, 151, 166–168, 170
  and Paraśurāma, 72–73, 166–169

Aśvatthāman (Droṇa's son) *(continued)*
possession by Śiva, 166
vengeance of, 71–77
and Yudhiṣṭhira, 71–72, 166
Aśvin twins (Vedic horse deities and physicians), 44, 86, 110
*Atharva Veda*, 37, 58, 90, 91, 151, 153, 187
Aurangzeb (Mughal emperor), 211
Aurva (Paraśurāma's ancestor), 61, 152–153, 198, 272*n*15
*Avadhūta Gītā* (attributed to Dattātreya), 33–34
Avalokiteśvara (*bodhisattva*), 117
*avatāra(s)*
Kalki, 74–76, 263*n*34
Kṛṣṇa. *See* Kṛṣṇa
Narasiṃha, 34, 201, 259*n*3
Paraśurāma. *See* Paraśurāma, as *avatāra*
Rāma. *See* Rāma Dāśarathi
Vāmana, 34, 254
Vasūdeva, 171–173, 266*n*16
of Viṣṇu, 34–35, 70

Babb, Lawrence, 190
Bacon, Francis, 14, 19
Bagchee, Joydeep, 48–49, 52, 260*n*16
Bāḷājī (Citpāvan Peśwā), 209, 211
Balamani Amma
*Maluvinte Katha* poem, 7, 40–42, 114, 165, 219, 221, 254
Bali/Bālika (demon king), 158, 188, 254–255
Ball, Phillip, 18
Bandyopadhyay, Sibaji, 168–169
Ban-Yatra pilgrimage, 247
Bappura family. *See* Bali/Bālika
Barasch, Frances, 128
Barnett, L. D., 93
Basham, A. L., 45
Bataille, Georges, 265*n*12
*bhadradipāpratiṣṭā* (rite), 119–120, 122
*Bhagavān Paraśurāma* (Munshi), 59
*Bhāgavata Purāṇa*, 65, 66, 95
Bhāgavatas, 275*n*32
Bhandare, Shailendra, 46
Bhandarkar, R. G., 275*n*32
Bharadvāja (Droṇa's father), 53, 202
*Bhāratabhāvadīpa* (Nīlakaṇṭha), 264n4
Bhargava, P. L., 184
Bhārgavakṣetra. *See* Paraśurāmakṣetra
Bhārgavas, 42–43, 62, 108, 185, 186, 221, 255
extermination campaigns of, 272*n*15
generosity of, 54
and Haihaya feud, 10, 152–154, 176, 181, 190, 198, 223
sacrificial suicide, 129
and *varṇa*, 156–157
Bhattatiri (caste), 201–202
Bhavabhūti, 75
*Bhāviṣya Purāṇa*, 46
Bhavsars (caste), 158, 189
Bhīṣma, 61–62, 160
and Ambā, 220, 239
Cirakāri story, 126
deathbed sermon, 47, 123
and Yudhiṣṭhira, 35, 124
Bhṛgu, 108, 186
power to raise dead, 81
and Satyavatī, 2–3, 35, 227
and Vitāhavya, 153–154
Bhṛguization thesis (V. S. Sukthankar), 42–43
Bhūtarāya Pāṇḍya (Perumāl), 200
Biardeau, Madeleine, 48–49, 98–99, 144, 225
bicameral mind. *See* Jaynes, Julian
blood and soil myth
Maharashtra, 208–217
Malabar, 194–208
United States, 215, 224
blood-guiltiness, 195–196, 208, 214

Blumenberg, Hans, 21
Booth, Wayne, 114
Bose, Girindrasekhar, 9
Bourdieu, Pierre, 21
Brahmā (god), 66, 171
Rāvaṇa-Paraśurāma conflict, 193
*brāhmahātya* (Brahmin-killing), 116
*Brahmāṇḍa Purāṇa*, 66, 71, 75, 192
Paraśurāma and Gaṇeśa, 118, 119–121
*Brahmavaivarta Purāṇa*, 118, 138
Brahmins
Bhārgava. *See* Bhārgavas
Citpāvan, 5, 11, 208–217, 234
cultural victory of, 48
Kṣatriya conflicts. *See* matricide, varṇicide
and Kṣatriyas. *See* Kṣatriyas
Nambudiri. *See* Nambudiris
Peśwās in Maharashtra, 210
regeneration of Kṣatriyas, after varṇicide, 4, 150, 199, 228, 239
Vaidika, 48
and Vena (king), 23, 65, 67, 221
*Bṛhaddharma Purāṇa*, 64–65, 67
Bṛhadratha (Mauryan emperor), 45
Brigurama. *See* Paraśurāma
Brinkhaus, Horst, 176
Bronkhorst, Johannes, 43, 48, 170
Brubaker, Richard Lee, 90, 96
Bryan, William Jennings, 162, 273*n*22
Buddha
in medieval France, 26–27
myth, 92
Buddhism, 37, 45, 73
and Rudra (Śiva), 117
wilderness and kingship, 91–92
Buffalo Sacrifice, 99
Bundy, Cliven (Nevada rancher), 57

Calasso, Roberto, xvi
Cartaphilus. *See* "Wandering Jew"
*caru* (rice pudding), 2, 36, 38, 75, 220, 224, 227
Cassirer, Ernst, 20
caste oppression, 22–23
Cattar (Nambudiri subcaste), 206
cattle raids, and kingship, 56–64
Cēra kingdom, 200, 205
and Nambudiris, 208
Ceramān Perumāl, 203
Charlottesville protest (2017), 215
Charpentier, Jarl, 193, 207, 269*n*16
Chavers (warriors), 205
*chekor* (fighter), 207
Chinnamastā (headless goddess), 10, 128–130, 248. *See also* Reṇukā
Chola kingdom, 200, 205
Cholavandan, Tamil Nadu, 86
*chora* (vessel), 90
Choudhary, Pradeep Kant, 186, 207
Christianity, 30–31, 73–74
Cirakāri, 9, 222
in *Mahābhārata*, 123–125, 127
in *Skanda Purāṇa*, 125–127
*cirañjīvin* (immortal), 4, 70
*cirañjīvin-avatāra* paradox, of Paraśurāma, 7, 64, 70–71, 78, 163, 226, 262*n*31–263*n*31
*Citpāvanabrāhmaṇotpattiḥ* (*Sahyādrikhaṇḍa*), 212
Citpāvans (Koṅkaṇastha), 5, 11, 208–217, 234
Citraratha (*gandharva* prince), and Reṇukā, 3, 53, 61, 92–93, 127, 180
*coincidentia oppositorum*, 71, 220
comparative mythology, 20
Cook, Captain James, 16
Creuzer, Georg Friedrich, 19
Cyavana (sage), 61–62

Dange, Sadashiv Ambadas, 93
Darrow, Clarence, 162, 273*n*22
Das, Anirban, 275*n*30

Das, Rahul Peter, 265*n*8
Dasgupta, Shamik, 165
Dattātreya (Deccan folk god), 8
  *Avadhūta Gītā*, 33
  "*neti, neti*" formula, 41
  and Paraśurāma, 55–56, 221
David, Jacques-Louis (painter), 27
Dawkins, Richard, xv
De, S. K., 275*n*32, 275*n*33
"Dead Mother complex," 5, 138–146
decathexis, 140–141
Decius Mus (Roman consul), 167
defilement of Reṇukā, and *akrasia*, 83–88, 96, 222
Dejenne, Nicolas, 34, 59, 130, 151, 258*n*2–259*n*2, 271*n*13
Derde, Willem, 48
Desai, Rashmi, 108
Deshpande, N. A., 212–213
Devī, 137–138
*dhanurveda* (science of archery), 11, 62, 205
Dhanvantari (sage), 178, 179, 276*n*40
*dharma*, 123
  Bhīṣma's lengthy deathbed sermon on, 123
  and sovereignty, 68–70
  violations of *varṇa* and, 202
Dharmaśāstras, 45
Dhṛṣṭadyumna (warrior), 54
divine violence, 105, 164
Doniger, Wendy, 1, 9, 29, 34, 80, 82, 131, 248
double negation, of Paraśurāma, 76, 221
Draupadī
  disrobing of, 265, 277*n*3
  and Pāṇḍavas, 1, 72, 170
Draviḍas (Brahmin clans), 212–213
Droṇa (warrior-sage), 4, 8, 22, 24
  Aśvatthāman and Pāṇḍavas, 54, 71, 166
  birth of, 53
  and Dhṛṣṭadyumna, 54
  and Drupada, 54
  and Ekalavya, 22–23, 26
  and Paraśurāma, 52–54, 221
Drupada (Kṣatriya king), 54
Dumézil, Georges, 44, 57
"Durgā complex," 138
Duryodhana, 71, 201, 264*n*6–265*n*6
Dvāpara Yuga, 150, 210
Dvivedi, Hazariprasad, 259*n*3

Edgerton, Franklin, 92
*The Edinborough Review*, 15
Eisenhower, Dwight D., 25
Eisler, Robert, 13–14
Ekalavya (archer)
  against caste oppression, 22–24
  and Droṇa, 26
Elias, Norbert, 163
Elmore, W. T., 112
Elst, Koneraad, 47, 260*n*15
eugenics program, in India, 157, 272*n*18
exorcism, Tamil (*pēy*), 9, 101, 222

Falk, Nancy, 91–93, 127
Feldhaus, Anne, 192
Feller, Danielle, 46
Figueira, Dorothy, 209
Fire Clan Rajputs, 11, 190, 223
Fitzgerald, James L., 46, 54, 124, 271*n*13
fluidity theme/motif, 38, 85, 99, 102, 112, 115, 129. See also *caru*; *karakam* pot
  in *Godāvarī Māhātmya*, 268*n*10
  in Hindu mythology, 82
forest representation, in Indian myths, 89
Frazer, James G., 165, 191
Frazier, Jessica, 29
Freud, Sigmund, 20, 30, 144, 245, 247
*friedlos* (man without peace), 169

Furui, Ryosuke, 67

Gādhi (king), 2, 36
Gail, Adalbert J., 121, 176
Gaitonde, Gajanan, 213
*gandharvas* (celestial musicians/forest spirits), 3, 9, 61, 222
  Bharadvāja and, 53
  characterization of, 92–93
  Citraratha (prince), 2, 3, 53, 61, 92–93, 127, 180
  in *Ṛg Veda*, 93–94
  in Upaniṣads, 92
Gandhi, M. K., 56
Gaṇeśa (god), and Paraśurāma, 118–121
Gauḍas (Bengali Brahmin clans), 212
Gelders, Raf, 48
genocide, 157–159. *See also* varṇicide
Ghṛtācī (celestial dancer), 53
Girard, René, 64
Glucklich, Ariel, 38, 69–70
*Godāvarī Māhātmya*, 268*n*10
Godse, Nathuram, 209
Gōkarṇa, 193
Goldman, Robert, 9, 42–43, 62, 81, 86, 108–109, 186, 260*n*12
*Götterdämmerung* ("Twilight of the Gods"), 170
*Grāmapaddhati* (Kannada), 204
Gṛdhrakūṭa Mountain (Vulture Peak), 175
Great Dissolution. *See* Mahāpralaya
Green, André, 5, 9, 139. *See also* "Dead Mother complex"
Griffin-Kremer, Cozette, 57
Grottanelli, Cristiano, 16
Gurumurthy, K. G., 109–110

Haberman, David, 246–247
Haihaya kings, 270
  and Bhārgava feud, 10, 152–154, 176, 181, 190, 198, 223
  Vitāhavya, 153–154
*Halloween* (film), 248–249
Hanumān (god), 70, 262*n*29
Hart, George, 205
Haṭha Yoga, 82
Hawaii, Makahiki festival, 16–17
Heesterman, Jan, 35, 44
Hegel, G. W. F.
  dialectics of, 31
  *The Phenomenology of Spirit*, 50–51
Hemacandra, Śvetāmbara Ācārya, 177
*Henry: Portrait of a Serial Killer* (film), 249
Hercules, 27–28
Hiltebeitel, Alf, 9, 43
Hinduism
  and Jainism, 178
  wilderness and kingship, 91–92, 133–137
Hiraṇyakaśipu (demon), 34
Hitchcock, Alfred, 249
Hobbes, Thomas, 68
Hodges, Sarah, 272*n*18
*homa* ritual, 95
Horse Sacrifice, 46, 97, 151, 192
  Aryans, 267*n*25
Hudson, D. Dennis, 172
Hughes, Aaron W., 17
Hunter, Lloyd A., 215–216
hypotheses, testing, 18

Indo-European societies, 44, 57
Indra (god)
  cattle raiding in *Ṛg Veda*, 58
  curse against women, 264*n*5
  and Kṣatriyas, 44
  Medhātithi and Ahalyā (Cirakāri story), 125–126
  and Varuṇa, 44
infidelity, of Reṇukā, 83, 97–98
"infinite contained within finite" (Vaiṣṇavism), 71, 220
*itihāsa* (history), 20

Jainism
and Hinduism, 178
Jamadagni-Reṇukā story in, 178
representation of Paraśurāma in, 10–11, 177–180
Śvetāmbara (White-Clad), 10, 177
Jamadagni (Paraśurāma's father), 3, 12, 37, 75, 83, 86
curse on disobedient sons, 106–107, 112–113
and Kārtavīrya, 58, 87–88, 227–228
and Reṇukā. *See* Reṇukā
and Viśvāmitra, 94
Jamison, Stephanie, 96–98
Janamejaya, and Vaiśampāyana, 150, 174
Jarāsaṃdha (king), 150
*Jay Paraśurām* (Pramad), 129
Jaynes, Julian, 52
John the Baptist, 146
Jonte-Pace, Diane, 81
Joyce, James, 16
Jung, C. G., 20
Jurewicz, Joanna, 90

Kakar, Sudhir, 9
*kalaripayattu* (martial art), 11, 62, 204–208
Kali Yuga, 74, 210
*Kālikā Purāṇa*, 107, 117
Kalita (caste), 158
Kalki (*avatāra*), 74–76, 263*n*34
*Kalki Purāṇa*, 73–74
*Kāma Sutra*, 85
Kāmadhenu (Wishing Cow), 3, 56, 58, 59, 142, 252
*Kāñcippurāṇam* (Tamil), 63, 88, 116
Kannada
*Grāmapaddhati*, 204
*karakam* pot, 90, 129, 248
Karṇa (warrior), 4
and Parasūrāma, 54, 73, 220, 261*n*20
Kārtavīrya Arjuna (king), 3–4, 12, 41, 48, 56, 99, 141, 151, 225, 236
and cattle theft, 58, 62, 106, 142, 229–230, 239
Citraśāla version of, 270*n*5
and Jamadagni, 58, 87–88, 227–228
and Rāvaṇa, 239–240
Kashmir, Vaiṣṇava theologians in, 5
Kaśyapa (Ṛṣi), 188, 198
Katz, Ruth, 170
Kauravas, 1, 71
Kauśika (caste), 62–63
Kāyastha (caste), 158, 189
Kerala
*kalaripayattu* (martial arts), 11, 62, 204–208
matrilineal succession, 195, 199, 277*n*7
Nambudiri. *See* Nambudiris
Onam festival, 254
Paraśurāma myth in, 194–208
Perumāls' rule, 195, 200, 223
*Keralamahātmya* (Sanskrit), 11, 194, 200, 223
*Kēraḷōlpatti* (Malayalam), 11, 194–204, 213, 223
Khaṇḍelvāl Vaiśyas, 11, 190, 223
Khatri (caste), 158, 189
Kierkegaard, Søren, 33–34
kingship
and cattle raids, 56–64
wilderness and, 91, 133–137
Kinsley, David R., 129, 248
*klinnāmbhasi* ("soaked in water"), 81, 85
Kosambi, D. D., 11, 185, 214
Kripal, Jeffrey J., 9
Kristeva, Julia, 9, 81, 89–90, 107
psychoanalytic interpretation of matricide, 133–137
*krodha* (wrath/anger), 152
*Kṛṣi Gītā* (Malayalam), 197

Kṛṣṇa (*avatāra*), 72, 150, 159
  and Rādhā solving Gaṇeśa-Paraśurāma conflict, 122
Kṛtavīrya (king). *See* Kārtavīrya Arjuna
*kṣatra*, 12, 236. *See also* Kṣatriyas
  as sacrificial remainder, 186–191
Kṣatriyas, 3–4, 186
  annihilation of. *See* varṇicide
  and Aurva, 153, 272*n*15
  Bhavsar, 158, 189
  clans, 158, 189
  Drupada king, 54
  extermination of twenty-one generations, 4, 41, 151, 184–185, 214, 225, 234, 251
  and Indra, 44
  Kauśika, 62–63
  Kāyastha, 158, 189
  Khatri, 158, 189
  Perike, 158
  regeneration by Brahmins, after varṇicide, 4, 150, 199, 228, 230, 239
  regional descendants of, 158
  relations with Brahmins, 43–50, 221
  Reṇukā life as, 7, 39, 86–87, 107, 113, 140
  Samanthar, 158
*kulasaṃkara* (mixture of clans), 62
Kuper, Leo, 159
Kurtz, Stanley, 9, 111, 133
  psychoanalytic interpretation of matricide, 133, 137
Kurukṣetra, 53–54, 107, 134, 175, 187
  Paraśurāma sacrifice at, 53, 198
  *staṃbha rovila* at, 210–211
Kuśika (king), 62

Lacan, Jacques, 9, 11, 81, 133, 135
Lajjāgaurī (headless goddess), 10, 130–132. *See also* Reṇukā
Lakṣmī (goddess), 171
land creation, 11, 38, 136, 184, 191–194, 207, 223, 234
Leopold, Joan, 157
Lévi-Strauss, Claude, 18, 20, 53, 191
Lincoln, Bruce, 16, 26, 29, 60, 155
  myths of Indo-European societies, 57–58
*liṅgam* (phallus), 109, 111, 136
Livius, Titus (Livy), 167
Logan, William, 195, 199–200, 203
Lucas, Henry Lee, 249
Lutgendorf, Phillip, 7, 70, 262*n*29

Macaulay, Thomas Babbington, 14–16
Maccoby, Hyam, 73
macromyth, of Paraśurāma, 1, 169, 232
Madhya Pradesh
  Akṣaya Tṛtīya festival, 269*n*3
magico-sovereign function, in Indo-European societies, 44
Magnone, Paolo, 175
*Mahābhārata*, 1, 4
  Ādi Parvan, 149–150, 199
  Āraṇyaka Parvan, 150, 259*n*7
  Aurva myth, 152–154
  Bhārgavas, 42–43
  Cirakāri story, 123–125, 127
  Critical Edition of, 35, 61, 77, 276*n*38
  Droṇa, 52–53, 66, 71
  Mausāla Parvan, 272*n*20
  Mokṣadharma Parvan, 47
  narration of varṇicide in, 149–152
  Nīlakaṇṭha (commentator), 9, 82, 244, 264*n*4
  Niṣādas, 22–24
  Paraśurāma myth. *See* matricide; varṇicide; Paraśurāma
  quasi-parricides in, 46
  Sabhā Parvan, 150

*Mahābhārata* (continued)
Śānti Parvan, 151, 169, 173, 187, 259*n*7
Sauptika Parvan, 71, 151, 170
varṇicidal campaign against Kṣatriyas, 149, 157
worldview, 25
Mahānubhāv sect, in Maharashtra, 275*n*34
*Sahyādri-lila*, 56
*Sutra-pāṭha*, 55
Mahāpadmānanda (emperor), 46
Mahāpralaya (Great Dissolution), 76
Maharashtra
Citpāvan Brahmins, 5, 11
Mahānubhāv sect in, 55–56, 275*n*34
Paraśurāma in, 11, 46, 68, 208–217
Peśwās in, 210
*Mahāvīracarita* (Bhavabhūti), 75
Makahiki festival (Hawai'i), 16–17
Malabar, Paraśurāma in, 11, 46, 68, 173–174
Malabou, Catherine, 21
Malamoud, Charles, 187
Malayalam
*Kēraḷōlpatti*, 11, 194–204, 213, 223
*Kṛṣi Gītā*, 197
*Maluvinte Katha*. See *Maluvinte Katha*
*Maluvinte Katha* (Balamani Amma poem), 7, 40–42, 114, 165, 219, 221, 254
*mandabhāgya* (bad luck), 72
Māriyamman (Reṇukā), 98
heteronormativity in rituals surrounding, 246
and Śiva, 132
*Mārkaṇḍeya Purāṇa*, 66
Mārtaṇḍavarman (king), 118–119
*maryāda* ("boundary/propriety"), 247
matricidal axe
Paraśurāma's, 40, 102, 114–116
in Śaivism, 116–123
matricide, 8, 29, 61, 79–81, 105, 222
abjection, repression and renunciation, 106–114
"broken pot," 79–103
Cirakāri story, 123–128
Dead Mother complex, 138–146
decapitation and resurrection, 114–116
defilement and *akrasia*, 83–88
headless goddess, 128–133
incontinence, 2, 13, 53, 61, 81–84, 88–89, 91, 95, 144, 222, 226, 245
matricidal axe, 114–116
psychoanalytic readings of, 133–146
psychological aspects of, 9
reading myth through ritual, 95–102
of Rudra (Śiva), 116–117
in Śaivism, 116–123
matrilineal succession, 11, 195, 199, 277*n*7
Matsubara, Mitsunori, 275*n*32
Mauryan Empire, 45
Mausāla Parvan (*Mahābhārata*), 272*n*20
McNaughton, John, 249
Medhātithi (sage), 124–125
Meghanāda (*vidyādhara*), and Subhūma, 179
Meloy, J. Reid, 253
Menon, Ramesh, 159
Menon, T. Madhava, 198, 200, 202
"metamyths," 42, 260*n*12
"miscegenation," 65
Mitra-Varuṇa, 44, 51
*mlecchas* ("barbarians"), 74, 211
modern society, and mythic ideas, 164–165
Mokṣadharma Parvan (*Mahābhārata*), 47
Monier-Williams, Monier, 247
mother-child relationship, stages in, 135–137
Mount Mahendra, 40, 54, 145, 165, 192, 204

*mṛtasaṃjīvinī vidyā* (resurrection spell), 108, 242
*Mukapiṭhavāsiṇī Śrī Reṇukā Mahātmya*, 130
Mulaka (Nārīkavaca). *See* Bali/Bālika
munificence, 88
Munshi, K. M., 59
*Mūṣakavaṃśakāvya*, 195
*Mūṣikavaṃśa*, 154
"muted third term" comparison, 17
myths
  and anxieties, 24–25
  cattle raids and kingship, 56–64
  defined, 19–20
  Kwakiutl, 20
  "making sense" of, 12–13
  as narratives, 21–23, 48
  paradoxes in, 34
  psychoanalysis, structure, and subjectivity in, 29–31
  reading through ritual, 95–102
  received and reproduced, 26–29
  ritual complex of Reṇukā, 131–132, 136
  speculative arguments about, 13–16
  structure of, 7–12
  *Tuirbe Tragmār*, 193
  and values, 23–24
  Wandering Jew, 8, 73, 221
  and worldviews, 25–26

Nabokov, Isabelle, 99–100
Nala (king), 166–167
Nambidi (Ambalavasi caste), 201
Nambudiris, 11, 119, 195
  Cattar (subcaste), 206
  and Cēra kingdom, 208
  in Malabar, 214
  and Paraśurāma, 194–208, 234
  water libations, 196
Nandī/Nandinī cow, 59
Napier, Macvey, 14–15
Nārada (sage), 72, 125, 126, 152
  and Reṇukā, 112–113
  and Vāsudeva, 172
  and Vyāsa, 72
Narasiṃha (*avatāra*), 34, 201, 259*n*3
narratives, and myths, 21–23, 48
National Convention in Paris (1793), 27
Nayars, 195, 202, 206
  adopting matrilineal succession, 199
Neevel, Walter G., 170
"*neti, neti*" ("not this, not that"), 33–34, 41
*The Neuro-Psychoses of Defence* (Freud), 245
*Nicomachean Ethics* (Aristotle), 83–84
Nietzsche, Friedrich Wilhelm, 214–215
"night raid" of Aśvatthāman on Pāṇḍavas, 71, 151, 166–168, 170
Nīlakaṇṭha (*Mahābhārata* commentator), 9, 82, 244, 264*n*4
*Nīlamata Purāṇa*, 174–175
*nirvikāra śiśu*, 118, 120–121
Niśāda (demonic figure), 65
Niṣādas (tribal group), and Pāṇḍavas, 22–24
*Nṛsiṃha Purāṇa*, 71

Obeyesekere, Gananath, 9, 17, 82, 119
Oedipus complex, 17, 133, 135, 139, 252
Olivelle, Patrick, 47
Oppenheimer, Robert, 164

*Pabūjī* (Rajasthani epic), 58
*Padma Purāṇa*, 184, 270*n*11
Padmasambhava (Tibetan tantric magician), and Rudra, 117
*paṇaghaṭa-līlā* (woman waylaid at the well), 80–81, 89
*pāncarātra* ("five nights"), 170, 275*n*33
Pāncarātrins, 10, 66, 152, 240
  mitigating Paraśurāma myth's violence, 169–177, 223

Pāṇḍavas, 1, 61
and Aśvatthāman, 71, 151, 166–168, 170
and Droṇa, 54, 71, 166
and Niṣādas, 22–24
Pāṇḍya kingdom, 200, 205
*Paraśarāma Caritra* (Vallabha), 11, 209–213
Paraśurāma, xvi
abjection, repression and renunciation of, 106–114
and Aśvatthāman, 72–73, 166–169
as *avatāra*, 6, 7, 12, 34, 71, 144, 226, 237
and Bāḷājī (Citpāvan Peśwā), 209, 211
blood-guiltiness of, 195–196, 208
Brahmin warrior motif of, 33–78, 241
*cirañjīvin-avatāra* nature of, 7, 64, 70–71, 78, 163, 226, 262*n*31–263*n*31
and Citpāvans, 208–217
and Dattātreya, 55–56, 221
as devotee of Śiva, 48, 116–118, 121, 175
dislocation, excess, and becoming symbols of, 50–64
divine violence, 105, 164
and double negation, 76
"doubling" of conception narrative, 12
and Droṇa, 52–54, 221
eternal exile of, 4, 53, 69, 134, 144, 187, 188, 226, 234, 255
first death of, 76, 228
and Gaṇeśa, 118–121
genocide/varṇicide. *See* varṇicide
in Jainism, 177–180
and Kalki, 74–76, 263*n*34
and Karṇa, 54, 73, 220, 261*n*20
Kārtavīrya's cattle theft and, 58, 62, 106, 142, 229–230, 239
Kerala, 194–208
land creation. *See* land creation
Maharashtra, 208–217
matricide. *See* matricide
mixed birth of, 2–3, 7, 38, 80, 224
on Mount Mahendra, xvi, 40, 54, 145, 165, 192, 204
and Nambudiris, 194–208, 234
negative personality traits of, 269*n*16
open-ended structure of, 12, 226
Pāncarātrins, 169–177
pilgrimage, 117–118
*point de capiton* (quilting point) of, 11, 193
practicing penance after varṇicide, 175, 204
compared to Pṛthu, 65–67
and Puṣyamitra, 45–47
quality of excess/saturation, 8, 64, 77, 221
and Rāma Dāśarathi, 71, 75, 76, 175, 220
and Rāvaṇa, 161–162, 193, 210
Reṇukā and Jamadagni. *See* Reṇukā; Jamadagni
resurrection rite on decapitated father, 109
sacrifice at Kurukṣetra, 53, 198
Śaiva-Vaiṣṇava dual identity of, 70–71, 163, 262*n*31–263*n*31
second Paraśurāma. *See* Mahāpadmānanda
as sovereign and *homo sacer*, 69, 221, 255
and Subhūma, 11, 177–180
and Subrahmaṇya, 193
temple in Pedhe, Mahararashtra, 75, 86
temporal and spatial exceptionalism, 8, 64, 77, 221
twenty-one-fold extermination of Kṣatriyas. *See* varṇicide
"Universal-Particular-Singular" split identities of, 7, 33–43, 220–221

vanishing mediator of "becoming," 8, 64, 77, 221
and Varuṇa, 193
and Viśvāmitra, 61–62, 221
Paraśurāmakṣetra, 195, 198
*Paraśurāmarāmāyaṇa*, 189
Parāvasu (Viśvāmitra's grandson), 151
Parikṣit (Pāṇḍavas), resurrection of, 72, 170
Parpola, Asko, 267*n*25
Pārvatī (goddess)
Gaṇeśa-Paraśurāma conflict, 118–121, 138
and Rādhā, 122
Pattanaik, Devdutt, 109
Paul, Saint, 84
Pauwels, Heidi, 89, 91
Pedhe, Mahararashtra
Paraśurāma temple in, 75, 86
Pentheus (Theban king), 146
Perike (caste), 158
Periyantavar (incarnation of Duryodhana), 267*n*26
Perumals, 11, 195, 200, 223
Peśwās, in Maharashtra, 210
Petrov, Stanislav Yevgrafovich, 123
*pēy* (sexualized demon), 99–100, 222, 245, 267*n*26
phallus (*liṅgam*), 109, 111, 136
*The Phenomenology of Spirit* (Hegel), 50–51
Pilate, Pontius, 73
Pillai, E. K., 203
Pippalāda tree. See *aśvattha*
Plato, xv, 186
*point de capiton* ("quilting point"), of Paraśurāma myth, 11, 193
Pollock, Sheldon, 185
Pōttu Rāja (buffalo king), 98, 138, 145
*pravargya* rite, 267*n*5
"primal scenes," 7, 12, 119, 144, 225, 235–236, 247
*Prokeria.com*, 217
Pṛthu (king), 23
and Paraśurāma, 65–67
*Psycho* (film), 249–251
psychoanalysis, of Paraśurāma myth, 30–31, 89, 107
Pulaya slaves, 195
*Puranānūru* (Tamil), 205
Purāṇas, 1, 9, 20. See also specific *Purāṇas*
Puṣyamitra (Śunga emperor), 8, 45–47, 221

"quasi-parricides," 46

Rādhā, and Kṛṣṇa solving Gaṇeśa-Paraśurāma conflict, 122
Raghavan, V., 275*n*33
*rajas* (female sexual fluid), 82
Rajasthan, Khaṇḍelvāl Vaiśyas in, 11, 190, 223
Rajendra II (Chola king), 277*n*9
Rāma Dāśarathi (*avatāra*), xvi
and Hanumān, 70, 262*n*29
lawsuit against, 163
and Paraśurāma, 71, 75, 76, 175, 220
quest to rescue Sītā, 1
Rāma Jāmadagnya. *See* Paraśurāma
Ramanujan, A. K., 9, 108
*Rāmayāṇa*, 1, 71
Kārtavīrya in, 239–240
Rāma and Paraśurāma, 53–54
regional versions of, 75
Rangappa, Babburu (poet), 189
*ratnahārin* ("jewel-bearer"), 60
Rāvaṇa (demon king), 1
and Kārtavīrya, 239–240
and Paraśurāma, 160–161, 193, 210
Ṛcika (Paraśurāma's grandfather), and Satyavatī, 2, 35–38, 224
re-description, of myths, 18

Reṇukā (Paraśurāma's mother), 3, 38–39
and Anantavīrya, 178–179, 276*n*41
decapitation of, 8, 10, 79, 114–116
as goddess, 12, 48, 56, 86, 98, 128–133, 248
incontinence (Kārtavīrya/Citraratha), 2, 13, 53, 61, 81–84, 88–89, 91, 144, 222, 226, 245
and Jamadagni. *See* Jamadagni
Kārtavīrya as younger son, 141, 144
as Kṣatriya, 7, 39, 86–87, 107, 113, 140
and Nārada, 112–113
resurrection of, 109, 115
Tamil myth-ritual complex of, 131–132, 136, 266*n*20
*Renuka Devi Mahatyam* (film), 94
*Reṇukāmahātmya* (*Sahyādrikhaṇḍa*), 212
Reṇukā-Yellama
in Belgaum, 109
at Savadatti, Karnataka, 86, 111, 134
renunciation, 111, 133
repression, 111
resurrection
of Parikṣit's slain fetus, 170
of Reṇukā, 108–109, 115, 133, 146, 233
of Jamadagni, 109
Śukra's spell of, 108
*Ṛg Veda*
*gandharva* in, 93
Indra's cattle raiding, 58
Jamadagni and Viśvāmitra, 94
pippal tree, 52
Ricoeur, Paul, 83
Rigopoulos, Antonio, 55–56
rites/rituals
*bhadradipāpratiṣṭā*, 119–120, 122
Buffalo Sacrifice, 99
*homa*, 95
Horse Sacrifice, 46, 97, 151, 192, 267*n*25
Human Sacrifice, 215
and myths, 95–102
*pēy* exorcism, 9, 101, 222
*pravargya*, 267*n*5
resurrections, 108–109
Snake Sacrifice, 174, 271*n*13
*varuṇapraghāsa*, 96–97
*yajnas*, 95
Rosella, Daniela, 89
Rudra. *See also* Śiva
matricide of, 116–117
Russon, John, 50

Śabalā cow. *See* Nandī/Nandinī cow
Sabhā Parvan (*Mahābhārata*), 150
"sacred executioner," 73, 241
sacrificial remainder, of varṇicide, 186–191
Sahlins, Marshall, 16–17
Śāhūjī (king), 209, 211
*Sahyādrikhaṇḍa*, 212
*Sahyādri-lila* (Mahānubhāv sect), 56
Śaivism, 9
axe murdering in, 116–123
*coincidentia oppositorum*, 71, 220
and Vaiṣṇava identity of Paraśurāma, 70–71, 163, 262*n*31–263*n*31
Śākta Pīṭhas, 268*n*13
Śākti (goddess worship), 55–56, 57
*śālabhañjikā* (woman-and-tree motif), 37
Samantapañcaka. *See* Kurukṣetra
Samanthar (caste), 158
*Samarāngaṇasūtradhāra*, 66
Saṃkarṣaṇa (*vyūha*), 107, 171–173
*Sanatkumāra Saṃhitā*, 173
Sanderson, Alexis, 47
Sangam Era, 205
Sanskrit, 43
*Keralamahātmya*, 11, 194, 200, 223
*śāntarasa* (peacefulness), 169
Śānti Parvan (*Mahābhārata*), 151, 169, 173, 187, 259*n*7

*Śatapatha Brāhmaṇa*, 51, 187
Sathaye, Adheesh, 42, 61, 271*n*13
*Sātvata Saṃhitā*, 172
Satyavatī (Paraśurāma's grandmother), 2, 36–39, 277*n*2
and Bhṛgu, 3, 35, 227
Ṛcika and, 2, 35–38, 224
ritual mistake of, 7, 39, 225, 233
Sauptika Parvan (*Mahābhārata*), 71, 151, 170
Savadatti, Karnataka
Reṇukā-Yellama at, 86, 111, 134
Schmitt, Carl, 8, 68, 77, 217, 221
second Paraśurāma. *See* Mahāpadmānanda
Sen, Aditi, 246
Senapati ("general"), 45
separation stage, in mother-child relationship, 135–136
*śeṣa* (sacrificial remainder), 187
Shāhjahān (Mughal emperor), 211
Shay, Jonathan, 271*n*14
Shulman, David Dean, 47, 63, 108, 186–187
Śiva (god), 34, 64, 71
Aśvatthāman's possession by, 166
Gaṇeśa-Paraśurāma conflict, 118–121
Paraśurāma as devotee of, 48, 116, 118–121, 175
Rāma and Paraśurāma, 75
Śivājī (Marāṭhā ruler), 208, 211
*Skanda Purāṇa*, 10, 121, 192, 208
Cirakāri story, 125–127
Sleeman, William, 15
Smith, Brian K., 156
Smith, Frederick M., 167
Smith, H. Daniel, 170
Snake Sacrifice, 174, 271*n*13
Soma (sacred substance), 93
South Asian cultures, 6
sovereignty, 8
*dharma* and, 68–70
and supplement, 64–70
Sprengnether, Madelon, 81
*śrāmaṇas*, 47
*Srimanmahābhāratam*, 152
Srinivasan, M. N., 43
Srinivasan, Perundevi, 95, 131–132, 136, 246
Srivastava, V. C., 266*n*21
*staṃbha rovila* (killing post), 210–211
Straus, Scot, 157–158
Strenski, Ivan, 18
Stutley, Margaret, 92–93
Subhūma/Subhauma (Jaina Paraśurāma), 11, 177–180
subjectivity, 29–30
Subrahmaṇya (god), and Paraśurāma, 193
Śudras, 260*n*14
matrilineal succession, 199
second Paraśurāma and, 46
Śukra (*asura* chief priest), 267*n*3
resurrection spell, 108
Sukthankar, V. S., 185
Bhṛguization thesis. *See* Bhṛguization thesis
Śunaḥśepa (Viśvāmitra's adopted son), 190, 264*n*2
Sundahl, Deborah, 265*n*9
Sūrya (god), 94
*Sutra-pāṭha* (Mahānubhāv text), 55
Svamin, Govindacarya, 275*n*32
Śvetāmbara (White-Clad) Jains, 10

Tagare, Ganesh, 258*n*1
*Táin Bó Cúailgne* (Irish epic), 57
Tamil
exorcism, 9, 101, 222
*Kāñcippurāṇam*, 63, 88, 116
*Puranānūru*, 205
Tamil Nadu
Cholavandan, 86
Dharapuram district festival, 98–99
martial arts, 11

Tampurāns, 195
*tapas* (asceticism), 36, 41, 116
"The Story of the Axe." See *Maluvinte Katha*
"Theses on Comparison" (Lincoln & Grottanelli), 16–17
Theweleit, Klaus, 102
Thomas, Lynn, 39, 269*n*3
"thrice seven." See *triḥsapta/ triḥsaptakṛtvaḥ*
Tibet
  Buddhist tradition of Rudra, 116–117
Tilak, B. G., 209
*Totemism* (Lévi-Strauss), 53
traversing fantasy stage, in mother-child relationship, 136–137
Tretā Yuga, 269*n*3
tribadism, 85
*triḥsapta/triḥsaptakṛtvaḥ*, 236, 270*n*7, 270*n*8
*trimukhī* (three-faced deity), 56
tripartite ideology, 17, 44
Tripurā (goddess), 55, 261*n*18
*Triṣaṣtiśalākāpuruṣacarita* (Hemacandra), 177, 181
*Tuirbe Tragmār* (Irish myth), 193
Tulu Nadu, 204
twenty-one generations of Kṣatriyas, extermination of, xv, 4, 41, 151, 184–185, 214, 225, 234, 251. *See also* varṇicide
"two deaths" concept of, 76, 166

Uberoi, Meera, 159
*ucchiṣṭha* (sacrificial remainder), 187
*uḍumbara* (tree), 35, 37
Ugraśravas (sage), 149
United States
  "blood and soil" mythologies in, 215, 224
"Universal-Particular-Singular" split identity, 7, 33–43, 220–221
unrelatedness, 17–18
Upaniṣads, 171
  *gandharvas* in, 92
Ūrvī (goddess), 188
Uśanas Kāvya. *See* Śukra

*Vādeśvarodaya-kāvya* (Viśvanātha), 193
Vaidika Brahmins, 48
Vaiśampāyana, and Janamejaya, 150, 174
Vaiṣṇavism, 5, 56, 71, 170
  "infinite contained within finite," 71, 220
  Pāncarātrins, 10
  and Śaiva identity of Paraśurāma, 70–71, 163
  and Śaivism conflicts, 122
  theologians in Kashmir, 5
Vaiśvānara (sage), 178
Vaiśyas, 44, 190, 223
Valan fishermen, 195
values, and myths, 23–24, 223
Vāmana (*avatāra*), 34, 254
van Buitenen, J. A. B., 152–153
Varadarajan, Siddharth, 272*n*20
*Vargav* (Dasgupta), 165
*varṇa* (ancient Indian class system), 7, 10, 47, 80, 156–158, 161–162, 221
*varṇasaṃkara* ("mixture of varṇas"), 62, 64
varṇicide, 7, 10, 27, 41, 54–56, 81, 154–163
  Aśvatthāman and Paraśurāma, 166–169
  Bhārgava-Haihaya feud, 10, 152–154, 176, 181, 190, 198, 223
  blood and soil myth, 194–217
  description in Purāṇas, 152
  extermination and regeneration of Kṣatriyas, 4, 149–182, 199, 228, 239
  Jaina Paraśurāma, 177–180
  and *Kṣatra*, 186–191

land creation, 11, 38, 136, 184, 191–194, 207, 223, 234
narrations in *Mahābhārata*, 149–151
"patron saint of total war," 163–166
sacrificial remainder, 186–191
uses and abuses of Paraśurāma, 184–186
violence in Pāncarātra tradition, 169–177
Varuṇa (god), 2
and Indra, 44
and Paraśurāma, 193
*varuṇapraghāsa* (rite), 9, 96–97
Vasiṣṭha (sage), 59, 175, 190
and Viśvāmitra, 59–64
*vāstu* (sacrificial remainder), 187
Vasūdeva (*avatāra*), 171–173, 266*n*16
and Nārada, 172
*Vāyu Purāṇa*, 75
Vedas, 5
"broken world" of Vedic sacrifice, 35
Puṣyamitra restoration of, 8, 45–47, 221
*varuṇapraghāsa* rites, 9
Vena (king), and Brahmins, 23, 65, 67, 221
Vico, Giambattista, 19
*vidyādhara* (celestial magician), 178–179
*vimānas* (flying chariots), 164
Viṣṇu (god), 6, 34
*avatāras* of, 70
*yugas* of, 39
*Viṣṇu Purāṇa*, 46, 66, 160
*Viṣṇudharmottara Purāṇa*, 48, 94, 152, 174–176
*Viśvaksena Saṃhitā*, 171–172
Viśvāmitra, 3, 8, 37, 42, 52, 190, 264*n*2
and Jamadagni, 94
and Paraśurāma, 61–62, 221
and Parāvasu, 151
and Vasiṣṭha, 59–64
Viśvāvasu (*gandharva*), 92
Vitāhavya (king), 153–154
Vyāsa (sage), 72, 74

"Wandering Jew," 8, 73, 221
Whitaker, Jarrod, 58
Wiesel, Elie, xv
wilderness, in Indian myths, 89, 91, 133–137
Wishing Cow. *See* Kāmadhenu
women
and Indra's curse, 264*n*5
*rajas* (female sexual fluid), 82, 85, 96, 247–248
representation in Indian mythology, 244
*The Wonder That Was India* (Basham), 45
worldviews, and myths, 25–26
Wotan, 73

*yajnas* (daily rituals), 95
*Yakṣas*, 9, 92–93
Yavana rulers, 211
and Brahmins, 210
Yudhiṣṭhira, 186, 187, 201
and Akṛtavraṇa, 35, 150
and Aśvatthāman, 71–72, 166
and Bhīṣma, 35, 124, 153
*yugas* (cosmic ages), 39
Dvāpara Yuga, 210
Kali Yuga, 74, 210
Tretā Yuga, 269*n*3

Zarrilli, Phillip B., 205, 206
Žižek, Slavoj, 7, 31, 34, 76, 220

www.ingramcontent.com/pod-product-compliance
Lightning Source LLC
Chambersburg PA
CBHW030128240426
43672CB00005B/65
*9781438480381*